Urban Growth Theories and Settlement Systems of India

About the Editors

Prof. Kalpana Markandey did her doctorate from Osmania University, Hyderabad and has been teaching at the Geography Department of the same University for the past three decades. She has been the Head of the Department and Chairperson Board of Studies of this Department with a credit of starting M.Sc. Geoinformatics at Osmania University. She has contribution of publishing nine books and around 35 research papers having successfully completed ten research projects. She is also member of numerous professional bodies.

Prof. Geetha Reddy Anant (also Geeta Reddy Anant & J. Geeta Reddy) is Director, Centre for Indian Ocean Studies Osmania University, Hyderabad having worked on issues of urban growth and life, informal economy, energy consumption and impacts etc. She is the author of *Urbanisation and Primate City Growth in the Indian Ocean Countries—1995, Planning and Regional Development—Towards Identification of Economic Potential—1996* as well as editor of *Problems of Hunger and Food Security in the Indian Ocean Region—2000, and Multilayered Cities and Urban System—2009.* She has also published over one hundred articles and research papers.

Urban Growth Theories and Settlement Systems of India

Essays by Prof. Manzoor Alam

Compiled and Edited by

Professor Kalpana Markandey
Professor Geeta Reddy Anant

CONCEPT PUBLISHING COMPANY PVT. LTD.,
NEW DELHI-110059

ISBN-13: 978-81-8069-739-5

First Published 2011

Published and Printed by

Concept Publishing Company Pvt. Ltd.
Regd. Office:
A/15-16, Commercial Block, Mohan Garden
New Delhi-110059 (India)
Phones : 25351460, 25351794, *Fax* : 091-11-25357109
Email : publishing@conceptpub.com,
Website: www.conceptpub.com

Editorial Office:
H-13, Bali Nagar, New Delhi-110 015, India.

Cataloging in Publication Data--*Courtesy:* D.K. Agencies (P) Ltd. <docinfo@dkagencies.com>

Urban growth theories and settlement systems of India / edited by Kalpana Markandey, Geeta Reddy Anant.
p. cm.
Includes bibliographical references and index.
ISBN 9788180697395

1. Cities and towns--India--Growth. 2. Metropolitan areas--India. 3. Land use, Urban--India. 4. Dwellings--Energy consumption--India. 5. Urbanization--India-Hyderabad. I. Markandey, Kalpana, 1956- II. Geeta Reddy, A.

DDC 309.15487 22

Foreword

I should like to begin this preface with a personal story. One day in 1976, I was walking along a street in Hyderabad with Dr. Manzoor Alam whom I had met briefly the day before at an energy conference organized by Administrative Staff College of India. As we walked, our attention was drawn to the large number of large depots selling fuelwood. Our reaction was immediate and very similar. At the conference we were discussing various sources of energy—oil, gas, coal, hydro, and nuclear—but here before our eyes was evidence of another form of energy that clearly provided important energy services for the very poorest, and whose exploitation had major ramifications for environmental sustainability. It was a short step from that realization to Dr. Alam's determination to examine the importance of this hitherto neglected source of energy, reported in Part 3 of this volume.

This incident illustrates several facets of Dr. Alam's characteristics that are amply illustrated in this book—his intellectual curiosity; his enthusiasm and responsiveness; his energy; his refusal to be constrained by the traditional bounds of his discipline; his concern for the well-being of the poorest sections of the population; and his ability to make connections between seemingly disparate events, especially as they affected the scale and scope of urban design. Though a distinguished member of traditional Hyderabadi society, his thinking was lively, penetrating and even radical.

As an expert in urban development, Dr. Alam has been professionally active in extraordinary times. When he started out as a young professor, London, Paris and New York were by far the largest cities in the world with populations around 8 to 10 million. Now they have been dwarfed by new rapidly growing cities throughout the developing and emerging world. To take a few examples, Mexico City, Sao Paulo, Mumbai and New Delhi now have populations twice as large, many living below the poverty line. Urban design and management designed specially for these new behemoths is urgently needed. There were no blueprints to go by. Dr. Alam through his careful analysis of the theory of urban growth, the settlement systems of India, and the provision of essential services to urban areas, has contributed to our understanding of these complex urban issues and to wise policy formulation.

This series of essays is an exciting journey of exploration, the fruit of a life time of careful analysis and perceptive and imaginative thought. My personal debt to Dr. Alam is immeasurable, and it is a great privilege for me to introduce the writings of this remarkable man to a wider audience.

February, 2009

Dr. Joy Dunkerley
Washington DC

Professor Manzoor Alam as viewed by a Peer

To recall memories about a person with whom I have literally grown up is indeed difficult, especially if the readers expect me to explain my mental connection with him. Swimming back in the stream of memory I recall meeting Manzoor in the early sixties as he came to give us a seminar in the department of Geography of Presidency College in Calcutta on the subject of his research degree from the University of Edinburgh on the emergence of Hyderabad city from its roots in the medieval capital at Golconda. I was then teaching in that college after getting my research degree from the London School of Economics and Political Science. At that time my preoccupation was to explore the complexities of agricultural economy in India and somehow thought farming is the essence of India. I was hit by Manzoor's gait with a solidly built body neatly dressed gentleman eagre to remind us of the urban antecedents of India. I will not be untrue to myself if I admit that my later involvement with urbanization had its root in that event in Presidency College. The need to explore the features of Indian urbanization as distinct from those of the Western civilization appeared worthy to pursue.

Shah Manzoor Alam was a distinguished personality in the Osmania University located in Hyderabad. Manzoor originates from north India, but spent his academic life in Hyderabad, reconfirming in a queer fashion the popular notion that Hyderabad is the southernmost city of North India as also the northernmost city of South India. Two distinct cultural realms have merged inseparably in Hyderabad. Manzoor's approach to life was also similarly blended after having married Banu Begam, a beautiful dignified woman from Hyderabad. She bore several children all exquisitely beautiful and had amazing ability in culinary practices. She and Manzoor loved to feed their friends. I cannot forget my delight from putting the food of his house in my mouth. Alas, she is no more there to sustain the pleasantries of eating. My gain from this situation was to get our two families together, which still lasts even when Manzoor lives in the United States of America and I stubbornly preferring to live in India.

Returning to Manzoor's academic pursuit, I should mention the impact on me from his seminal article on Ibn Khaldun's Concept of the Origin, Growth and Decay of Cities. Till then my scholastic formulations were based on writings in English. The article on Ibn Khaldun revealed how important it is to consult writings in other languages. Needless to mention, this importance arises just not from the language used in those foreign texts, but from the cultural bearing of the users of those languages that reflected their respective historical experiences. It is good to see at some you love through many eyes of others. This approach has profited me a great deal.

To keep reminiscence brief is a virtue by itself. I will only state that every article Manzoor wrote was enjoyable as some were enlightening and some others controversial. The collection of essays that Manzoor's students are bringing out would be a testimony on the varied range of interests that he had. He is by habit a researcher and that has not changed as yet. After taking retirement from the academy, he persisted with his search on Indian geographical reality. One output of remarkable importance is the work on energy consumption in metropolitan Hyderabad. Now he is preparing excellent material to impart education. Hope he continues enjoying his works.

April 15, 2009

Satyesh C. Chakraborty
Professor (Retired)
Indian Institute of Management,
Calcutta

Professor Shah Manzoor Alam : Teacher, Researcher and Administrator

Prof. Shah Manzoor Alam had a very fruitful teaching and research career at Osmania University, spanning almost four decades. He joined the Department of Geography at Osmania University in 1950 and has been a towering personality and a beacon of light in the Department of Geography at Osmania University, preoccupied with teaching and research. In fact he gave a head start to the 'research' tradition in this department, which had otherwise been only a teaching department. He was a teacher with exceptional distinction, qualities of discipline and indepth knowledge, flowing from his extensive research driven by rare intellectual ingenuity. This made him stand out in the teaching fraternity and earned respect for him from the student community and admiration from his peers. He had a rare knack of teaching, where the subjects taught by him left a lasting impression on the minds of the students. His classes were always looked forward to and were attended in full strength and with rapt attention. Besides, the subjects taught by him also became the most popular and sought after specializations. In this way the Geography Department of Osmania University came to be identified with urban geography and all subsequent research and studies on Hyderabad by individuals and institutions took cues from his works and commenced with reference to his work. Prof. Alam was a rare visionary and he could chart and steer the future of the department towards a chequered destination. The courses that he started have saleability even after forty years. His work and determination brought the Special Assistance Programme to the Department from the University Grants Commission. With this extensive infrastructure was added to the Department. His persistently positive approach and definite mission enabled him to emerge as an institution builder par excellence. He also set up the Centre for Area Studies at Osmania University in 1982 and was its Founder-Director. He has been a very capable administrator and always led by example and from the front. He was punctual and did not take easily to any kind of misdemeanour at the work place. He was a strict disciplinarian and always went by the rule book. He had a rare eye for identifying the right people while recruiting staff and the staff recruited by him have emerged as assets to the various departments. Prof. Alam has also been an advisor with the World Bank from 1982 onwards. When the call came in 1984, he served as the Vice Chancellor of Kashmir University at Srinagar, where he introduced many new courses and revived others. Prof. Alam has also been a very widely travelled person, both in India and abroad. Even post-retirement, he has been very active in research and tried to decode the secrets of the *Dead Sea Scroll* from English translations of Hebrew. He tried to look for the unifying factors of the different religions in these. He has also written a book entitled 'war on terrorism' or American Strategy for Global Dominance: Islamic Perspective on the Afghan-Iraq war about the Iraq conundrum in the recent past.

Prof. Alam's research and publications in the field of geography have substantially expanded the scope of the subject adding innovative approaches to understand development from geographic perspective and yielded such outputs as the Planning Atlas of Andhra Pradesh, the first comprehensive study of Hyderabad and its region, national primate cities, and national settlement system of India on the one hand, and energy as a critical input to urbanization and the geopolitical significance of the subregions of India as well as the Indian Ocean region on the other. He has more than fifteen books to his credit, both written and edited; this is apart from over fifty research papers. His contribution to the launch of Cartography as a specialized discipline through the formation of the Indian National Cartographic Association in 1978, initiation of post graduate diplomas in Geographical Cartography and Urban and Metropolitan Planning at Osmania University are other significant contributions. Although urban studies received an initiation in the 1920s in the west, in India it is only in the 1950-60s that efforts in the direction of urban studies commenced, and Alam is one of the torch bearers in this direction. He worked consistently for over six decades, exploring new realms and making signal contributions to knowledge. Such a combination of academic brilliance, administrative efficiency, and outgoing personality are extremely rare.

Kalpana Markandey and Geeta Reddy Anant
(Former Students of Professor Alam)

Professor Shah Manzoor Alam–1928

Manzoor Alam is buried neck deep in the study of the *Dead Sea Scroll*. Scrutinizing the English translations of these Hebrew and Aramaic texts, Alam's aim is to decode the principles which unite religions that are contained in these works. It was a write up in *Edit* a newsletter of the University of Edinburgh in 1997 that led Alam towards the historical richness of these traditional texts. Identifying and creating a unique niche of works is not new to Alam.

When Alam joined as a lecturer at Osmania University in 1950, the Department of Geography was languishing in obscurity. It was a department tucked way out in the south and stood isolated from the heartland of Geography which held sway in the north. Intellectually the university was impoverished, as two-third of its faculty had fled to Pakistan as an aftermath to the partition of India. It is here that Alam built a department which the University Grants Commission recognized as a Centre of Excellence way back in 1978. This is not all, Alam is the founder of the Centre for Area Studies in 1982. Its objective to bring together the countries of Indian Ocean to a common platform for research was unprecedented not just to the State of Andhra Pradesh and the University of Osmania but to India as a whole. Invited to the Vice Chancellorship of the University of Kashmir, Srinagar in 1984 was Alam's other arena where he displayed talent. In the exceptionally hot soup of political challenges which embroiled Kashmir valley, Alam introduced half a dozen new courses of study and revitalized many which had virtually gone defunct. His vision was not merely to guard the chair, but to use his position in fostering close ties between Kashmir and the rest of India. A Talent Promotion Scheme wherein each winter vacation more than twenty teachers of the university were funded to tour and research in any part of India was a scheme whose goodness is still remembered. Laudable were his works with the World Bank from 1982 to 1997, that till date he remains a consultant in their file.

How did Alam accomplish all this? Alam had no intellectual mentor in India, he has a doctorate from the University of Edinburgh. Born on the first day of the year in 1928 in a small town of Ghazipur about 75 kilometres to the north of the city of Banaras, Alam does not hail from an elite family of political, economic or academic repute. It was from St. Andrews College of Gorakhpur that Alam did his intermediate. Academics was not one of the Alam's first career options, to commission as an officer in the defence forces was his desire. A graduation and a post graduation from the University of Aligarh in 1948, did not add feather to his cap. A short year as a lecturer in an intermediate college at Jaunpur in 1949 and a term of teaching at the National Defence Academy were not pads for a launch of any sorts. Filled with pride and dignity, Alam is far from the type who networked or begged favours. What then was the chemistry to Alam's success? Innovative research in Geography, is what catapulted him into the stage of spotlights.

Availing the British Council Travel Grant and the University of Edinburgh Scholarship, it was under the tutelage of Watson, chairperson at the department of Geography, Edinburgh that Alam had completed his doctorate in 1962. Do the Theories of Hoyt, Harris and Burgess on the urban evolution of America explain the morphology of Asian city was the interesting question Alam addressed in his doctorate. His results are truly penetrating, very revealing, and original contribution to urban Geography is what Wreford Watson writes in the preface of Alam's published thesis: *Hyderabad-Secunderabad—A Study in Urban Geography* in 1965. Alam's use of a mixture of theory, common sense and inferences drawn from data challenged the established models and led him to the conclusion that "all cities are too much the children of their cultures to be alike, each speaks in a unique way of the history and geography of the region it expresses". Studies on urban Geography were not new to the academic landscape of Indian Geography, but Alam's work was a departure from the kind of urban studies prevalent in the country at that time. His research so stirred the academic community that Alam could not be ignored. Invitations of visiting professorship poured in from as far as the University of Massey at Palmerston, New Zealand; and the University of Macquarie, Sydney, Australia, where he spent six months each in 1972 and 1974 respectively. The Planning Atlas of Andhra Pradesh—the first of its kind in 1976 in India, was Alam's next turf of success. Bringing together three diverse departments:

State Planning Department of Andhra Pradesh, Survey of India and the University of Osmania the thrust of the Atlas held a strong message—administration can understand planning better through maps. The acclaim acquired through the Atlas invigorated Alam towards another unusual creation—the Indian National Cartographic Association in 1978. It was Alam's brainchild. When Joy Dunkerley, the economist with the United States senate was in search of an anchor for her project on fuel wood Alam was an obvious choice. This paved the way to a series of projects on urban energy with the World Bank through 1994 to 1997. Writing five books, editing another ten and publishing fifty research articles—it is in the harvest of innovative works in Geography that Alam reaped his bounties.

Creative people like sensitive species tend to retreat rather than adapt when the environment gets hostile. Even though nurtured with personal care when conferences turned more political than professional Alam preferred to limit his days of attendance. When political meddling interfered with his vision of a Vice Chancellor, Alam forwarded his resignation.

How does Alam peg himself ? Reticent and humble he attributes his works to the will of God. Little wonder that Alam has found another unique niche—to make active the secrets of the *Dead Sea Scroll.*

Professor Anu Kapur
Department of Geography
Delhi University

Professor Shah Manzoor Alam : A Short Profile

Shah Manzoor Alam was born in Ghazipur City, Uttar Pradesh, on January 1, 1928. He completed his schooling from that city in 1942. and joined St. Andrews College, Gorakhpur for Intermediate or Pre-University education which he finished in 1944 and subsequently joined the Aligarh Muslim University to pursue higher studies.

Dr. Manzoor Alam obtained his Master's Degree in Geography from the Aligarh Muslim University, India, and Ph.D. from Edinburgh University, U.K. He is a distinguished social scientist who retired as Vice Chancellor, University of Kashmir. Prior to that he was Dean, Faculty of Social Sciences, Head, Department of Geography and Founder Director of Centre for Area Studies, Osmania University, Hyderabad.

Dr. Alam is an eminent geographer specializing in urban geography and regional planning. His research contributions in these disciplines have been path breaking and trend setting. The importance of his research contribution was nationally recognized when he was selected as National Lecturer in Geography in 1977 by the University Grants Commission in India.

He is the only Indian scholar to have developed a theory of urban growth for Indian cities. He highlighted the uniqueness of Indian cities while comparing them with urban growth theories for cities in the West, particularly in Western Europe and North America. His contribution in the field of urban geography was internationally recognized. He was invited by Massey University, New Zealand and Macquarie University, Autralia, as Visiting Professor to lecture on Urban and Regional Planning. He was also a member of the

Commission on Urban Development and National Settlement Systems of the International Geographical Union (IGU) from 1972 to 1980. He has lectured extensively in his field of specialization in universities in Malaysia and in Eastern and Southern Africa.

The Planning Atlas of Andhra Pradesh, India, was another trend setting scholarly work pioneered by Alam. Its publication in 1976 attracted the attention of the Planning authorities of other States in India and many of them attempted to emulate the model set by the Andhra Pradesh Planning Atlas.

He was attracted to energy studies in the early eighties by Dr. Joy Dunkerley, an eminent British energy economist. They jointly worked on a project "Fuel Wood in Urban Markets" funded by the Resources for the Future, a Washington based organization. The findings of this research study were published by the Concept Publishing House. The success of this project deepened his interest in energy studies and led to the establishment of the Institute of Energy and Environmental Studies in Hyderabad in 1990. Subsequently, in 1994, the Institute took up a World Bank funded project on "Household Energy Consumption in Urban India—Case Study of Metropolitan Hyderabad." The project was jointly directed by Dr. Alam and Dr. Douglas Barnes of the World Bank.

He has a rich and diversified experience as academic administrator which culminated into his appointment as the Vice Chancellor of the University of Kashmir where he set high standards of academic excellence. Alam's expertise as academic administrator was utilized by the Government of India. He was appointed Member of the Executive Council of a number of Central Universities managed by the Government of India. His most challenging appointment was on the Executive Council of the North Eastern Hill University, Shillong, Meghalaya, during its foundation years. He played a key role in shaping its development programmes in the formative stage of the University.

Alam's services as a social scientist were utilized by UNESCO to work on a project on Vulnerability and Resilience of Cities in India. He also served as a Member of the Indian Council of Social Sciences Research (ICSSR), Ministry of Human Resources, since its inception from 1972 to 1975 and then again from 1988 to 1991.

He has published more than fifty research articles in Indian and international professional journals. He is an author of distinction. He has authored four books one of which, namely *Hyderabad-*

Secunderabad, Twin Cities: A Study in Urban Geography (Allied Publishers, 1965) is a unique contribution to urban studies in India. Professor Watson of Edinburgh University, in his Foreword to this book, wrote that he "has made a most original, interesting, and valuable contribution to urban geography" and added in conclusion, "All who are interested in cities, in history and geography, in the growth of cultures, and in systems of philosophy will find Dr. Alam's study extremely stimulating and thought provoking."

Alam has recently written a book titled *War on Terrorism or American Strategy for Global Dominance—Islamic Perspective on Afghan-Iraq War*. It has been published by Vantage Press of New York, U.S.A.

Contents

PART III

URBAN INDIA : HOUSEHOLD ENERGY CONSUMPTION—POLICY ISSUES

PART IV

OTHER TOPICAL THEMES

Introduction

This book, an ensemble of select essays written by Prof. Shah Manzoor Alam, independently and collectively with other co-authors, portrays the diverse fields into which Prof. Alam forayed in the quest of knowledge. The sixteen essays are divided into four parts based on specific themes. Part one focusses on the 'Theories of urban growth', Part Two deals with the 'Settlement systems of India', Part Three highlights 'Urban household energy consumption—Policy issues' and the last Part discusses largely `Historical and Geopolitical` issues.

Part One

Prof. Manzoor Alam has traced *Ibn Khaldun's Concept of the Origin, Growth and Decay of Cities* in the very first chapter of this volume. This opening chapter has set the tone for the other chapters in this volume as well as it has traced the growth of cities in a timeline context. Ibn Khaldun, a fourteenth century scholar, made a detailed study of cities as the dwelling places of man. He gave a historical, strategic, geographical, social, economic and ecological interpretation of cities. The fundamental ecological processes of competition, co-operation, conflict, dominance and succession operate also in shaping the human society according to him. Ibn Khaldun made signal contributions to urban geography with the help of a critical and analytical method. The organismic concept of the development of human society led him to apply the ecological principles in studying and understanding the genesis, growth and decay of human civilization.

The setting of a city, however, requires certain favourable natural factors for its future growth and expansion. In all probability the political factors in the age of Ibn Khaldun were so paramount and predominant that other factors could be safely overlooked. He, however, analysed carefully and examined critically the various factors—cultural and natural—contributing to the origin, growth and expansion of cities. To him cities represented a vital aspect of civilization performing a variety of specialized functions in the economic and cultural fields. The city, he recognized, was a product of time and the impress of each period was indelibly marked on its life structure.

The city reflects the characteristics of its age, carries the impress of its past and epitomizes the ideals of the civilization it represents. It, therefore, forms an inevitable link in the evolution of human society. The city passes through the early stages of pioneer dwelling, village, town, city and metropolis, before it reaches its present self-suffocating condition. Ibn Khaldun recognized three major stages in the evolution of cities and society: Youthful, Maturity and Senility. Ibn Khaldun formulated the norms and enunciated the principles which applied in assessing critically the various stages of evolution of the human society. He considers civilization to be cast in the mould of constant change and continuous movement.

Alam maintains that Khaldun's intellectual contributions lie in his approach to the study of human society as illustrated by the character, form, function and transitions of cities. His ingenuity lies in projecting the city as a consequence of man's social and cultural development as an individual and as a member of a group and the respective institutions, together with their respective attendant attributes. The emphasis on ecological principles in Khaldun's appraisal of city growth is more recently explored by Philip Armesto Fernandez exhaustively. The essence of cooperation to promote city growth and civilization of any kind is well brought out in the Muquaddimah (Prologomena). Alam lauds the links between climate and resources and cities, the cause of defence and fortifications, the urban-regional interdependence, cities as socio-political structures imprinted by time and their locational advantages. Alam compares Khaldun with al-Farabi and others, especially Khaldun's concept of rise and fall of cities to the western perspectives as also classification of cities, definitions, of cities etc. Alam brings out Khaldun's ingenuity in coherence and scientific approach and upholds Khaldun's work as highly intellectual and visionary.

In the chapter on *Masulipatnam—A Metropolitan Port in the Seventeenth Century,* Prof. Alam finds that one cannot just imagine the prosperity or even the decline of Machilipatnam, called by various names—Maisobs, Masalia, Masuli, and studied by Sinnopah Arasiratnam, and which has been in existence since the Satavahanas (first century). In tracing the growth of Masulipatnam, Alam appears to have the objective of explaining the growth of Hyderabad as well as the rise and fall of cities as expressions of the regional set-up. Masulipatnam, the eastern counterpart of Surat, and a port of international importance precedes Hooghly and Madras (now Chennai). It was the chief port of the Golconda kingdom and is stated to have the most plural, multicultural and cosmopolitan populations, economy and culture by virtue of being the confluence of people of diverse backgrounds from West Asia and the Far East who met there for trade and commerce. Its growth and decline in response to the progress and prosperity of the kingdom of Golconda ratifies the strong city-region relationship, the stability of Golconda kingdom and the existence of the natural harbour. Its defeat to new technologies, larger ships, catering to increasing volume of trade and changing global political equations proved to be its bane. The ruin of the port is also attributed to misadministration.

In *The Concept of Islamic City and the Planning of Islamabad* it is found that the Islamic city is not a city of the past. It is a continuous presence of the philosophy of Islam, translated into cultural practices and determined by the religious beliefs. Its presence extends to all such countries that promote and follow Islam as a religion either partially or completely. Damascus, Islamabad, Shahjahanabad, Baghdad and the countries of Indonesia and Malaysia boast of some very typical examples. In the essay *The Concept of Islamic City and the Planning of Islamabad*, Shah Manzoor Alam contoured the Islamic cities in all their dimensions tracing their genesis, growth and the structure and form. The religious moorings and cultural underpinnings reflected in the layout of the settlements, architectural forms and housing design demonstrate the past and existing lifestyle. The conformity of every Islamic settlement and houses to the Islamic tradition and way of life reflects the concept, design and plan, with time and space as no inhibitors. Alam is critical in this chapter that Islamabad does not conform to the basic planning principles of Islamic cities such as Shahjahanabad in Delhi, Hyderabad in Andhra Pradesh and Lahore in Pakistan.

The first written research document and consistent research on Hyderabad and its hinterland is by Shah Manzoor Alam. *The Growth of Hyderabad—A Historical Perspective*—comprises an explanation of the genesis and growth of Hyderabad as a planned city as the statements of Tavernier and Thevenot explain and the remains of the city today substantiate. The extensive narration of the demographic, socio-cultural and politico-economic details of Hyderabad and its residents from inception to emergence as the capital of the linguistic State of Andhra Pradesh is the first of its kind and a source of reference to subsequent writers. This essay forms a prelude to the subsequent extensive research undertaken by Alam during his active academic career which few can lay claim to.

In *Indian Cities and Western Theories of Urban Growth—An Empirical Appraisal,* Prof. Alam has placed the twin cities of Hyderabad and Secunderabad within the framework of the morphological classification of Dickinson, Burgess and Hoyt and has examined the applicability of these western models in the context of the cities of the developing countries. He has, meticulously, placed each of the morphological units of Hyderabad and Secunderabad within the outline of these models giving due cognizance to their social and cultural moorings. Hyderabad is envisioned a socio-cultural unit, influenced by political, religious and linguistic factors and it is viewed within this milieu vis-à-vis the western cities which are commercial and industrial cities. The characteristics which tell apart Hyderabad from the American cities similarly distinguish other Indian cities from them. It is thus found that Indian cities have a distinct history, culture and social structure of their own and hence their course of expansion, growth and development differ from the Western cities.

Prof. Alam's work on *Indian Cities and Western Theories of Urban Growth* has added fresh dimension and new direction to urban studies in India. In his Foreword to Alam's work published in 1965: *Hyderabad-Secunderabad (Twin Cities)—A Study in Urban Geography*, Professor Wreford Watson of Edinburgh University wrote that scholars "will find Dr. Alam's study extremely stimulating and thought provoking such as should lead to many new fields of research and the whole enrichment of geographical knowledge."

Part Two

In the path breaking chapter *Metropolitan Hyderabad—Its Pattern of Regional Influence and Delimitation of Its Planning Areas*

Prof. Alam has highlighted the primacy of Hyderabad in the State of Andhra Pradesh. This city has a functional primacy as well and interacts strongly in a spatial, social and economic sense with its hinterland. It, thus, cannot be planned in isolation of the region and at the same time the Hyderabad Metropolitan Area is a very extensive area to be treated as a Primary Planning Area. Hence, a scientific delimitation of the area for planning becomes crucial. The region has been largely delimited by means of the traffic shed apart from other techniques pertaining to the supply zones of various perishable commodities and the service areas of certain services. The area of influence is by and large confined to a 40 km radius from Hyderabad and this has been found to be the most appropriate area for the economic planning at the micro level. This area is further divided into three zones—the metropolitan core, the peri-urban zone and the rural hinterland. This is the hard core area of urban impact within the Primary Planning area which is delimited based on the Principal Elements like suburban transport, retail, water supply etc. and Reflective Elements like villages with more than 50 per cent of the population in non-agricultural activities, villages with more than 1,000 units of electricity consumption etc. This chapter highlights the need for an integrated rural-urban planning in this area in order to stem chaotic growth which if left unchecked will snowball in the future. Prof. Alam predicted as far back as 1972 that this Primary Planning area will be extensively urbanized in the future leaving little scope for regulated development. There has been a manifold escalation in the land values in this area owing to commercialization of agriculture and henceforth all land transactions should be with the approval of the planning authorities. An integrated rural-urban land use plan should come up which is aimed at the development of satellite towns, setting a physical limit to the extension of water supply, sewerage, electricity, and telephone lines and also the establishment of planning and administrative machinery for the Metropolitan District.

The chapter on *Distortions in the Settlement System of India* brings about a correlation between the economic system and the settlement system. The settlement system evolves in response to the politico-economic system and the level of economic development. The political twists have warped the settlement systems which have evolved over a period of time and have made for new spatio-economic bonds. The relationships may take time to get forged and may require proactive policy interventions and till such time remain as distortions in the settlement system. Examples of this have been cited from Rajasthan where the urban system had evolved around the princely states of Jaipur, Jodhpur and Udaipur and the lower order centres had tuned themselves to the supremacy of these larger primate cities in their respective kingdoms. They had aligned themselves around these centres from a spatial as well as a functional angle, but after the reorganization of India on linguistic lines, all the three regions became part of the poly-nucleated settlement system of Rajasthan and could not take on the degree of spatial cohesiveness that is expected in the case of a mono-nucleated hierarchical settlement pattern. So has been the case with Andhra Pradesh where settlements belonging to different systems were realigned to a new economic, political and administrative nucleus centred on Hyderabad. In this situation political, administrative and cultural integration is possible but economic integration is a difficult task more so as the settlements were linked to a larger and economically more dominant centre—Chennai (then Madras). The case of Calcutta (now Kolkata) is also unique as it was part of and at the apex of the East Indian Settlement system. After East Pakistan (present day Bangla Desh) broke off from east India the links of the settlement system in this area were disturbed and Calcutta had to realign itself all over again with the rest of east India, now through a very constricted passage in the northern part of West Bengal.

The transport routes and the inter-city linkages that they forged, further brought about a hypertrophy in the settlement system of India. This led to the dominance of the markets of sub-dominant centres rather than those of the rural areas. The central places in the rural hinterlands are unevenly distributed resulting in a distorted system of hierarchy. Distortion in the settlement hierarchy of India was found to be the direct outcome of the colonial policy to concentrate investments and administrative and political power in a few large urban centres. This thwarted the development of a system of towns which would embrace the entire settled space of the country and also prevented the development of a regional urban sub-system.

To create a more dynamic urban and metropolitan economy, the government must mediate and contain the role of finance capital, check polarized development of metropolitan centres, hasten the growth and development of middle order urban centres and initiate public policy to encourage the percolation of developmental impulses to the lowest level of settlements in the system.

The National Settlement Systems of India was commissioned by the Commission on National Settlement Systems of the International Geographical Union. It was published in the book *Urbanization and Settlement Systems : International Perspectives*, by the Oxford University Press in 1984. Dr. Alam has brought together and synthesized in this chapter his research findings on the settlement systems of India as outlined and explained in the articles on this theme, most of which are included in Part Two of this volume. This chapter brings out the uniqueness of the evolution of settlement systems in India because of the interplay of its distinct historical, political and cultural factors. While maintaining its distinctiveness the impact of global economic and cultural currents are clearly visible in the contemporary development of Indian Metropolises.

This chapter brings out the poly-nucleated urban apex of the hierarchy of settlements in India. The colonial past has a lot to do with the urban system of India. Calcutta and Bombay have been strong flag bearers of the colonial economy as they interacted with the imperial power. After independence, Madras and Delhi have been tagged on at the apex of this multinodal system of cities. Most of the investments were concentrated in them and they have now formed systems around them organizing the space in their economic environs. The Calcutta system still has a primate city pattern. There is a marked absence of lower order settlements in this system. Even a study of inter-settlement distances brings out this fact in no uncertain terms. The Bombay, Delhi and Madras systems have a relatively low index of primacy. As the States of India have a wide diversity, they display variations in the city size structure also. Three distinct systems have been identified: (i) Primate City Distribution as in Andhra Pradesh, West Bengal, Maharashtra, Tamilnadu, Karnataka and Gujarat. Primacy is relatively high in the context of these States which have either had a feudal past or where they had ports under the sway of the British colonizers. The capital cities have a concentration of high order educational, medical, banking and other services. They also have the main transport routes radiating out from them. (ii) Lognormal Distribution in Uttar Pradesh and Rajasthan where their focii—Kanpur and Jaipur, respectively have not been overwhelmingly dominant in their respective regions. (iii) Decentralized Distribution as in Madhya Pradesh, Bihar, Orissa, Kerala and Punjab. Barring Punjab, the other States have a low level of development.

Prof. Alam observes that urban growth in India is Metropolitan oriented. The metropolitan settlements of India have grown under four distinct socio-economic, political and administrative situations and these situations in turn define the processes of urbanization operative in India : (a) Politico-administrative processes of urbanization, where new capital cities like Chandigarh or Gandhinagar were created or alternatively the status of district headquarters like Kohima or Gauhati was upgraded to the level of the State capital. (b) Agro-based urbanization, which is giving rise to dynamic balanced development. Examples of this occur in the Krishna, the Godavari and the Kaveri Deltas, plains of Punjab, Haryana and western Uttar Pradesh. (c) Polarized Industry oriented urbanization, has picked up the pace and vastly expanded since independence. It is found in regions like Ranchi—Hatia, Bokaro, Rourkela and Bhilai besides Ramagundam and Visakhapatnam. Most of them have national and international links but lack local moorings. Hence the rural-urban divide gets intensified and induces in migration to the central city and its periphery. (d) Multi-functional metropolitan oriented urbanization, where the combination of higher order market, industrial, transport and service functions generates an urban force which has helped the growth of big cities. These cities also have a distinct concentration of quaternary functions. On the periphery of these cities sub-urbanization is active and large industrial satellites came up as in the case of Hyderabad or Bangalore. Prof. Alam has used the example of Hyderabad to show as to how these metropolitan magnets prevent the articulation of the settlement system at both the micro and meso regional level. The magnetic pull of Hyderabad has not allowed services to develop in its micro region and its powerful shadow effect does not allow even lower order metropolitan settlements in Telangana like Warangal and Nizamabad to come out of its silhouette.

The chapter highlights that like any developing country India has also experienced the concentration of investments and higher order administrative and political functions in few large urban centres. An upshot of this was hypertrophy of the urban system and deterrence to the development of a system of towns embracing the entire settled space of the country. The control of monopolistic production and finance capitalism of the metropolitan economy has continued even after independence and hence the pattern of urban and metropolitan development in independent India is not much different from that of the colonial times. This type of metropolitan development also comes in the way of the diffusion of technology, causes stagnation of the hinterland economy, prevents adequate articulation of a hierarchical system of settlements and leads to outmigration of people from the peripheral rural areas and middle level urban centres. The intervention of the government is required here to discourage the concentration of investments in metropolitan settlements, encourage the growth of middle order urban settlements and initiate policies to promote permeation of developmental impulses to the lowest level settlements in the system.

In the chapter *Regional Planning : Functional and Nodal*, Prof. Alam, brings out the inherent differences between two types of territorial systems—the functional organization of a region which is based on the homogeneity and specialization of functions in an area on the one hand and integrative nodal regions on the other. He has traced the concept of regional planning in the framework of the Five Year Plans of India and found that it gained cognizance with the planners only from the Third Five Year Plan onwards, when the key role of urbanization in stirring up social and economic transformation was appreciated. It was then that the master plans for select urban areas were prepared. The Fourth Five Year Plan, further stressed on regional and metropolitan planning. During the Fifth Plan period small towns and new urban centres were promoted and a National Urbanization Policy laid down.

This is more of a review paper of the many regional surveys conducted throughout the length and breadth of the country. Also a number of studies on Market towns, Growth Pole or Metropolitan Oriented studies on regional Planning in India have been re-examined and Prof. Alam feels that though a number of studies find nodal regions as a more realistic approach to regional planning yet no effort has been made to understand the totality of the urban system of India and the role that metropolitan settlements can play in integrating the economy. Thus the main task is to identify the National Urban System of India along with its sub-systems. This would help take appropriate steps to hasten intra-regional development and lessen inter-regional inequality. This would lead to the formulation of a national policy for the development of counter-magnets to check the growth and decrease the magnetic pull of national metropolises.

In the chapter *Metropolitan Dominance Atrophies Rural-Urban Integration* Prof. Alam points out that Metropolitan Dominance is a characteristic feature of the urban scenario of all developing countries.

These metropolitan cities have a concentration of administrative and economic functions and thus emerge as primate cities in their respective regions but are also parasitic in nature. They dominate at the national as well as at the State level. They are better connected to other metropolitan cities than to the region of their location, though they build up a symbiosis with their hinterland.

There was a remarkable increase in the urban population of India during 1971 and 1981. This is largely due to the sharp increase in the population of Class I cities. These cities attracted a substantial proportion of the population of the smaller towns leading to the decimation of the population of the latter. Even among the Class I towns it is the four largest i.e. Delhi, Calcutta, Bombay and Madras which have shown a noteworthy increase. They have a very large concentration of the labour force of the country as well as that in the secondary, tertiary and quaternary activities. They also have an enormous concentration of banks, deposits and advances. Furthermore, they contribute to trade in a remarkable way.

Hyderabad is one such case in point which is likely to continue as a primate and also a parasitic city. It is better linked with urban centres outside the State than with settlements in its own region. In addition the transport network and the concentration of central government jobs in these centres favour their growth and development. This in turn has led to increased immigration into these centres.

This study concentrates on the cases of Hyderabad as a primate city in Andhra Pradesh and Bombay (now rechristened Mumbai) in Maharashtra. It is found that there is a hyper concentration of migrants employed in senior professional and managerial cadres in both these cities. The grip of these metropolises on the national economy is such that the prices of perishable food items of consumption in these metropolises are determined by the national demand pattern. They also cater to the demands of such products in the non-metropolitan areas, thus stunting the development of the hinterland of the latter.

Metropolitan dominance has inhibited the integration of the rural economy with the urban system. Integration, wherever visible, is only with regard to the city and its hinterland. If distortions in the national economic system are to be eradicated, the process of rural-urban integration has to be hastened. This can be done by a phased redistribution of the tertiary and secondary activities from the metropolitan cities to lower order urban settlements and a revamping of infrastructure facilities in rural India, minimization of wage differential between the metropolis and lower order settlements. This is essential to bring rural India into the vortex of the national economic system so that it is not deprived of the developmental benefits.

Part Three

The issue of household energy and fuel wood studies were first initiated by Manzoor Alam who provides a socio-economic and spatial dimension to an otherwise essentially science and technology related subject matter. Alam in his numerous research projects has drawn attention to energy as a household item, as a driver in urbanization and as an environmental factor, which needs to be examined from the geographic perspective.

Part Three includes three essays on household energy. Research studies on these issues were carried by Alam and co-authors of the respective chapters.

The essay *Fuel Wood in the Context of Developing Countries: Two Case Studies from India* co-authored with Joy Dunkerly, and Amulya Kumar Reddy, is about fuel wood consumption of Bangalore (now renamed Bengaluru) and Hyderabad. They examine the fuel wood consumption patterns, demand and sources of supply besides the impact of prices of other available energy carriers. In the examination of fuel cycle of the two settlements in terms of generation, distribution and use, parallels are registered in mode of supply, procurement by consumers, trade and sales patterns, and supply besides consumption differentials in actuals and estimates. Two significant geographic inputs to fuel wood estimates are distance as a factor of time and volume. The transportation means, distribution channels and kind of consumers constitute important additions to fuel wood evaluation surveys. The variations in costs of fuel wood and between fuel wood and other energy carriers, consumer competition, demand conflicts, facilitate a clear evaluation of fuel policies which are the strengths of the study.

Fuel Wood as a Source of Domestic Energy in Urban India—The Case of Metropolitan Hyderabad and Raipur is a joint contribution by Alam, Joy Dunkerley, Molly Macauley and Naimuddin. The study projects fuel wood as a persistently important source of energy with a sustained demand despite the implosion of modern fuels. The assessment of supply and demand trends gains clarity with the examination of the constraints, fuel mixes, compositions, demand and supply preferences, transitions, purchasing power variations and changes, cultural inhibitions that determine choices. The impact of monetization and commercialization on fuel choice in rural and urban sectors as well sectoral demand impact the choice and consumption levels significantly. Hence the urban demand for fuel wood persists at a high level of 50 per cent. While per cent term decline in number of consumers is registered, the actual consumption has increased and is likely to persist in the foreseeable future. Hyderabad varies in area, population size and character from Raipur, and hence some differences are noted in the catchment area of fuel wood supply (200 km versus 100 km), slower energy transitions and slower population growth. According to the authors, fuel wood will continue to be the principal energy source for the urban poors. In view of the diminishing free sources, the need for constant monitoring of supplies, devegetation controls, plantation propagation are recommended. It is noted that the trends observed in Hyderabad and Raipur are applicable for the rest of India.

This is more extensively examined and explained in the essay *Urban Household Energy Use in India : Efficiency and Policy Implications*, by Alam, Jayanth Sathaye and Douglas Barnes. The authors of the chapter stress that household energy consumption and transitions are products of resources' availability, changes in policies, price-parity and consumer's socio-economic disposition. The need for inter-fuel substitution and fuel-ladder—income-education connection is amply demonstrated. Tracing the need to enhance modern fuel access and availability, driven by human health and welfare concerns, prompted government interventions through subsidies, the authors appraise consumer preferences for cleaner fuels, accessibility of modern fuels, and government's policy pursuits. The comparisons of 1980-2000 trends include approval of government-private initiatives in energy supplies and pricing. Addressing government's Public Distribution System, they recommend targeting of subsidies to the needy, reforestation to check devegetation trends and improvement of energy markets through stringent measures. They opine that changes in policies and prices and availability of fuels and household disposition (socio-economic etc.) are impacting factors for inter-fuel substitution on the one hand and energy ladder as determined by income and education, on the other. The need to enhance modern fuel access and availability, driven by health concerns for users, prompted government interventions through subsidies, require targeting the low income groups as against the high income groups which currently are the greater beneficiaries. This is apart from aggressive revegetation and controlled deforestation together with improvement of energy markets.

Part Four

Alam's research and publications transcend the limits set by disciplinary boundaries. His examination of the role of boundaries, territory and territoriality in development and urbanization as well as the growth and decline of regions and settlements illustrates his trans-disciplinary approach to research and problem solving.

Geopolitical Importance of the Indian Ocean is an important exploration of the Indian Ocean from a historical and resource perspective to trace the transformations in linkages and networks between nations and regions as determined by economic and commerce interests on a mutually complementary basis and the gradual transformation in these in consonance with the geopolitical climate to a progressively exploitative nature and use of critical locations as defence and espionage launch pads. Underscoring the importance of the Indian Ocean Region as a resource rich region with geo-strategic locations, connecting the largest number of countries in the shortest possible distances, Alam illustrates the present and future significance of this ocean and region underscoring the need to study it. Highlighting the trends in progress and prosperity, Alam argues on the requirements of greater defence forces and security for the Indian Ocean countries as well as those traversing its waters and land, from a security and safety perspective. The land and sea lanes of communication, centres of marketing, nodal settlements, sea ports as soft targets with rim, littoral countries as well as heavy investment arenas for the Americas, Europe and other Asian counterparts, trace the economic interactions preceding the first century A.D. with Europe and East and West Asia. A forecasting and prescriptive approach for mutual development and coexistence is projected with multiculturality as a means of achieving it. Presumably in view of the aforesaid factors Alam established the Centre for Area Studies for Indian Ocean Region at the Osmania University

Changing Geography—Redrawing India's Internal Spatial Structure is all about the political game play driven by economic interests and foreign influx for annexing and looting. In the earlier essay India's stakes as a regional power are very adroitly spelt out. In this essay India's responsibility to its own citizens and India's role in regional power play is analysed. Alam examines the internal; politico-economic structures in this essay. Driven by the need for autonomy vis-à-vis control and decentralization, specially with respect to the border States a review of existing federal political system is recommended to ensure mitigation of development imbalances, and satisfaction of Indian citizens. Alam criticizes the 'linguistic jingoisms" and divisive tendencies in the States. He highlights the importance of English language as a binding force and education as an important propeller of development.

Critical of the federal polity of the country which has encouraged dualism in our political and economic system which has accentuated tension and friction in the State-Centre relationship. Alam suggests the need to develop a political system which, while eliminating the existing dualistic system of government, will allow democracy to percolate down to the grass root level and where the people will genuinely feel that they have a share in the management of the country. In his view this may be feasible if the federal structure is replaced by a unitary system, the States are abolished and the district is made the basic political and administrative unit of a national system of administration. The modern system of communication which is being effectively used to centralize political and administrative powers in the capital cities of the States can be used with equal effectiveness to decentralize it. The telephone, teleprinter and wireless network can instantly link the district headquarters with the national capital.

The chapter concludes that transformation of the federal polity of India into a democratized and decentralized unitary system will, on the one hand, eliminate divisive tendencies and, on the other, maximize economic development and reduce socio-economic disparities at all levels. The abolition of the states of India and the emergence of the districts as the planning, administrative and political entities is envisioned. It will transform radically the political, social and economic setting of the country. The national capital can be strongly linked to the district headquarters by modern means of communication and transportation from where the developmental impulses can effectively trickle down to the village level. There will be no State and Central sectors, no concurrent and State lists, and no Central and States' services. All these anomalies will vanish and will give way to a well articulated and highly democratized national system with, distinct but well coordinated national policies on education, administration, industrial and agricultural development, etc. The plurality of Indian culture will flourish but it will be subsumed by a broader national culture and will be perceived in the national context.

The Historical Deccan—Geographical Appraisal—The evolution of the concept of the historic Deccan has been critically examined in this chapter. Alam highlights the fact that the historic Deccan as perceived by the historians did not exist during the Vedic period. All territories south of the Vindhyas were called Dakshinapatha. The concept of the historic Deccan evolved with the expansion of Aryan imperialism and culture to the south of the Vindhyas. In order to assert the unity of India all the imperial powers of the north from Asoka to Aurangzeb attempted to annex territories south of the Vindhyas to control them politically. Analysing these succession of north Indian imperialistic invasion of the territories and the extent and magnitude of their territorial control, Alam divides the Deccan Peninsula into three distinct geopolitical units: (1) Marchland or area of political cultural assimilation by the North; (2) Heartland or area of political control and domination by the northern imperial powers; and (3) Peripheral Land of the Deccan in the extreme south where the political control and cultural influence of the North was minimal. The chapter concludes that in Independent India the historic concept of the Deccan has lost its validity. India's security is now threatened more from the sea than from land. This geopolitical compulsion demands that in order to protect itself India must develop a powerful navy. This point has also been stressed in the first chapter in this Part.

Prof. Kalpana Markandey
Prof. Geetha Reddy Anant

Part I : Theories of Urban Growth

1

Ibn Khaldun's Concept of the Origin, Growth and Decay of Cities

Ibn Khaldun, a distinguished, bold and independent Arab scholar of the fourteenth century appeared on the intellectual horizon of Islam when the Islamic power and prestige and its intellectual brilliance, having passed their meridian of glory, were revealing signs of decay on all sides. The intellectual legacy of Ibn Khaldun thus remained in oblivion for centuries, both in the East and the West. It was only towards the end of the seventeenth century that Ibn Khaldun was introduced to European scholars by D'Herbelot[1] but western thought showed no interest in his works till the beginning of the nineteenth century when Sylvester de Sacy[2] published a lengthy biography in 1816 and Von Hommer Purgstall[3] studied critically Ibn Khaldun's theories on the decline of states and published a German translation of some passages of the Prolegomena. However, the real resurrection of the intellectual achievements of Ibn Khaldun was brought about in 1858 with the publication in Paris of the Arabic version of his Prolegomena by Quatermere[4] and in the same year in Cairo by Shaikh Nasr Alhurainy. A decade later with the publication in Paris of M.D. Slane's complete translation of the Prolegomena [*Les Prolegomenas de Ibn Khaldun (1863-68)*] in French, appeared in diferent languages as critical studies of Ibn Khaldun as a philosopher of history (Kultur Historical), economist, sociologist and geographer were written by scholars of repute. Unfortunately, none of these scholars has critically appraised, evaluated and compared Ibn Khaldun's concept of urbanization, although the entire fourth chapter of the Muqaddimah is devoted to a discussion of the factors contributing to and the principles governing the origin, growth and decay of cities. Scattered references to this aspect are also found in the first, third and fifth

Published in *Islamic Culture*, Hyderabad, April 1960, pp. 90-105.

chapters. Muhsin Mahdi's[5] excellent study of Ibn Khaldun is probably a solitary exception. The following is an attempt at a critical analysis and a comparative study of Ibn Khaldun's exposition of the principles of urbanization.

Ibn Khaldun's Basic Approach to the Study of Human Society

It would not be beside the point here to refer to the basic approach of Ibn Khaldun to the study of human society as that would assist a better appreciation of his analysis as regards the characteristics, forms and functions, and growth and decay of cities.

Ibn Khaldun claimed to be a scientific historian, and to him history "is information about human social organization which itself is identical with world civilization. It deals with such conditions affecting the nature of civilization... and with all other institutions that originate in civilization through its very nature."[6] The scope of history was thus widened and its concept changed from a mere faithful chronicling of events in time perspective to a "record of man's social development dependent on natural causes, and resulting from the impact of environment and the reaction of individual and group".[7] This comprehensive nature of history covers every aspect that contributes in giving shape to human civilization, stage by stage and age by age. In fact it is all pervasive, for he surveys that human scene in its entirety to understand the principles that govern the evolution of human fundamental unity among the social, political, economic and spatial aspects. In the interpretation of his concept, he reasserts his view-point in the following words: "I omitted nothing concerning the origin of races and dynasties, concerning the synchronism of the earliest nations, concerning the reason for change and variation in past periods and within religious groups, towns and hamlets...sciences and crafts, gains and losses, changing general conditions, nomadic and sedentary life, actual events and future events, all things expected to occur in civilization. I treated everything comprehensively and exhaustively and explained the arguments for and causes of its existence."[8] While treating everything exhaustively and comprehensively, he pursued the scientific principles of keen observation and comprehensive accumulation of facts, their careful sifting, rational classification and accurate description without prejudice and partisanship. He fully realized that proper understanding of any single human phenomenon would necessarily entail an appreciation of other connected factors, because each is, inevitably and inseparably, linked with the others. Ibn Khaldun emphasized the basic and underlying unity of all the branches of knowledge and attempted their synthesis in his exposition of human society. He adopted the critical and analytical method only to sift the truth from the spurious. He was essentially interested in discovering the essence of civilization, and to express that his inventive genius and creative intellect introduced the "Sciences of culture". This proved a penetrating medium to explore the causes and express the interrelationships that bind together the various cultural aspects, and the culture with the environmental factors. To him human society was essentially dynamic and organic, undergoing continuous change, manifesting discernible patterns and following discernible causes.

Application by Ibn Khaldun of Ecological Principles

The organismic concept of the development of human society led him to apply the ecological principles in studying and understanding the genesis, growth and decay of human civilization. He observed and reflected upon the structure of its life history which comprises three distinct phases—juvenile, adult and senile. Human society, although tempered with cultural factors, is peculiarly symbiotic in character, since it passes through all those phases and possesses all the characteristics which comprise the life cycle of an organic substance, plant or animal. Ibn Khaldun himself observes, "The world of elements and all it contains comes into being and decays. This applies to both its essences and its conditions—minerals, plants, all the animals including man and other created things and specially the conditions that affect man. Sciences grow up and then are wiped out. The same applies to craft and to similar things".[9] Human society has to experience the biotic processes because of man's intimate association with the organic world for his food and shelter. Like plants man is in need of nutrition, growth and generation, and as in the case of animals, his appetites and choleric power seek correct adjustments. "Those needs and desires are strong drives that direct human action and intention. They may be elemental and primitive, but they are powerful and persistent."[10] His emphasis on the submission of man to the general laws, which govern animals, shows his awareness of the principles of ecology. He at the same time understood that human behaviour was not simply determined only by this intimate relationship of man to the physical environment and the world of organism. There are other factors too. Man is distinguished from animals by four distinctive qualities as enumerated by Ibn Khaldun:[11] (a) Ability to think, (b) Restraining influence of a strong authority, (c) Man's need for food and his efforts to make a living, and (d) Civilization. He too, like Park, recognized that "human society, as distinguished from plant and animal society, is organized on two levels, the biotic and the cultural. The cultural superstructure rests on the basis of the symbiotic substructure, and the emergent energies that manifest themselves in the biotic level in movements and actions reveal themselves on the higher social level in more subtle and sublimated forms."[12] Man's relation, therefore, to the world of intelligence and his rational approach to the problems of his society impart a purposeful motive to human movements. Man sets before himself certain ideals which manifest themselves in the shape of evolving civilizations. It is this idealism of man that lifts him above the animal plane, yet the cyclic character peculiar to plant and animal life is a dominant characteristic in the evolutionary process of human society as well. "Society is nothing but awhile in the universal current of things; it goes away as everything does. Life is like a rhythm; every change necessitates the contrary, every rise is followed by a fall".[13]

Further elaboration of the ecological principles applied by Ibn Khaldun is obtained when he discusses the origin of society and rise and fall of dynasties. The fundamental ecological processes of competition, co-operation conflict, dominance and succession operate also in shaping the human society. Eorge Simmel observes : "Society exists wherever a number of individuals enter into reciprocal relations with one another". Ibn Khaldun also in the fourteenth century had expounded a similar basis for society. He considered co-operation essential for the emergence of social organization even in its most primitive stage : "God created and fashioned man in a form that can live and subsist only with the help of food. He guided man to natural desire for food and instilled in him the power that enables him to obtain it. However, the power of the individual is not sufficient... Thus he cannot do without a combination of many powers from among his fellow beings... Through co-operation, the needs of a number of persons, many times greater than their own number, can be satisfied."[14] Co-operation is thus at the root of every social organization. Co-operation on an intensive basis confined to a restricted number generates that dynamic force of human organization; group feeling is the creative force governing the evolution of civilization. Its initial vigour unleashes a force of intense competition and conflict through which society registers marked progress. The emergence of a dominant group imparts stability to the social organization, thereby allowing full play to the creative ability of man leading to the development of optimum civilization. This stage of civilization may be compared with the climax condition and the dynamic equilibrium obtained at a maximum biological potential of the dominant plant species. The climax having been reached, civilization ceases to grow and stagnation sets in. The forces which contributed to the phenomenal growth of civilization, lose their vitality and begin to decline at an accelerated pace. The zenith of civilization marks the culmination points of its evolution. It generates such forces at its height that civilization begins to recede and decline. During this final stage the people are prone to live luxuriously and "luxury corrupts the character... the soul acquired diverse kinds of evil and sophisticated customs... This points towards retrogression and ruin... The dynasty shows symptoms of dissolution and disintegration. It becomes affected by the chronic diseases of senility and finally dies."[15] The death of one ushers in a fresh, vigorous and youthful current of civilization and the ecological processes of competition, dominance and succession reassert themselves. This natural process of disintegration is essential if the dynamic processes of change and growth in the structure of civilization are to be maintained. Ibn Khaldun considers civilization to be cast in the mould of constant change and continuous movement. In the words of Professor Flint, "He expresses himself repeatedly and in various forms the general truth that history is a collective continuous movement, an incessant and inevitable development."[16] Ibn Khaldun formulated the norms and enunciated the principles which applied in assessing critically the various stages of evolution of the human society. He was primarily interested in discovering the effect of position,—both time and space, upon human institutions and human behaviour. He recognized the internal bonds that unite the manifold aspects of civilization and that during the rise and fall of civilization influence and casually determine each other. He fully appreciated "the complex dynamism of the rise and fall of civilization", and the "need to inquire into the manifold relationships...as they manifest themselves during the different stages of its development".[17] And thus Ibn Khaldun's 'Science of Culture' like the modern human ecology is "fundamentally an attempt to investigate (1) the processes by which the biotic balance and the social equilibrium are maintained once they are achieved; and (2) the processes by which the biotic balance and the social equilibrium are disturbed, the transition is made from one relatively stable order to another"[18] These complex forces and processes of civilization reveal themselves distinctly in urban forms and functions. The city reflects the characteristics of its age carries the impress of its past and epitomizes the ideals of the civilization it represents. It, therefore, forms an inevitable link in the evolution of human society. Realizing its significance, therefore, Ibn Khaldun has at length dealt with the manifold aspects of urbanization in the Muqaddimah.

The growth of a city, in the view of Ibn Khaldun, is a natural stage in the evolutionary cycle of civilization. It is a physical manifestation of the social growth. It expresses the humanized aspects of the spatial phenomena. Mumford and Vidal de La Blache express similar views. The former thinks that the 'city is primarily a social emergent,[19] and the latter remarks that "a city, in the full sense of the word, is a social organization of much greater scope; it is the expression of a stage of civilization...[20] Ibn Khaldun treats the city and its institutions as an important aspect of civilized culture and its existence, according to him, is "for the satisfaction of man's desire for luxury, refinement and leisure."[21] The capital cities are ostentatious manifestations of the glories and the majesty of a state. In them are concentrated the best that civilization has to offer. They are homes "of the highest achievements of man in art, literature and science."[22] They represent the optimum stage in the development of human society.

Ibn Khaldun treated the cities not only as historical facts and social phenomena but considered them as physical entities as well. He, therefore, analysed carefully and examined critically the various factors, cultural and natural, contributing to the origin, growth and expansion of cities. To him cities represented a vital aspect of civilization performing a variety of specialized functions in the economic and cultural fields. The city, he recognized, was a product of time and the impress of each period was indelibly marked on its life structure. He equally appreciated the city as a geographical phenomenon and in his analysis of the distribution and size of the cities he made it abundantly clear that they were closely linked with the climate and the resources of their respective regions.

Origin of Cities

The development of cities is next in the stage of hierarchy to the Bedouin civilization. It is only when the nomads have reached a certain level of civilization and have raised themselves above the subsistence level that they turn their attention to comforts and conveniences and consequently "they build large houses, and layout towns and cities for protection".[23] There are certain prerequisites to the establishment of a city: (1) The peaceful and steady progress of civilization; (2) a sustaining force to guarantee peace; and (3) an agency to remove the state of insecurity of the cultured, yet defenceless, people of the city as a further guarantee to progress and prosperity. Thus royal authority precedes the evolution of cities. "This because when royal authority is obtained by tribes and groups, the tribes and groups are forced to take possession of cities for two reasons. One of them is that royal authority causes the people to seek tranquillity, restfulness and relaxation, and to try to provide the aspects of civilization that were lacking in the desert. The second reason is that rivals and enemies can be expected to attack the realm, and one must defend oneself against them."[24] Thus royal authority, defence and the existence of peace, in the opinion of Ibn Khaldun, are the major contributory factors in the origin of a town. This analysis by Ibn Khaldun of political factors being paramount is fully corroborated by Mumford, a great authority on medieval town-planning: "The political necessity for town making arose earlier than economic need. In the humble beginnings of the new towns of the Middle Ages, military considerations are always paramount. A strong ruler conquered a district adjacent to his old dominions or wished to defend his frontiers against neighbouring enemy. He built rude fortresses, and encouraged his subjects to live in them."[25]

Apart from the political and geographical factors conditioning the site of a town, the famous author of the Prolegomena seems to betray complete ignorance of the economic, strategic and inertia factors that also played quite a prominent role in the location of medieval towns. That he was aware of the significance of accessibility in determining the geographical extent of any kingdom is clear from his statement that "each dynasty has a certain amount of province and lands, and no more."[26] And yet the fact that he fails to appreciate this is all the more surprising. He is aware that the capital city is the nerve centre of a kingdom "The centre is like the heart from which the vital spirit spreads. Were the heart to be overrun and captured, all the extremities would be routed."[27] In spite of his keen appreciation of the role of the capital city, he makes a vague statement about the regeneration of certain capital cities: "Frequently it happens that after the destruction of the original builders of a town, that town is used by another realm and dynasty as its capital and residence... The life of the new dynasty gives the town another life. This has happened in contemporary Fez and Cairo."[28] This statement seems to suggest that only political accidents dictate the choice of capital cities. Probably the political factors in the age of Ibn Khaldun were so preeminent and predominant that other factors could be safely overlooked.

Location of a Town

The city is a product of expanding human needs. It is, therefore, a rational expression of the cultural aspects of man. The setting of a city, however, requires certain favourable natural factors for its future growth and expansion. With the changing requirements of society the site and situation of the city also are altered and only those sites and situations which constantly respond favourably to the expanding needs of human society have the potentialities for optimum development.

During the age of Ibn Khaldun the location of a town pivoted on and was conditioned by physiographic factors. Towns were dwelling places as also places of defence. "Therefore, it is necessary in this connection to ensure that harmful things are kept away from the towns by protecting them against inroads by them, and that useful features are introduced and all the conveniences are made available in them... one should see to it that all the houses of the town are situated inside a protective wall. Furthermore, the town should be situated in an inaccessible place, either built upon a rugged hill or surrounded by the sea, or by a river so that it can be reached only by crossing some sort of bridge...In connection with the protection of town against harm that might arise from atmospheric phenomena, one should see to it that the air where the town is to be situated is good, in order to be safe from illness."[29] Thus protection against external enemy and security against harmful atmospheric effects were the primary considerations in locating a town. Having enunciated the general principles on the lines of Aristotle, Ibn Khaldun enumerates the various geographical factors that are to be kept in view while deciding upon the site of a city: "The place should be on a river, or springs with plenty of fresh water facing it. The existence of water near the place simplifies the water problem for the inhabitants, which is urgent", but marshy areas which pollute the atmosphere and are breeding ground of harmful germs should be avoided. "Another utility in town for which one must provide is good pastures for the livestock of the inhabitants. Every householder needs domestic animals for breeding, for milk and for riding. These animals require pasturage. If the pastures are nearby good, then that will be more convenient for them, because it is troublesome for them to have the pastures away. Furthermore, one has to see to it that there are fields suitable for cultivation. Grain is the basic food. When the fields are near, the needed grain can be obtained more easily and quickly.

Then, there is also the problem of woods to supply firewood and building material. Firewood is a matter of general concern. Timber, too, is needed for roofing and for many other necessities for which timber is employed.

"One should also see to it that the town is situated close to the sea to facilitate the importation of foreign goods from remote countries. However, this is not on the same level with the afore-mentioned requirements. All the requirements mentioned differ in importance according to the different needs and the necessity that exists for them on the part of the inhabitants."[30]

Ibn Khaldun was probably not the first Arab scholar to deal with the subject. We have it on the authority of Enan[31] that al-Farabi had also elaborated on these aspects but his treatment was purely philosophic, whereas Ibn Khaldun's is empirical and social. His statement, therefore, pertaining to the physiographic requirements for the town planning is candid, and concise and covers the fundamentals governing the location of cities. He also realized that requirement patterns vary from region to region as is evident from his discussion on the coastal and border towns.[32] He is, however, silent about the physical aspects of town planning. The value of his statement on town planning would have been greater had he thrown light, like Aristotle, on the principles that govern the town patterns, the laying out of the major arteries of the city and the direction of its physical expansion. If he had dwelt upon these aspects, we would have been in possession of a valuable critical appreciation of the Arab concept of town planning. Anyway this should not detract from the merit of his careful analysis of the environmental factors affecting town location. It would be too exacting to expect him to throw light on the modern requirements, because today, social results are the outcome of mechanical shocks. In his age they were the products of simple human attitude and behaviour. That he could perceive the requirements of his age correctly and present them in proper perspective, is indeed a great tribute to his genius.

He could not conceive of a city, and very rightly too, existing as an isolated unit totally cut off from its surroundings. He imagined the city and the desert as an integrated and interdependent unit. It is very clear from his statement that the cities were not so remorselessly urban in character as the modern cities are. According to Ibn Khaldun, the city and its immediate hinterland comprised four zones: (1) the central built-up area; (2) the pastoral zone; (3) the agricultural belt, and (4) the forested tract, arranged either in almost concentric zones or wedge and sector pattern and easily accessible from the central zone where most of the population was concentrated. The order of proximity of these zones is not rigidly fixed by Ibn Khaldun. It is liable to change, for instance, if an agricultural tribe inhabits the city, then the members of this group would prefer a location in close proximity to agricultural land, which will thus replace the pastoral zone in order of proximity. The forested tract always occupies the periphery in this rural-urban continuum. Ibn Khaldun envisages a complementary rural urban association "city in continuous need of fresh supplies of inhabitants and mercenary soldiers, who must be drawn from the desert and the countryside. It is also in need of the foodstuffs produced by the countryside adjacent to it. The inhabitants of the desert and the countryside on their part come to desire the enjoyment of some of the conveniences offered by the city. They offer their produce or services in exchange for these conveniences."[33] This rural-urban interdependence is borne out even more prominently by modern researches. Hallenbeck expresses this fact as follows: "Because of the interdependence of the urban nucleus and the adjacent countryside, it is impossible ecologically, economically, or politically to divorce the urban from the rural aspect of a community or to consider either singly with any possibility of genuine understanding."[34] To Ibn Khaldun the existence of populous rural suburbs was a prerequisite for the continuity in the life of any town after the collapse of the dynasty that founded it "The dynasty that has built a certain town may be destroyed. Now the mountainous and flat areas surrounding the city are desert, the word 'desert' here implies open pasture grounds inhabited by nomadic tribes that constantly provides for an influx of civilization. This fact then will preserve the existence of the town, and the town will continue to live after the dynasty is dead."[35] A city, situated in isolation and cut off from its hinterland, is doomed to decay and destruction. "It may happen that a town founded by a dynasty now destroyed has no opportunity to replenish its civilization population by a constant influx of settlers from a desert near the town. In this case, the destruction of the dynasty will leave it unprotected. It cannot be maintained. Its civilization will gradually decay, until its population is dispersed and gone."[36]

The Age of a City and the Stages in its Development

The life of a city depends on the following factors as explained by Ibn Khaldun : (1) The life of the dynasty which founded the city; (2) the city and its hinterland; and (3) the inherent pull of the city.

The city comes into existence when groups acquire the power of establishing it. This is thus inevitably linked with the formation of a state and the rise of a dynasty. The city is a visible manifestation of a growing civilization. Royal authority and civilization are inseparable like form and matter. The shape of civilization is preserved by the sustaining force of royal authority and crystallizes in the form of a city. As it is impossible to imagine a civilization without a dynasty, similarly the existence of civilization is unimaginable without an urban base. The city represents the pulse of the dynasty and the civilization and in turn life in a city is conditioned by the force of the civilization. Therefore, the fall of a dynasty and its civilization disturb the city's equilibrium and disrupt the fabric of its life. Thus the life span of a dynasty is also the life span of a city. The ruins of Damascus, Marrakesh and Baghdad, during the time of Ibn Khaldun provided positive proof to his general concept and enabled him to generalize thus: "We have found out with regard to civilization of the city that is the seat of the ruler of that dynasty also crumbles, and in this process often suffers complete ruin. There hardly ever is any delay."[37] Not agreeing with this sweeping generalization of Ibn Khaldun, one has however, to admit that this factor operates even to this date in the rise and fall of capital cities. Confirmation and general echo of this view are also found in the scholarly study of Ibn Khaldun by Prof. Taha Hussain.[38] However, there are other factors that may act as a brake in the process of complete disintegration of the city after the fall of the dynasty. An intimate association of the city with its hinterland is one of them. He refers to the populous suburbs feeding the city proper with population in case of disintegration, and thus saving it from decline. He is, however, vague as to the forces that would attract this suburban population when the royal authority is removed.

Lastly, there are certain cities which have a geopolitical pull and thus even after the fall of one dynasty they are being retained as the political centres of the succeeding dynasties and by virtue of this they, escape the death, that in the view of Ibn Khaldun, haunts every capital city—small or great. It is in such cities that the sedentary culture is firmly rooted, urban characteristics are prominent, and progress is continuous.[39] Vidal de La Blache strikes a similar note. "... In others progress has never entirely ceased. Such regions have never suffered alarming breaks in continuity. For there has been an uninterrupted sequence of related political systems."

The appearance of a city and its culture is not a miraculos phenomenon but an evolutionary process. True to his organismic concept of the evolution of societies, Ibn Khaldun applies it to study the rise and decline of cities. His passage on the stages in the evolution of a city compare favourably with the description of the city of Lebanon and New Hampshire by E.N. Torbert.[40] The evolutionary stages of a city are described by Ibn Khaldun in the following words:

> "It should be known that when cities are first founded, they have few dwellings and few building materials, such as stones and quicklime, or the things that serve as ornamental coverings for walls... Thus at that time the buildings are built in Bedouin style, and the materials used for them are perishable.
>
> "Then the civilization of a city grows and its inhabitants increase in number. Now the materials used for building increase because of the increase in available labour and the increased number of craftsmen. This process goes on until the city reaches the limit in that respect...

"The civilization of the city then recedes, and its inhabitants decrease in number. Thus it entails a decrease in the crafts. As a result good and solid buildings and the ornamentation of buildings are no longer practiced. Then the available labour decreases because of the lack of inhabitants. Materials such as stones, marbles and other things, are now being imported scarcely at all, and building materials become unavailable. The materials that are in the existing buildings are reused for building and refinishing. They are transferred from one construction to another,....The same materials continue to be used for one castle after another and for one house after another, until most of its is completely used up. People then return to the Bedouin way of building. They use adobe instead of stone and omit all ornamentation. The architecture of the city reverts to that of villages and hamlets. The mark of the desert shows in it. The city then gradually decays and falls into complete ruin, if it is thus destined for it."[41]

This vivid and living description of city evolution reminds one of Griffith Taylor, who has very much improved upon this concept of city evolution and has provided it with a real scientific base. Griffith Taylor believes in a "Cycle of Town Evolution" but doubts if geographers "shall ever be able to analyse and synthesise the data of city development so adequately that we can produce as logical a concept of a Cycle of Town Evolution," as that of the geomorphological cycle. Yet, "We can but try for one thing we are dealing with the irrational actions of Man, rather than with the inevitable actions of nature. Hence the City Cycle cannot be as clear as the Landscape Cycle."[42]

Ibn Khaldun recognized three major stages in the evolution of cities and society: Youthful, Maturity and Senility. Griffith Taylor retaining these three stages adds the infantile stage,[43] preceding the youthful one. Like Ibn Khaldun he also considers relevant the symbiotic process in the growth of cities and compares the growth of a city with that of a tree. "But it is something like the way a young tree grows. Its trunk and branches increase by a sort of expansion, while quite new characters such as flowers and fruits appear as it reaches maturity."[44] Every great city of today had a small beginning and in his own words: "The giant city, unwieldy and unaesthetic as it is, has passed through the early stages of pioneer dwelling, village, town, city and necropolis, before it reached its present self-suffocating condition."[45] Griffith Taylor's analysis of the city of Toronto[46] unfolds clearly the variations, from age to age, in the types of buildings and the materials used, for their construction and bears close resemblance with that of Ibn Khaldun cited above. It may further be added that Ibn Khaldun's brilliant analysis of city evolution does contain the germs of the 'Zones and Strata' concept which was later scientifically nurtured and perfected by Griffith Taylor. This is, however, not to suggest that Prof. Taylor was in any way influenced by the ideas of Ibn Khaldun. It would be dangerous to draw the analogy too far. There is a basic difference in the approach of the two scholars, as there is a wide divergence between the periods of which they are the products. Ibn Khaldun studies the city essentially as a social phenomenon and considers it an outcome of the rise of the dynasty and the state. Griffith Taylor, on the other hand, attempts to unravel all the complex forces and factors—social, political, economic, cultural and physiographic—which are involved in the inevitable Cycle of Urban evolution. Griffith Taylor, besides describing the general urban characteristics, is also busy evolving a scientific system of classifying cities according to their functional categories and discovering the discernible patterns of city-development on a global basis as conditioned by the physiographic factors. The modern city rests on complex mechanism and is not so simple as to collapse with the fall of the ruling power. It has a sounder economic base and can withstand political upheavals. The modern economic and commercial metropolises overshadow the political capitals if they are not identical. That Ibn Khaldun could not analyse on the lines of Griffith Taylor is conceivable but that he could suggest the line of approach, later perfected by the latter, is indeed creditable.

Size, Classification and Characteristics of Cities

The expansion of the physical size of the city, the growth of its population and the development of its institutions, its prosperity and luxurious manners of life are entirely dependent on the continuous political patronage and protection that could be offered by strong, capable and stable political power.

The size of a city and the monuments it contains are in direct proportion "to the importance of (the various dynasties). The construction of cities can be achieved only by united effort, great number and the co-operation of workers. When the dynasty is large and far flung, workers are brought together from all regions and their labour is employed in a common effort. Often, the work involves the help of machines, which multiply the power and strength needed to carry the loads required in building (unaided) since human strength would be insufficient."[47] The size of a city, both physical and in density of population will depend on the continuity of sedentary culture, the age of the city and the size of the kingdom that the city commands. A kingdom of vast dimensions will provide the city with vast and diverse resources, both natural and human, which enhance the prestige and position of the city. A city which has been the political capital for centuries has its built-up area so vastly increased and population so multiplied that it looks an aggregation of urban centres.[48]

Ibn Khaldun not only classifies cities on the basis of their size and density of population, but he had also some notion of the functional classification of urban centres. He introduces the idea of the superiority or hierarchy of cities on the basis of crafts.[49] "The activities required for the necessities of life, such as those of tailors, carpenters, and similar occupations exist in every city. But activities required for luxury, customs and conditions exist only in cities of highly developed culture... Among such activities are those of glassblowers, goldsmiths, perfumers, cooks, coppersmiths, biscuit bakers, harisah bakers, weavers of brocade and the like".

These differential activity patterns in the cities are in accordance with the increase in the customs of sedentary culture and requirements of luxury conditions; there originate crafts especially for this kind of luxury requirements. The crafts of this kind will thus exist in a particular city, but not in others... Public baths... exist only in densely settled cities of a highly developed civilization... Therefore, public baths do not exist in medium sized towns".[50] The growth of a city is a slow process of accretion and with the passage of time it not only increases in physical dimensions but also accumulates a variety of functions. Thus the hierarchy in size and functions of a town will depend on the period for which sedentary culture had persisted there. There is a wide range of variation in the age of cities even within a realm and, therefore, they differ, among themselves, both in size and functions. "The quality and the number of the crafts depend on the greater or lesser extent of civilization in the cities and on the sedentary culture and luxury they enjoy."[51] Thus there are small-sized towns exhibiting a slight improvement over the nomadic life, the medium-sized town with just a few luxuries developed, and the large sized ones, existing as expressions of superior civilizations and products as it were the results of accumulated progress",[52] having concentration of highly developed crafts and scientific pursuits because of the availability of surplus labour, leisure and capital resources.

A scientific definition of the city is yet to be discovered. It has been consistently eluding the urban ecologists. A uniform quantitative system is inapplicable, since the pace of urbanism is not universally uniform. What is applicable to one is inapplicable to many others. For instance, the quantitative approach to define the cities of the United States does not fit into the urban structure of either Europe or India. It was in sheer desperation that Wilbur C. Hallenbeck pronounced: "A city is what a city does" and thus he has very much hit the nail on the point. To distinguish one city from another, and to distinguish between the urban and rural centres, it seems logical that in either case the distinguishing characteristics should be analysed and presented. Ibn Khaldun adopted this technique throughout while discussing the evolution of urban centres.

Distinguishing the urban from the desert civilization, he states: "It has been stated by use before that desert civilization is inferior to urban civilization, because not all the necessities of civilization are to be found among the people of desert. They do possess some agriculture at home, (but) they do not possess (all) the materials that belong to it, most of which depend on crafts. They do not have any carpenters, tailors, blacksmiths, or other (craftsmen whose crafts) would provide them with the necessities required for making a living in agriculture and other things . . . likewise, they do not have (coined) money—dinars and dirhams. They have the equivalent of it in harvested grains, in animals, and animal products such as milk, wool of animals, camels, hair, and hides which the urban population needs and pays the Arabs money for."[53] Making another fine distinction, he says that "the desert people live mainly on agricultural and pastoral occupations which do not take them beyond the subsistence level," and contrary to this, "sedentary people means the inhabitants of cities and countries, some of whom adopt the crafts as their way of making a living, while others adopt commerce. They earn more and live more comfortably than Bedouins, because they live on a level beyond the level of bare necessity, and their way of making a living corresponds to their wealth."[54]

Cities are centres of production, trade and commerce, they are "the world's market place. All kinds of merchandise are found in the market and near it. The wealth of the nation is accumulated in the city and its free circulation in urban regions contributes to the prosperity of the city."[55] Cities are the great producers of surplus products. "This surplus provides for a population far beyond the size and extent of the actual one and comes back to the people as profit which they can accumulate. Prosperity thus increases and conditions become favourable"[56] for concentration of wealth.

With its gradual evolution, a new social structure develops in the city. The tribal sense of 'group feeling' which had prevailed in small, closely knit and relatively isolated communities tends to disappear. Individual families live in isolated residences and become strangers to one another. "The highly differentiated demands for specialised goods and skill tend to create specialized groups of artisans and traders. The various classes comprising the city, the rulers, the bureaucracy, the artisans and traders as well as the learned tend to group themselves according to their political and economic interests rather than their blood relations."[57]

The city is a concentration of labour, leisure and wealth. It, therefore, encouraged development of highly specialized crafts and sciences. Scientific pursuits require both wealth and leisure and the availability of either only in large cities, confines these pursuits to large sized cities only. "We, at this time, notice that science and scientific instruction exist in Cairo in Egypt because the civilization of (Egypt) is greatly developed and its sedentary culture has been well established for thousands of years."[58] "The development of specialized crafts and instruction in various branches of science attract people from the desert regions where technical knowledge is non existent, to cities to seek scientific instruction."[59]

The city culture, having reached the apex, turns senile by the self-effecting processes of urban luxuries. They breed laxity of morals and corrupt customs. The vitality of desert life and its integrity and honesty are totally annihilated. The city in its senile stage develops the characteristics of slums and blighted areas of large and modern urban centre. "Immorality, wrong doing, insincerity, and trickery for the purpose of making a living in a proper or improper manner, increase among them... People are now devoted to lying, gambling, cheating, fraud, theft, perjury and usury."[60]

The Decay of Cities

"The highest peak of civilization is generally its turning point. Thence begins the step backward—thence commences the decline of the State". Thus, summarized Khuda Bux,[61] Ibn Khaldun's concept of the decline of civilization after attaining the climax. The decline of the State is sharply reflected in the deteriorating economic conditions of the capital cities. "A city with a large civilization (population) is characterized by high prices in business and high prices for its needs."[62] The prices are sky rocketed during the senile stage of the State, since (owing to its mounting expenditure and shrinking frontiers and resources) the royal authority is compelled to levy customs duties. The progressively declining economic conditions reduce the purchasing capacity of the people and consequently there is general slump in business.[63] Fall of business spreads squalor and poverty. Prosperity deserts the city, leaving behind heaps of slums. Depopulation sets in and ultimately dehumanization completes the process of the ruin of a city.

Wrong choice of locations, either in relation to natural features or cultural ones, may also contribute in the decline of urban centres. A city by the side of a marshy areas, or located in isolation, cut off from its natural and population resources, is doomed to ultimate decay. Ibn Khaldun considers decay of cities and civilization quite natural in the cycle of urban evolution. They have a natural span of life. All the great cities have their origin in humble hamlets and, having reached the climax, they revert to their original status. Cities being an inevitable link in the growth of civilization cannot escape the rigours of the laws of nature. His contentions are substantially supported by the modern researches of Griffith Taylor. Even Vidal de la Blache echoes the voice of Ibn Khaldun while describing the evolution of civilization. "Even in some countries of advanced civilization a mode of life once achieved is a closed circle . . . The same old habits persist without perceptible change. So that after having shown signs of an evolution capable of reaching a stage of relative perfection, there comes a certain impotence, an incapacity to advance farther in the same direction or to start off in any other . . . A time comes, when all effort ceases... A period of stagnation follows that of progress..."[64] and finally the chain of progress is broken.

Conclusion

Ibn Khaldun was the first among the ancient and the medieval scholars to have made a coherent and scientific study of cities. Prior to him Aristotle also discussed the growth and functions of cities in his *Politics*,[65] but his cities are meant only for "those who are members of the state and form part of it". Ignorant of the ecological processes, Aristotle introduces rigid zoning of functional areas, completely segregating one from the other, in order to create the most beautiful city. He is so busy combining magnitude with good order that he signally fails to take into account the social and economic forces that operate so powerfully in the growth of cities. His account of the growth and functions of cities lacks coherence and is far from being scientific. Ibn Khaldun, on the other hand, fully appreciated the social basis and the economic character of the urban order and, therefore, paid considerable attention to observe the character and development of these features in the urban set-up. To him the city was the concrete manifestation of the rising level of human civilization. In the constantly shifting scenes of city development he tried to observe the general laws and principles operating upon the growth and development of the city structure. He fully "recognized the superiority of sedentary culture, the goal of all of man's efforts to become civilized". He equally appreciated the urban characteristics, the close rural-urban relationship and the impact of environmental factors on city growth. He, however, had only dim apprehension of the ecological patterns of a city. This may partly be due to the fact that during the age of Ibn Khaldun the functional areas, excepting the royal palaces, were not well differentiated and defined and, therefore, they did not possess sharply distinguishing features to invite the attention of the author of the Prolegomena, and partly due to the fact that he studied the cities as an inevitable stage in the cycle of civilization. He was, therefore, in search of urban synthesis and thus was not interested in dissecting the individual cities. Moreover, the quantitative methods now developed to investigate the complicated urban patterns, were beyond the intellectual resources of Ibn Khaldun. It is not, therefore, expected of him even to suggest an attempt on the modern lines. In spite of this handicap, he did suggest and approach to the study of cities on the line of Griffith Taylor, and it was no mean achievement considering the age when the Prolegomena was written. That he had many failures, it has to be admitted. Those were the failures not of his intellect, observation and appreciation, but of the age of which he was the product. Yet in the Muqaddimah he re-evaluates, in a systematic way practically every single individual manifestation of a great and highly developed civilization. The Muqaddimah accomplishes this, both comprehensively and in detail, in the light of one fundamental and sound insight, namely, by considering every thing as a function of man and human social organization. He was indeed a man with a great mind who combined action with thought, a man of vision and penetrating intellect who always looked ahead of his age.

REFERENCES

1. D'Herbelot: *Bibliotheque Orientale*—1697.
2. Sylvester de Sacy: *Biography Universettle*—1816.
3. Von Hammer Purgstall: 'Ubenden Verfall des Islams nach den evslen drey juhrhunderter dev Hidschrat'. 1812.
4. In 1858, the *Prolegomena* appeared in Paris in three volumes, edited by Quatermere after a manuscript of Royal Library, within the collection known as "Notices ti Extraits des Manuscripts de la Bibliotheque due Roi," occupying Volumes XVI to XIX.
5. Muhsin Mahdi: *Ibn Khaldun's Philosophy of History*: Chapter I, pp. 209-16 George Allen and Unwin, London, 1957.
6. *Muqaddinah* (tr) F. Khaldun, Rosenthal, Vol. 1, p. 71.
7. N. Schmidt: *Ibn Khaldun, Historian, Sociologist and Philosopher*, (New York, 1930), page 16.
8. *Muqaddimah*: Vol. 1, p. 18.
9. *Muqaddimah*: Vol. I, p. 278.
10. M. Mahdi: *Ibn Khaldun's Philosophy of History*, p. 192.
11. *Muqaddimah*: Vol. I, p. 84.
12. R.E. Park: Human Ecology: *The American Journal of Sociology*, Vol. XLII, July 1936, p. 13.
13. M.A. Enan: *Ibn Khaldun, His Life and Work*, Sh. Ahammad Ashraf, Lahore, India.
14. *Muqaddimah*: Vol. I, p. 90.
15. *Muqaddimah*: Vol. I, p. 341.
16. R. Flint: *The Philosophy of History*, p. 169. (William Blackwood & Sons—Edinburgh, 1893).
17. Muhsin Mahdi: *Ibn Khaldun's Philosophy of History*, p. 203.
18. R.E. Park: Human Ecology, *The American Journal of Sociolog*, Vol. XLII, July 1936, p. 15.
19. L. Mumford: *The Culture of Cities*, p. 6.
20. Vidal de la Blache; *Principles of Human Geography*, p. 471.
21. Muhsin Mahdi: *Ibn Khaldun's Philosophy of History*, p. 209. (George Allen & Unwin, London)
22. *Great Cities of the World*: Ed. W.A. Robson, (George Allen and Unwin, London, 1954), p. 195.
23. *Maqqaddimah*: Vol. I, p. 249.
24. *Ibid.* Vol. II, p. 237.
25. Mumford: *Culture of the Cities*, Secker and Warburg; (1945), p. 25.
26. *Muqaddimah*, Vol. I, p. 327.
27. *Ibid.*, Vol. I, p. 329.
28. *Ibid.*, Vol. II, p. 237.
29. *Muqaddimah*, Vol. II, pp. 243-44.
30. *Muqaddimah*, Vol. II, pp. 246-47.

31. M.A. Enan: *Ibn Khaldun—His Life and Work*, pp. 140-142, p. 137.
32. *Muqaddimah*: *Ibid.*, Vol. II, p. 243.
33. Muhsin Mahdi: *Ibid.*, p. 212.
34. W.C. Hallenbeck: *American Urban Communities*, Harper Brothers and Publishers, New York, 1951, p. 99.
35. *Muqaddimah*; Vol. II, p. 236.
36. *Muqaddimah*, Vol. II, p. 236.
37. *Muqaddimah*: Vol. II, p. 297.
38. Dr. Taha Hussain: *Ibn Khaldun* (Original in French) into Urdu by Maulana Abdul Salam Nadqvi from an Arabic version, Maarif Press, Azamgarh (India), 1940, p. 205.
39. *Maqaddimah*, Vol. II, pp. 216-88.
40. Torbert, E.N. The Evolution of Lebanon, *Geog. Review*, 1935.
41. *Muqaddimah*: Vol. II, p. 270-271.
42. G. Taylor: *Ibid.* p. 7.
43. Griffith Taylor: *Ibid.* pp. 76-77.
44. Griffith Taylor: *Ibid.* p. 73.
45. Griffith Taylor: *Ibid.* p. 73.
46. Griffith Taylor: *Ibid.* pp. 73-76.
47. *Muqaddimah*: Vol. II, pp. 238-39.
48. *Ibid.* Vol. II.
49. *Ibid.* Vol. II, p. 302.
50. *Muqaddimah*: Vol. II, p. 302.
51. *Ibid.* Vol., pp. 434.
52. Vidal de la Blache, *ibid.*, p. 320.
53. *Muqaddimah*: Vol. pp. 308-9.
54. *Muqaddimah*: Vol. I, pp. 249-50.
55. *Ibid.*, Vol. II, pp. 286-87.
56. *Ibid.*, Vol. II, 281.
57. Muhsin Mahdi, pp. 213-14.
58. *Muqaddimah*, p. 434.
59. *Ibid.* p. 434.
60. *Ibid.*, Vol. II, p. 293.
61. *Ibn Khaldun and History of Islamic Civilization*, By Khuda Bux, Islamic Culture (Hyderabad Dn.) Vol. I, No. 4, October 1927.
62. *Muqaddimah*, *ibid.*, Vol. II, p. 292.
63. Abdul Quader M.
64. Vidal de la Blache: (Tr.) Human Geography, pp. 325-26, (Constable).
65 *Aristotle*, Vol. II, Great Books of the Western World Series No. 9, pp. 530-535. (*Politics*: Book VII, Chapters 4 & II). Published by Encyclopedia Britannica, Chicago, 1952.

2

Masulipatam–A Metropolitan Port in the Seventeenth Century

During the seventeenth century Masulipatam or Matchlibandar was the most prosperous port on the east coast of India and was in every respect a rival of Surat, the chief port of the Moghul Empire on the west coast. Masulipatam was already a port of international importance when Hooghly was coming into prominence and Madras was an unknown factor. The metropolitan nature of this port is corroborated by a British factor, who in 1659 called it 'the Metropolitan port and factory'.[1] This 'chief port of the Kingdom of Golcunda' had become 'the most famous mart of the whole Coromandel Coast' and merchants from Europe and Asia used to assemble here to transact business; and thus the port, in the words of a Dominican friar, was 'resembling Babel in the variety of tongues and the differences of garbs and costumes.' Tavernier also found this port in a flourishing state since it could accommodate ships of large tonnage. He says, 'this place is renowned merely on account of its anchorage, which is the best in the Bay of Bengal'. He further endorses its international status as a port, since he found Masulipatam to be 'the sole place from which vessels sail for Pegu, Siam, Arkan, Bengal, Cochin, China, Mecca and Hormuz and also for the islands of Madagascar and Sumatra and the Manilas'.[2]

The town and port of Masulipatam had a meteoric rise and its history as a port of considerable and international importance could be linked with that of the rise of the Kingdom of Golcunda. The trade conditions at Masulipatam fluctuated with the political affairs of the state, and the rise and fall of the trade curve at Masulipatam in the

Published in *Indian Geographical Journal*, Madras, July to December 1959, pp. 33-42; also in *Islamic Culture*, July 1959, pp. 169-187.

seventeenth century represented stable or chaotic conditions, respectively, within the state. Any invasion of the kingdom by the Moghul forces was always marked by a slump in the trade conditions at Masulipatam.

As to the origin of Masulipatam, there is no reliable or authentic information available. It has a Sanskrit name Matsyapura 'from an old tradition of a whale having been washed on to the shore'. This testifies to its existence and traces its origin from very ancient times, but probably during that period it was a minor fishing town. However, the author of the *Tuzaki Walajahi* in a footnote writes as follows; "The port is said to have been founded in the fourteenth century by the Arabs. In 1478 it came to be occupied by the Bahmani Sultan Mohammad II.[3] Another author also ascribes its origin to the Arabs, 'who 400 years ago…, as they say, founded Masulipatam."[4] During the fifteenth or early sixteenth century when the Bahmani kingdom had not disintegrated and its boundaries stretched from the west coast to the east coast across the Peninsula, Goa was its chief and unrivalled port. The town of Golcunda was only headquarters of an outpost of the kingdom. Business of the kingdom naturally gravitated to Bidar and Gulbarga, its two premier cities, and the products of the state found their outlet through the port of Goa. During this period Masulipatam, therefore, remained a minor and an unimportant port of the kingdom.

The rise of Golcunda as an independent kingdom towards the early half of the sixteenth century and its gradual stabilization to prosperous conditions in the latter half of the same century heralded also the rise of Masulipatam as quite the most important mart all along the Coast of Coromandal. The kingdom of Golcunda producing a rich variety of products, both raw and manufactured, and commanding an extensive coast line was bound to develop a number of ports to cover the trade of this highly productive hinterland, and Masulipatam by virtue of its situation became the premier port of the region.

Masulipatam was not a port gifted with the natural facilities of a harbour, and in fact as a port it had many disadvantages. Although it is on the bank of a river, yet it is unfit for ships or pinnaces to enter, being shallow and also narrow; the ships which come here namely ours and English must be about a mile offshore because it is absolutely flat. The ground is very soft; the ships lie in 3 and 4 fathoms. The town is situated about half a league up the river'.[5] The defects in its location are further pointed out by Methowld, who describes it as 'a small town... ill built and worse situated; within all the springs are brackish, and without overflowed with every high sea for almost half a mile about.'[6] These statements pinpoint the disadvantages of Masulipatam as a port. There was no direct land communication between the ships and the town, as the intervening land area was morassy and marshy and thus passage was difficult. This isolation of the ships from the trading centre and the absence of communication facilities except by boats were felt keenly by the English factors when their ships were totally cut off from their factories in the town by local officers who 'had countered all attempts to get off goods and men by stopping communication between the ships and the shore with the result that English ships were suffering for want of water and provisions'.[7] Further, most of the ships required for their berthing and anchorage a minimum depth of 3 to 4 fathoms, whereas the depth of water in the river channel fluctuated between 3 and 8 feet and, therefore, the ships had to anchor in the open and were thereby open to the hazards of weather; and the Coast of Coromandel was notorious for bad weather in the months of November and December when it was frequented by severe cyclonic storms causing great damage to the ships in the roadstead of Masulipatam.

It had certain advantages also, one of which was its comparative freedom from silting. Consequently, the river channel was free from bars and islands and, therefore, plying of boats all the year round without the assistance of any pilot was possible. During that period the Krishna Delta was encroaching towards the south, and Masulipatam being located on the northern branch of the river, was not disturbed by this deltaic advancement.

However, the disadvantages of its site were more than offset by the remarkable situation that it commanded. On its back was the most fertile tract of the Deccan forming its hinterland; and port itself was directly linked with the great capital of the kingdom, Golcunda, which served as an insatiable market for the wide variety of goods imported into the country. The proximity of the large ship-building centre, Narasapurpeta, was an added advantage.

The hinterland of Masulipatam, i.e., the Kingdom of Golcunda, was proverbially known for its abundance in provisions and produced a wide variety of goods, both raw and manufactured, highly valued in the international market. Testifying to the fertility of the region, one anonymous author states that 'the coast for ten or twelve leagues inland abounds in provisions, the abundance increasing as one goes north's,[8] and John Crandon, the penman to the English East India Company, found in Masulipatam 'the only delightful place to live in on all the coast, but not a little expensive; although victual is pretty cheap'. If for nothing else Masulipatam would have earned international fame 'for the beautiful fabrics produced upon this coast'[9] and these fabrics commanded a wide market in Europe, West Asia and South East Asia. Masulipatam as an emporium for calicoes and paintings stood unrivalled all over the country, and in the words of Methowld, 'the paintings of this Coast of Coromandal (are) famous throughout India, and are indeed the most exquisite that are seen, the best wrought all with pensill, and with such durable colours that, notwithstanding they be often washed, the colours fade not whilst the cloth lasteth.'[10] The rich diamond mines of Kollur, employing 30,000 workers daily, were only 108 miles inland from the port. Iron ore and steel of excellent quality were obtained in Nirmal and Indur. Indigo of the finest variety, matching in quality with Lahore indigo, was produced in the region adjoining Masulipatam, Kondapalli and Ellore. Salt, tobacco and saltpeter were the other important products of the state. Saltpetre provided an important raw material for the manufacture of cartridges. Thus the diverse products of Golcunda could cater to the needs of an extensive geographical area from thc tropics to the temperate region.

Narsapur Peta was the greatest ship-building centre of the region and its closeness to Masulipatam assured easy, efficient and low cost repairing facilities to ships coming from long distances. Schorer gives the following description of Narsapur and its ship-building industry: 'A place called Narsapur Peta lies 10 to 12 leagues beyond Masulipatam... Here there is a river, where the Moslems, the Portuguese and the Gentus build their ships because timber, iron and other necessary materials are available and the wages are low'.[11] This statement is further corroborated in the *Anonymous Relations*:.[12] 'The river of Narsapur Peta is very large, wide and convenient. Ships of as much as 200 tonnes can be sheathed or built in it... Ships of even larger tonnage displacements used to be built here as the native merchants of Masulipatam used ships of 600 tonnes or even more in their overseas trading operations. Normally only merchant ships were turned out from this centre. They were managed by sails and used to be oval shaped, allowing thereby ample space for the stowage of provisions and other mercantile commodities. These ships were mostly built of teak growing plentifully in the interior of Narsapur Peta.

Cables and other cordage for ships were made of coir imported from Ceylon and the locally available iron ore provided the raw material for the manufacture of anchors. There are frequent references to this ship-building centre, also called Emaldee, in the English Factory Records, and ships when damaged by storms or the wafts of the sea are found returning to this port for necessary repairs. The Advice, a ship of the English East India Company damaged in a stormy weather off the coast of Masulipatam, was sent to Narsapur Peta for trimming (October 1641).[13] Another ship of the company *Winter Frigate*, which the company had ordered to be sold, 'had been refitted at Narsapur' and was later sent 'on a voyage to Achin.'[14] The proximity of this ship-building centre further facilitated the coastal trading operations of the trading nations since local junks were handy and could easily be engaged for collecting goods from other centres along the coast.

The availability of credit facilities was a great advantage at Masulipatam. Numerous records are available to show that when foreign merchants were in difficulty regarding funds, they could borrow from local merchants on easy terms. Sometimes they could even get interest free loans.[15] In 1643 English factors are found 'endeavouring to borrow money at Masulipatam to begin an investment for England' and in the same year most of the treasure received from England at Madras was sent to Masulipatam 'where the money is to be used in satisfying the most pressing of their creditors.[16] Borrowing was not possible in Madras, as the chief at Madras wrote categorically to the Company in England in 1650 that 'no money can be borrowed here to make the necessary investment.'

The Persians, Arabs and the Gentus were the business communities of Golcunda. The Gentus had little hand in the foreign trade of the country, as they did 'not go much to sea', and it was primarily controlled by the Persians who were specially invited by the ruler of the Kingdom to settle in his domain and many of them settled at Masulipatam to engage themselves in profitable business. The sea-borne trade of the region received further impetus when contacts with the trading nations of Europe were developed. Merchants from Armenia, Arabia, Persia, England, Holland, Portugal, France, Denmark, Bengal, Siam, Malaya and East Indies not only made Masulipatam their operating base for trading along the coast and in the hinterland of Masulipatam, but also extended their range of activity even beyond the domains of Golcunda, as a factor of the English East India Company at Masulipatam wrote in 1623 that 'goods are carried hence chiefly to Bijapur, Burhanpur and Agra.' Merchants from Armenia and Persia used to come annually to Masulipatam for conducting trade and business in the territory of Golcunda and even beyond. Tavernier in May 1652, embarked on a ship at Gombroom bound for Masulipatam and he had as his co-passengers 'about 100 merchants, both Persians and Armenians, who were going for trade.[17]

The trading activities at Masulipatam covered a wide range both in the nature of business conducted and the geographical area traversed. Prominent among the trading activities were coastal and inland trading operations both by the foreign and the native merchants, although the native merchants had an edge over the foreigners in this respect. The foreigners, however, had monopolized the lucrative business of carrying freight goods of the local merchants between Masulipatam and Persia and also to the Red Sea, Malaya and the Indies.

Coastal trading was very brisk along the east coast and ships of the native merchants as well as those of the foreign companies were engaged in this operation. Realizing the importance of coastal trading, the English factors at Masulipatam requested their Company in England to send them 'also two small vessels for the port to port trade,[18] to enable them to collect cargo of pepper and cloth from Tanjore and other ports of the south for stocking them at Masulipatam. There was a very lucrative trade between Masulipatam and the Bay ports and, therefore, 'the products of Bengal were readily obtainable at Masulipatam.' Silk, sugar, saltpeter and gumlack of Bengal were highly valued in the Masulipatam market and a sizeable stock of these articles was always available for re-export to foreign countries. In an attempt to partake of this profitable trade the English factors, with Masulipatam as their operating base, initiated in 1630 'to go to the Bay ports' carrying rich cargo of spices, calicoes and steel goods. And to the ports of coast south of Masulipatam ships used to 'sail from Masulipatam in January for Arrimgaon, Pulicat, St. Thome, Tegnapatam, Porto-Novo, Negapatnam and on to Ceylon as far as Cochin'[19] for the sale of Masulipatam wares, consisting of coarse cloth and steel goods, and collection of the return cargo of pepper, coir for cordage and some varieties of cloth for local consumption as also for export from Masulipatam. Thus the geographical range of coastal trading from Masulipatam was up to Hooghly in the north and Cochin on the west coast. The diverse products of all these regions were well stocked in the Masulipatam and from there they were distributed to various parts of the world.

Within the hinterland of Masulipatam the City of Golcunda was the greatest market, consuming most of the articles and also the costliest ones imported from foreign countries. 'Costly English cloths of £ 18 or £ 20 a *cloth* would sell at the Court of Golcunda,'[20] reported an English factor to the Company in England. The city was a great manufacturing centre of the kingdom and provided a number of exportable commodities. Some of the finest varieties of cloths, like guldars and ferrat cannes, wrought with gold, silver and silken threads, could be obtained only in and around Golcunda and were in great demand in Persia, Bengal, Siam and the Philippines. Further, diamonds above 10 carats could be produced only at Golcunda, as the trade in this commodity was a monopoly of the King. Similarly, the capital city was the greatest market for bezoar stones (stones of medicinal properties in the paunches of a particular species of goats found in the North Eastern region of the Kingdom) and in the words of Tevernier: 'Golcunda ...is the place where there is the most considerable sale' (of bezoar) and he 'purchased about 60,000 rupees worth of bezoar.'[21] Moreover, license for trading in the territory of Golcunda could be obtained only at the capital and, therefore, a permanent representative of each of the foreign countries trading in the kingdom was kept at Golcunda to negotiate trading concessions with the court and also to control trading operations in the vicinity of the capital. And thus in 1669, a French representative Mons. Marcara was ' in Golcunda negotiating his business at court for procuring a firmaund from the king like to ours or the Dutches......'[22] For making their business, which had expanded, more profitable, it had become imperative for the foreign merchants to have a few factories established in the interior of the kingdom to enable them to procure things at source, since prices of goods coming to Masulipatam from the interior used to rise to such an extent that the purchase of these goods at Masulipatam, on account of the keen competition from the native merchants, proved an unprofitable proposition. The following quotation will substantiate this statement:[23] 'In Golcunda it is very pertinent likewise that you keep a continual residence, for diverse requisites do strongly depend thereon. As first, the sale of all your Europe, Southward and Persian commodities which may be thither transported in 10 or 12 days time... clear of all the duties on the way (which amounts to no less than 30%) and there sold to far greater profit than can be ever expected in this town (Masulipatam). Secondly, it will be the mainstay to the quite of your business to have an able man at all times so near the king's elbow... for quick settlement of differences. But that which does yet more precisely press the setting of your people in this city is the investment for Persia, for in some town near adjacent thereunto is the greatest part of the goods made that is more proper for that trade. And it is far more beneficial for the Company to have their comities bought there at the best hand than to contract for the same here at Masulipatam, after it has paid at least 30 per cent customs on the way, besides the profit that the seller will justly expect to put into his own purse, which difference of price will amount yearly to a large sum of money in the laying out of £ 15,000 or 20,000.'

The transport of freight goods carried, mainly by the Dutch and the English ships, was one of the important overseas trading operations performed by the foreign trading companies stationed at Masulipatam. The freight trade was found highly profitable and the natives also appreciated this gesture, since European vessels were better equipped for safe and speedy navigation. They were thus attracted to transport their goods through these foreign ships to Gombroon. The English factors found this 'experiment of carrying freight goods from Masulipatam to Persia . . . a success . . . for . . . the resulting receipts were nearly £ 3,000'[24] In 1655, the Persian freight trade had brought so much profit to the English trade on the coast that 'the money brought from Persia had discharged all debts and left a considerable surplus'. There was thus a great boom in freight trade for the foreign companies functioning at Masulipatam, since the sea-borne trade of the natives was not confined to Gombroon and Mocha but also extended to Pegu, Tennasserim, Kedah, Jambi, Achin and many other ports in the East Indies. The nature of the profit which accrued from freight trade, is further evident from a complaint that Winter[25] lodged with the English East India Company that 'Buckkeridge had done the Company an ill-service by refusing to allow George and Maratha to be hired out for a voyage to Tennasserim, instead of lying idle at Masulipatam. A sum of 2000 pagodas had been offered... while the Company's estate left in Siam was to be transported gratis.'[26] The English East India Company used to commission one ship every year exclusively for this freight trade.

By virtue of its central situation on the east coast and because of convergence of ships both from Europe and Asia, Masulipatam had also some time the English factors used it as an operating base for promoting their trade in the Bay area. The natives also with 'ships of 600 tonnes or more... traffique ordinarily to Mocha, the Red Sea, to Achin upon Sumatra, to Arakan, Pegu and Tennasserim on the side of the Gulf'[27] and there was normally a sizeable stock of the wares of these regions at Masulipatam for re-export to other centres. It is observed from the English Factory Records that most of the ships of the English East India Company while proceeding to the Coast and the East Indies first assembled at Masulipatam and from there proceeded to their respective regions of operations; and further, after contracting business in their respective spheres of activity they returned to Masulipatam to proceed to new destinations. A letter from Fort St. George to Bantam records as follows: "The pinnace *Advice* left Balasore on November 7, and reached Masulipatam ten days later with cargo... Having landed her goods and taking in other for Bantam... The *Hopewell* quitted Balasore on December 1, with goods together with passenger and freight goods... she got to Masulipatam... took in freight for Persia".[28] In 1648, the English East India Company sent two ships to the Coast and from Madras both the ships were redirected to Masulipatam with all their cargo of merchandise and treasure and from there laden with coast goods one left for Jambi and Bantam and the other was homeward bound. Ships from Gombroom to Bantam or *vice versa* had to go via Masulipatam to carry its exports and re-exports to the respective centres. This port was a great centre for the distribution of rubies, chinawares, lead, gumlack and spices. 'The rubies are distributed largely from Masulipatam into the interior as far as Persia, where they are sold to great profit'.[29] And lead which formed an item of import at Masulipatam was re-exported to Mocha. Smithson says: 'I...do very well know that all or most of the lead went to Moho (Mocha) where it was sold at above cent per cent profit'. Gumlack of various varieties and from different countries could be purchased at Masulipatam, as is evident from a letter: "This sorte (gumlack on sticks) cometh all from Bangala where it is cheap and plentiful...Masulipatna, we think, should also supply you with that which cometh from Arrecan and Pegu, which doth afford to our knowledge a far deeper tincture and... be more valued".[30] As regards the stocking of goods at Masulipatam, a letter from the Company in England to the Chief at Madras gives the following information: "*The Madras Merchant*... had been directed to which was to be left at Masulipatam for shipment to England. For the same purpose the Bengal factors had been directed to keep Masulipatam supplied with saltpetre; also with sugar which would sell there with a profit of 50 per cent".[31] Further evidence to the fact that Masulipatam road served as the confluence of ships trading in the Orient is obtained from a letter by the Agent at Madras early in August and the Discovery about a fortnight later; both proceeded to Masulipatam to take in cargoes, the former for Macassar and the latter for Jambi, for which place she sailed on September 17. To Masulipatam came also the *Marigold* (24th September) which had returned from Macassar and (20th October) The *Merchant Adventure.* The Anne from Achin got into the roadstead on October 25... a considerable assemblage of vessels at Masulipatam".[32]

An idea of brisk entrepot trading and the stocking of goods at Masulipatam is gathered from a report submitted by the Agent of the English East India Company at Madras to the Company at Home: "The *Endeavour* seems to have got back to the Coast from Pegu some time in the spring or early summer, and on August 6 she sailed from Masulipatam for Bantam, arriving there towards the close of November... The *Expedition* also reached the coast from Gombroon sometime in summer, leaving again for Surat and Persia at the beginning of October. Another incoming vessel was the *Dove* from Bantam, which was thereupon employed in a voyage to Pegu".[33]

The range and regional distribution of sea-borne trade of Golcunda was extensive and the commodities exchanged were of diverse nature. There was never a dull season at Masulipatam and never was it to be found empty of ships. It was always bristling with activity. The ships were to be found there in every season either to unload the cargo or to be laden with fresh cargo for their new destinations. The foreign trade of the kingdom was handled by the Moores, the European trading companies and private merchants from Europe. Among the Moores, the Persians had a major share in the sea-borne trade of the Kingdom.

The Moores of Golcunda were an adventurous and enterprising people and even prior to the arrival of European merchants they had commercial contacts with many countries of the Indian and the Pacific Oceans stretching from East Africa in the west to the Philippines in the east. Their ships used to sail for 'Bengal, Arakan, Pegu, Tennasserim, Achin, Priaman, Queda and Perak usually...in September for if they wait longer they are in danger of missing their voyage. The Mecca ship usually sails in January or the end of December'.[34] The natives had very great interest in the spice markets of the East Indies and the impact of their competition was very keenly felt by the European traders, as one complained that the 'competition of Bengal, Masulipatam and Pegu merchants much hindered the purchase of return cargo.[35] Even Mir Jumla of the Kingdom of Golcunda had personal interest in the export and import business of the country. He owned a number of junks which used to carry his goods annually for sale to Pegu, Mocha and Gombroon. In 1647 the President and Council at Madras reported to the Company in England that 'last year a junk, called '*Derry Dowlat*' sailed from this place to Mokha...Mir Jumla is about to send another junk to Pegu laden with his own freight and goods.[36] The enterprising Moores of Golcunda had extended their sphere of trading activity even to Siam and the Philippines, where they came into contact with merchants from China, Japan and even Peru. Pertaining to this, Tavernier has to say as follows: "But concerning this commerce by sea between America and the Philippine Islands, the people of Bengal, Arakan, Pegu, Goa and other places carry thither all sorts of cloths, and a quantity of worked stones, such as diamonds and rubies, with many manufactured articles of gold and silver, silken stuffs and Persian carpets.[37] Tavernier does not directly refer to the merchants of Masulipatam, but the nature of the articles of commerce which were carried to the Philippines clearly point to their inclusion in this trade, and their exclusion is just unimaginable. As regards their trade with Siam, the President and Council at Madras of the English East India Company wrote to the Company at home that 'the Moores at present do supply that place with fine goods per via Tennasserim, but they carry them 40 days by land and pay several customs; and are at above 50 per cent charges more than the goods that go by shipping'. The port of Ayuthia in Siam was the meeting place of ships coming from Japan, Cochin, China, Macau and Manila and thus offered a great opportunity for the exchange of rich variety of things, and the chief articles imported from Ayuthia were silk, gold, copper tuttanague (zinc), amber, damask, Benjamin (benzoin), eagle-wood, tin porcelain wares and aloes. The relations of Golcunda with Siam were not only confined to the level of trade but had also reached the diplomatic stage since in 1664 the King of Siam dispatched an ambassador, with rich present of elephants and other goods, to the Court of Golcunda.[38] The most lucrative overseas trade of the natives, however, was with Persia where Golcunda cloth and diamonds, Bengal sugar and tropical spices were in great demand and in return Persian horses, carpets and *attars* were highly valued in Golcunda. The balance of trade, as between Persia and Golcunda, was probably always in favour of the latter, since the native merchants always returned with surplus treasure, from their Gombroon voyage.

Among the European nations participating in the sea-borne trade of Golcunda were the Dutch, English, Portuguese, Danes and French. Each of these trading nations of Europe annually sent a fleet or caravan of ships carrying treasure for investment and goods for sale in Golcunda. The strength of the caravan varied with the capital resources of the trading nations and their conditions of trade of the coast. Of the European nations transacting business at Masulipatam or along the coast, the Dutch were the most prosperous and were doing excellent business. Dr. Nihar Ranjan Ray[39] has summarized the trading activities of the Dutch on the coast in the following words: "The trade of this country being considered very important, orders were given that every means should be employed to increase it, due economy was to be practised in consequence of the enormous sums laid out by the Company. And on account of the profitable business they were carrying on, the Masulipatam factory was to be maintained". Great importance was attached by the Dutch to the Persian trade and it 'was considered the most important of all for the Company', and since Masulipatam goods were highly valued and profitably vendible in Persia it was but natural that they attached great significance to the trade with Golcunda. The magnitude of their trading operations can be gauged from the fact that they paid annually 3,000 pagodas as customs charges at Masulipatam, besides giving large sums as *piscashes* to the King. During the same period the English East India Company paid only 800 pagodas as customs charges and when the Dutch factors offered a *piscash* of 1500 pagodas to the King in 1660, only a third of this amount was expected of English factors. It appears from a perusal of the *English Factory Records* that the representatives of the English East India Company posted on the Coast were very jealous of Dutch prosperity and complained time and again to the Company in this connection. 'But how this poor trade here will maintain the charge cannot be apprehended by the former of us…for the Dutch are grown so potent that they have gotten the whole Coast trade in their own possession and have so dispersed their moneys that we cannot get cloth for money,[40] complained an English factor to the Company in England. The financial superiority of the Dutch over the English was well established and they could always drive the English out of the market on sheer strength of their capital resources. A letter from Masulipatam to England has to say the following in this respect: "The Dutch abounding so with means and having given out such great quantities to merchants and weavers that little or nothing is procurable there...... If the Dutch succeed in securing control of Coast line from Pulicat to Ceylon they will quickly oust the English from trade in Golcunda parts by outbidding them for piece goods. The Dutch had the monopoly in cloves, nuts and mace and by reason of this they had a great advantage over the English in the Masulipatam market as 'great quantities of cloves, nuts and mace sold there at very great profit, and brings (*sic*) them in gold, which is there much preferred to rialls or the silver.[41]

The English East India Company was a very active participant in the foreign trade pf Golcunda. Its trade was in a flourishing state, and its annual investment in the hinterland of Masulipatam increased almost ten times within a decade (1631: £ 10,380; £ 10,500) and thereafter it fluctuated between £ 80,000 and £ 90,000[42] annually. The figures quoted above represent the investments made from the amount directly received from England and do not include the profit procured through the freight trade nor the amounts received from Bantam and Surat. The bulk of the cargo received from England was in gold or silver and only 25 to 30 per cent consisted of merchandise. Broad cloth, lead, alum, tin, coral and wine were the chief items of goods brought to Masulipatam. The return cargo consisted of chintz, calicoes, spices, gumlac, steel goods, saltpeter and indigo. The policy of exporting bullion was a profitable proposition, since gold, when minted into the new pagodas, yielded a net profit of 10 to 12 per cent. Golcunda and Masulipatam were great marts for gold and a stock of this valuable metal could always fetch ready money for immediate investment. The profitable trade of the natives at Mocha was based on exchange of gold for goods. Silver was not rated as high as gold and it was many a time devalued on the coast[43] and consequently foreign merchants sometimes suffered severe setbacks in their business. To avert such a catastrophe the President of the English East India Company at Surat wisely advised the Company to direct 'hither the greater part of treasure extended to the Coast to be here converted into rupees and passed by exchange to Masulipatam.[44] The rupee had always an edge over the pagoda in exchange value, being the currency of the Moghul Empire.

The participation of the European nations in the commercial

activities of Masulipatam had vastly increased the geographical limits of its range of trading and commercial contacts and had further improved the stock position of Masulipatam both in quantity and diversity. The ships from Europe not only brought Masulipatam into direct contact with the major ports of that continent but also with those of Japan and China, since their ships extended their sphere of activity to those countries. The number of ships voyaging between Masulipatam and Gombroon as well as between the Bay ports and the East Indies had also increased. There was also an increase in the frequency of voyages undertaken by these ships. As a consequence, the status of Masulipatam as an international mart had considerably enhanced.

The inclusion of these foreign merchants in the commercial operations of Masulipatam had provided great impetus to the productive activities within the territory of Golcunda. Moreover, the hinterland of Masulipatam was capable of adequately meeting the special requirements in cloth of West Europe, West Asia and South East Asia. The manufactures of the state, therefore, were being encouraged by them; and on account of keen competition among the Europeans as regards the purchase of these wares, there was a great boom in the prices of the articles. The cloth industry of the state had attained its apex. Export and import business at Masulipatam was very brisk and progressive, and the collection of customs duty from the English East India Company alone had registered over five-fold increase within a period of six years (1630-35).[45]

Masulipatam as an international trading centre, abounding in wares of various climes, had assumed great importance. Its hinterland alone was capable of providing suitable cargo along the coast for both the temperate and the tropical regions. Therefore, the capital investments laid out by the European nations were of enormous proportion. The British factors considered the area safe for investment and, therefore, most of the treasure received at Madras used to be sent to Masulipatam as in 1660 'the gold brought from Guinea by the *Truro* and the *Brabados Merchant* totalled £ 17,500... out of this £ 15,000 was to be spent in providing cargoes for those vessels to carry to Jambi and Macassar, while the *Concord* which brought only about £ 8,300 was to go to Persia with a cargo costing £ 4,000 or 5,000'[46] The trade boom in Golcunda is further borne out by the optimism of British factors who in 1636 'dare confidently promise the return of £ 80,000 sterling (if not more) yearly from this Coast,[47] and the distribution of this amount for providing cargo to different regions was to be in the order of £ 20,000 each for Persia and Bantam and £ 40,000 for England.[48] The prosperity of British trade reflected the general prosperous business conditions along the coast.

However, this prosperity was not an everlasting one and Masulipatam like any other trading centre suffered from cycles of boom and slump in its trade. Depressions in business conditions normally followed either a natural calamity like famine, or chaotic political and administrative conditions on account of war with the Moghul forces or with the neighbouring kingdoms of the Deccan, and also owing to the highhanded policies of corrupt native officials. Anglo-Dutch wars in Europe also adversely affected the business at Masulipatam.

The territory of Golcunda was scourged thrice by catastrophic famines within a period of 75 years (1612-1686). The 1630 famine was described as 'a great and mortal dearth which began three years hence and still increaseth'[49] and 'those lands which had been famous for their fertility and plenty now retained no trace of productiveness'.[50] The sense of tragedy is further heightened when it is observed 'that life was offered for a loaf but none would buy, rank was to be sold for a cake but none cared for it: the ever bounteous hand was now stretched out to beg for food; and the feet which had always trodden the way of contentment walked about only in search of sustenance (*Badsahnama*)'. Another famine in 1648, though it only affected the region south of Masulipatam, had greatly disturbed the peace and tranquillity of the state so essential for the prosperity of the kingdom. However, the last great famine, prior to the dissolution of the kingdom in 1687, occurred in 1659. It had brought the country to a state of virtual ruin and the trading operations to a standstill.

The insane, unwise and highhanded attitude of the native officials at Masulipatam had contributed in no small measure to the ruin of the port. The British factors at Masulipatam were compelled by their antagonistic attitude of shift their chief factory from Masulipatam to Madras, since they were living there under conditions of perpetual insecurity and 'fear of the morrow'. The obstinacy of the local Governor in 1647 in not allowing 'any merchant to buy any goods' seriously hindered open and free trading at Masulipatam.

The turmoils and troubles of war made the situation worse. The hinterland of Masulipatam was plundered and pillaged in 1661 by Bijapur forces and the army of Aurangzeb burnt Masulipatam to ashes in 1664. It had not recovered from these shocks when the process of decay was brought to a climax by Aurangzeb. His forces reduced

Masulipatam in 1687 in order to expel the Dutch and thereafter it was totally surrendered to the forces of decay and destruction.

Meanwhile the centre of business activity on the East Coast was creepingly migrating to the Hooghly where the fertile plain of the Ganges opened out immense possibilities of profitable investment. The unstable conditions at Masulipatam further accelerated the pace, and after 1662 definite instructions were issued by the English East India Company to its Agent at Madras to invest the greater proportion of the treasure advanced by the Company from year to year in purchase of goods from the Bay ports. After the incident of 1687 Masulipatam was just a shabble of ruins, its business supremacy having passed to Hooghly, and in course of time it reverted to its original status of being a port and town of insignificant stature having only local importance. The town of Masulipatam, however, still bears the traces of its past and the ruins of the colonies of European merchants vividly remind us of the glory that this metropolitan port of the Kingdom of Golcunda and 'the most famous mart of the whole Coromandel Coast' was.

Seldom has the life history of a port so well coincided with the rise and fall of the kingdom which it served so well.[51]

Tabulary Summary of the Sea-borne Trade of Golcunda which operated from Masulipatam

Range of Trading from Masulipatam			*Shipping Season*	
Region	*Country*	*Port*	*Ships arriving at Masulipatam*	*Ships departing from Masulipatam*
A. Europe	1. England	London	Jul-Aug.	Dec-Jan
	2. Holland	Amsterdam	Jul-Aug.	Dec-Jan
	3. Portugal	Lisbon	Jul-Aug.	Dec-Jan
	4. Denmark	Copenhagen	Jul-Aug.	Dec-Jan.
	5. France	Marseilles	Jul-Aug.	Dec-Jan.
B. West Asia	1. Persia	Gombroon	Jul-Aug-Sep.	Oct-Nov-Dec.
	2. Arabia	Mocha	Jul-Aug-Sep.	Oct-Nov-Dec.
C. South-East Asia	1.Burma	(a) Tennas-serim	Apr-May.	Aug-Sep.
		(b) Pegu	Apr-May.	Aug-Sep.
	2. Malaya	(a) Kedah	Feb-Mar.	Aug-Sep.
		(b) Perak		
		(c) Malacca		

(Contd.)

Range of Trading from Masulipatam			*Shipping Season*	
Region	*Country*	*Port*	*Ships arriving at Masulipatam*	*Ships departing from Masulipatam*
	3. Sumatra (a) North (b) South	Achin Jambi	Sep-Oct.	May-Jun. Sep-Oct.
	4. Java	Bantam	Jul-Aug.	Sep-Oct.
	5. Celebes	Macassar	Jul-Aug.	Sep-Oct.
	6. Philippines	Manila	Jul-Aug-Sep.	May-June.
	7.Siam	Ayuthia.	Jul-Aug.	May-June.
D. Bay of Bengal	1. Bengal	Hooghly	Oct-Nov.	Jul-Aug.
E. Indian Ocean	1. Ceylon	Fort De Galle	Jul-Aug.	Oct-Nov.
F. Arabian Sea	1. Malabar	Cochin	Jul-Aug.	Oct-Nov.

Note: The native merchants used to go via Tennasserim following an overland route.

GOODS EXCHANGED

Exports from Masulipatam	*Imports into Masulipatam*
Coarse cotton cloth, silk, calicoes, painted clothes, spices, saltpeter, diamonds, rubies, indigo, steel, cotton yams, bezoar stones, gumlac, tobacco, etc.	Alum, lead, tin, broadcloth, quicksilver, coral, vermilion, brimstone, paper, gold, silver, etc.
Saltpetre, pepper, indigo, long-cloth, chintz, calicoes, steel, gumlac, diamonds, tobacco, etc.	Silver and gold in small bars, coral, vermilion quicksilver, paper, woollen and cotton fabrics, etc.
Calicoes, chintz, beethyles, coral, lead, gumlac, sugar, steel, diamonds, rubies, sapphires, spices, saltpeter, guldars, ferrat cawnes, etc.	Runas, rosewater, almonds, pickles, leather, simoranees, carpets, silk, hazelnuts, raisins, pistachees, musk, horses, gold, silver, etc.
Calicoes, longcloth, spices, steel goods, lead, sugar, diamonds, steel, rubies, tobacco, etc.	Gold, silver, dates, coffee, musk, horses, etc.
(a) Spices, sandal-wood, cotton yarn (red and white), tobacco, calicoes, indigo, chinawares, diamonds, silver, glass, steel goods, etc.	Embroidered quilt, pitch, benzoin, china root, gold, gumlac, rubies, sapphires, brimstone, rice, etc.
(b) Tobbacco, calicoes, steel goods, indigo, beethyles, diamonds, silver, spices, sandal-wood, ginger, cordage, etc.	Gold, tin, quicksilver, eagle-wood, sappan wood, martabans, nippa (a Drink), 2 elephants, bell metal, etc.

(Contd.)

Exports from Masulipatam	*Imports into Masulipatam*
Painted cloth, coarse cloth, calicoes, steel goods, rice, diamonds etc.	Sulphur, camphor, silk, tin, pepper, dammar or resin, etc.
Rice, calicoes, coarse cloth, silk, painted cloths, gumlac, iron, steel goods, indigo, etc.	Pepper, cloves, sulphur, tin, tortoise shells, copper, nutmegs, maces, etc.
Calicoes, coarse cloth, cinnamon, steel goods, rice, cloth for sail, cordage, indigo, saltpeter, salt, etc.	Gold, silver, copper, sugar, tugenague (zinc), nutmegs, maces, cloves, benzoin, camphor, sugar, porcelain, sandal-wood, tortoise shells, etc.
Rice, calicoes, coarse cloth, painted cloths, silk, diamonds, steel goods, indigo.	Clovers, nutmegs, maces, pepper, sulphur, etc.
Calicoes, painted cloth, saltpeter, iron, steel goods, indigo, gumlac, silk, carpets, diamonds and rubies (cut and polished), articles of gold and silver.	Gold, silver, sulphur, tutenague, silk, copper, porcelain, camphor, sappan wood, benzoin, etc.
Red cotton yarns, beethyles, calicoes, paintings, diamonds, indigo, rubies, steel goods, saltpeter, carpets, satins, etc.	Raw silk, china, velvet, twisted china silk, damasks, aloes, tin, copper, tutenague, benzoin, camphor, elephants, sappan wood, porcelain, etc.
Tobacco, indigo, calicoes, steel and steel goods, tin, spices, silk, carpets, chintz (paintings), etc.	Sugar, rice, butter, silk, saltpeter, white cloth, gunny alyjahs, gumlac, beeswax coarse and fine iron, etc.
Coarse cotton cloth, sugar, salt, steel goods, etc.	Cinnamon, fine mats, precious stones, coir, etc.
Gumlac, benzoin, camphor, coarse cotton cloth, salt, steel goods, etc.	Pepper, cashew nuts, areca nuts, coir, etc.

REFERENCES

1. Foster: *English Factory Records*—1655-66, p. 261.
2. Tavernier: *Travels,* Vol. I, p. 141
3. Burhan's *Tuzuk-i-Walajahi;* Part 1; Page: 39, (Madras University, Islamic Series No. I).
4. A dissertation on the *Establishments made by Mohammadan Conquerors,* p. 147
5. Hakluyt Society: *Relations of Golcunda,* p. 55
6. *Ibid.*
7. Foster; *English Factories in India/66/-64*, p. 173
8. Hakluyt Society: *Golcunda Relations* (Anonymous).
9. Hugh Marray: *History of British India*, p. 145.
10. Hakluyt Society: *Golcunda Relations* (Methowld).

11. Hakluyt Society: *Golcunda Relations* (Schorer).
12. *Ibid.* (Anonymous).
13. Foster: *English Factory Records*, 1637-41.
14. *Ibid.*
15. Foster: *English Factory Records*, 1646-50: XXVIII.
16. *Ibid.* p. 120.
17. Tavernier: *Travels*—Vol. I, p. 205.
18. Foster: *English Factories in India*. 1634-36, p. 296.
19. Hakluyt Society: *Golcunda Relations* (Schorer).
20. Foster: *English Factories in India*, 1630-33, p. 296.
21. Tavernier: *Travels*, Vol. II, p. 116.
22. Foster: *English Factories in India*, 1668-69, pp. 288-89.
23. Foster: *English Factories in India*, 1634-35, p. 46.
24. Foster: *English Factories in India*, 1630-33, p. XXV.
25. Chief Factor at Masulipatam and later an Agent of the Company at Madras.
26. Foster: *English Factories in India*, 1661-64, pp. 378-79.
27. Hakluyat Society: *Golcunda Relations* (Methowld), pp. 36.
28. Foster: *English Factories in India.*
29. Hakluyat Society: *Golcunda Relations* (Schorer), pp. 62-63.
30. Foster: *English Factories in India*, 1634-36, p. 146.
31. *Ibid.*, p. 255 (footnote)
32. *Ibid.*, p. 256.
33. Foster: *English Factories in India*, 1645-50.
34. Hakluyt Society: *Golcunda Relations* (Schorer), p. 59-61.
35. Foster: *English Factories in India*: 1642-45.
36. Foster: *English Factories in India*, 1646-450.
37. Tavernier: *Travels*, Vol., p. 83.
38. Foster: English Factories in India, 1661-64, p. 363.
39. Calcutta University has edited a book entitled Dutch Activities in the East.
40. Foster: *English Factories in India*. 1642-45; p. 191.
41. *Ibid.* 1622-23, 10-338.
42. *Ibid. English Factory Records*, 1630-1669.
43. Foster: *English Factory Records*, 1650-54, p. 350.
44. Foster: *English Factories in India*: 1637-41, p. 287.
45. *Ibid.*, 1634-36, p. 318.
46. Foster: *English Factories in India*, 1655-60, p. 400.
47. *Ibid.*, 1634-36, p. 325.
48. *Ibid.*, 1634-36, p. 48.
49. *Ibid.*, 1630-33, p. 77.
50. *Ibid.*, p. xiii.
51. See Tabular Summary of the Sea-borne Trade of Golcunda on pp. 183-187. (Anonymous).

3

The Concept of the Islamic City and the Planning of Islamabad

Introduction

The concept of fraternity and equality which Islam engendered, the vertical and horizontal mobility in every aspect of life which Islam ensured, the vigorous public life which Islam enjoined upon the Muslims, encouraged community and corporate life, and privacy of family life which Islam insisted upon had tremendous impact on urban planning and design in the Islamic world. These concepts and ideas made the Islamic cities distinct entities very different from cities in area located outside the Islamic belt.

Islamabad, the city of Islam or the city of peace, is the most recent creation as the capital of Pakistan, one of the largest Islamic states of the world. The main object of this chapter is to highlight the basic concepts of urban planning applied in the principal Islamic cities, assess their relevance to modern urban planning and examine objectively if they have been observed in Islamabad.

Basic Characteristics of Islamic Cities

The all pervasive character of Islam profoundly influenced and shaped the social, political and economic ethos of Islamic societies. Most of the activities in Islamic countries were pivoted around a mosque which consequently occupied a focal position in Islamic polity and made it essentially urban in character and spirit. The focal role of the mosque induced social, economic and political mobility in Islam which is borne out by the close relationship that the political elite, the *'ulama'*

Published in *Islamic Culture,* Hyderabad, Vol. 59, No. 3, July 1985, pp. 180-202.

and the bourgeoisie maintained among themselves, the freedom one enjoyed to shift from one profession to the ease with which one could rise in ranks provided one merited it, Islam never encouraged any distinction based on caste, colour, ethnicity and wealth. In an Islamic society the rise of schools of thought and *madaris* (sing. *Madrasah*) focused around the mosques proved most conducive to such a development. These schools of thought and *madaris* in Islamic urbanization contributed towards detribalization of Islamic population by fostering the feeling of brotherhood and community consciousness cutting across tribal lines. Unlike the other religions, Islam never encouraged the rise of a class of clergies which is amply demonstrated by the fact that on occasions such as births, deaths and marriages the presence of priests is not obligatory. In a mosque which is the house of God all are treated equal irrespective of their caste, colour and social status. Similarly, in the *maqamah* or halls of residence attached to mosques and institutions of higher learning, individuals drawn from diverse walks of life irrespective of their colour and tribal affiliations lived together amicably. All the institutions which developed under Islamic inspiration stressed on communal harmony, equality of man, and equality of opportunity for all under the banner of Islam. Being supported by these factors Islamic urbanization developed unique characteristics which were abundantly reflected in the Islamic cities and gave them a distinctive personality.

The "Islamic city" like the "Roman"or the "Greek" city developed under three basic conditions. Either they were originally new camp settlements (*amsar*) which emerged as major urban nuclei such as Busra, or they were superimposed on already existing urban settlements such as Damascus and Constantinople, or they were planned new settlements such as the round city of Baghdad, Shahjahanabad and the city of Hyderabad, the civil capital of the kingdom of Golcunda in South India. Irrespective of the circumstances under which they were founded and the geographical areas in which they were located, the Islamic cities were marked for their common institutional characteristics. These (institutions) constituted the foci of Islamic cities. For instance, the institution of congregational prayers on Friday led to the rise of the concept of the cathedral or the *jami'* mosque which also attracted the rise of a central shopping area around it called the *suq* (pl. *aswaq*). These central mosques and the *aswaq* were not only the places of worship and trading transaction, but "were also centres of social and literary activities."[1] Besides being the religious, political and intellectual centre the *jami'* mosque in the early phase of Islam had emerged also as a pre-eminent centre of political authority. The first four caliphs of Islam, after the death of the prophet Muhammad, were elected to the Caliphate in the central mosque of Madina. The *jami'* mosques and the *aswaq* or the main shopping centres, therefore, became the integrating elements in the planning of Islamic cities. The residence of the head of the Islamic State occupied a distinct location as a called settlement beside the *suq* or was sited as a separate entity in the form of a citadel away from the city centre as in Shahjahanabad (Delhi).

The residential quarters of the Islamic city were marked for their ethnicity or tribal distinctiveness, and were inward looking, for Islam advocated "a clear separation between public and private life, private life turned inwards towards the courtyard and not towards the street."[2] The natural residential areas or quarters *khitat* (siag. Khutah), looked towards the mosque and the religious schools of thought for their social and political guidance. These schools of thought had their adherents spread over different tribes cutting across tribal loyalties. The cohesion lent by the common normative order prescribed in the Qur'an was reinforced by the activities of the '*ulama*'—the people learned in the literature, doctrines and laws of Islam. They were *par excellence* prayer leaders, scholars, teachers, judges, consultants on the laws and functionaries of the mosques. The regulation of the markets was entrusted to them. They were in addition the managers of the city's educational religious and philanthropic institutions.[3]

In view of this peculiar type of religious and social developments, the fabric of the Islamic city, according to Hourani, was spun around four basic components[4]:

1. First, there would be a citadel, very often a place on some natural defence work.
2. Secondly, there might be a royal city or quarter which might have grown up...as a royal enclave.
3. There would be a central urban complex which would include great mosques and religious schools and the central markets with special places assigned for the main groups of craftsmen or traders.
4. There would be a core of residential quarters, marked by at least two special characteristics—the combination of local

with ethnic or religious differentiation and the relative separateness or autonomy of each quarter or group of quarters.

The four basic characteristics ascribed to Islamic cities by Hourani are also broadly corroborated by Samuel V. Noe who specifies the following four principal characteristics[5]:

1. The city is walled with several gates. Main roads from the gates lead to the Central Area where the major religious institute, the *jami'*, is located.
2. The palace or administrative area may be located in the centre of the city, near the *jami'* or on the periphery. In the latter form it is usually in the form of a fortified citadel.
3. Markets or bazars are located in linear patterns along the major roads and are segregated according to commodities offered.
4. There is a clear separation in the city between public and private areas.

Of these components of the Islamic city, the residence of rulers, the *jami'* mosque and the *aswaq* constituted the key elements irrespective of the pattern of development of the Islamic city. For instance, Scanlon points out that Damascus which was conquered by the Islamic power was remodelled and adapted "to accommodate peculiar Islamic demands particularly the erection of Friday mosques and central government buildings."[6] Even when the growth is spontaneous the Friday mosques and *Dâr al-Imârah* or the Chief's residence are advantageously located in a prominent place. Raphail Wahaba points out that in planning the "new capital in Askar Cairo they followed the familiar principles. They build the mosques, the Government and other places and around those the city grew."[7] Those striking similarities characterizing the Islamic or "Arab cities makes them unmistakably Arab (or Islamic): The mosque 'maidan,' the 'suk' or 'bazar,' the craftsmen's quarters, the residential courtyard are features lending a special character to the traditional Arab (Islamic) city."

Janet Abu Lughod also emphasizes this character of the 'Islamic city' and remarks that "along this main street or at least in easy connection with it were the main congregational *madrassaite* mosques, perhaps the *maqama* (halls of residence) and certainly many of the public buildings for government and or market administration."[8]

The importance of mosques and market places in the urban culture of Islam, and in the making of Islamic cities has always been emphasized by scholars of the Islamic law, history and architecture. Ali Safak, a distinguished scholar in Islamic law, asserts that "when a city is established by Muslim people the place of the government court, the central mosque and central square should first be fixed and constructed. Market places and square have always been established as the city is founded."[9] Emphasizing the unifying role of the mosques, he observed that mosques should be constructed to unite the public. In Islamic cities mosques were built at fixed distances from one another, the central mosque being the largest one for Friday prayers.[10]

The privacy of residential areas in Islamic cities is emphasized by all scholars. August de Montequein suggests that "the traditional Muslim city is based upon the privacy of life and the religious sense of that life."[11] Hourani also stresses "a clear separation between public and private life, private turned inwards towards the courtyards and not towards the street—but a life where the basic units of the families touched externally without mingling to form a civitas."[12] Scanlon also notes that "housing was always oriented away from the streets, doors seldom faced one another for the citizen sought to maintain his privacy and achieve as complete a withdrawal from the public as possible."[13] Supporting this Islamic concept of residential privacy strongly, Abu Lughod points out that "emphasis in Islamic cities upon semi-private space was undoubtedly the pattern of sex segregation—In Islam maximum segregation between the sexes is required outside the kin group. Private space is safe and secure."[14] Acclaiming the privacy of residential sector, Francois Auguste remarks, "the classical city of Islam in its sense of privacy, neutrality and religiousness represents a supreme symbol of the equality of all Muslims in the eyes of God."[15]

Planned Islamic Cities

It is clear form the aforesaid that the central mosque had a crucial role to play in the Islamic polity, culture and in the development of Islamic thought. It assumed a focal role in unifying urban life in Islamic cities. Hence, its location occupied as great an importance as the location of the Caliph's residence itself. These two, together with the *aswâq,* normally constituted the core round which the Islamic cities evolved. In the evolution of Islamic cities the distinction between private and public life was well maintained. This resulted in the segregation of residential areas away from the busy thoroughfares. We propose now to look into the planning of some of the medieval Islamic cities such as Baghdad, Lahore, Shahajahanabad (Delhi) and Hyderabad founded by Muslim rulers to see if they conformed to the basic principles of Islamic urban planning as outlined above.

The round city of Baghdad was founded by Caliph al-Mansur in A.H. 145/A.D. 762 as the administrative centre of his kingdom. The major business centres were deliberately kept out of the main city. Nonetheless, shops were lined along the main streets of the town to meet the basic needs of the community living within the walled city of Baghdad. Despite the administrative and military outlook of this capital, the mosque occupied a prominent focal location. Besides the residence of the Caliph, "the cathedral mosque and the bureau" were also located in the centre of the city. It expresses an intimate relationship between religion and state, with an additional dignity bestowed on the state.[16]

Samuel Noe made a specific and detailed study of Lahore as an Islamic city. He first identified the basic characteristics of an Islamic city in general, and compared them with the structure and layout of Lahore. He concluded that Lahore conforms basically to the pattern of Islamic cities despite the fact that the mosque while remaining a primary institution in the walled city "has largely lost its educational role. The informal integration of the religious leadership into the secular life of the city is also diminished."[17] Noe observed that the commercial streets, residential quarters and the street patterns conformed to the Islamic pattern and thus "comparison of these features of Lahore with those of the Islamic city reveals many similarities."[18] Since the economic structure of the walled city of Lahore has hardly changed, "the disposition of bazars remains strikingly similar to that discussed in the literature. The overall pattern of street network is also identical to the prototype in the hierarchy of types, scale and expression of the separation of public and private portions of the city. The configurations of walls, gates and fortresses are of course also prototypical".[19] He noticed, however, that outside the walled city, the "prototypical Islamic social structures and institutions in Lahore are being eroded by the process of industrialization, technological change and establishment of formalized civil administration."[20]

Shahjahanabad or the walled city of Delhi is another classic example of conformity in conception, design and planning to the basic characteristics of Islamic cities as identified by Hourani, El Ali, Ali Safak and Samuel Noe. The imperial quarters and the mosque are the two key components occupying prominent location. While the citadel was withdrawn from the humdrum of the city, the central mosque or *jami' masjid* occupied location as an integrative element around which grew the old city. The hierarchy of streets is strikingly similar to that of Lahore and the residential segregation from the shopping centres is well marked. Bazars are identified by the commodities sold in them, and the residential areas by artisan class living in them. A wide variety and range of goods are sold in the bazars round the *jami' masjid.*[21] Here too, the mosque has lost its educational function. Nonetheless, the Friday congregation occasionally assumes political significance for the leader or *imam* of the mosque or of the congregational prayer sometimes uses this platform for political purposes. Another example of an Islamic city is the city of Hyderabad, the capital of the kingdom of Golcunda. It was founded in 1591 as a civil capital and twin settlement town of fortress town of Golcunda. It was planned on a grid pattern with the royal palaces and the central mosque, *jami' masjid* (called Mecca Masjid) located centrally but in the opposite sectors. In fact, Hyderabad has two *jami'* mosques, one bigger than the other. Both occupy central location. The bigger mosque was built 30 years after the foundation of the city to accommodate the ever increasing congregation. Because of the existence of a royal citadel in the fort of Golcunda, the royal palaces were not separated from the rest of the settlement. The city was divided into four quarters. "Of its four quarters, the north-western was set apart for the royal palaces and state offices, and the north-eastern for the residences of the nobles."[22] According to contemporary sources, "the city was divided into 12,000 precincts *(mohallahs)* and its main thoroughfares were lined with 14,000 buildings including shops, mosque, rest houses and *madrasas*."[23] The pattern of residential segregation from the main and busy commercial thoroughfares was set by the royal palace which had its main entrance turned away from the main street. The continuity of shops was broken by the deliberate and planned location of an enclosed open space in front of the palace gate. The residential quarters were segregated by communities such as Iranis and Mughals, and the shopping centres by commodities. The city plan provided for an open space called the *chawk,* around which developed the central shopping area.

It may be pointed out, therefore, that the cities, planned and built by Muslim rulers, whether in Iraq, Egypt or India, had some major characteristics in common. They signify the universality of Islamic influence on urban planning irrespective of the clime or region in which they were founded.

The Planning of Islamabad

With the growth of modern science and technology, the transformation of global economy and society, the planning of Islamic cities will be subject to strong technological and extra-Islamic cultural influences. Therefore, it would be naïve to expect even the Muslim architects, most of whom being trained in the Western style of architecture, to design and plan the exact prototype of Islamic cities. For instance, the degree of residential segregation enjoyed in the medieval period is inconceivable today when people take to living in multi-storied buildings. Similarly, a modern university with its extensive space requirement cannot be located in the heart of the town in proximity to the *jami'* mosque. Despite this global socio-economic transformation and emergence of new principles in urban planning, there are certain aspects in the planning of Islamic cities which can stand the test of time and can be used with effectiveness even in modern urban planning. The residential areas in modern cities are stratified according to class, income group, caste and ethnic group. The role of the mosque and the *madaris* attached to them has to cut across this ethnic and class barrier in order to promote equality, fraternity and unity. The *aswaq* in Islamic cities with pedestrianisation of their pathways were centres of politics and culture besides being places of business. They fostered a high degree of socialization at all levels. The urge for fraternization in Islamic cities, irrespective of caste, clan or colour, was maximum and Islamic cities were the prime agents to promote it. It is against this backdrop of the planning concept of an Islamic city that we shall look into the planning and development of Islamabad.

In order to understand and appreciate the philosophy of the foundation of the new capital of Pakistan, the goals and ideals set by its founding fathers, the hopes and aspirations of the nation associated with it, and the planning concepts employed in its design and development, we have relied mainly on official plan documents issued by the National Capital Development Authority, and on the planning proposals and programmes prepared by Doxiadis and associates.

Pakistan, a newly established independent country (1947), initially adopted Karachi as its capital but in due course felt the need to shift the capital from the port town to an inland and central location. The need to shift was genuine, for Karachi was bound to grow to enormous proportions, being the only sea outlet for international trade. The Government of Pakistan appointed a Commission in February 1959, to propose a site for the new capital of Pakistan. On the recommendations of the Commission, the Potwar Plateau was selected as the site for the new capital. It was in October 1961, that the construction work commenced, and the first digging was made on the ground in what is commonly known as the Aabpara neighbourhood. Exactly after two years, in October 1963, the new city came to life with the shifting of the pioneer residents.[24] The capital was named Islamabad.

Regarding its role and functions, the planners visualized that, besides the administrative hub of the nation, the national capital will "become the centre of culture and education and a real centre of national expression, contributing to the development of the people, the economy and culture of Pakistan" and that it will eventually emerge "as symbol of the new state and of the nation towards which the eyes of the whole people will look for unity and guidance for the consolidation of their new state."[25] While elucidating further the role of the capital city, the capital plan document states that the "capital of a country is not merely just another city, it is a leader among cities. To this come leaders of the administration and polities, commerce and trade, literature and art, religion and science. From this city flows the inspiration which pulsates life into the nation. It is a symbol of our hopes. It is a mirror of our desire. It is the heart and soul of the nations. It is, therefore, essential that the environment of the capital should be such as to ensure continued vitality of the nation.[26]

These noble sentiments echoing the Doxidian concept of a dynapolis, which is more technology-oriented, reduce the human scale despite its claim to "include all social and income groups and all types of functions, satisfy all human needs on the basis of the principle of unity of purpose."[27] It was, thus planned as a modern metropolis in conception and design and from this angle it is one of the world's best planned metropolises, even better than Canberra, the capital of Australia.

The plan document does not visualize that the city could be the expression of both the religious philosophy and social outlook of the nation. Its secular approach to urban planning ignores the spiritual content and, therefore, does not think that religion has a role to play in planning. The Romans, the Ancient Indians and Sumerians, the Babylonians and the medieval urban planners, whether in India or West Asia, all recognized the significant role assigned to religious symbolization in the planning of towns.

Due to this secular Doxidian approach, religion has been assigned only a peripheral role. The mosque has been deemed to be a mere place of worship. It hardly enters as a planning concept in the structure plan of Islamabad. The only reference to the mosque in the official plan document of Islamabad is on page 202, para 700 of volume 2, part 2, wherein it is cursorily observed that "a community class IV centre is defined by the number of families needed to keep up the elementary functions of the daily life such as market, a place of worship, a secondary school...etc." Even the document issued by the Capital Development Authority merely states that a "series of mosques at suitable points with various congregation capacities have been built to serve the needs of self-contained residential neighbourhoods."[28] That the mosque has a distinct social, cultural and political role in Islamic culture has not been even perceived of by the planners. It is noticed that all elements of national culture, viz., the national museum, the national library, the national bank and the central business district are located in the heart of the town. The central or *jami'* mosque, around which the great Islamic cities have stemmed, has no place in the centre of Islamabad. The King Faisal Mosque, with its Islamic Research Centre which is a magnificent structure, could have occupied the heart of Islamabad. It would have infused new spirit to the planning and development of the capital of Pakistan. The location of the central mosque in the heart of a modern Islamic capital city would have established its relevance and validity in modern town planning. It would have provided impetus to the Islamic researchers to stress the contribution of Islam to the development of modern science and knowledge. The location of mosque on the periphery, isolated from the mainstream of city life, prevents it from playing a positive role in shaping the lives of the city folk. This has not been realized at all by the Capital Development Authority. They have demonstrated total lack of perception of the role of a national mosque in Islam, for they make a bland statement that "the Master Plan provided construction of a grand national mosque on a scale and excellence befitting the city of Islam. A suitable site was earmarked at the foot of the Margalla hills which is located on a high terraced land on the axis of Shahrah-e-Islamabad.[29] It is an irony in modern Islamic town planning that the central mosque which should have been rightly in the heart of the national capital, guiding its spirit and dominating its form, has been cast aside with peripheral location. The planners of Islamabad have discarded this most interrogative urban element of Islamic cities.

Similarly, the planning of the central business district of Islamabad lacks imagination. The mechanical scale is so prominent that human scale has been dwarfed in entire planning process of Islamabad. The shopping malls and arcades, and the pedestrianisation of the central business districts of Western cities have been derived from the *aswaq* of Islamic cities. While the West is adopting these concepts to their advantage, the Muslims are ignoring them. Thus, they are exhibiting total lack of imagination in urban planning. They are not able to appreciate the value of their own Islamic legacy and heritage in city planning. Janet Abu Lughod stresses the point that "in many western cities portions of the central business district are being redesigned to create pedestrian malls that are highly reminiscent of the *aswaq* of medieval Islamic cities. And the latest design of shopping centres is to enclose them as well as to bar vehicular traffic."[30] This is also confirmed by an AID report which describes that "there are striking similarities between what are now considered most up-to-date site planning approaches and traditional Egyptian neighbourhood patterns. The 'clustered plan' which in the old city grew naturally over hundreds of years is defined by narrow streets and open spaces *(rihab)*. This arrangement restricts heavy traffic inside the clustered dwellings, separates heavy traffic from pedestrians and at the same time has proved 20 per cent lower in cost than the grid system."[31] It was left to Francois Auguste, a European scholar, to highlight the virtues of Islamic planning and to lament over the fact that they are being abandoned in the Islamic world. He points out that "the Muslim Madina a traditional island of pedestrian circulation in the heart of the city can be excellent source of inspiration for the urban centres of the future—shopping malls and local markets are a tradition in Middle East, they provide scattered work opportunity for the low income segment of the neighbourhood and inhibit, therefore, slum generation and social decay."[32] He further says that "at a time when every

European city is introducing pedestrian zones particularly in their historic centres, the Islamic cities with their incomparably rich pedestrian oriented fabric are subject to dissection by traffic routes or suffocation by automobiles."[33]

Conclusion

In conclusion, it may be observed that some of the basic aspects of planning of the Islamic cities are still valid and relevant to modern town planning despite astonishing progress in science and technology. In the planning of Islamabad, the planners and architects of Pakistan had a challenging opportunity to stress this fact and to re-live the legacy of Islamic planning by creating a metropolis which would have been modern in substance and Islamic in spirit. They could have made Islamabad true to its name; an urban centre imbued with Islamic culture and spirit and a liveable city noted for its human scale and values. Instead, Islamabad has been designed after outmoded Westernized concepts of planning which will promote segmentation of its urban form and structure as against the integrative role the Islamic concepts of urban planning stimulate. Consequently, Islamabad being alienated from the basic principles of Islamic urban planning will, no doubt, stand out as modern metropolis but will not be able to perform the noble integrative and humanistic role of Islamic cities which the founders expected it to perform.

REFERENCES

1. EL Ali, "The Foundation of Baghdad," *The Islamic City,* ed. A.H. Hourani and S.M. Stern (Cassirer Oxford, 1970), p. 89.
2. A.H. Hourani and S.M. Stern, *The Islamic City* (Cassirer, Oxford, 1970), p. 24.
3. I.M. Lapidus, "Muslim Urban Society in Mamluk Syria," *The Islamic City,* pp. 1-7.
4. Hourani and Stern, pp. 21-22.
5. Samuel, V. Noe, "In Search of 'the' Traditional Islamic City, An Analytical Proposal with Lahore as a Case Example," *Ekistics,* Vol. 47 (Feb. 1980), No. 280, pp. 69-75.
6. George T. Scanion, "Some Aspects of Medieval Islamic Public Service", *The Islamic City,* p. 180.
7. Raphail Wahabe, "Cairo," *The New Metropolis in the Arab World,* ed. Morroo Berger (Allied Publishers, Bombay, 1961), p. 26.

8. Saba George Shibber, "Planning Needs and Obstacles," *The New Metropolis in the Arab World*, p. 167.
9. Janet Abu Lughod, "Contemporary Relevance of Islamic Urban Principles," *Ekistics,* Vol. 47 (January to February 1980), No. 280, pp. 6-10.
10. Ali Safak, "Urbanism and Family Residence in Islamic Law," *Ekistics,* Vol. 47 (Jan-Feb. 1980), No. 280, pp. 23-24.
11. Francois Auguste de Montequein, "The Islamic City—Its Traditional Environment and Physiognamy," *Ekistics,* Vol. 47 (January to February 1980), No. 280, p. 37.
12. Hourani and Stern, p. 24.
13. George T. Scanion, p. 162.
14. Janet Abu Lughod, p. 8.
15. De Montequin, p. 3.
16. El Ali, pp. 93-94.
17. Samuel Noe, p. 70.
18. *Ibid.,* p. 73.
19. *Ibid.,* p. 74.
20. *Ibid.*
21. Jag Mohan, *Shajehanabad*, Vikas, New Delhi, 1977.
22. S. Manzoor Alam, *Hyderabad-Secunderabad, Twin Cities* (Allied Publishers, London—Bombay, 1965), p. 3.
23. Manzoor Alam, p. 3.
24. S.A.T. Wasti, *Islamabad—The City of Peace* (Directorate of Public Relations Capital Development Authority, Islamabad, 1979), p. 12.
25. *Islamabad: Programme and Plan,* Vol. 1, document 2, p. 27, para 79.
26. *Ibid.,* p. 160.
27. *Ibid.,* p. 108, para 282.
28. *Ibid.*
29. Wasti, p. 58.
30. Abu Lughod, p. 10.
31. Laila Ali Ibrahim, "Traditional Designs and the Requirements of Modern Islamic City," *Ekistics,* Vol. 47 (Feb. 1980), No. 280, p. 17.
32. De Montequein, pp. 37-39.
33. *Ibid.,* pp. 37-38.

4

The Growth of Hyderabad City : A Historical Perspective

Hyderabad City, in its growth from the capital of the medieval state of Golcunda to the status of a modern metropolis, has passed through many historical phases, each of which has left a strong imprint on the City's structure and character. The object of this chapter is to focus the growth and development of Hyderabad in historical perspective and to evaluate the impact of each historical period on its physical growth and functional development.

The history of the growth of Hyderabad City can be conveniently divided into six clearly identifiable stages:

I.	The Qutb Shahi Stage	1591-1687
II.	The Transitional Stage	1687-1725
III.	The Early Asaf Jahi Stage	1725-1798
IV.	The Residency Stage	1798-1874
V.	The Railway Stage	1874-1908
VI.	The Modern and Metropolitan Stage	1908-1963

These stages indicate the occurrence of a significant political event or the introduction of new economic factors having a marked influence on the forms and functions of Hyderabad.

I. The Qutb Shahi Stage, 1591-1687 (Map 4.1)

The city of Hyderabad was founded by Muhammad-Quli Qutb Shah,

Published in *Dr. Ghulam Yazdani Commemoration Volume*, Edited by Prof. H. K. Sherwani, Maulana Abul Kalam Azad Oriental Institute, Hyderabad (India), 1966, pp. 212-220.

the fifth ruler of the kingdom of Golcunda in 1591, on a desirable site on the south bank of the river Musi, four miles east of the citadel of Golcunda. No other place near the fortress-town combined the favourable factors of an open, gently sloping, well drained land, a location on the main commercial highway of the kingdom and a large perennial tank (Jalpalli) available for domestic use.

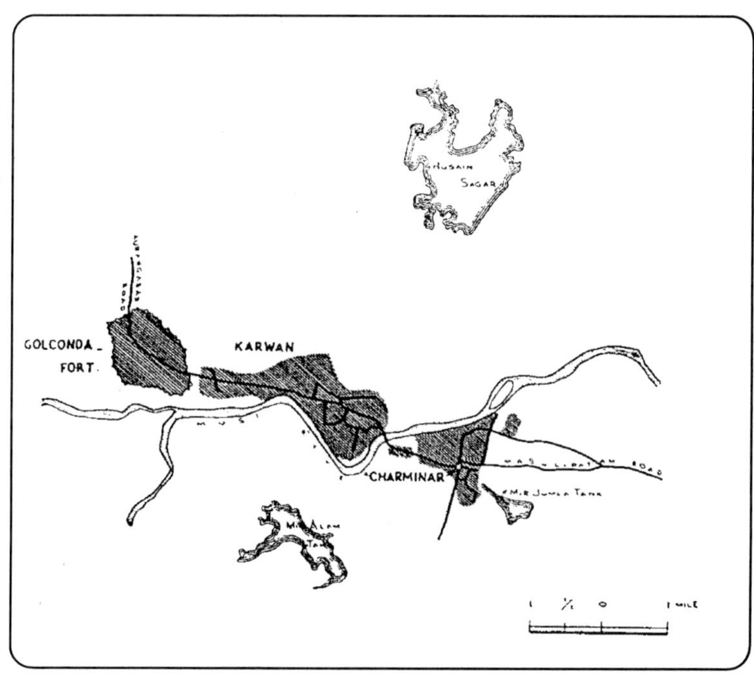

Map 4.1: Hyderabad—Growth of Settlement Area : 1687

The city of Hyderabad was planned on a grid pattern consisting of two main roads, running East-West and North-South and intersecting at Charminar, the City Centre. It thus formed four quarters. According to contemporary sources the main thoroughfares of the city were lined with 13,000 shops and with mosques, rest houses and madrasas or schools. Of its four quarters, the north-west was set apart for royal palaces and state offices, and the north-eastern for the residences of the nobles. City building during this period was stimulated by the king who constructed numerous palaces, laid out beautiful gardens in the city and suburbs, patronized men of letters and commerce which resulted in a phenomenal growth of the city.

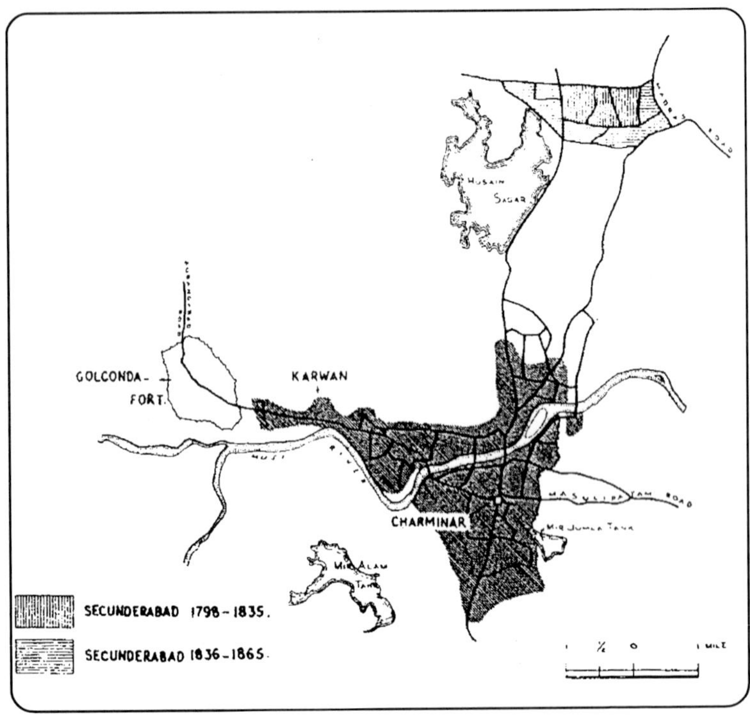

Map 4.2 : Hyderabad-Secunderabad—Growth of Settlement Area : 1865

This explosive growth of Hyderabad is testified by Tavernier who visited the town in 1652 and found it "nearly the size of Orleans, well built and opened out"[1]. We, however, owe to Thevenot, who visited Hyderabad 17 years after Tavernier, a precise account of the city growth and its suburban extension. Thevenot entered Hyderabad from the Karwan side and after crossing the bridge he "marched quarter of an hour (or one mile) through a long street with houses on both sides"[2]. During Tavernier's time only the right side of the road was built. As regards the total expansion of the town, Thevenot records "that the town makes a kind of cross, much larger than broad… having adjusted my measures I found Bagnagar was 5,650 paces in length (2.7 miles) 2,450 paces (1.1. miles) from the bridge to the Tower and from thence 3,200 paces to the Gate (1.6 miles) which leads to Masulipatam. There is beyond that gate a suburb 1,100 paces (917 yards) long"[3]. Although the built up area of the City had considerably expanded, the settlement was nevertheless centred principally round four nuclei: (1) Royal Palaces in the NW quarter, (2) Haveli of Mir Momin (now called the Purani Haveli) and Daru'sh-Shifa, (3) Mughalpura, near Mir Jumla Tank, and (4) Husaini Alam. Besides these emerging settlements, Karwan, between Hyderabad and Golcunda, was a thickly populated suburb about two miles long, though "only built up of earth and thatched with straw...so low and ill-contrived that (the houses) can be reckoned no more than huts," it was "where all the merchants, brokers and artisans dwell"[4].

Within a short period of its foundation Hyderabad became the commercial metropolis of the kingdom of Golcunda. Tavernier found local businessmen transacting with foreign traders and de Thevenot was surprised to see in this city the number of rich merchants, bankers, jewellers and skilful artisans "not only native but also Persians and Armenians"[5]. In 1672, Abbe Carre observed that this "large town...Bagnagar (is) full of strangers and merchants. That trade is carried on by foreigners and others without any restrictions as to their nationality or particular business. There is such a concourse of every kind of people, merchandise and riches that the place seems to be the centre of all trade in the East"[6].

Thus the Qutb Shahi stage of development was a period of virulent growth for the city of Hyderabad. Founded as a civil capital, Hyderabad rapidly outshone its sister capital, the fortress of Golcunda, and became the nerve centre of the kingdom, directing its administrative, intellectual, cultural and commercial activities. Golcunda's rock was difficult of access and the walls of the citadel constricted the opportunities for city growth which the increasing stability of the kingdom, its growing military power and rising commerce demanded. On the construction of the bridge (now the Purana Pul or Old Bridge) in 1578, the possibility for expansion towards the south bank had been opened out and thus Hyderabad soon supplanted Golcunda both in size and function. Hyderabad's growth along with that of Golcunda was, however, suddenly halted by the annexation of the kingdom to the Mughal Empire in 1687.

II. The Transition Stage : 1687-1725

This period began with a breakdown in the organic development of Hyderabad city. It was divested of its capital status and the seat of authority was shifted to Aurangabad which was made the headquarters of the vast Southern Province of the Mughal Empire. Meanwhile Aurangabad suffered from political instability and consequently the situation at Hyderabad was also unstable. Towards the end of 1724 political conditions settled down, Nizamul-Mulk Asaf Jah founded the Asaf Jahi dynasty (which lasted right up till 1948), took firm control of the Deccan and of Hyderabad city. A significant event of the period was the completion of the city-wall which defined precisely the city limits, provided for the safety and the security of the people and thus made possible the return of the population which had shifted back to Golcunda in 1687.

III. The Early Asaf-Jahi Stage : 1724-1798

This period in the morphological development of Hyderabad is characterized by two distinct phases, one of (a) inhibition (1724-63) and the other of (b) acceleration (1763-98).

(a) Period of Inhibition : 1724-63

The period of inhibition was one of great economic stress and strain for Hyderabad. Aurangabad had become the premier city of the Deccan and most of the powerful land-holders had migrated there. The death of Asaf Jah I in 1748 and the Anglo-French struggle for supremacy in the Deccan (1750-60) renewed political uncertainty which adversely affected Hyderabad's growth. Even the construction of the Ruler's palace Salabat Jung's (south of Mecca Masjid) and his ministers' mansions in the south-west quarter of the city could not check the stagnation set up by the other factors. Excepting the north-west quarter, the city was only partially filled, the nobles' houses were largely empty and its major and minor shopping centres were half empty. The north-west quarter, where once stood the royal Qutb Shahi buildings, was full of dwellings of poor quality, narrow roads and crooked lanes. There was hardly any suburban expansion. In fact, Hyderabad was rapidly stagnating and all the symptoms of decadence were there.

(b) Period of Acceleration : 1763-98

The phase of acceleration started in 1763. Sometimes decisions of rulers play a great part in shaping the future of a city. It was one such decision by Nizam Ali Khan, the Viceroy of the Deccan, that salvaged the declining city of Hyderabad. The Nizam became the Viceroy of the Deccan in 1761. He first consolidated his position and then shifted his headquarters permanently to Hyderabad in 1763. It is difficult to state precisely the reasons for this shift. Nevertheless it appears that the proximity of Aurangabad to unfriendly Marhatta States, the emergence of the British as the chief political power in the south, the meteoric rise of Hyder Ali in Mysore and the consequent threat to the Nizam's state might have influenced him to make Hyderabad the capital of his domain. The emergence of Hyderabad as a capital city again after an eclipse of more than three quarters of a century, infused the city with new life, vigour and energy.

The fate of a capital city in a feudal state is inevitably linked with the ruler's presence and that of the nobility. If the capital city loses its status its vitality is sapped for its entire economy and functional importance pivots round the ruler and the dignitaries of his state. The Nizam's decision, therefore, was of historic significance for the economic and physical growth of Hyderabad. With the Nizam his nobles also returned to Hyderabad, resulting thereby in a great concentration of power and wealth in the city. The Deccan Province was twice the area of the kingdom of Golcunda and much more prosperous than that. The developmental activities of the city were naturally spurred on. Old and dilapidated buildings were razed to the ground, replaced by mansions of the nobles. The entire walled city was thus face-lifted. Development outside the city-wall, within a radius of two miles, was equally substantial. In the south this extra-mural extension consisted mainly of nobles' pleasure houses and gardens, while in the north developed an extensive business locality of Begam Bazaar, parallel to the river bank east of the Karwan. Commerce and business also reacted favourably to this economic and physical growth of the city. It had only four bazaars and one grand bazaar (Chauk) in 1761 but in 1798 it included twelve bazaars, three grand bazaars and a large wholesale business centre (Begam Bazaar). Thus between 1763-98, the city of Hyderabad considerably regained its past political stature, and economic and commercial importance.

IV. The Residency Stage : 1798-1874

In 1798, two significant political decisions were taken, namely (a) the Nizam's permission for the construction of the British

Residency on the north bank in proximity to the walled city; (b) the Subsidiary Alliance of the Nizam with the East India Company in 1798 which created Secunderabad, profoundly altered the course of the city's development.

(a) Construction of Residency and its Impact on the Growth of Hyderabad

The Residency buildings were completed in 1806 and following its construction, "there came into existence around (it) a cluster of shops and dwelling houses of the *bona fide* subjects of the Ruler of the State" and over which "the Nizam's government accorded to the Resident unreserved power, jurisdiction in civil and criminal matters"[7]. This settlement, being efficiently administered, enjoyed peace and security. The native bankers, resident in Karwan who were being molested by the free-booters there, were thus also attracted to it. This is corroborated by Temple who wrote that "a native banker came to see me and said that he lived in Karwan, a sort of suburb of Hyderabad, which was formerly full of bankers, but that many of them had left…and had come to Chadarghat to be near the protection of the Residency"[8]. Moreover, the native civil servants of the Nizam's government also moved to Chadarghat "preferring probably our sanitary and police arrangements to their own"[9]. Besides these colonies of native merchants and civil servants a large colony of Europeans and Eurasians had also sprung up in Chadarghat, West and North-West of the Residency. Confirming this, Saunders said that "a large European Society which has grown up in the vicinity of Hyderabad holds a (respectable) position among the inhabitants of the (Residency) Bazaar"[10].

This European-Eurasian Colony adjacent to the walled city was a valuable addition to Hyderabad's cultural development. European style residences, Christian Churches and Missionary Schools dominated Chadarghat. The first native Christian Colony was established by the French round the Gun Foundry located here which served as a nucleus for the growth of Christian settlement, and it is within 1,000 yards of the foundry's radius that Hyderabad's Christian population, churches and convent schools are still concentrated.

The inflow of bankers and civil servants into the Residency area stimulated its banking and commercial activities. Bilgrami and Willmot record that "Residency Bazaars are great trading centres, there are to be found branch houses and representatives of all the native banking firms in India who are prepared to grant (*hundies*) for the largest sums upon any town from Peshawar to Madras"[11].

As a result of this expanding business activity and extensive colonization by the European, Eurasian and native civil servants the settlement area around Residency expanded to over 9 sq. miles by 1874.

The dynamic growth of the Residency area was also reflected in the city proper and its southern and northern suburbs. In the south the extensive suburbs of Jahan-Numa and Doodh Baoli had emerged while in the north the suburbs extended to the Chadarghat Bridge (Oliphant Bridge, constructed in 1839) to finally merge into the Residency settlements. Within the city proper the density of dwellings and of population and also considerably increased and is evident by the addition of a thriving bazaar (Mandi Mir Alam) in the north-east quarter of the city.

This rapid development of the walled city and its suburbs and of the Residency areas stimulated contacts between the two and generated movement of people and goods in either direction. This was further assisted by the addition of two bridges across the Musi at Chadarghat and Afzalgunj in 1839 and 1857 respectively.

The setting of the Residency thus within the vicinity of Hyderabad contributed to the latter's physical expansion and also introduced a critical change in its pattern of growth. The Chadarghat area which was during the Qutb Shahi period a vast tract of garden and grove was replaced by populous bazaars and houses largely European in style. A northward shift in Hyderabad's axis of growth was clearly discernible for towards the end of the Residency period the Charminar-Afzalgunj Road had become the principal retail thoroughfare (Shah Rah) replacing the old Purana Pul-Charminar Road.

V. The Railway Stage : 1874-1908

The coming of the railway in 1874 into the rapidly expanding city of Hyderabad and its subsequent extension into the hinterland of the city had a profound impact on its growth and economic structure. Regionally the railways linked Hyderabad with its rich cotton producing areas of Marathwada and expanded its commercial activities. They also made a tremendous difference by transferring the trade of Hyderabad from Masulipatam to Bombay and Madras. Locally, their effect was no less powerful. They accelerated the northward expansion of Hyderabad, assisted its industrial development, and established it as a regional business centre.

The growth of Hyderabd south of the Musi was practically halted and its axis of growth was definitely turned northward. The expansion of settlement area in the north was explosive, and in the words of Valentine Prinsep (*Madras Times*, 1884): "The city of Hyderabad...has grown with exceeding great growth. From the Musi to Afzalgunj, from Afzalgunj to Chadarghat and from Chadarghat to Saifabad, the city has gone on spreading. Thousands of houses valued at many lacs have been built and every hillock has been availed for a nobleman's residence.

Excepting household and cottage industries Hyderabad had no large scale industrial establishments before 1874. But within 15 years after the advent of the railways a couple of industrial nuclei emerged. The establishment of a Mint and its workshop in 1878, on the south bank of Hussain Sagar, near Khairatabad village, gave great impetus to the growth of that "neat well-populated opulent village. The development of cotton textile and tile factories by 1895, east of the Tank Bund initiated rapid urbanization of the adjacent villages of Bhoiguda, Kavadiguda, Bholkagudam and Mushirabad.

This period of growth, like the preceding one, was also one of extensive residential and commercial development. The functional base of the city was being broadened and its link with the hinterland was being strengthened.

VI. The Modern Age and Metropolitan Development : 1908-1963

The modern era in Hyderabad's growth was ushered in by a catastrophic flood in 1908, and its metropolitan development commenced with the completion of the rail and road network by 1936. The former allowed scope for the internal reorganization of the city, while the latter stabilizes its regional relations and diversified its functional base.

The devastating flood of September 1908, though it disrupted civic life, brought in its wake a strong move by the newly established City Improvement Board in 1912 to reorganize, structurally, the whole city. With a view of this the Board sponsored a large scale house building activity, clearance of slums, widening of roads and improvement of shopping facilities. As a result many of the congested areas in the city were opened, slums were demolished and converted into model residential neighbourhoods and roads were widened to take in vehicular traffic. To the flood also the city owes its existing improved system of sewerage and water supply. The most significant events, however, from the morphological standpoint were the shift of the Nizam's residence in 1914 and of the state offices to the north. This shift made the walled city stagnant and in contrast accelerated residential and commercial developments in the Chadarghat and its adjoining areas where, however, until the introduction of the city and suburban bus services, only interstices were being filled up and there was no lateral expansion of the settlement area.

The metropolitan growth of Hyderabad, although initiated and sustained by improved regional and city and suburban transport systems, has been also greatly strengthened by political factors. The radiating regional rail and bus routes from the capital enhanced its administrative and economic control over the State of Hyderabad. Commercially, it became the nucleus of wholesale business activity for the State. Its industrial development was also speeded up, and by 1940 Hyderabad claimed two large industrial districts within it and in the suburbs.

The City and Suburban rail and bus services were started in 1928 and in 1932 respectively. They now traverse extensively within a radius of 17 miles from the city centre, the Moazzam Jahi Market. The two advanced the various urban functions, and new residential neighbourhoods and business centres have emerged. This rapid expansion of suburban transport saved the part of Hyderabad south of the river from depopulation, urbanized adjoining villages, made possible the development of functional suburbs such as industrial (Sanatnagar, Kukatpalli and Maula Ali), educational (Osmania University, Adikmet), recreational (Zoological Gardens—Mir Alam Tank), and has increased the sphere of direct and dominant metropolitan influence.

The political events too have much strengthened this metropolitan phase in Hyderabad. The "Police Action" on the state of Hyderabad in 1948 and the Reorganization of States in 1956 are the two political events of historic significance. Of these the latter has influenced more the social and economic structure of Hyderabad city. The emergence of Hyderabad as the capital of the enlarged State of Andhra Pradesh brought about a large immigration of population and financial and economic activities in it. This influx spiralled up land values in Hyderabad city and caused a boom in its city building activities. Every available space in the city is being rapidly swallowed by diverse urban land uses. The astonishing rapidity of increase in built up area is exemplified in and around Chikadpally, near Mushirabad, a large and sparsely populated locality until 1956. This is now packed with decent two storeyed dwellings. It was this area, east of the Tank Bund, which Dr. Balfour, in 1865, described as "an unending stretch of paddy fields,"[12] but this same area now is metamorphosed beyond recognition as an endless pile of lime and stone, brick and mortar. Here has been such an explosive growth that the settlements of Hyderabad and Secunderabad have fused into each other and these two, along with their suburbs, have developed into a unified, though complex, urban settlement.

Conclusion

During its life span of three and three quarter centuries the city of Hyderabad and its environs have undergone total metamorphosis. Each historical period has left it deep impression on the architectural expressions and forms and functions of Hyderabad. During each period of its growth it absorbed new cultures, functions. These cultural and functional changes are reflected in its morphology for every new form of the city preserved its past and reflected its age. The dynamic city of Hyderabad is thus a unique cultural landscape in this ancient tableland of the Deccan.

REFERENCES

1. Jean, B. Tavernier: *Collection of Travels through Turkey into Persia and the East Indies,* Book I, Part II, pp. 63-64; translated from French by J. Phillips and Edmund Everard, London, 1680. Words in brackets within quotes, right through the paper are additions by the writer.
2. Monsieur'de Thevenot: *op. cit.*, p. 94.
3. Monsieur'de Thevenot: *op. cit.,* p. 94. [For "Bagnagar" see Sherwani, "The Bhagmati Legent", *Journal of Indian History,* April 1961, pp. 119-130 Ed.].
4. Jean, B. Tavernier: *op. cit.,* p. 63.
5. M. de, Thevenot: *op. cit.* p. 97.
6. Abbe, Carre: *Travels of the Abbe Carre in India and the Near East,* 1672-74: tr. From the MS Journal of his travels by lady Fawcett, Ed., Sir Charles Fawcett, Hakluyt Society, Series No. XCV, 1947.
7. Anonymous: *A Note on the British Residency in Hyderabad,* p. 1, (year of publication not mentioned—copy: British Museum).

8. Sir R. Temple: *Journals kept in Hyderabad, Kashmir, Sikkim ad Nepal,* p. 3, London, 1867.
9. Charles, Saunders: *Administration Report,* 1869-70, *of the Resident of Hyderabad to the Government of India,* p. 149.
10. Charles, Saunders: *op. cit., Administration Report,* 1870-71, p. 194.
11. Bilgrami &Willmot: *Glimpses of the Deccan History,* Bombay, 1884.
12. Dr. S. Balfour: *Medical Report on the British Cantonment in Secunderabad and Bolarum*—1865.

5

Indian Cities and Western Theories of Urban Growth–An Empirical Appraisal

Studies on urbanization and urban development in Western Europe and North America have led to the formulation of a number of theories of urban growth. Scholars in Western Europe including the British Isles have discussed the more formal regions within a city in relation to broad morphological characteristics. For instance Dickinson in his study of West European Cities observed their common tendency to grow in concentric zone of distinctive build and character.[1] American scholars on the other hand have generalised the land use pattern for American cities as influenced by the ecological processes. These have resulted into the formulation of concentric zone theory by Burgess,[2] and sector theory of residential neighbourhoods by Hoyt.[3] The object of this chapter is to critically examine the land use development of Hyderabad, a historic city and an emerging Indian metropolis in the light of these western theories of urban growth. In a general discussion on the relevance of these theories for Hyderabad examples from other Indian cities will also be cited.

Hyderabad with its population of nearly 2 million is the fifth largest city of India. From its foundation in 1591 A.D. as the capital of the medieval feudal state of Golcunda to its rise to the status of a modern metropolis, Hyderabad has passed through many historical phases each of which has left a strong imprint on the city's structure and character. The dynamic political and economic changes, since its inception, have significantly altered its axis of growth, have radically transformed its morphology and have notably influenced its demographic composition and economic and social structure.

Published in *Urbanization in Developing Countries* – Indo-Soviet Vol., Editors Manzoor Alam and V.V. Pokshishevsky, Osmania University, Hyderabad, (India), 1976, pp. 455-473.

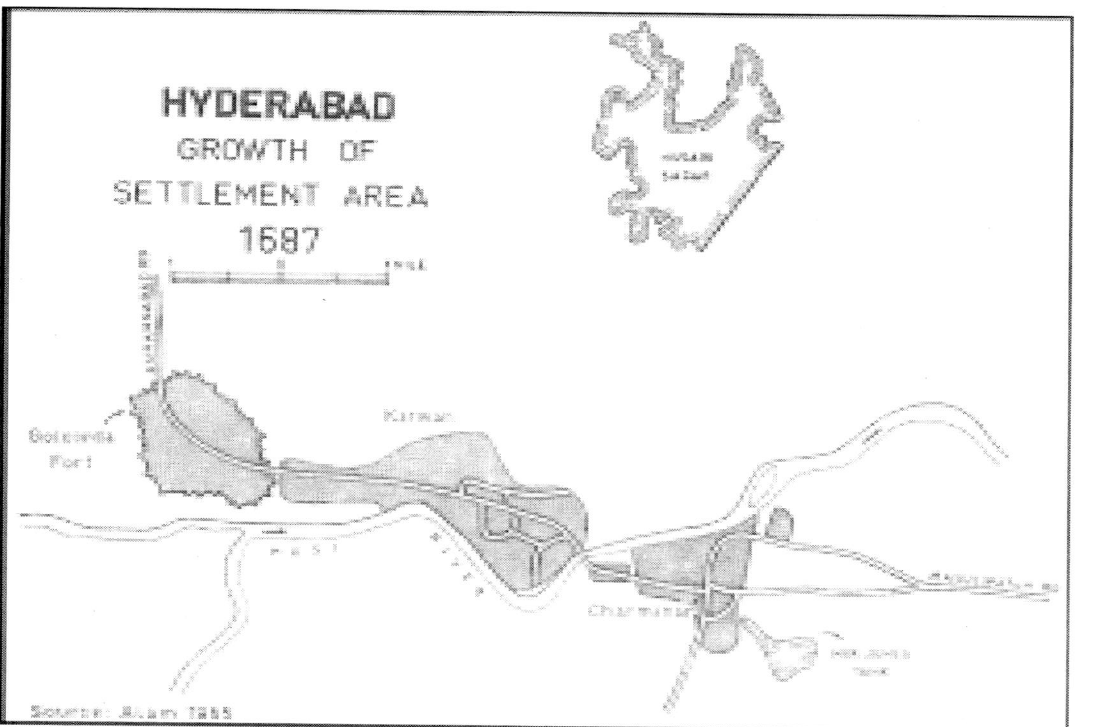

Fig. 5.1 : Hyderabad : Growth of Settlement Area, 1687

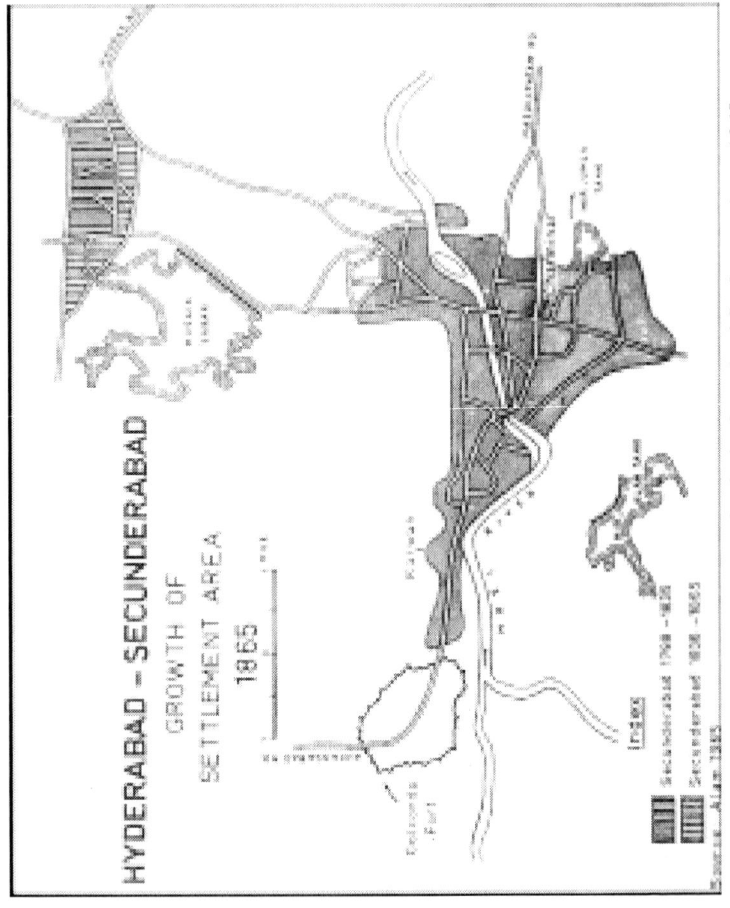

Fig. 5.2 : Hyderabad-Secunderabad : Growth of Settlement Area, 1865

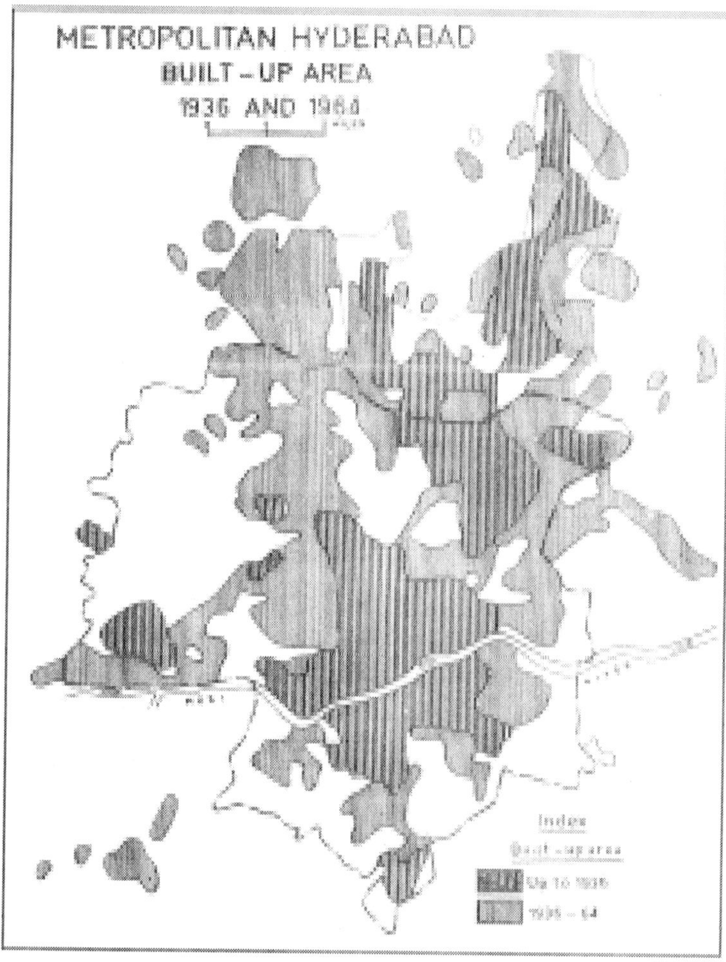

Fig. 5.3 : Metropolitan Hyderabad : Built-Up Area, 1936 and 1964

The political changes in the capital city caused the shift of axis of growth from west-east to north-south (Figs. 5.1-5.3). The northerly growth of metropolitan Hyderabad was accentuated and stabilised to such an extent with the location of British Residency and Secunderabad cantonment in the north, the extension of rail facilities, and the development of modern industries that the economic core was also eventually attracted to the north. Consequently the historic core has been left out of the orbit of growth and is tending to stagnate.

The impact of political changes is also strongly marked on the morphological evolution of Hyderabad city. The morphology of Hyderabad was radically transformed after 1687 A.D. when the political control of the city passed from the hands of Qutb Shahi dynasty to that of the Asaf Jahi dynasty. The city was walled and that part of the city where the Qutb Shahs of Golcunda had built their palaces was destroyed, and subsequently occupied by people of middle and low income group (Fig. 5.4 and 5.5). The new palaces for the Asaf Jahi kings were built in the south-western quarter of the city.[4]

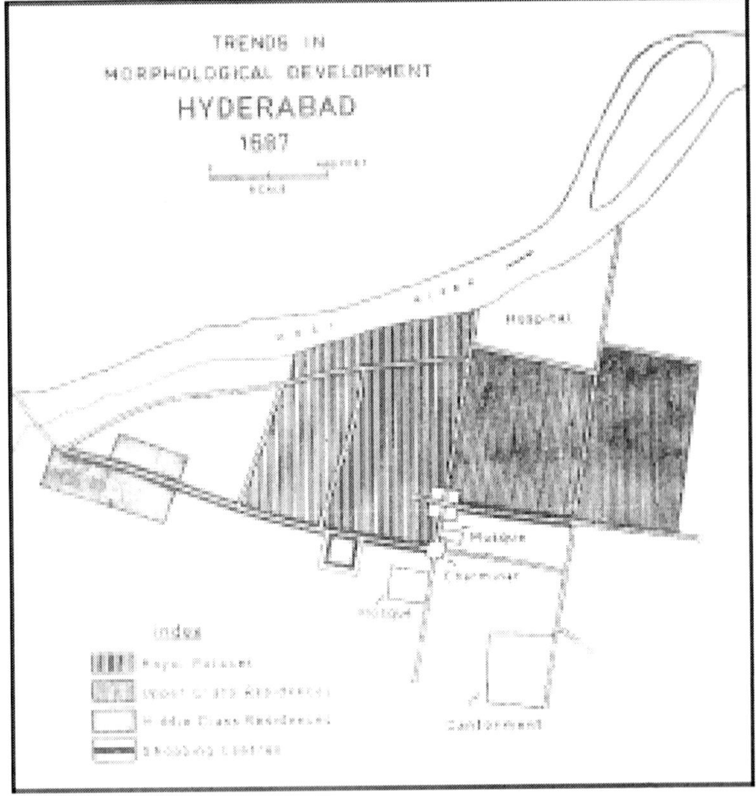

Fig. 5.4 : Trends in Morphological Development : Hyderabad, 1687

The location of British Cantonment of Secunderabad in the north and of the British Residency along the north bank of the river, besides attracting the axis of the growth to which are highlighted in Fig. 5.6.

The Residency area, north of the river emerged, with its establishments of banking and educational institutions modelled after the British system, as a nucleus of modern development and a centre for innovation. Even the residences of the local elite in this area were designed after the British style.

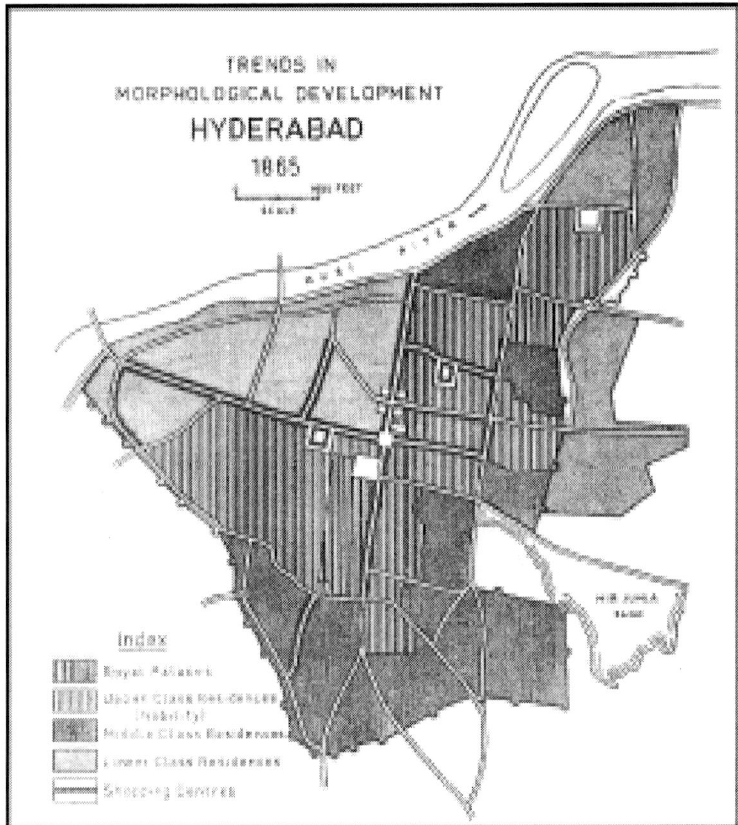

Fig. 5.5 : Trends in Morphological Development : Hyderabad, 1865

Hyderabad is noted for its confluence of cultures but until 1948 it was essentially an island of north Indian culture in a predominantly southern region because of being under the political control of a north Indian ruling dynasty. Since its becoming the capital of the reorganised Telugu speaking State of Andhra Pradesh in 1956, the demographic composition has changed considerably and Telugu, a south Indian language of Dravidian stock, is fast replacing north Indian languages, Urdu and Hindi. This has aggravated the cultural hiatus between the economically strong and politically dominant migrants from Coastal Andhra and Rayalaseema regions and the economically weak and politically subdominant citizens of the historic core.

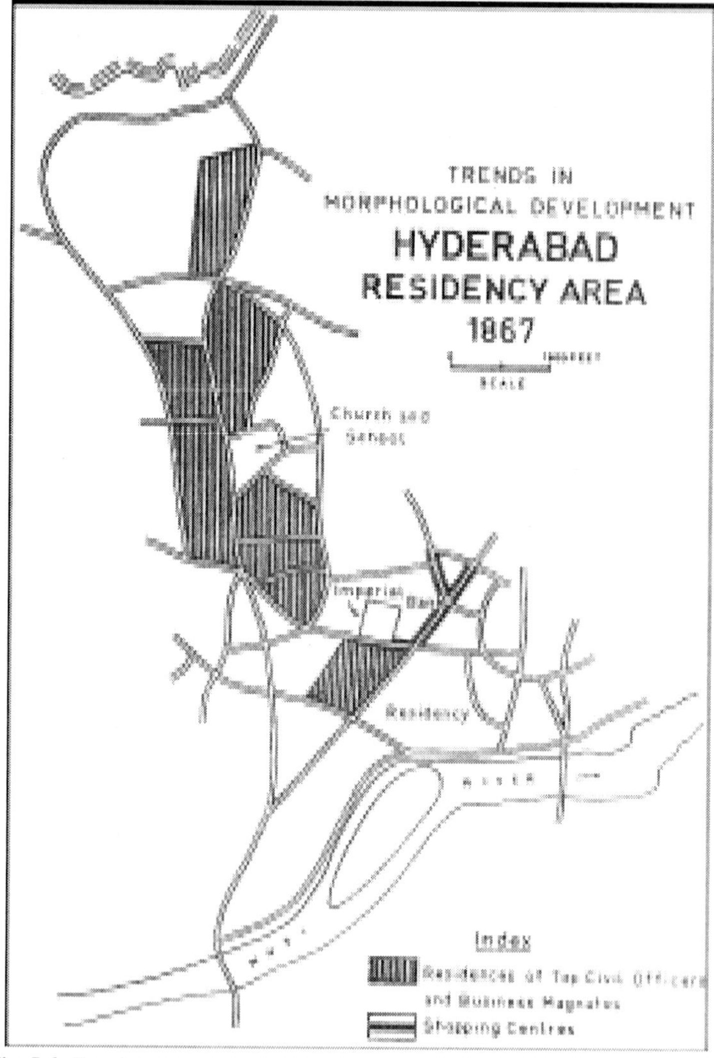

Fig. 5.6 : Trends in Morphological Development : Hyderabad Residency Area, 1867

This brief background has been presented for a proper perspective of the historical, political and economic forces which shaped the growth and morphology of metropolitan Hyderabad. This will help us in understanding the forces which have influenced Hyderabad's morphology and in appreciating the differences and similarities in the morphological pattern between Hyderabad city and those of Western Europe and North America.

Morphological Patterning of Hyderabad and Dickinson's Scheme of Morphological Classification

The West European cities according to Dickinson can be generally classified into three concrete morphological zones :

1. "the central fully built up zone, which is the core of the modern city;
2. "the compact and fully built middle zone that was erected mainly during the nineteenth century; and
3. "the outer, partly built-up (suburban) zone in which urban and rural areas are mixed, and to which urban areas have penetrated mainly during this century;"[5]

The core of the city in Dickinson's classification includes the historic city, and the city always grows outward from this historic core. The growth of the West European cities was thus centred round the historic core and more so because the commercial core of the modern metropolis itself budded out from it. As a result the historic core never ceased to be a part of the growing metropolis and its existence was maintained. Such continuity of association has thus imparted to the West European cities, their characteristic pattern of growth.

In the case of Hyderabad there are both differences from and similarities to, the historic West European cities. It differs in that it lacks the continuity of historical and cultural association, emotional integration and the superimposition of the present upon the past that European cities seem to manifest. The similarity in the growth pattern of Hyderabad with West European cities is reflected in its well marked ring development in each of its three major historic phases of development the Qutb Shahi of Golcunda, the Asaf Jahi of Hyderabad and the British, each of which represented different cultures.

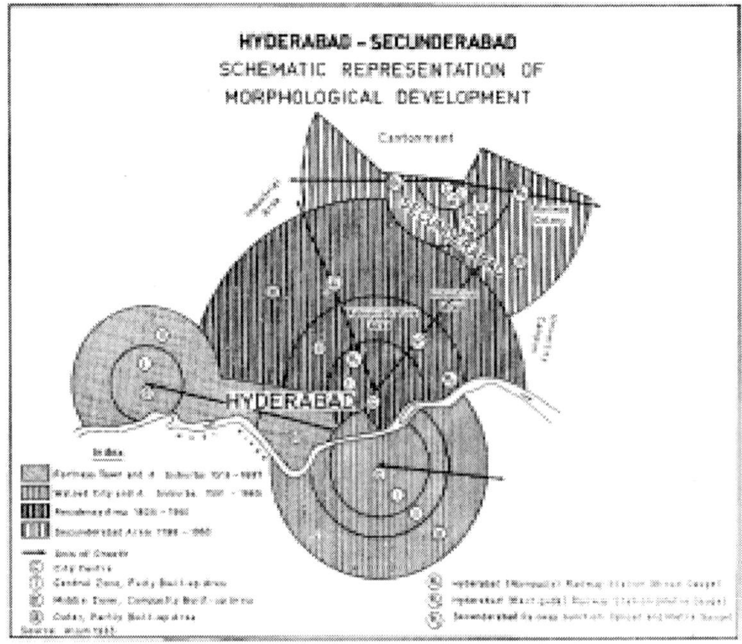

Fig. 5.7 : Hyderabad-Secunderabad : Schematic Representation of Morphological Development

Figure 5.7 a generalised schematic representation, illustrates the pattern of urban growth within the present urban complex of Hyderabad since the origin of Golcunda. It is thus clear that the city within its boundaries includes three distinct urban units represented by the ruined fortress town of Golcunda, the decaying Walled City and the dynamic Chaderghat including the British Residency area which until 1931 was a separate municipality. These urban centres were the products of different political, cultural and economic systems, and thus were separate in foundation and emotional associations. As a result the newer did not fuse into the older, but maintained its discrete identity through the creation of new cultural and economic activities. This naturally caused the decline of the older settlements and accounts for the ruin of Golcunda. Founded in 1518, Golcunda continued to develop along with Hyderabad city from 1591 to 1687, when both fell to the Moghul forces. With the succession of the Asaf Jahi dynasty in Hyderabad in 1725 the fortress town of Golcunda finally lost its political, cultural and administrative importance, while Hyderabad was walled and made the capital. This was followed by the depopulation of Golcunda and a complete shift of its administrative and economic activities to the Walled City which under the Asaf Jahis was an urban unit reborn, different in spirit from the Hyderabad of Qutb Shahis. The decay of the Wall City in turn has not been caused so much by the change in political rule as by the introduction of new economic developments, notably the coming of the railways and the use of mechanical power for factory production. These new factors in the economy of Hyderabad set new demands on land which the Walled City could hardly meet. Moreover, for political reasons the terminal of the railway systems were located by the British in the north near the Secunderabad cantonment. This naturally diverted by industrial growth away from the area was located near Secunderabad and attracted the later industrial development to the north-west and north-east along the railway lines.

These trends have been further accentuated since the formation of Andhra Pradesh in 1956 for the crowded Walled City offers no attraction to the enterprising immigrants from Andhra who are more interested in developing the modern commercial core in the north and also in the vacant lands in that same section of the city for residential use. These immigrants have no cultural and emotional ties with the southern part of the city, which for them is a relic of decadent feudalism, the very antithesis of progressive trends which they represent. These breaks in emotional ties and cultural links have created tension between the two settlements and they are pulling apart. The older, being thus isolated from the forces of growth and expansion, is hardening against change, its population is clinging fast to outmoded traditions and economic systems which might lead to its decay and ultimate ruin.

Thus not all parts of Hyderabad are vitally active. While the Walled City in the south is reacting negatively to the current cultural and economic changes, Residency area in the north is reacting positively and these are demonstrated in functions, land value trends, and patterns of land use.

We need a morphological classification for the city which would express characteristics that Dickinson's scheme of classification may fail to bring out. For instance Dickinson's "central fully built up zone" includes the city's commercial core as well as the historic city whereas in Hyderabad, the three main components have their respective historic cores. And even if we grant the Walled City as the "historic" city of Hyderabad yet the commercial core of the metropolis lies outside it.

Although Dickinson's generalised morphological classification is inapplicable to Hyderabad city as a whole, yet the three component units of the city—Golcunda, the Walled City, and Chaderghat—if examined separately, reveal a morphological development similar to those of the West European cities. This is shown in Fig. 5.7 from which it is seen that each unit developed its own nucleus round which urban development was concentric. Each of these three includes commercial and historic cores in their "central fully built up zone". For instance in Chaderghat this central zone contains the original and "historic" buildings of the area such as the Residency, Churches, and the Nizam's palace, and has come to include the CBD. But as an urban complex Hyderabad city has to be viewed as a whole, and not merely as three separate entities.

Consequently, the following classification has been devised. This classification denotes the general character of each region irrespective of functions, for a number of distinct functional regions will be included under each classification.

(a) The Derelict Region,
(b) The Static Region,
(c) The Region of Internal Dynamism, and
(d) The Region of External Expansion.

Figure 5.8 representing these morphological regions shows them to be distributed in a succession of layers, while the Derelict region and Expansion areas lie in opposite direction from the present city centre.

(a) The *Derelict Region* is that old area of Golcunda and Karwan which had developed even before the founding of Hyderabad city. In this area the ruined Fort, the tombs of Qutb Shahi kings, empty mansions and caravan *sarais* speak of the region's former prominence. Although now largely deserted, in the sixteenth and seventeenth centuries the Fort of Golcunda and Karwan were prominent centres of political, economic and cultural activities and were thickly populated. In the few settlement areas still inhabited in this region most dwellings are old, dilapidated and shabby, they lack amenities of modern living and are insanitary.

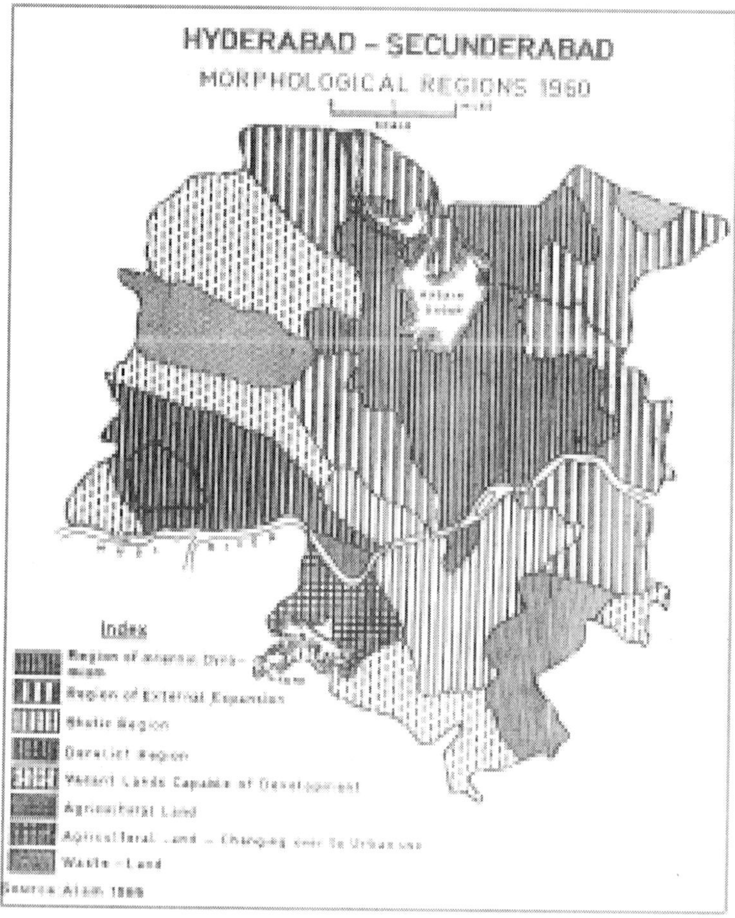

Fig. 5.8 : Hyderabad-Secunderabad : Morphological Regions, 1960

(b) The *Static Region* includes a large area of the Walled City, the immediate area surrounding the city-walls in the south and a small area adjoining the derelict region east of the Purana Pul (Old Bridge). It was developed mainly between the seventeenth and early nineteenth centuries. It contains well-preserved historic buildings of both Qutb Shahi and Asaf Jahi periods such as Charminar (the four minarets), Macca Mosque and Panch Mahal (Five palaces).

In the Static Region are found the worst slums with crimes and diseases. Its dwellings are crowded with low income groups; it is an area of few economic opportunities and it offers only low-paid jobs in small industries, shops and few minor government offices. Its dwellings which are generally small, low built though not in a ruinous state, belong architecturally to a decadent age. Its commercial streets lack the tempo of business which would be a marked feature of a growing area. These social and economic conditions have set in here a general state of regression leading towards rapid decay and deterioration.

(c) The *Region of Internal Dynamism* shows the greatest intensification of land use, and includes a large part of north central Hyderabad and a small portion in the south surrounding Charminar. Excepting the Charminar area, which has been in existence from the city's origin, lands in the dynamic region were largely, developed from 1806 onwards in its central part in and around the Residency area the dynamic region is compactly built up the density of dwellings decreases considerably towards its periphery in the north-east and north-west. In this region lies the city's central business district (CBD) containing its principal central functions such as banking, wholesaling, retailing, administration, education and entertainment. It is in this region that the shopping complexes of the city (a recent development) have emerged. And thus economically this region is most dynamic, characterised by high land values and keen competition for parcels of land among different uses. Rapidly expanding commerce is pushing out residential use from the main thoroughfares and their adjoining areas and is encouraging vertical development of sites. Under economic pressure notable residences are being put to new and dynamic uses. For example near Charminar in the Haveli (mansion) of the late Sir Salar Jung, (prime minister of Hyderabad State between 1930 and 1935) is now located a cooperative store

(Kalpalatha or Super Bazar); the Hill Fort palace, a former residence of the eldest son of the last Nizam is now a luxury hotel (Ritz), while another has become an Administrative Staff College conducting courses for senior executive officers in government service and leading private business firms. Lands are fully serviced in this region. Immediately outside the central business district (CBD) residential land use gains prominence. Even in these residential areas detached single storeyed houses with large compounds are fast receiving additional storeys and new dwellings are generally double storeyed flats with hardly any compound. All vacant plots are being built up. Slums and derelict buildings are also being caught up in a process of renewal. In brief the Dynamic Region is the focus of the city's metropolitan functions and of its developmental activities in banking, commercial, administrative and residential functions which are not matched in any other morphological region of the city.

(d) The *Region of External Expansion* shows the strongest horizontal or lateral spread and is located peripherally to the east, north-east and north-west of the built up area. The three main directions of Hyderabad's expansion are: (1) in the north west along the road leading to the Sanathnagar industrial area and beyond in the direction of Kukatpally and Balanagar; (2) in the north-east along the roads leading to Uppal, Maula Ali and Charlapalli suburban settlements where large scale industrial development commenced since 1966; and (3) in the east along the road to Vijayawada and Masulipatnam. In this region, with the incorporated area, the development has been mainly residential; commerce is only slowly advancing in this direction along the arteries of traffic. The developing residential areas are separated from one another by long distances and consist both of planned and unplanned neighbourhoods, inhabited mostly by middle income groups from among the immigrants from Andhra. Small single storeyed dwellings with small compounds predominate. Most of the vacant plots are sold speculatively by the land-owners of their agents. Although it lacks the intensity of development of the Dynamic Region, yet compares favourably with regard to the tempo of development. The prevailing trends in building construction and land values in the Expansion Area contrast sharply with those of the Static Region.

Outside the built-up area lands capable of development predominate and waste lands not liable for development in the foreseeable future occupy a comparatively small area to the west around the Banjara hills and the Fort of Golcunda. Cultivated lands devoted mostly to vegetable and fruit farming survive in the river bed and on the periphery of the town.

Morphological Regions of Secunderabad

Secunderabad is the twin settlement of Hyderabad. It was established as an independent British Cantonment in 1798. Although it has now physically fused with Hyderabad and has been incorporated within the Hyderabad Municipal Corporation, it nevertheless retains some of its distinctive cultural and morphological characteristics, since it was administered directly by the British until 1947. Since Secunderabad did not experience all the historical, cultural and political forces which shaped Hyderabad, the four fold morphological classification outlined for Hyderabad cannot be validly applied in its case. Accordingly our scheme of morphological classification is meaningful here. It can be broadly divided into the following three morphological zones :

(a) The Central, Fully Built Up Zone, (1798-1874)
(b) The Middle, Compactly Built Up Zone, (1874-1930)
(c) The Outer, Partly Built Up Zone, (1930-)

(a) The Central, Fully Built Up Zone, (1806-1874)

Developed between 1798 and 1875, this occupies the core of the city including the General Bazaar, the city's first native settlement. The few historic buildings in Secunderabad such as the first Arsenal of Secunderabad Cantonment (1806), Mahakali Temple (1810) and the first clock tower of the city (1844), are found in this zone. This is the commercial nucleus of the city and economically its most dynamic part, but it lacks the vitality of the Dynamic Region of Hyderabad.

This zone is occupied largely by low income groups, has the highest density of houses of any area in either of the two cities, and is marked for its poor housing bordering on slum conditions.

(b) The Middle, Compactly Built Up Zone, (1874-1930)

The growth of this zone started after the railways came in 1874 and ended around the 1930's. This zone comprises most of the railway colony on the east, a large portion of south Secunderabad, and a small area to the west. It contains the city's principal centre of administration and its wholesale markets for foodgrains and vegetables which were moved from General Bazaar to the vicinity of the railway station in 1881. The quality of its residences towards the east is much better than any other part of the zone and its residential density is below that of the city's core. The proportion of middle and upper income group residential neighbourhoods increased appreciably in this zone.

(c) The Outer Partly Built Up Zone, (1930-)

This includes large peripheral lands to the west and east and smaller areas to the north and south. Although development started in the early 1930's most of it took place after 1947. Its settlements, except in Maredpalli, are scattered, residential density is low and its thoroughfares are of only minor importance to business. As in Hyderabad the new residential neighbourhoods are inhabited largely by immigrants from Andhra, but different income groups dwell in various parts of the zone. Some neighbourhoods are planned, some are not. To the east dwell middle and low income groups, in detached or semi-detached small houses and tenements built by the Housing Board; to the north in Maredpalli there has been a combined development for three different income groups, the upper predominating; but to the west along the Airport Road leading to the western bank of Husain Sagar is an exclusive modern upper class residential neighbourhood consisting of large detached single-storeyed houses.

Burgess' Theory of Concentric Zones and Hoyt's Sector Theory of Residential Neighbourhood

While Dickinson's classification deals with morphological

development in terms of historic system of growth, the theories of concentric zones and of radiating sectors generalise the processes and patterns of ecological change, based on the struggle of different functions for the use of the land. These two theories will, therefore, be examined in the background of Hyderabad's development and the factors involved. Secunderabad will be excluded here because a substantial portion of its land is not open to competitive use, being parcelled for specific uses such as the railways and aerodrome, and besides, its boundaries are so rigidly circumscribed that there is little scope for the free play of urban processes. These complications would call for many exceptions to the general principles proposed by either Burgess or Hoyt, with the result that their theories would be so distorted that to apply them would become hypothetical and meaningless.

Burgess's Concentric Zone Theory

Burgess was the first American scholar to illustrate the "typical processes of the expansion of the city by a series of concentric circles which he "numbered to designate both the successive zones of urban extension and the types of areas differentiated in the process of urban expansion". His ideal construction representing the tendencies of any city to grow outward from its central business district consists of the following concentric zones.[6]

I. "The Loop" of the central business district.
II. The "Transition Zone" of business, light manufacture and deteriorated housing.
III. The Zone of industrial workers' home.
IV. The Zone of high class apartment buildings or of exclusive "restricted" districts of single family dwellings.
V. The Commuters' Zone—suburban areas or satellite settlements.

Burgess's theory was based on the study of American cities, especially of Chicago, which were rapidly growing due to a high degree of technological development. He thus assumed a great measure of mechanization and accelerated activities in the central business district which are located at the convergence of routes. This concentration of activities generated the process of urban expansion through invasion and succession, and also initiated the antagonistic and yet complementary process of decentralisation. Decentralisation led to further physical growth, but was possible only with the extension of technical services. The great public utilities such as transportation, electricity, water and sewerage systems were a "part of the mechanization of life in great cities" and made city life "liveable". The development of concentric zones of residence, commerce and industry was a process of social and economic readjustment to city-growth, and especially to competition for land. Since Burgess assumed mobility and mechanization at the core of his theory he also implied the rise of a highly productive society with a high level of income and expenditure. He clearly set out socio-economic conditions under which American cities could assume the forms they did in the 1920's and about which he theorised.

In contrast to this is the socio-economic setting of Hyderabad, dominated until 1948 by the jagirdars (feudal lords) whose main revenue was derived from landed property.[7] Their incomes were high, their expenditure were marked by luxurious living and their investments were negligible whether in agriculture or industry. This non-productivity together with high consumption largely of imported luxury goods drained the wealth of both the city and its hinterland. It could hardly be conducive to the type of urban growth experienced in American cities. Mechanization, which has been prominent in the growth of American cities, has been of only slight importance in the development of Hyderabad. This is evident from the inadequacy of the network of city transport and of water, sewerage and electricity, and also from the absence of skyscrapers and lack of suburban development. With a population of nearly 2 million, Hyderabad has only 12,000 cars and motor-cycles, and of its 250 miles of road less than 50 per cent are covered by public transport routes. Although bus routes coverage in the central business district are stimulating a marked centralization there, the CBD lacks that intensity of land use, so characteristic of a highly productive economy which is marked by a great concentration of wealth. The utility services diminish with distance from the present city centre and are non-existent in suburban areas except in the newly developed industrial suburbs. Despite extensive and large scale industrial development since the sixties Hyderabad's economy is still dominated by the non-productive inefficient traditional economic sector. This is substantiated by its low per capita income of Rs. 594 only.[8] It is a city inhabited by people with very low standards of living and is inadequately equipped with the conveniences of modern civilization. It does not fulfil the conditions which Burgess considered essential for the "typical" process of concentric expansion matched by readjustments, social and economic.

Burgess, further, allotted a subservient role to individual or social "man" in this machine age for "in the expansion of the city a process of distribution takes place which sifts and sorts and relocates individuals and groups by residence and occupation". For this mechanistic approach Burgess has been strongly criticised by numerous American scholars who feel that man fills a more positive role in sifting and sorting of groups". This positive role of "man" is more prominent in Hyderabad where the machine has not assumed the dominance it has in American cities. Social organisations are not entirely subordinate to the rigour of rising economic forces and are based more on communal associations of religion and language. There are only a few areas in the city where residential segregation is determined by economic status, but there are many areas segregated on a linguistic basis such as Marathi and Telugu speaking residential neighbourhoods. Within this framework of culture groups there is, however, a tendency of residences to segregate according to economic grades. The separation of home from work-place which has gone deep into the urban structure of American cities is only in its embryonic state in Hyderabad, although it gained sufficient strength outside the central business districts. In view of these fundamental socio-economic differences functional zones in Hyderabad would be markedly different in character from those in American cities.

For an examination of the city we have used the Social Area Analysis based on the socio-economic data provided by Census of India (1961) (Fig. 5.9) and income data (1960) furnished by the Hyderabad Municipal Corporation. These are further supplemented by the functional land use map which gives the distribution of principal functions and of residences by income groups (Fig. 5.10). These together provide a suitable basis for the examination of the theory.

(i) Zone I of Burgess—The Central Business District (CBD)

Hyderabad has a well defined central business district and to this extent the city has felt the inward and outward pressure of land competition. As in American cities, it occupies the site of maximum coverage of routes in the city. However, there the comparison ends. It does not feel the pressure in any even way. It is neither circular nor semicircular. Its peculiar shape has followed certain cultural and historical axes, later seized on by the bus routes first developed in north Hyderabad. The CBD of Hyderabad also includes a few non-conformal functions as well. Some of the premier educational institutions of the city which developed in the late nineteenth and early twentieth centuries are located in this zone.

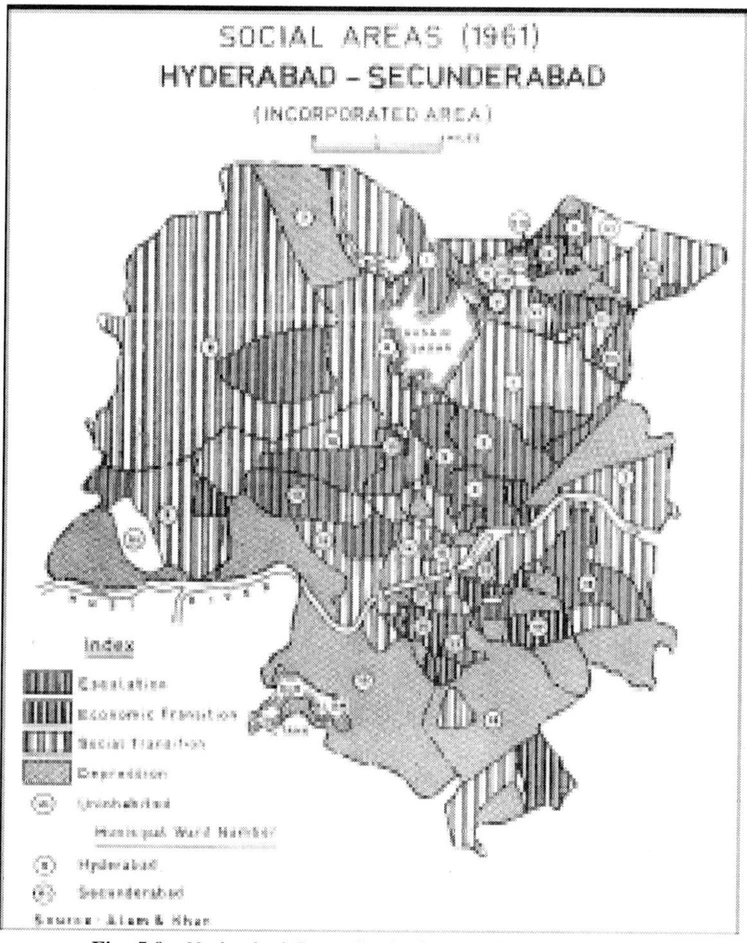

Fig. 5.9 : Hyderabad-Secunderabad—Social Areas of 1961 (Incorporated Area)

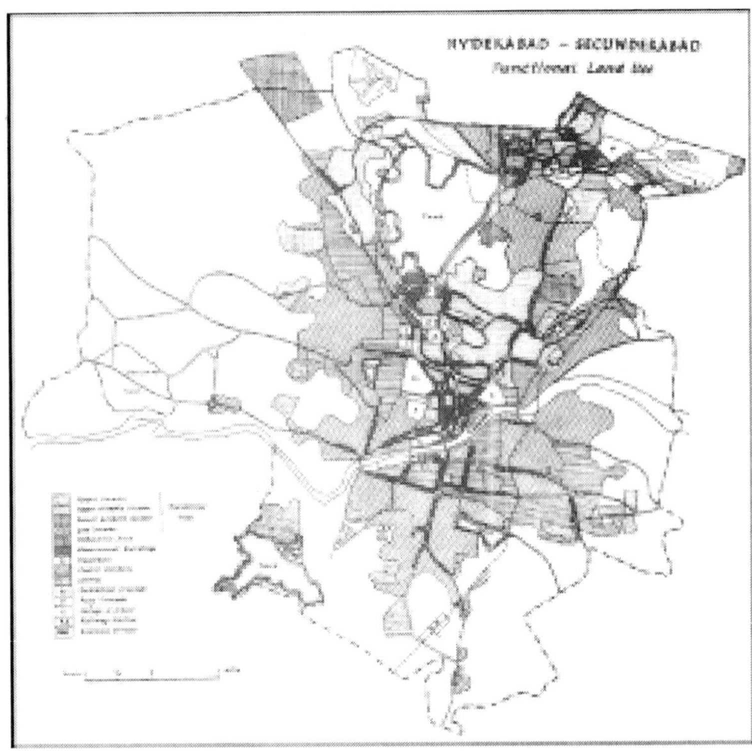

Fig. 5.10 : Hyderabad Secunderabad—Functional Land Use

(ii) Zone II of Burgess—The Manufacturing Area

In Hyderabad the zone around the central business district does not have manufacturing, and includes mainly non-migrant population. In contradistinction to the American city it includes the area of Social Escalation dominated by people with relatively high social and economic status. It is largely the upper middle income group which resides here. Most of the members of this income group are employed in the CBD, do not possess their personal transport and would, therefore, like to live as close to the work centres as they possibly can. The nearness to the CBD provides them with easy access to the shopping and educational facilities. What is "Shatter belt" or the area of the under world in Burgess has emerged as an upper-middle income group residential area. It is interesting to note that the Social Areas of Depression in Hyderabad which would correspond with the deterioration zone of Burgess are concentrated on the periphery of the city in the south or in the north-western industrial area of Sanatnagar.

(iii) Zone III of Burgess—Working Men's Residence

In Hyderabad Zone III consists of area of Social and Economic Transitions which include both the working class and the lower middle income groups. Ironically it is in one of sectors of this zone that the best residential address of the town is located. It is in this zone also that the historic walled city with its traditional economy and deteriorated residences is located. Pockets of underworld are identified here and consequently the incidence of criminality and juvenile delinquency are high in this zone.

(iv) Zone IV of Burgess—Higher Class Apartment Buildings

It is predominantly an area of Social Depression dominated by the illiterate or semi-literate members of the working class belonging to low social status. However, in certain sectors of this zone are concentrated the migrants from Andhra who belong predominantly to the middle income group. Consequently a large number of cooperative housing colonies of these migrants have also developed here.

(v) Zone V of Burgess—Commuter's Zone

The suburban development based exclusively on the residences of the elite is not to found at all in Hyderabad. The very concept of living on the periphery of the metropolis has not been accepted by the elite.

The periphery of Hyderabad, outside the incorporated area, consists either of dormitory urban or rural suburbs or of extensive industrially developed areas with residential colonies attached to them (Fig. 5.11).

Before concluding this discussion on the concentric zones it may be pointed out that this generalised model of land use cannot be found valid for some other Indian cities as well. It can be observed in Fig. 5.12 that in New Delhi, a planned city founded in 1911, the middle and the upper income groups occupy the sectors adjacent to the central business district—Connaught Place.[9] An examination of the land use pattern of Varanasi (Banaras) presents a totally different picture (Fig. 5.13) Varanasi is a settlement of great antiquity and of historic and religious importance. The economic core of this city has also shifted away from its historic core of the fort area. The concentric growth of Varanasi is evident but what is significant to note is that the central area of the city or the loop is occupied by old upper class residences displacing the commercial or economic core to the next zone i.e. Burgess' zone of transition.[10] The examples cited above and the detailed examinations of Hyderabad do testify that the urban land use models presented by Burgess cannot be validly applied to Indian cities. Nevertheless it must be pointed out that in their current phase of development all the principal metropolitan cities of India are experiencing rapid technological changes and strong economic pressures, which are evident from the spiralling of land values in the CBD and the growth of high rise buildings. These trends in future may shape differently the ecological structure of Indian cities.

LAND USE DEVELOPMENT MODELS

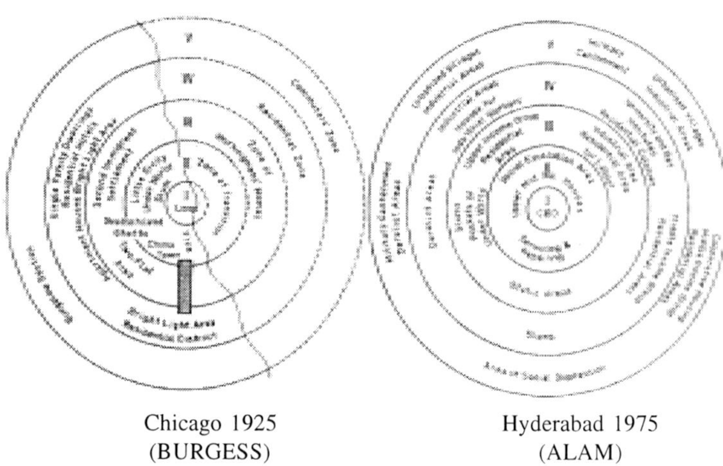

Chicago 1925 (BURGESS) — Hyderabad 1975 (ALAM)

Fig. 5.11 : Land Use Development Models

Hoyt's Sector Theory: The sector theory of residential neighbourhood was first propounded by Homer Hoyt in 1939.[11] Hoyt holds that the different income groups of American cities tend to be located in distinct areas which could be thought of as sectors of a circle focusing on the central business district.

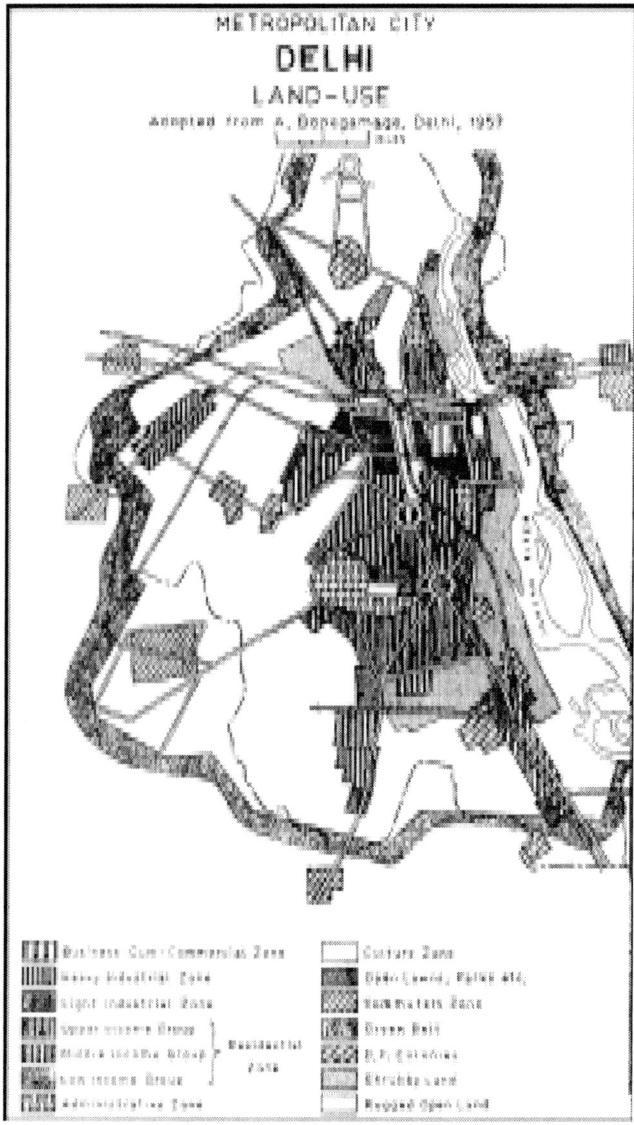

Fig. 5.12 : Metropolitan City Delhi—Land Use

In his detailed investigations of the distribution of residences by rental groups in 142 American cities, Hoyt discovered certain failings of the Burgess theory. Concerning the land uses allotted by Burgess to Zone II and III Hoyt wrote that the "manufacturing zone does not necessarily surround the CBD. Moreover, "with the increasing use of the automobile working men no longer need to live close to factory districts ...[12]. Qualifying the Burgess theory, Hoyt wrote that he found "general pattern of rent areas that applies to all cities. This pattern is not a random distribution ... it is not in the form of successive concentric circles, with the lowest rent areas near the centre and the highest on the periphery. Rent areas in American cities tend to conform to a pattern of sectors rather than of concentric circles."[13] Hoyt deduced his generalisations from the following common tendencies in the cities he investigated :

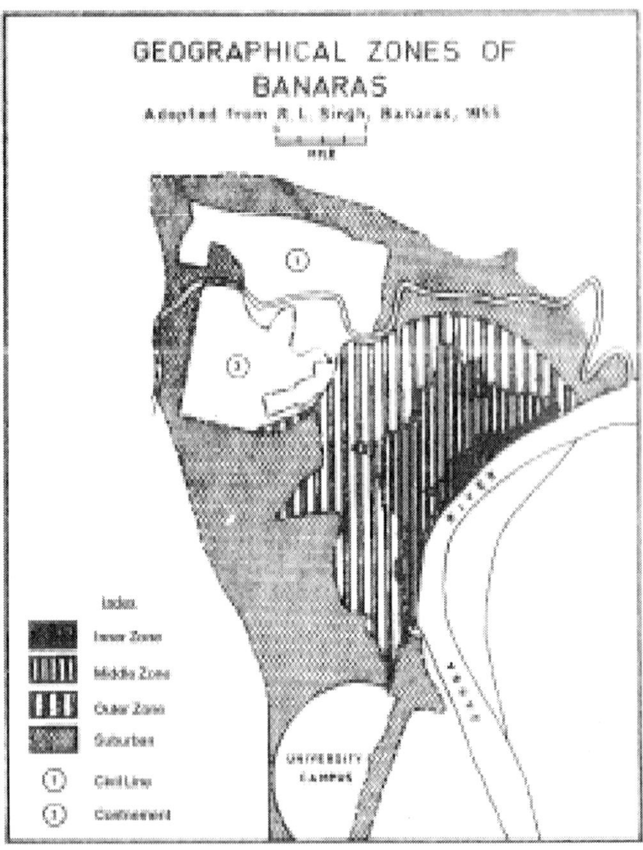

Fig. 5.13 : Geographical Zones of Banaras

(a) A tendency towards segregation in residential areas according to income groups and social position;
(b) Sectors in the use or low or middle income residences tend to remain perpetually so;
(c) Residences of varying income groups would arrange themselves like wedges along radial lines from the centre to the fringes; and
(d) High class residences move outward from the centre in the same sector along the line of fast transportation.

The sector theory is not a complete alternative to that of Burgess. Hoyt confined his study to the growth pattern of residences of different grades of rent and did not closely examine the whole range of land use, as Burgess had done. However, this theory like that of Burgess is mechanistic and has been criticised for this by Walter Firey[14] and Emrys Jones,[15] Brian Berry[16] and others. Even Hoyt in one of his later articles has advocated revision of his theory for "the principles of city growth and structure, formulated on the basis of experience in cities in the United States in 1930, are thus subject to modification—as a result of dynamic changes in the United States in the last few decades."[17]

Hoyt postulates the dominance of economic forces in patterning residential development in American cities. The economic and social forces which have shaped Hyderabad's morphological pattern have been explained earlier while discussing the Burgess' theory. In Hyderabad, among others, religion and language as factors influencing residential segregation are more prominent than in Western cities. In view of this, residential areas in Hyderabad would segregate primarily on linguistic and religious bases rather than economic status and arrange themselves in distinct sectors based on languages and religion. Thus Hoyt's generalization, modified to conditions in Hyderabad, has a reasonable application.

Movement of Upper Class Residences

With the help of historical accounts and old maps of Hyderabad it has been possible to trace and map the development of upper class residential neighbourhoods.

In Fig. 5.14, a, b, c, d and e show that upto the end of the nineteenth century high grade residences were closely linked with the royal palace. In a feudal state such as the kingdom of Golcunda and Hyderabad State the nobles were deeply involved in palace intrigues and their prestige and position depended upon the influence they could exercise upon the ruler. Hence the absence of speedy transport led the nobles to build their houses as close to the king's palace as possible. By 1880, the power of the Nizam had much weakened in the city because of the influence exercised by the British Residents, the representatives of the paramount power in India. The British Residency in Hyderabad thus became a focal point for the development of a new high grade residential district.

In 1912, the Nizam transferred his residence to the north, to the King Kothi Road. This later attracted a large section of the nobility from the south. The invasion of commerce along the Mahatma Gandhi Road from Residency to Tank Bund led the nobles to move outward from the Residency area. Meanwhile the introduction of the automobile, the telephone, electricity and piped water enabled them to settle on the western banks of Husain Sagar and also on the Banjara Hills, now no longer waterless, and both of them desirable landscapes and cooled by the tank breeze. These two areas have now consolidated their population as the best residential addresses of the city, and in them are now found the Raj Bhawan (Governor's House), residences of State ministers, important State officials, and of business magnates of the city. Most of the foreigners resident in Hyderabad live in this area.

As shown in Fig. 5.14 a, b, c, d and e, upper class residences in Hyderabad have tended to grow outward, in the same sector, from centre to the periphery, but this tendency cannot be wholly explained on a mechanistic basis. And whereas until the end of the nineteenth century the movement of high grade residential areas was linked to that of the seat of authority, the exodus to the Banjara Hills and the western bank of Husain Sagar was largely on the ground of desirable landscape and was also assisted by the extension of civic amenities. Thus it may be observed that political expediency, desirable landscape, extension of civic amenities and economic pressures were among the principal factors which influenced the growth and movement of upper class residences in Hyderabad, and that economic pressure was by no means the chief force involved.

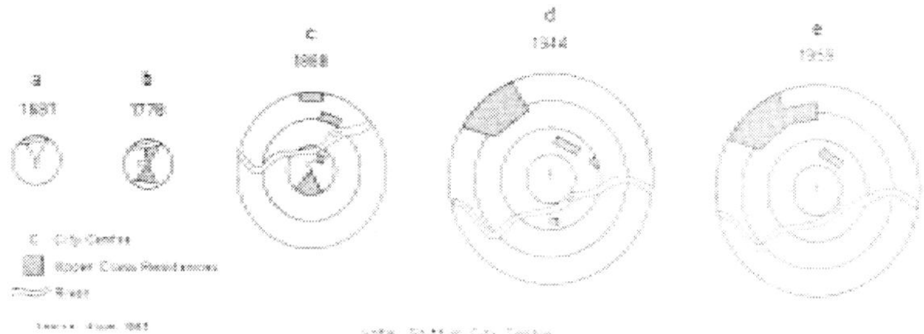

Fig. 5.14 : Hyderabad City: Schematic Representation of Growth of Upper Class Residences, 1591-1959

Before concluding this discussion on the two theories it may be pointed out that recent researches have demonstrated that the western cities contain elements of both concentric zone and sector patterns of developments. Robson in his study of Sunderland observed concentric development to the north of the river and sectoral patterning of residences to its south.[18] Berry points out that the western cities reveal "three dimensions of variation (in their internal structure): (a) the axial variation of neighbourhoods by socio-economic rank; (b) The concentric variation of neighbourhoods according to the family structures; and (c) and localized segregation of population by ethnic groups".[19]

Conclusion

The city of Hyderabad is a socio-cultural unit strongly influenced by political, religious and linguistic factors, and it is in this matrix that its patterns of growth can be studied. The functions of the city and the physical distribution of its occupations and residences are markedly influenced by its social and cultural values. Owing to these factors in Hyderabad, its morphological developments and ecological distribution is different from the commercial-industrial cities of Western Europe or America.

The socio-economic tendencies in Hyderabad, though widely different from American cities, are common to most Indian cities being the outgrowth of India's social and economic situation. Thus the characteristics which distinguish Hyderabad from American cities also distinguish other Indian cities from them.

In view of this, we may generalise that most Indian cities lack the social mobility and economic vitality of American cities and, therefore, the processes involved in the physical expansion and in the ecological patterning of cities in the United States are not equally effective in India. However, it remains to be seen if the universalisation of the economic processes of urbanisation which are strongly indicated in the urban growth pattern of India, should eventually lead to a broad similarity in their growth pattern to those of the cities of the west.

REFERENCES

1. R.E. Dickinson: *West European City*, London, 1951.
2. R.E. Park, E.W. Burgess and R.D. Mackenzie (Ed): *The City*, Chicago, 1925.
3. Homer Hoyt: *The Structure and Growth of Residential Neighbourhoods in American Cities*, Washington, U.S. Government Printing Office, 1939.
4. Hyderabad City was walled in 1744 A.D. for detailed account of the growth of Hyderabad refer to pp. 1-16 in Manzoor Alam: Hyderabad refer to (Twin Cities)—*A Study on Urban Geography*, (1965), Allied, India.
5. R.E. Dickinson: *op. cit.*
6. Robert F. Park, Earnest, W. Burgress and R.D. Mackenzie (Ed.): pp. 47-62, *op. cit.*
7. The "Jagir" was a free grant of land of one or more villages from the ruler of the state to the grantee as a reward for some conspicuous service, either military or otherwise. The grantee, called the Jagirdar, had the right to collect land revenue and generally retained the whole of it without passing it on to the state.
8. S. Manzoor Alam, Waheeduddin Khan: *Metropolitan Hyderabad and its Region (1972)*—Asia Publishing House, Bombay, p. 125.
9. Bopegamage, Delhi: *A Study in Urban Sociology*, Bombay, 1957.
10. R.L. Singh: Banaras—*A Study in Urban Geography*, Banaras 1955.
11. Homes Hoyt, *op cit.*
12. Arthur W. Weimar, and Homer Hoyt: *Principles of Real Estate*, p. 350, Roland Press, New York, 1960.
13. Homes Hoyt, *op. cit.*
14. Walter Firey: *Land Use in Central Boston*: Cambridge Mass; 1974.
15. Emrys Jones: *A Social Geography of Belfast*, London, 1960.
16. B.J.L. Berry: Internal Structure of the City, pp. 97-103 in Larry S. Bourne (ed.), *Internal Structure of the City*, 1971, London.
17. Homer Hoyt: Recent Distortions of Classical Models of Urban Structure in Larry S. Bourne, *Internal Structure of the City* (1971), London, p. 96.
18. B.T. Robson: *Urban Analysis—A Study of City Structure* (1971), Cambridge, pp. 128-129.
19. B.L.J. Berry, *op. cit.*, pp. 100-101.

Part II : Settlement Systems of India

6

Metropolitan Hyderabad : Its Pattern of Regional Influence and Delimitation of its Planning Areas

Introduction

Hyderabad, the capital city of Andhra Pradesh, is a leading metropolitan centre of India and a primate city in Telangana. Its importance as a metropolitan centre is evident from the fact that it is a premier centre of the country for highly specialized and advanced medical and educational services. Besides, the Osmania and Agricultural Universities it has advanced research and training centre of national and international importance in Chemistry, Geophysics, Nutrition, Electronics, Public Enterprise, American Studies, Community Development, Small Industries, Forensic Medicine, Banking and Personnel Management, and Survey and Photogrammetry. It has two branches of almost all the leading national banks, is the headquarters of the State Bank of Hyderabad (a subsidiary of the State Bank of India) and the Andhra Bank, and the regional headquarters of the State Bank of India. The Reserve Bank of India has recently opened a branch here. The headquarters of one of the railway zones (South Central) is located here. With the location of major industrial units such as the Bharat Heavy Electricals, Synthetic Drugs, Hindustan Machine Tools, Hindustan Aeronautics Ltd., and Electronics Corporation of India, etc., it has emerged as a leading industrial metropolis of the country.

Published in *Vyastanick,* Moscow University (Moscow), *1972, pp. 85-88;* also published *in Economic and Socio-Cultural Dimensions of Regionalization—* An Indo-USSR Collaborative Study, Census Centenary Monograph No. 7, 1972, pp. 117-146.

In the functional hierarchy among the major metropolitan centres of India, it now certainly leads Bangalore and ranks next only to the four premier metropolises of India—Calcutta, Bombay, Delhi and Madras.

Hyderabad's primacy over the Telengana region is highlighted by the fact that its population of 1.8 million in 1971 was nearly nine times the population of the region's next ranked town Warangal. The headquarters of all the leading industries of Telangana such as the Sirpur Paper Mills and Sirsilk, the Nizam Sugar Factory, the Singareni Collieries etc., are located in this city which thus controls and directs their productive activities. The influence of metropolitan Hyderabad over Telangana is more directly exercised by its distributive activities such as circulation of newspapers, wholesaling in tea, textiles, general merchandise, timber, drugs, and pharmaceuticals, and centralized services such as education and medical.

Within this wider area of influence of metropolitan Hyderabad can be identified a core area surrounding the metropolis (Metropolitan Region) with which the metropolis strongly interacts spatially, socially, economically. The productive activities of this Region are dependent on the consumer and industrial demands of metropolitan Hyderabad. Fluctuations in the metropolitan economy have a direct bearing on the Region's development. This strong interaction between the Regions' and the metropolis is reflected in the supply and demand of vegetables, milk and fruits (especially grapes) and in the movement of traffic. Metropolitan Hyderabad, therefore, cannot be planned divorced of its Region which has to be defined first so as to facilitate an integrated social, economic and physical planning of the metropolis.

In addition to the socio-economic planning problem of the Metropolitan Region, the increasingly complex land use development and planning problems of metropolitan Hyderabad have to be tackled urgently. Building activities have extended rather chaotically far beyond the incorporated area of Hyderabad/Secunderabad. In order to prevent this chaotic growth of the metropolis and for the formulation of an integrated and rational urban and rural land use development policy its Primary Planning Area has to be identified. The Hyderabad Metropolitan Region, as will be observed later, is far too extensive to be treated as the Primary Planning Area. Hence the delimitation of this area based on scientific principles has become imperative.

In view of the aforesaid the objectives of this chapter are :

(a) to define the Region and explain the generalized pattern of metropolitan influence over the Region; and
(b) to identify the Primary Planning Area (Metropolitan District) within the Region and explain the technique of its delimitation.

SECTION I

Delimitation of the Metropolitan Region and Generalised Pattern of Metropolitan Influence over the Region

Delimitation of the Region

In a recent study on Metropolitan Hyderabad diverse indices such as newspaper circulation, distribution of Resident University Students, Regional accessibility, and supply zones of such essential commodities as vegetables, milk and fruits have been employed to define its region (I.A.S. 1959, Ch. 2). Of these variables regional accessibility, based on the frequency of bus services and passenger traffic flow, has been the prime factor in defining the region. The other variables more or less corroborate the findings based on accessibility as can be observed on Map 6.1. In view of its importance the regional accessibility factor has been detailed out below.

Regional Accessibility and Traffic Divide

The accessibility factor is very important in determining the range and degree of metropolitan influence. This factor can be determined by a study of (a) the frequency of transport services and (b) the flow of passenger traffic. Of these two indices the traffic flow is the more refined, since it clearly defines the traffic-divide or the line beyond which the traffic shades off the metropolis.

Range and Frequency of Bus Services (Maps 6.2 and 6.3)

Nearly 90 bus services operate daily along the nine highways radiating out of Metropolitan Hyderabad carrying, each way, over 14,000 passengers. Through these services the metropolitan influence is spread into the region but the degree of its influence declines with distance as will be observed later.

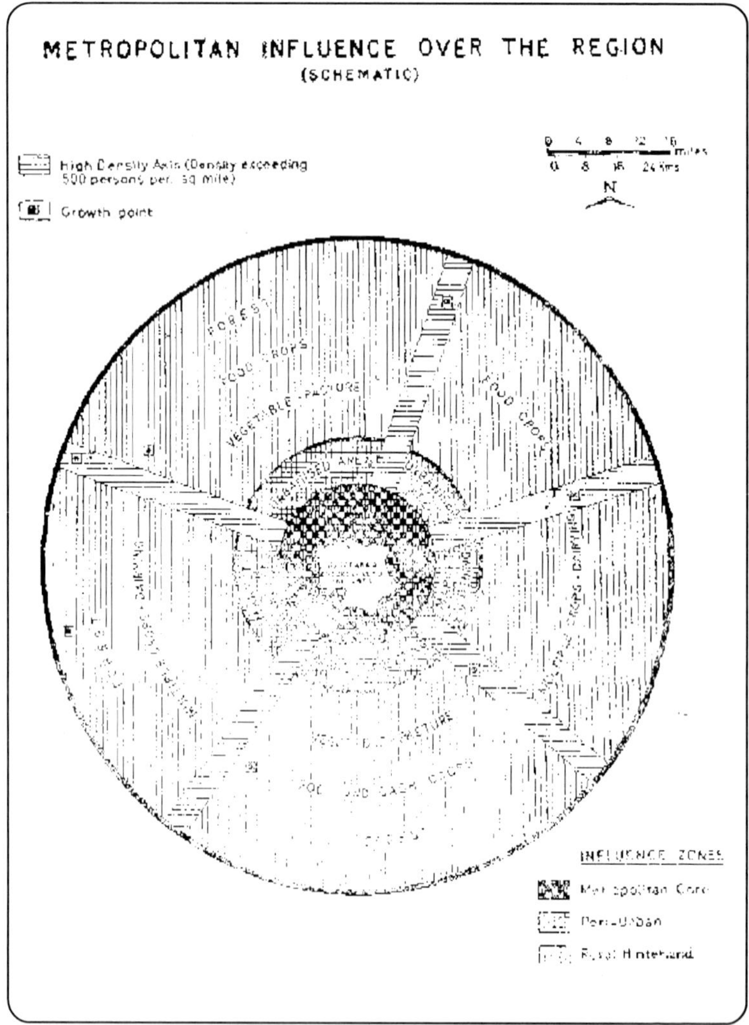

Map. 6.1 : Metropolitan Influence over the Region (Schematic)

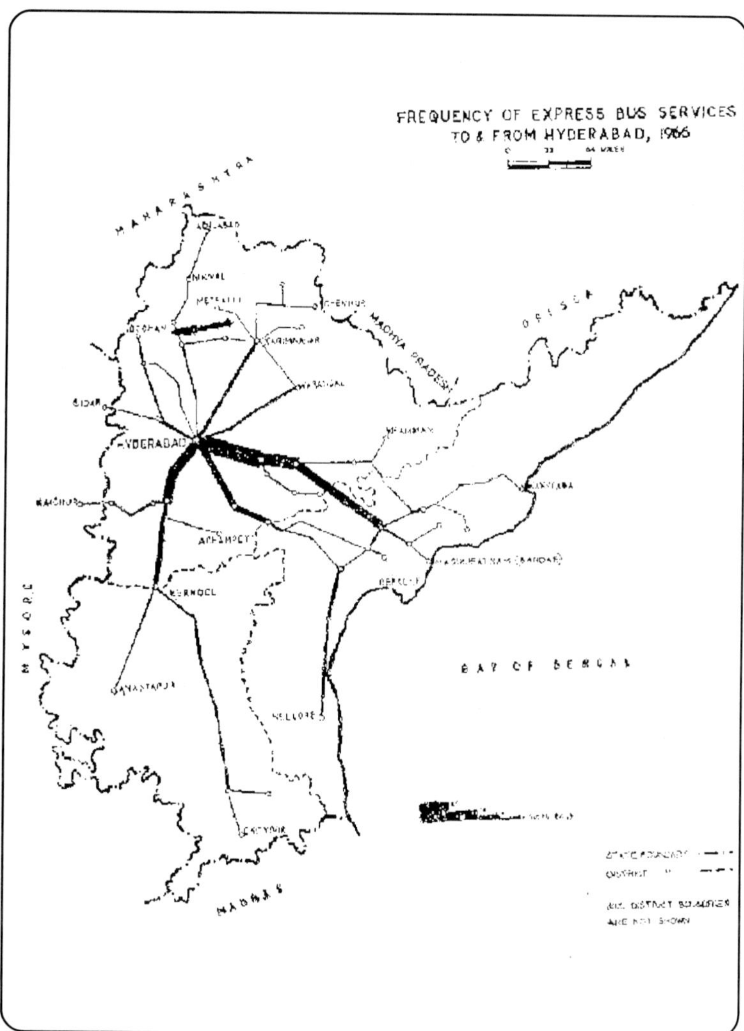

Map. 6.2 : Frequency of Express Bus Services To and From Hyderabad, 1966

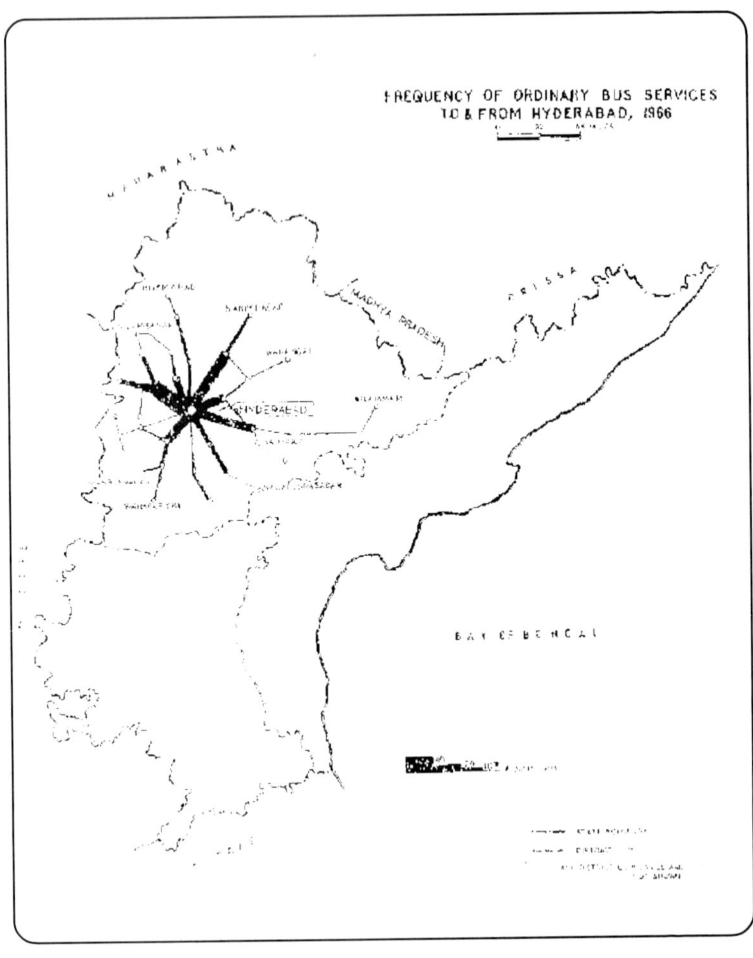

Map 6.3 : Frequency of Ordinary Bus Services To and From Hyderabad, 1966

The Road Transport Corporation runs express, passenger and local night bus services from the city. Of these the express services are less significant than the other two as an index of regional influence, not only because of their low frequency and fewer halting points, but also because they link the State capital only with either the district headquarters or major tourist or religious centres in the State. It is very revealing to note that of the services operating from the metropolis, the express bus services operate almost over the entire

State whereas the passenger bus services with the exception of the route to Khammam ply within a radius of 10 miles from the metropolis. The passenger services through their higher frequencies and more frequent halts are more reflective of city-region relationship (Map 6.2).

A perusal of Map 6.3 reveals a pattern of high frequency of bus services radiating out in all directions. The highest frequency of 21 services daily (either direction) is on the Hyderabad-Sangareddy route and the lowest, of 4 services daily (either direction) is on the Kalwakurthy route. While high frequency of services indicate strong linkage, sharp breaks in frequencies point out the weakening of the links.

Table 6.1: Frequency of Ordinary Bus Services to and fro Hyderabad—1965

Route	*Frequency Break Point*	*Frequency*		*Distance range of high frequency (miles)*
		To Hyderabad	*From Hyderabad*	
Hyderabad-Karimnagar	Siddepet	12	12	65.0
Hyderabad-Warangal	Bhongir	11	11	37.2
Hyderabad-Mahbubnagar Shadnagar	Shadnagar	12	12	31.2
Hyderabad-Nizamsagar-Zaheerabad	Sangareddy	21	21	38.6
Hyderabad-Nagarjunasagar	Deverkonda	05	05	77.0
Hyderabad-Nizamabad	Kamareddy	05	05	67.5
Hyderabad-Nalgonda-Suryapet	Narketpally	10	10	51.0
Hyderabad-Medak	Narsapur	09	09	32.0
Hyderabad-Kalwakurthy	Kalwakurthy	04	04	53.6

Source: Compiled from the Road Transport Corporation's Time Table.

An examination of Table 6.1 shows that high frequency route sectors and sharp breaks in frequency are concentrated within distances less than 40 miles and a few exceptions apart frequencies are low on sectors outside 40 miles radius. It may not be wrong, therefore, to assume that the regional influence of metropolitan Hyderabad as revealed by the analysis of frequency of passenger bus services varies between 30 and 40 miles. This is further corroborated by the fact that the range of operation of local night bus services which connect stations having strong contacts with the Metropolis on a daily basis, also coincides with the distance range of high frequency services and break of frequencies (Table 6.2).

Table 6.2 : Operational Range of Local Night Bus Services, 1965

Route	*Local Night Bus Service Destination*	*Distance from Metropolis (in miles)*
Hyderabad-Nizamsagar	Sangareddy	38.6
Hyderabad-Medak	Narsapur	32.0
Hyderabad-Nizamabad	Tupran	42.0
Hyderabad-Karimnagar	Gajwel	42.5
Hyderabad-Warangal	—	—
Hyderabad-Nalgonda	Choutuppal	32.0
Hyderabad-Nagarjunasagar	Kurmed	42.0
Hyderabad-Mehbubnagar	Shadnagar	31.2
Hyderabad-Kosgi	Chevella	22.0

Source: Same as Table 6.1.

Traffic Flow and Traffic Shed (Bus and Train)

In addition to the bus services, the city is linked with the region by four trunk rail routes. On an average, nearly 3,000 passengers come in and go out of the city daily by train. The major sub-regional centres on these routes are Nizamabad, Warangal, Mahbubnagar and Tandur. An examination of the flow of traffic between these sub-regional centres and the metropolis clearly shows that the flow of traffic tapers off with increasing distance from the metropolis (Map 6.4). The significant points on these routes, are those from where the passengers either cease to be gravitated to the Metropolis, or the metropolitan proportion of traffic is much less compared to that of the other centres. Thus at these points the intensity of traffic is directed away from the metropolis.

Table 6.3 : Traffic Shed Points along Rail Routes

Route	*Traffic divide points*	*Distance from metropolis (in miles)*	*Travel from metropolis hrs. mts.*
Hyderabad-Nizamabad	Mirzapalle	45.0	2-26
Hyderabad-Mahbubnagar	Balanagar	37.0	2-26
Hyderabad-Warangal	Aler	50.7	2-59
Hyderabad-Tandur	Vicarabad	45.6	2-25

Source: Compiled from Time Table and Passenger movements data supplied by the Commercial Superintendent, S.C. Railways, Secunderabad.

An analysis of the flow of traffic by bus points to similar results. A comparison of the traffic divide points on rail and road routes shows that while on the former (Table 6.3) the traffic divide occurs between

40 and 50 miles, in the case of the latter (Table 6.4) it is between 30 and 40 miles (Map 6.5).

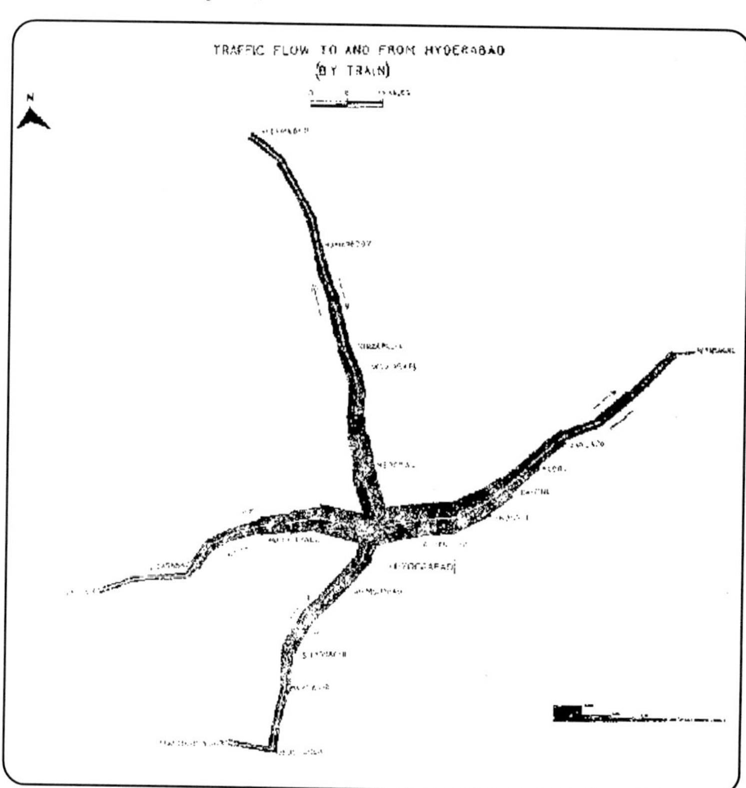

Map 6.4 : Traffic Flow to and From Hyderabad (By Train)

Table 6.4 : Traffic Shed Points along Bus Routes

Route	*Traffic shed point*	*Distance from Hyderabad in miles*	*Travel time from the city hrs. mts.*
Hyderabad-Nizamsagar	Sangareddy	38.6	2-25
Hyderabad-Medak	Narsapur	32.0	2-00
Hyderabad-Karimnagar	Gajwel	42.5	2-45
Hyderabad-Warangal	Bhongir	37.2	2-30
Hyderabad-Nalgonda	Choutuppal	32.0	2-00
Hyderabad-Nagarjunasagar	Kurmed	41.0	3-00
Hyderabad-Mahbubnagar	Shadnagar	31.2	2-00

Source: Same as Table 6.1.

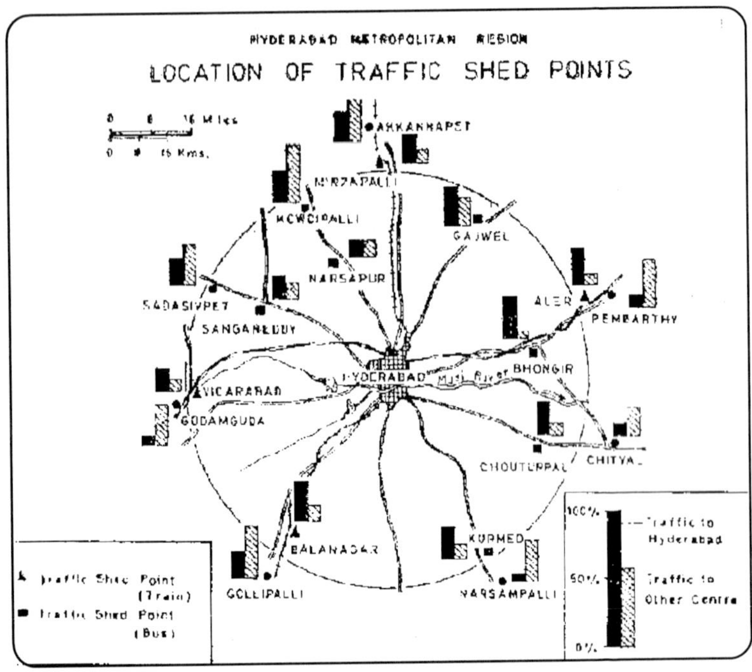

Map 6.5 : Hyderabad Metropolitan Region : Location of Traffic Shed Points

One significant point, however, is that in both cases traffic divide points are located within 2 to 3 hours isochrones (Map 6.6). It may not, however, be wrong to infer that 2 to 3 hours seem to be that critical time distance within which the direct metropolitan influence is dominant. It follows, as a corollary, that beyond the traffic-shed line, the rigors of economy and the friction of travel time reduce the intensity of the metropolitan pull.

The metropolitan dominance over the region extends to a radius of 40 miles from the metropolis. Thus defined the region extends over an area 4,733 sq. miles with a population of nearly 2 million (1961 Census) distributed between 6 small urban and 1,563 rural settlements. This region has a low level of communication facilities and hence cannot be treated as a Primary Planning Area for metropolitan Hyderabad. Nevertheless because of the dominant pull of the metropolis over the region it should be the most appropriate unit for economic planning at the micro level.

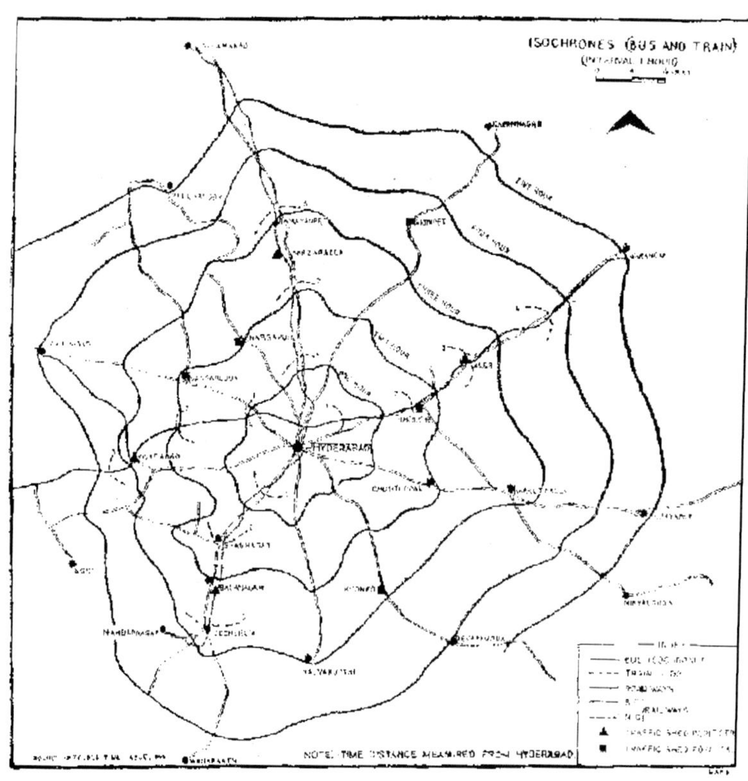

Map 6.6 : Isochrones of Bus and Train

Generalised Pattern of Metropolitan Influence (Fig. 6.1)

Despite a certain degree of interdependence between metropolitan Hyderabad and its region, the influence of the former over the latter is all pervasive and is spread into all aspects of the regional economy and even demography. Consequently a distinct pattern of demographic and economic development has emerged within the region. This is strikingly brought out by Figure 6.1, which represents schematically the generalised pattern of metropolitan influence over the region. The metropolitan region can be distinctly divided into three concentric zones: (I.A.S. 1969, Ch. 4).

1. The metropolitan core,

2. The peri-urban zone, and
3. The rural hinterland.

The Metropolitan Core extends within a radius of 6 to 8 miles from the core of the city and is by and large urbanised. All the urban settlements outside the incorporated area which are included within the Town-groups are located in it. For instance, Hyderabad Town, Group includes the following settlements: Secunderabad Cantonment, Malkajgiri, Fatehnagar, Alwal, Osmania, University, Macha Bolaram, Lalaguda, Attapur, Zamistanpur, Bowenpalli and Kandikal. It is a zone of high density of population exceeding 1,000 persons per square mile. Cultivation is not entirely non-existent but is subordinate to urban development. Cropped area is predominantly under vegetables and fruits.

The Peri-urban zone extends to a radius of 16 miles is marked by three characteristics :

(a) Axial development of high density population areas along lines of high accessibility;
(b) Development of highly urbanised sectors in the NW and NE; and
(c) Predominance of multiple cropped area dominated by commercial crops.

This zone is in effect, an extension of the rapidly developing metropolitan core.

The Rural Hinterland extends up to the 40-mile radius. It is a low density population zone (300 persons per sq. mile) and is predominantly agricultural with food crops dominating the cropping pattern.

The continuity of this zone is interrupted by the urban areas of high population density and multiple cropping and dairying sectors in the west and east. The emergence of these intensively cultivated sectors while reflecting the strong metropolitan impact in their development also suggest the possible line of development for the entire region. In the rest of this zone pastoral and agricultural activities dominate. Pastoral activities decline with the increase in distance from the metropolis. The forests have receded to the periphery of the zone and in the rest of the area food crops are prominent.

This generalised pattern may be valid for all metropolitan centres in India which are of the economic and population status of metropolitan Hyderabad.

SECTION II

Primary Planning Area : Its Delimitation

The Hyderabad Metropolitan Region as has been observed in the previous section is too extensive to be treated as a Primary Planning Area for an integrated and detailed urban and rural land use plan for Metropolitan Hyderabad. There is, however, a hard core area of metropolitan impact within the Region which is getting rapidly urbanised. This area is served by the metropolitan based central services such as transport, retailing, water supply, electricity and others. This is the area, therefore, of direct participation in the key metropolitan functions and can be treated as the Primary Planning Area of Metropolitan Hyderabad.

In order to precisely delimit the Primary Planning Area the impact zones of the following key urban functions called the 'Principal Elements' have been determined :

(a) Suburban Transport Service,
(b) Commuting Areas of Workers to Factories,
(c) Retailing,
(d) Water Supply,
(e) Electricity,
(f) Telephones, and
(g) Postal Service.

In addition to these key functions, the impact of metropolitan influence in the immediate rural hinterland can also be measured through certain demographic and occupational characteristic which are susceptible to urban influence and reflect the intensity of urbanization trends. These may be termed as 'reflective elements' and have been used to supplement the 'principal elements' in delimiting the Primary Planning Area.

Reflective Elements

(a) Villages with over 50 per cent of non-agricultural workers;
(b) Villages with electricity consumption exceeding 1,000 units per month;
(c) Villages with a density exceeding 640 persons per sq. mile—(318 persons per square mile is the average density of population of the Metropolitan Region of Hyderabad—A radius of 40 miles);
(d) Villages with a population-growth rate of 22 per cent or more in the census decade 1951-61 (national growth rate : 22 per cent for the decade 1951-61);
(e) Villages with a sex ratio of 951 or less females per 1,000 males (951-1000 is the average sex ratio for urban Andhra Pradesh); and
(f) Villages with a population exceeding 2,000 persons.

Electricity service, in this chapter, has been treated both as a 'principal' and 'reflective' element. As a source of bulk supply of power to growing urban industrial nuclei it is a 'principal element'. It is a 'reflective element' as regards its consumption in rural areas which only reflects urban influence.

Impact Zone of Principal Elements

A. Suburban Transport Services

The strongest physical and economic link between the city and its suburbs is provided by transport. The degree of linkage is indicated by the frequency of services and the volume of passenger flow.

(i) Train Service (Map 6.7)

For Metropolitan Hyderabad, of the two systems of suburban transport, buses and trains, the former are more important because these radiate in all directions and make the city influence pervasive. The movement of trains is rather restricted to a range of 17 miles in either direction, north-south of Secunderabad on the metre gauge, and to a distance of 6 miles in either direction, east-west of Hyderabad on the broad gauge.

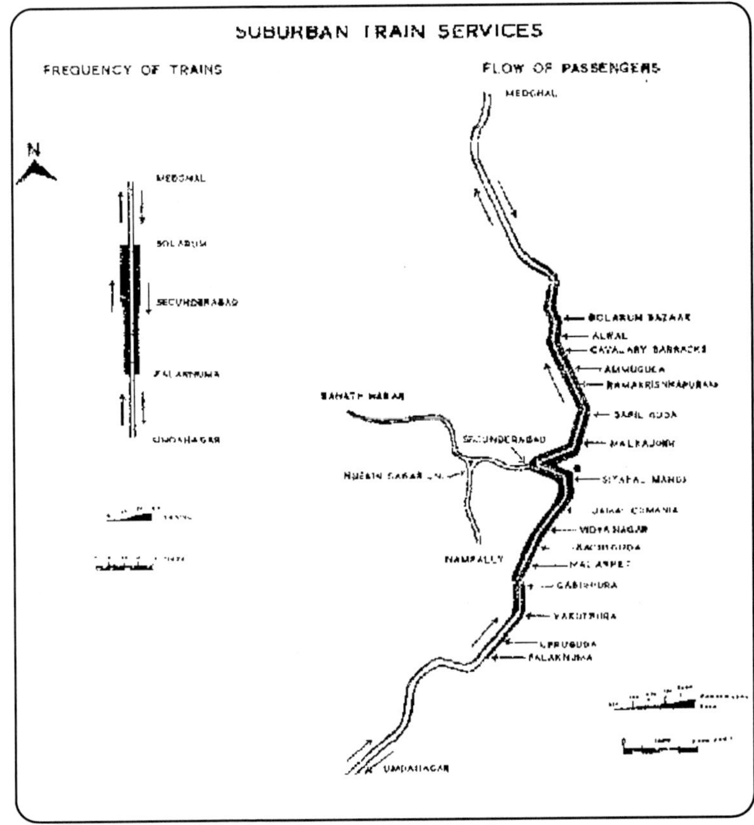

Map 6.7 : Suburban Train Services

The two important suburban centres outside of Metropolitan Hyderabad which are linked by train services are Shamsabad in the south and Medchal in the north. The extension of the metre gauge suburban train services to these centres seems to be of a supplemental character only, since they are also served by express and passenger bus and train services leading to Nizamabad in the north and Mahbubnagar in the south. Table 6.5 gives the frequency of express and passenger bus and train services passing through Medchal and Shamsabad.

A good portion of the commuting traffic from Medchal and Shamsabad is captured by these non-suburban services to these centres and the low flow of traffic on these services.

Table 6.5 : Daily Frequency of Express and Passenger Train and Bus Services passing through Medchal and Shamsabad

	Distance from (in miles)		*Daily Frequency of Express & Passenger Trains*				*Daily Frequency of Express & Passenger Buses*			
	Sec'bad	*Kachi-guda Hyd'bad*	*To*		*From*		*To*		*From*	
			Ex.	*Pas.*	*Ex.*	*Pas.*	*Ex.*	*Pas.*	*Ex.*	*Pas.*
Medchal	16.5	21	1	3	1	3	2	4	2	4
Shamsabad	17.5	13	1	3	1	3	4	3	4	8

Source: Compiled from the S.C. Railway's and Road Transport Corporation's Time Table.

Table 6.6(a) : Daily Frequency of Suburban Train Services

Section	*Distance (in miles)*	*Frequency of services*	
		To	*From*
1. Secunderabad to Umdanagar	17.5	1	1
2. Secunderabad to Medchal	16.5	2	2
3. Umdanagar to Medchal	34.0	1	1

Source: Compiled from S.C. Railways' Time Table.

The metre gauge suburban services on the Medchal-Shamsabad route carry daily to and fro, nearly 13,000 passengers. Of this total the percentage share of suburban traffic contributed by Medchal and Shamsabad is only 4.5 per cent. This is not a very significant proportion but it does indicate that nearly 300 persons commute daily from Medchal and Umdanagar each to work in Hyderabad-Secunderabad.

Table 6.6(b) : Passenger Traffic at Terminus Stations (Metre Gauge)

Section	*Distance from Sec'bad (in miles)*	*Number of Passengers*	
		Boarded	*Alighted*
1. Umdanagar	17.5	311	292
2. Medchal	16.5	245	284

Source: Commercial Superintendent, Railways, Secunderabad.

The broad gauge run of suburban train services is limited between Secunderabad-Hyderabad-Sanathnagar. The daily incidence of traffic on this route in either direction hardly exceeds 500 persons. The main traffic on this route is between Hyderabad and Secunderabad (242 passengers daily) and the daily traffic to Sanathnagar, the only suburban station on this route, seldom exceeds 20 persons from both Hyderabad and Secunderabad.

Table 6.6(c) : Daily Movement of Passengers—Broad Gauge Suburban Trains

Section	Distance	Number of Passengers
Hyderabad to Sanathnagar	6.2	15
Hyderabad to Secunderabad	5.6	212
Secunderabad to Sanathnagar	6.5	16

Source: Commercial Supdt., S.C. Railways, Secunderabad.

Although the maximum commuting distance by trains exceeds even 30 miles, the actual commutation range seldom exceeds 20 miles. One significant point which emerges on examination of figures 6.2 and 6.3 is that the medium commuting distance for a large section of the working population seldom exceeds 11 miles even under such favourable conditions of accessibility as are available through the railways.

(ii) Bus Services

Suburban buses radiate in all cardinal directions and their influence is all pervasive. They bring the central city in contact with such distant rural settlements as Ramachandrapuram in the north-west (17 miles), Ghatkesar in the north-east (13 miles), Gundipet in the west (12 miles) and Hayatnagar in the east (12 miles).

The frequency of suburban buses along certain routes is very high, but routes on which it is relatively low are well supplemented with district bus services. While considering the degree of accessibility of suburban routes the frequency of district bus services cannot be ignored as is evident from Table given in Annexure I.

It may be observed from the above Table that even some of the recognized suburban settlements such as Gundipet and Narsingi have a lower frequency of bus services than the aforesaid four rural settlements. It may also be added that these rural settlements are linked with the metropolis almost on an hourly basis between 7 a.m. and 6 p.m. and, therefore, for all practical purposes form part of the suburbs of the metropolis. Because of the varying intensity of contacts provided by the suburban services all the suburban centres cannot be included in its impact zone. The following criteria have, therefore, been used to define the impact zone of suburban train and suburban bus services. This zone will include only those settlements which: (a) are within an hour's journey from either Secunderabad or Hyderabad; (b) have a combined frequency of suburban and district transport services not less than 12 per day, and (c) are within a mile from the bus routes and railways. The last criterion is based on the assumption that residents outside the mile range distance may not avail of the suburban transport facilities for commuting to work.

B. Labour Commuting Areas (Map 6.8)

The range of daily commutation of workers to work centres is one of the best indicators of the intensity of interaction between the metropolis and the surrounding area. To determine this, 6 industrial units were randomly picked up, Cols. 2 to 7, of Table in Annexure II). Three of these are located in the central city (col. 5, 6, 7) and the other three on the periphery. Residential localities of the workers were obtained from factory records. It is evident from the Table that the central city itself is the principal feeder of labour to industrial units in both the central and peripheral locations. A majority of the workers reside in Secunderabad and in northern Hyderabad. Only a small fraction lives in southern Hyderabad or in the peripheral villages.

The central city being the source of labour supply, the median distance of labour attraction for the peripheral and the city industrial locations differ widely (Table 6.7a).

Table 6.7(a) : Work Place-Residence-Median Distance

	City units	*Peripheral units*	*Difference between a & b*
	a	*b*	*c*
Median distance in miles	1.13	4.66	3.53

The difference in the distance range is not highlighted with regard to their modal points on account of residential colonies set up by the Housing Board, adjacent to some of the peripherally located industrial units established in the 40s, such as the Hyderabad Allwyn Works and the Asbestos Cement Company located in Sanathnagar.

If examined individually it may be observed that the modal and median distances of city units do not differ widely from one another but those of the peripheral units do.

Table 6.7(b) : Modal and Median Distances of Work Place from Residence

Name of the unit	*Distance (in miles)*	
	Median	*Mode*
Industrial Units within the city:		
1. D.B.R. Mill	0.73	1.03
2. Vazir Sultan	0.831	0.99
3. R.T.C. Workshop	1.18	2.17
4. All units within the city	0.81	1.13
Industrial Units on the Periphery:		
1. Allwyn Metal Works	0.05	4.15
2. Hyderabad Asbestos	0.05	1.31
3. Hindustan Machine Tools	7.32	7.04

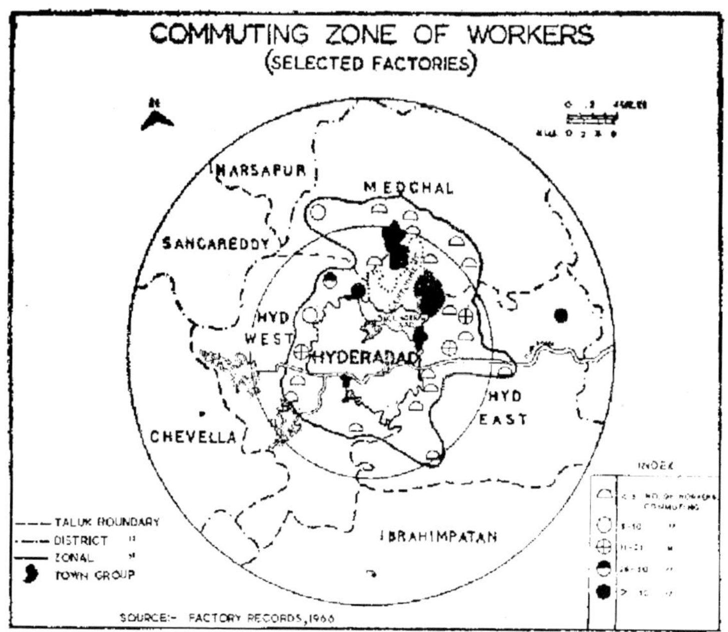

Map 6.8 : Commuting Zone of Workers (Selected Factories)

Among the city units the Road Transport Corporation records the highest modal and median distances of labour catchment.

This deviation from the average may be due to the free travel facility in Corporation buses made available to its employees by the Road Transport Corporation. Median distance among the peripheral units vary widely, while the modal points are the same in two of the three units.

The abnormally high modal and median values in the case of the Hindustan Machine Tools may be because of the transport facilities provided by the unit to its workers, most of whom live in the city. While the general tendency of the workers is to live close to the work centres as is indicated by both the modal and median values of the city units: the median values, however, seem to be directly related to the transport facilities available, the nature of the jobs and the pay scale offered by the units.

Of the two values, modal and median, the latter is perhaps a better indicator of the maximum desirable distance for journey to work. In other words all those villages which are within this median range are likely to be brought directly under the influence of the industrial centres developing in the periphery. It would not be wrong, therefore, to assume that all those industries will further improve their shares and will become increasingly urbanised with the extension of transport facilities. They cannot, therefore, be excluded from the area of direct metropolitan impact.

C. Retail Service Zone (Map 6.9)

The retail service linkage of Metropolitan Hyderabad with the surrounding region has been established in many ways :

(a) The retailers from the peripheral villages move into the metropolis and buy wares to be sold to the consumers in the villages;
(b) The local distributors move out to the villages supplying consumer goods to the retailers;
(c) The consumers themselves make direct purchases; and
(d) Along the highly accessible routes the retailers or commission agents residing in the metropolis move into the weekly markets to sell wares and to buy cattle.

These types of retail service linkages between the central city and its surrounding region testify to the daily interaction that exists between the two.

The boundary of retail service zone on Map 6.9 shows the maximum range of retail servicing. The map also shows the types of retail service relationship existing between the central cities and the surrounding villages. It may be observed that only medium to large sized villages (2,000-5,000 and above 5,000) which are economically progressive and highly accessible (within the range of suburban transport) and at the same time are performing some key functions in the rural setting, send consumers daily; otherwise the daily contact is normally through retailers. The impact zone of retail service, therefore, includes centres which have retail linkages only under the first-two categories (*a*) and (*b*) mentioned above. (Based on field work)

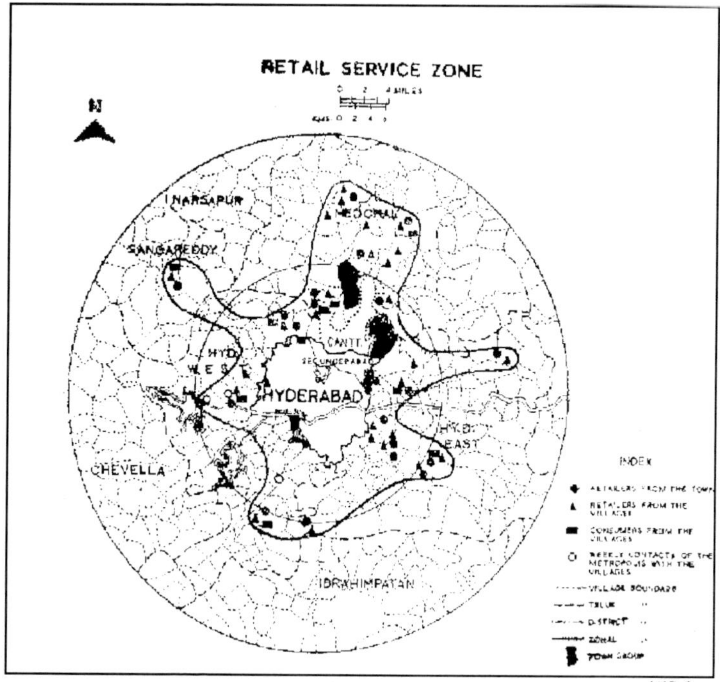

Map 6.9 : Retail Service Zone

D. Water Supply

Supply of filtered water is an essential service and is extended only to those centres which are either integral parts of the metropolis or whose growth is considered essential for the growth of the metropolis itself.

Metropolitan Hyderabad has three major sources of water supply: Himayatsagar, Osmansagar and the River Manjira, situated at 8, 13 and 36 miles respectively from the metropolis in a westerly direction. The first-two sources are in operation and together supply 46 million gallons of water daily. Water from the Manjira is expected to be supplied in two phases to be completed in September 1966 and 1967 respectively. When completed the Manjira Project will provide daily additional supply of 45 million gallons of water. In addition to the incorporated area of Hyderabad Secunderabad, water from Osmansagar and Himayatsagar is also supplied to the following suburban settlements :

1. Osmania University,
2. Cantonment, and
3. Rajendranagar.

Table 6.8 : Villages receiving or likely to receive water supply under the water supply scheme for Metropolitan Hyderabad

Localities/Taluks	Distance from	
	Hyderabad (Nampally)	*Secunderabad (Ranigunj)*
1. Ramchandrapuram	17.4	15.0
2. Lingampalli	12.5	13.8
3. Kukatpalli	8.7	6.0
4. Fatehnagar	5.8	4.1
5. Musapet	6.3	6.1
6. Balanagar	6.3	4.6
7. Dundigal	6.8	3.2
8. Moula Ali	9.0	7.8
9. Uppal	5.4	6.6
10. Mianpur	11.6	10.4
11. Hakimpet	13.2	9.6
12. Charlapalli	10.7	0.5

Source: Office of the Supdt. Engineer, Headquarters Circle, Water Works, P.W.D., Andhra Pradesh.

With the completion of the first and the second phase of the Majira water supply scheme for Metropolitan Hyderabad, the range of water supply outside of the incorporated area will further extend to such distant though industrially developing centres as Ramachandrapuram, Kukatpally, Balanagar, Dundigal, Moula Ali and Uppal. Thus the area dependent on Hyderabad city water works for water supply will have considerably enlarged. The water supply distribution area shown on the map includes all suburban and peri-urban areas which are either receiving supplies from the city water works or have been earmarked for supply under the Manjira Water Supply Scheme.

E. Electricity Supply

Hyderabad city falls within the Andhra Pradesh Electricity grid system and power is fed to the city from the following generating stations :

1. Hussain Sagar Thermal Power Station,
2. Nizam Sagar Hydel Power Station,
3. Ramagundam Thermal Power Station, and
4. Machkund Hydel Power Station.

From these generating stations, power is received by the channelling station at Erragadda and distributed through a chain of sub-stations located within and outside of the city. Because of the growing industrial importance of Hyderabad 130 KW high tension circuit line is being laid around Metropolitan Hyderabad extending up to Ramachandrapuram. This will eventually form the main distribution circuit for the expanding industrial requirement of Metropolitan Hyderabad. This line encircles almost all the developing industrial suburbs of Hyderabad. All potential major consumers of electrical energy will have to be located close to this circuit if use of power has to be efficient and economical. The impact zone of electricity supply is essentially formed by this high tension wire circuit. Most of the centres receiving bulk supply of power for industrial consumption are located within it.

F. Telephone Service

Telephone service provides immediate and direct contact. While trunk calls indicate the regional linkage, the local call zones under automatic dialling system mark out those areas which need direct and speedy communication with the metropolis and directly depend on it for their efficient functioning. The automatic dialling areas of metropolitan Hyderabad fall under two categories :

(i) *Category A* : Automatic dialling areas with local telephone rates of 15 P. per call; and
(ii) *Category B* : Automatic dialling areas with special telephone rates higher than the local rates.

The automatic dialling system under category 'A' includes all those areas which are within the 6 km operating range of either the main (MAX) or subsidiary (SAX) automatic exchanges of the Hyderabad Telephone District.

Areas outside of this zone are brought under automatic-dialling system if only they :

1. are directly dependent on the metropolis for their efficient functioning; and
2. are capable of paying higher telephone rates. Outside of the 6 km radius operational charges on the battery separated telephones become very excessive.

Ramachandrapuram and Ghatkesar are the principal centres which fall under category 'B' of the automatic dialling system. The strong telephone linkage of these centres with the Metropolis is indicated by Table 6.9.

Table 6.9 : Telephone Calls to Hyderabad-Secunderabad (January-March 1966)

From	*Number of Calls*
1. Ramachandrapuram	24,850
2. Ghatkesar	3,920

Source: District Manager of Telephones, Hyderabad.

It can be observed from Table 6.9 that the telephone contact of Ghatkesar with the metropolis is not as intense as that of Ramachandrapuram. It is because that contact with Ghatkesar is restricted to only one industrial unit i.e. the Brooke Bond Tea Factory, whereas in Ramachandrapuram the Bharat Heavy Electricals Private

Limited have a number of lines, and telephone connections there have been extended to residences as well.

Moreover, a subsidiary telephone exchange linked to the Main in Secunderabad is going to be located shortly in Gangawaram, near Ramachandrapuram to cater to the increasing demand of telephones in that area. Ramachandrapuram will thus eventually come under direct dialling category 'A'. In view of this the boundary of the impact zone has been extended to include all areas under direct dialling category 'A' and Ramachandrapuram.

G. Postal Service Zone (Map 6.10)

The creation of postal districts for the convenience of mail delivery is a function only found in large urban centres which are either metropolitan centres or are emerging as metropolises. Postal delivery districts are not found in towns with less than 100,000 population. The General Post Office (G.P.O.) of Hyderabad city acts as the main clearing house for all the incoming and outgoing mail of its postal district. All the postal zones within the district fall within the mail van distribution range of the G.P.O. This is perhaps one of the significant indicators of daily interaction between the city and its suburbs. There could not, therefore, be any doubt that all those peripheral villages which are within the postal district of the metropolis are also within its impact zone.

A list of villages under the direct delivery range of the G.P.O. Hyderabad, is given in Table in Annexure III.

Generalised Distribution Pattern and Intensity Ranges

A superimposition of the zonal boundaries of the distribution of these principal elements reveals a strong formation of boundary girdle within 10 miles radius of Metropolitan Hyderabad. These boundaries are extended axially along the transport routes in the Ramachandrapuram (West), Medchal (North), Ghatkesar (East), and Shamsabad (South) sectors (Map 6.11).

The impact of these principal elements within the 'impact zone' is not of equal degree in all directions. It seems to be directly related to the proximity to the metropolis and oriented along the principal lines of communication. As such the impact zone has been broadly divided into 'high' and 'low' intensity ranges based on the following method.

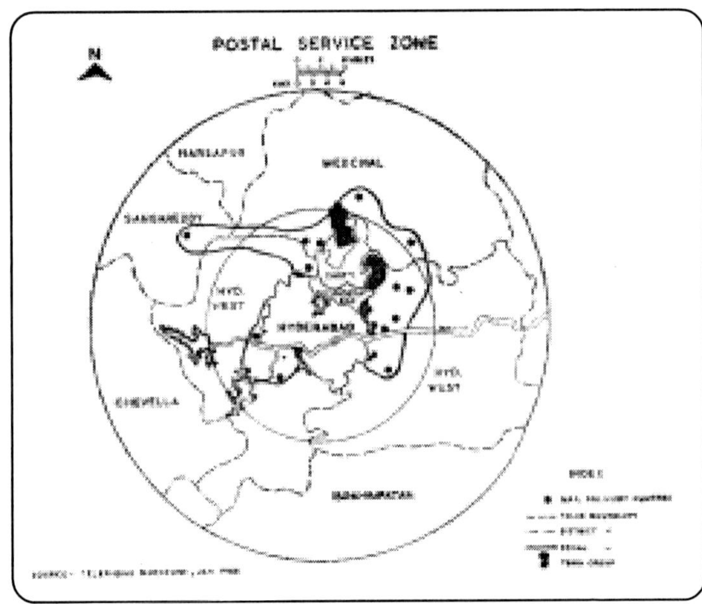

Map 6.10 : Postal Service Zone

Of the seven principal elements listed below the first-three relate to 'accessibility' and are thus ranked above the remaining four which can be categorized as 'utility service'. Each of these elements has been assigned a weighted score to mark its rank. Suburban transport provides high degree of accessibility and thus, being the most effective in transmitting Metropolitan impact over the surrounding areas, has been ranked first and assigned the highest weight. The lowest rank and score have been assigned to 'telephone service', which, in the present context, is not as effective as the others ranked above it. The rank and weighted scores of the seven 'principal elements' are given below :

S. No.	*Element*	*Rank*	*Weight*
1.	Suburban transport	I	7
2.	Commuting	II	6
3.	Retail Trade	III	5
4.	Water Supply	IV	4
5.	Electricity	V	3
6.	Postal services	VI	2
7.	Telephones	VII	1

All villages with a weight score of 10 or above are included under high intensity range. This implies that while villages with any two of the principal elements under 'accessibility' can be categorized under high intensity range, a village reached only by 'utility services' must have all the four services to be so categorised.

Villages with high intensity range are concentrated within the 10 miles radius in the north-western, northern and north eastern sectors of the metropolis (Map 6.11). They are, however, extended beyond this radius close to the 20 miles circle along the major lines of communications and, therefore, have emerged such important centres as Ramachandrapuram, Medchal, Hayatnagar, Ghatkesar and Shamsabad. These centres have started developing their own functional base. While Medchal and Hayatnagar are administration oriented, Ramachandrapuram and Shamsabad are supported by industries and commerce respectively. Each of these can, in future, serve as nodes of development.

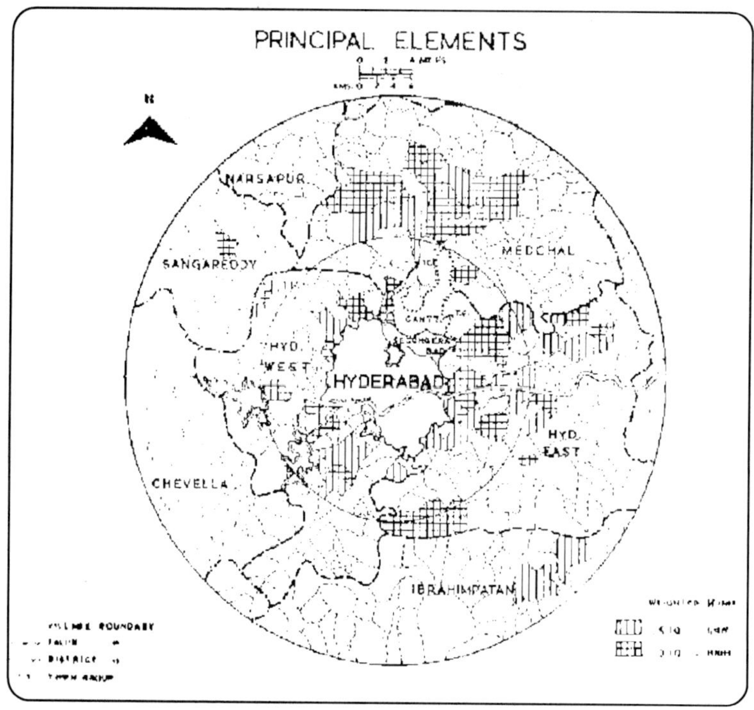

Map 6.11 : Principal Elements

Lack of uniformity of development in the impact zone of metropolitan Hyderabad is clearly revealed by a composite distribution map of all the principal elements. The generalised boundary of this map is crooked, ill-defined and extended disproportionately along the lines of communication (Map 6.11).

Areal Distribution of Reflective Elements

As explained earlier the 'reflective elements' relate to those socio-economic aspects which respond to urbanising impulses of the metropolis. Of the 'reflective elements' selected the following five are of basic character in the sense that they reveal direct relationship with urbanisation trends :

(a) Villages with over 50 per cent of the working population engaged in non-agricultural occupation;
(b) Villages with a density exceeding 640 persons per square mile;
(c) Villages with electricity consumption exceeding 1,000 units per month;
(d) Villages with a population growth rate exceeding 22 per cent in the decade 1951-61; and
(e) Villages with a sex ratio of 951 or less females per 1,000 males.

The sixth reflective element: (f) 'Villages with a population of 2,000 or more in 1961' is rather of a supporting character and has been used to link two high density villages if it intervenes between them. (Census, 1961 and Electricity Board, 1965-66).

A brief analysis of the maps relating to each of the aforesaid reflective elements is given below :

(a) Non-Agricultural Workers exceeding 50 per cent (Map 6.12)

This is one of the most significant variables indicating the impact of urbanisation. Map 6.12 clearly reveals direct relationship between Metropolitan Hyderabad and villages with high percentage of non-agricultural workers.

Out of a total of 37 villages with non-agricultural workers exceeding 50 per cent of the working population, almost 30 are ringed

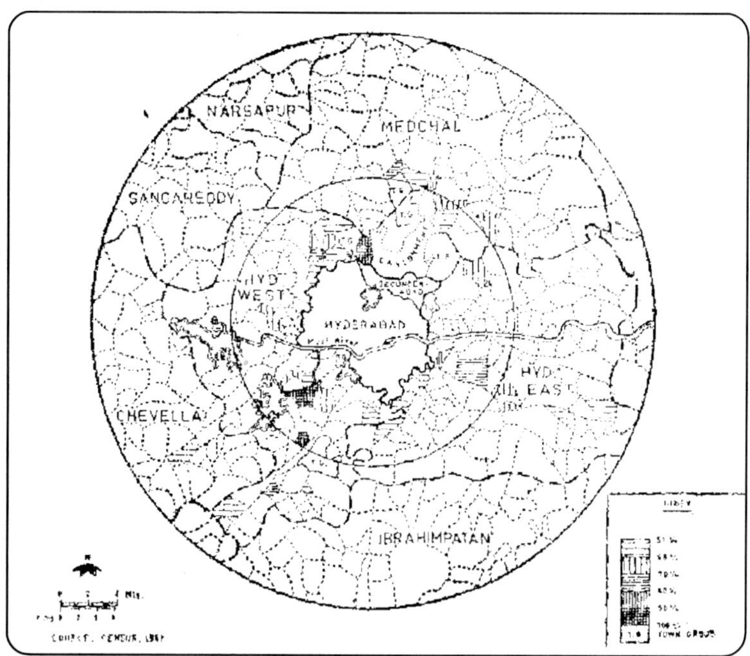

Map 6.12 : Distribution of Villages with Non-Agricultural Workers above 50%

around the metropolis. This ring seems to be well developed in the north, north-west and north-east because of the location of the cantonment and of important industrial areas in those sectors and is likely to strengthen further.

(b) Density of Population exceeding 640 Persons Per Square Mile (Map 6.13)

The areal pattern of distribution of density exceeding 640 persons per square mile as indicated in Map 6.13 has a strong resemblance with that of the distribution patterns of workers in non-agricultural occupations (Map 6.13).

The Hyderabad Metropolitan Region is an agriculturally poor area because of the low average annual (25" to 30") and highly variable rainfall, lack of irrigation facilities and poor soil. Consequently, it can support only a small population which is indicated by its low average density of population i.e. 318 persons per square mile. For a region so poorly endowed with agricultural resources a density of population approximately twice that of the region could be achieved, perhaps, only through urban influence.

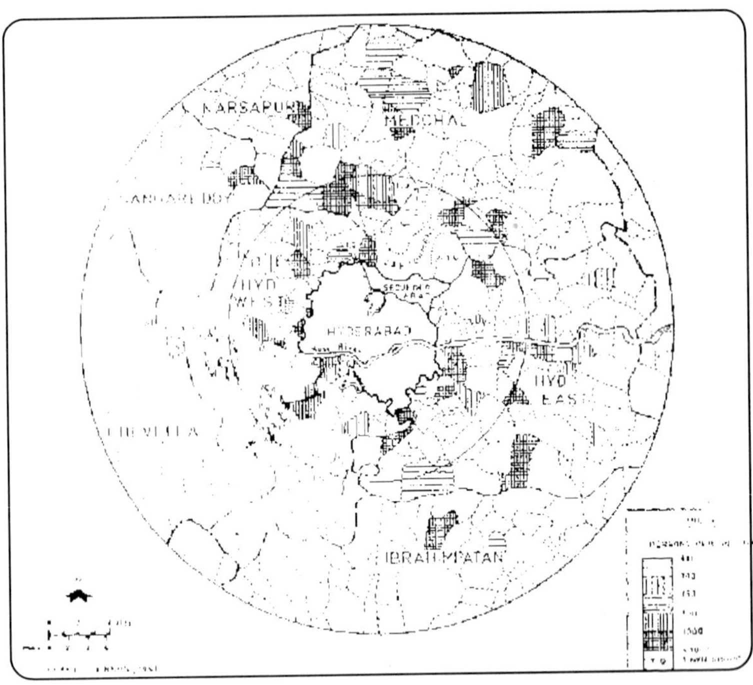

Map 6.13 : Population Density—640 Persons Per Sq. Mile and Above

This assumption is further corroborated by the fact that 75 per cent of the villages with high density of population are concentrated in the industrialised northern sectors within a radius of 10 miles (Centre : Nampally Railway Station) from the heart of the metropolis.

(c) Villages with Electricity Consumption exceeding 1,000 Units Per Month (Map 6.14)

Electrification of rural areas is being systematically carried out under the rural development programmes of the Five Year Plans. Nevertheless there seems to be a direct relationship between rural electrification and proximity to the metropolis.

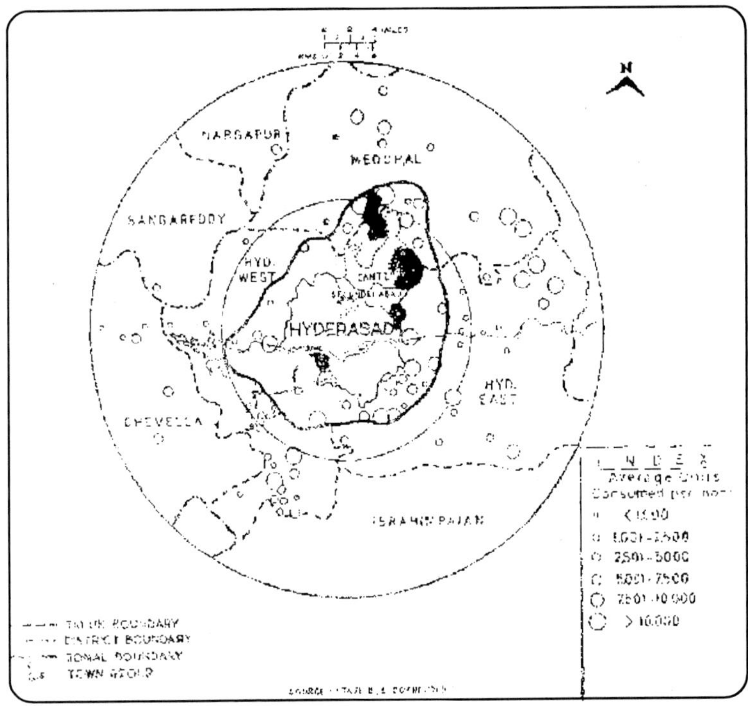

Map 6.14 : Electricity Consumption in Rural Areas

Table 6.10 : Number and Percentages of Electrified Villages by Talukas (March 1966)

	Taluka	No. of Villages Electrified	Percentage of total villages in Taluka
1.	Ibrahimpatnam	20	14.1
2.	Medchal	45	52.8
3.	Hyderabad East	49	25.0
4.	Hyderabad West	54	30.1
5.	Chevella	33	26.4
6.	Vicarabad	15	7.5
7.	Pargi	5	3.3

It can be seen from Table 6.10 that talukas adjoining the metropolis (Medchal, Hyderabad West and Hyderabad East) have a larger proportion of electrified villages. This tendency seems to be more pronounced with regard to the unit consumption of electricity.

It is evident from Map 6.14 that in the region surrounding Metropolitan Hyderabad there is a ring of villages where the consumption of electricity exceeds 1,000 units per month. It is also within this ring that villages consuming 500 units or more of electricity per month are concentrated. High consumption of electricity is either linked with industrial use or with irrigation for the production of crops which have high marketable values in the metropolis such as vegetables and fruits. Market gardening is the most important economic activity in these rural areas especially in the southern, south-eastern and eastern sectors.

There is a rapid decline in consumption of electrical energy outside of this zone of high consumption. There are also three other isolated modes of high energy use, one each in the north, south and east. These are all oriented to railways and highways.

(d) Percentage of Variation in Population 1951-1961 (Map 6.15)

The rural population of the Metropolitan Region of Hyderabad (40 miles radius) was 1.53 million in 1961, an increase of 17.1 per cent over 1951. This percentage increase in population is less than the national average (21.9) but slightly higher than the State average which is 15.6 per cent. It has been assumed here that increase in population in the Metropolitan District of Hyderabad above the national average may be due to migration. It is further assumed that a population growth rate higher than the national average is a function of the urbanising influence of the metropolis.*

This assumption seems to be corroborated by the fact that the growth rate of rural population within the 20 miles radius of Hyderabad decreases with the decrease in radial distance from the metropolis. It can be seen from the Table in Annexure IV that the average growth rate within 20 miles radius is only 21.3 per cent which is even slightly less than the national average, whereas in the 10 miles zone the average growth rate is as high as 27.40 per cent and, in its industrially developing region north of the Musi it is 28.31 per cent.

Of the 390 villages within the 20 miles zone, there are 154 villages which recorded a population growth of 22 per cent and above during the last census decade. That such a high proportion of rural settlements

---

* In order to apply a rigorous test the national rate of growth has been preferred over the State growth rate.

have experienced growth rates well above the national and regional average only indicated that a factor or a combination of factors not operative in the region at large was at work within a 20 miles radial range during the census decade 1951-61.

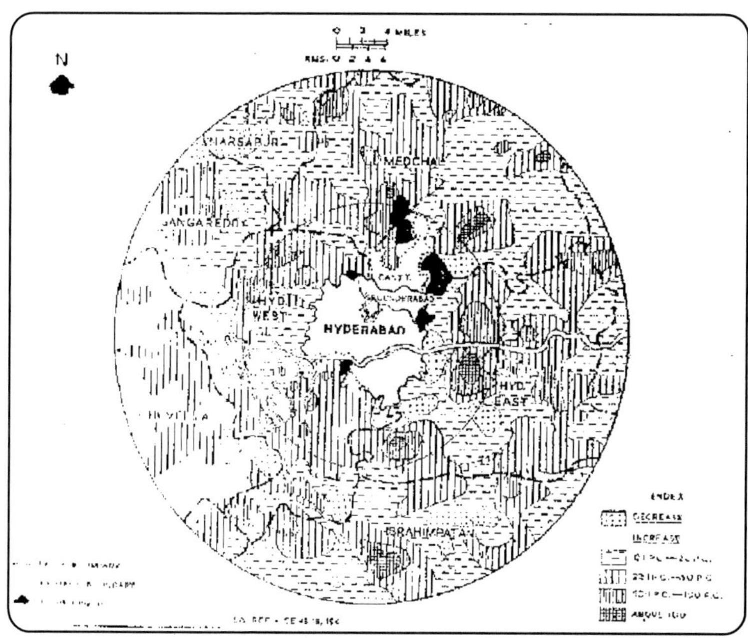

Map 6.15 : Percentage Variation in Population, 1951-1961

An analysis of Map 6.15 further highlights the aforesaid points and corroborate the fact that almost all the villages with very high percentage of increase in population (above 25%) are located closer to the metropolis. Most of these are concentrated in the relatively more urbanised sectors.

(e) Sex-ratio—Females 951 or Less Per 1,000 Males (Map 6.16)

Sex ratio (females per thousand males) in urban India is not as susceptible an index of urban influence as it is in western countries, and, therefore, cannot be rated as significant as the first four variables are. Nevertheless it cannot be completely ignored for the reason that the sex ratio (females per 1,000 males) in urban India is much lower (846/1000) than the corresponding figure for rural India (961/1000).

Within 20 miles radius of Hyderabad there are 107 villages which have lower number of females per 1,000 males than the average sex ratio for urban Andhra Pradesh. Of these 25 villages have sex ratio even lower than urban India. An examination of Map 6.16 reveals that in general most of the villages with lower number of females are clustered round the urban units. Moreover, there is a greater clustering of such villages in the industrial north than in the south. It may, therefore, not be incorrect to infer that there are more male immigrants in the north than in the south.

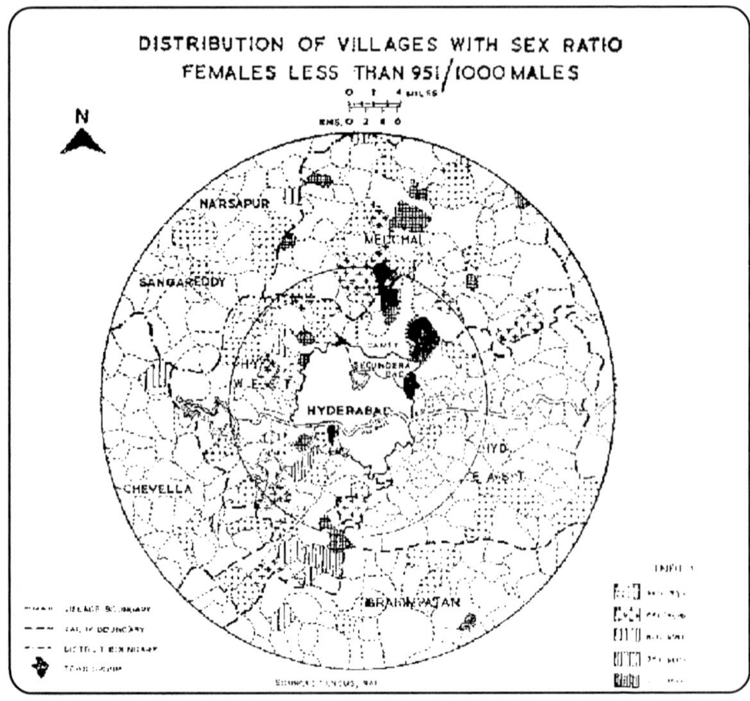

Map 6.16 : Distribution of Viallages with Sex Ratio—Females Less than 951 per 1000 Males

General Distribution Pattern of Reflective Elements and their Intensity Range

The 'reflective elements' are distributed over a larger area than the 'principal elements' but lack the compactness of development of the latter. Each element seems to have developed as an independent variable and, therefore, boundary girdles are exception. Nevertheless, the distribution pattern of reflective elements largely confirms the trend of development indicated by the distribution of principal elements. The major areas of concentrated distribution here too, as in the case of 'principal elements' are localized in narrow sectors in the north-west, north and north-east and east.

Like the 'principal elements' 'the reflective elements' too are not uniformly distributed and vary in their range of intensity around the metropolis. The range of intensity has again been broadly categorized into 'high' and 'low'. The following method has been adopted to determine the intensity range of 'reflective elements'.

Each of the five elements has been given different weights and the total 'weighted score' of these five elements is 15. The distribution of weighted score is as follows :

Elements	*Weight*
(a) Non-agricultural workers	5
(b) Electricity consumption	4
(c) Density	3
(d) Population variation	2
(e) Sex ratio	1

Weights have been assigned to the above elements according to their importance in revealing the urban character and urban way of life. Thus, the element 'Non-agricultural Workers' which is considered to be the most reflective of urbanization has been given the highest weight while the sex ratio, the least reflective have been given the lowest weight.

The 'weighted score' of each of the villages was computed and plotted on the Map 6.17.

All villages with a weighted score of 7 and above have been classified under high intensity range. This implies that a village to be included in this range must have at least two of the five reflective elements selected for weighting and one of which must be either 'non-agricultural' or 'rural electrification', the two highest ranked elements.

A composite map showing the distribution of all the 'reflective elements' reveals a badly defined and generalised distribution pattern as in the case of 'principal element'. Disproportionate extension along communication lines and the concentration of high intensity zones in narrow north-west, north and north-east sectors are further emphasized by this map.

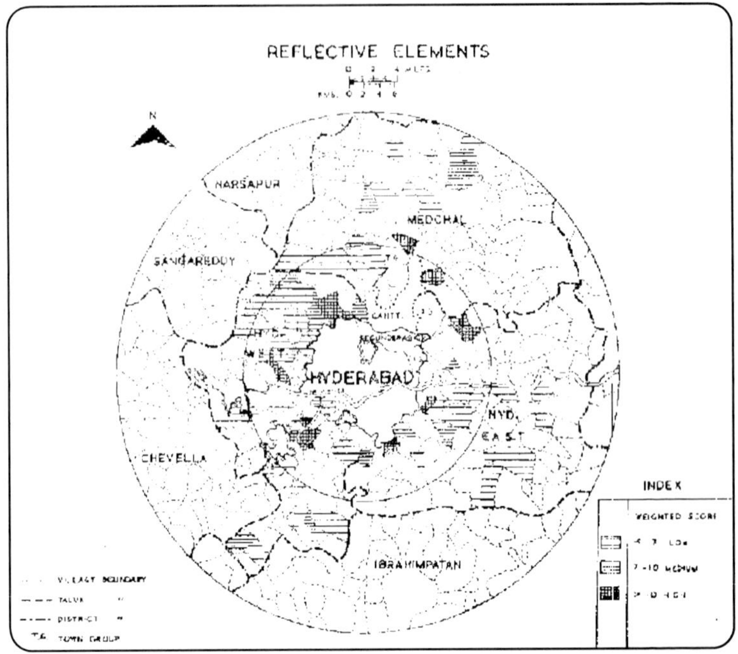

Map 6.17 : Reflective Elements

Significantly all the principal peripheral nodes of development have not yet developed reflective characteristics but are likely to do so within the actionable future because of the expansion of industries in that direction.

Two significant points emerge out of the foregoing study on the delimitation of the Primary Planning Area (Metropolitan District) of Hyderabad :

1. The high intensity range zones of the 'principal' and 'reflective' elements and the continuously built up areas outside of the incorporated area are all concentrated within a radius of 10 miles, measured from the broad gauge railway station, Hyderabad; and
2. Immediately outside of the 10 miles zone, villages with high intensity range, having strong daily interaction with the metropolis, have developed in sectors with strong lines of

communication such as Ramachandrapuram, Medchal, Ghatkesar, Hayatnagar and Shamshabad.

An integrated development of these high intensity peripheral sectors with the Metropolis and the 10 miles zones around it are the key determinants in delimiting the Primary Planning Area.

The Primary Planning Area of Metropolitan Hyderabad will thus incorporate the following territory and will cover an area of 381.86 sq. miles (including the area of Hyderabad Municipal Corporation) containing a population of 1.4 million (Map 6.18 and Table 6.11).

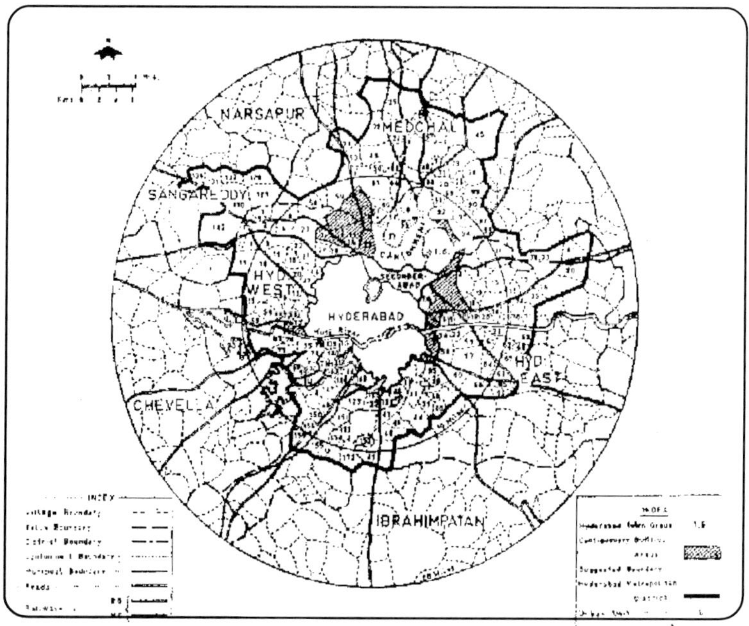

Map 6.18 : Suggested Boundary—Hyderabad Metropolitan District

(a) The Hyderabad Town Group (Census 1962);
(b) All the villages and urban units within the 10 miles radius;
(c) Villages and urban units with high intensity range outside of the 10 miles radius but contiguous to it; and
(d) Non-contiguous villages and urban units located along the highways and railways and between 10 and 20 miles radii exhibiting high degree of metropolitan influence.

Table 6.11 : The Hyderabad Metropolitan District thus delimited will have the following Area and Population Component

Unit	*Number of Villages*	*Area in sq. miles*	*Population*
1. Hyderabad/Secunderabad Municipal Corporation	—	69.40	1,118,553
2. Hyderabad Town Group excluding (1)	—	15.68	132,566
3. Medchal Taluk	40	69.40	40,248
4. Hyderabad East	64	77.61	42,909
5. Hyderabad West	80	128.22	54,546
6. Sangareddy Taluk	8	21.55	9,438
	192	**381.86**	**1,398,260**

Source: Census of India 1961, Vol. II Part II-A General Population Table and District Census Hand Book, 1961.

Conclusion

While the delimitation of the Metropolitan Region is vitally important for an organic social and economic development of the metropolis, the delimitation of the Primary Planning Area has to be done on a priority basis in order to prevent haphazard growth of metropolitan Hyderabad.

The pre-eminent trend of this area is its rapid urbanization. Extensive areas outside of the Municipal Corporation boundary in the North-East and North-West have been built ever since 1956 for residential and industrial functions. The existing pattern of development is, however, chaotic and has generated an axially elongated growth of built up area which is not conducive to a balanced physical development. It may, however, be pointed out that this area is still a relatively less densely populated (density of population varying between 300 and 500 persons per square mile), and even the urbanised areas have not expanded so extensively as to preclude the possibility of integrated and rational planning. In fact, there is plenty of scope to model the urban and rural land uses in accordance with the scientific principles of planning and in keeping with the physical and functional needs of the dynamic central city. The rapidity with which this area is urbanising suggests that in the next two decades it will be extensively urbanised leaving thereby little scope for regulated development. Consequent upon this trend and that of commercialization of agriculture land values have increased several fold in its rural areas. Land values in the villages now range between Rs.2,500 and Rs.10,000 per acre (decreasing with distance from the central city) whereas prior to 1956 they hardly exceeded Rs. 2,500. In order to prevent speculation in land and spiralling of land values, the boundary of the Primary Planning Area should be notified forthwith and all transactions in land without the approval of the planning authorities should be forbidden. An integrated urban and rural land use plan should be prepared for this area and a well defined policy may be formulated in regard to:

(i) The development of satellite towns;
(ii) The physical limit for extension of water supply, sewerage, electricity and telephone services; and
(iii) The establishment of planning and administrative machinery for the Metropolitan District.

NOTE

Institute of Asian Studies (1959): "Economic Characteristics and Strategy for Regional Development" in Final Report to Hyderabad Metropolitan Research Project. Osmania University, Hyderabad. (mimeographed)

ANNEXURE I

Daily Frequency of Suburban and District Bus Services, 1965

	Code No.	Taluk	Distance in miles from		Suburban Bus Service		District Bus Service Passenger & Express	
			Hyd'bad city Bus Station	Sec'bad (Ranigunj)	To	From	To	From
Suburban Settlements								
1. Kukatpally	27	Hyderabad West	8.7	6.0	25	25	21	21
2. Ramachand-rapuram	130	Sangareddy	17.4	15.0	12	12	21	21
3. Moula Ali	—	Hyderabad East	9.0	7.8	42	42	—	—
4. Lalapet	—	Hyderabad East	6.0	5.4	46	46	—	—
5. Ghatkesar	80	Hyderabad East	13.8	15.0	2	2	11	11
6. Pahadi Sharif	49	Hyderabad East	7.8	10.8	24	24	4	4
7. Shamsabad	155	Hyderabad East	10.0	13.4	6	6	4	4
8. Hakimpet	48	Medchal	13.2	9.6	6	6	12	12
9. Narsingi	57	Hyderabad West	9.0	12.0	15	15	—Friday only—	
10. Osman Sagar	—	Hyderabad West	10.8	14.2	4*	4*	4*	4*
11. Uppal	9	Hyderabad East	5.4	6.6	42	42	14	11
12. Saroonagar	28	Hyderabad East	5.0	8.5	24	24	11	11
13. Hayatnagar	65	Hyderabad East	9.0	12.6	1	1	11	11
Rural Settlements								
1. Shamirpet	45	Medchal	16.4	12.8	—	—	10	10
2. Dhundigal	20	Medchal	16.8	13.2	—	—	9	9
3. Patancheru	136	Sangareddy	20.3	17.9	—	—	21	21
4. Ibrahimpatnam	82	I'Patnam	14.9	17.3	—	—	9	9

Note: * On Sunday and Public Holiday only. *Source*: Compiled from data supplied by the Road Transport Corporation and field work.

ANNEXURE II

Labour Residential Groups of Selected Industrial Units in Metropolitan Hyderabad (Sector-wise), 1966

	H.M.T. Narsapur Road	*H.A.M.W. Sanathnagar*	*H.A.C. Nagar*	*V.S.T. Musheerabad*	*A.P.R.T.C.W.S. Musheerabad*	*D.B.R.M. Tank Bund*	*T.S.W.M. N. Road*	*H.R.F.M. Moula Ali*	*Total*
(1)	*(2)*	*(3)*	*(4)*	*(5)*	*(6)*	*(7)*	*(8)*	*(9)*	*(10)*
Hyderabad	838	1,099	634	740	363	707	19	28	428
Hyderabad South	92	69	26	53	52	50	—	4	381
Secunderabad	318	321	140	260	612	869	30	23	2,579
	1,248	1,489	800	2,058	1,057	1,626	55	55	8,388
Peripheral Villages	5	46	68	4	15	10	—	27	241
TOTAL	1,253	1,535	868	2,062	1,072	1,636	121	82	8,629

H.M.T. — Hindustan Machine Tools
H.A.M.W. — Hyderabad Allwyn Metal Works
H.A.C. — Hyderabad Asbestos Cement
V.S.T. — Vazir Sultan Tobacco Co.
A.P.R.T.C.W. — Andhra Pradesh Road Transport Corporation Workshop
D.B.R.M. — Dewan Bahadur Ramagopal Mills
T.S.W.M. — Telangana Spinning and Weaving Mill
H.R.F.M. — Hyderabad Roller Flour Mills

Source: Compiled from data supplied by the various industrial concerns.

ANNEXURE III

Hyderabad Postal District—Centre Outside Municipal Corporation and Cantonment

	Village Code No.	Village	Taluk	Distance in miles		Postal Zone No.
1.	121	Balapur	Hyderabad West	7	Hyderabad	5
2.	60	Bandalguda	Hyderabad East	4.8	Hyderabad	5
3.	43	Kothapet	Hyderabad East	7	Hyderabad	5
4.	52	Karga HSW	Hyderabad West	5.4	Hyderabad	8
5.	68	Himayatsagar	Hyderabad West	9	Hyderabad	30
6.	33	Alwal	—	8.9	Secunderabad	10
7.	—	Asafgram	—	8.8	Secunderabad	10
8.	30	Balanagar	Hyderabad West	8	Secunderabad	11
9.	93	Ammuguda	Medchal	8	Secunderabad	15
10.	2	Mallapur	Hyderabad East	—	Secunderabad	17
11.	1	Malkajigiri	Hyderabad East	7.2	Secunderabad	17
12.	1	Mirzalguda	Hyderabad East	7.2	Secunderabad	17
13.	77	Ibrahimbagh	Hyderabad West	7.2	Hyderabad	3
14.	130	Ramachandrapuram	Sangareddy	17.4	Hyderabad	32
15.	—	Balanagar Township	Hyderabad West	9	Hyderabad	37
16.	—	H.M.T.	Hyderabad West	9.5	Hyderabad	37
17.	—	Telangana Spinning Mills	Hyderabad West	9	Hyderabad	37
18.	9	Uppal	Hyderabad East	5.6	Hyderabad	13
19.	—	Osmania University	Hyderabad East	4.3	Hyderabad	7
20.	—	R.R.L.	Hyderabad East	4.6	Hyderabad	9
21.	3	Necharam	Hyderabad East	6.3	Hyderabad	13
22.	40a	Hakimpet	Medchal	13.2	Secunderabad	14
23.	—	Putomguda	Hyderabad East	—	Secunderabad	14
24.	—	Saroonagar	Hyderabad East	5.0	Hyderabad	35
25.	—	Rajendranagar	Hyderabad West	8.1	Hyderabad	31

Source: Telephone Directory—January, 1966 and Office of Supdt. of Post Offices, Hyderabad Circle.

ANNEXURE IV

Rate of Growth of Rural Population, 1951-1961 Sector-wise

20 miles radius	*No. of villages 1961*	*Population 1961*	*Percentage Share of villages 1961*	*Percentage share of population 1961*	*Population on 1951*	*Percentage variation 1951/1961*
1	*2*	*3*	*4*	*5*	*6*	*7*
North of the Musi	203	190,563	52.0	55.3	156,268	21.94
South of the Musi	187	154,063	48.0	44.7	127,655	20.68
	390	344,626	100.0	100.0	283,923	21.31
10 *mile radius*						
North of the Musi	36	51,915	50.9	55.8	40,461	28.31
South of the Musi	54	41,046	49.1	44.2	32,506	26.27
	90	92,961	100.0	100.0	72,967	27.40

Source: Basic Data from District Census Hand Books, Andhra Pradesh, 1951 and 1961.

7

Regional Planning : Functional and Nodal*

Regional Planning attempts to analyse the territorial systems which are based on the functionally homogeneous characteristics or are organized around settlement nodes which command exchange regions of heterogeneous character. These two basic types of territorial systems are not mutually exclusive but Indian scholars have tended to treat them separately and consequently there are very few studies which have analysed a territorial system in terms of both its functional specialization and nodal exchange characteristics. Of the two territorial systems Indian scholars have paid greater attention to the functionally homogeneous regions without discussing the integrating role of urban centres. There are indeed very few studies which have discussed the functional, cyclical and nodal aspects within a single region. It is proposed to review in this chapter some important studies relating to both the functional and the nodal regions. In the concluding section of this review paper some suggestion will be offered with regard to the type of studies which may be sponsored to understand the organization and functioning of the system of nodal regions of India.

Five Year Plans and Regional Planning

Initially the regional approach to planning was not accepted by the Planning Commission and consequently we find scant reference to it in the first two Five Year Plans. The concept of regional planning and balanced regional development as understood by the Commission

---

* The author gratefully acknowledge the benefit of discussion with Prof. C.D. Deshpande while revising this chapter.

Published in *The Indian Journal of Social Work,* Vol. 36, Nos. 3 & 4, October 1975 to January 1976, pp. 317-329.

then merely implied "a judicious location of new industrial units with due emphasis on balanced regional development as a vital step in the direction of wider diffusion of employment opportunities. (Planning Commission, 1952: 20). It is in the Third Five Year Plan (1961-66) that the Planning Commission approved the regional approach to planning and commended this approach to the planning of large industries which will serve as focal points of development for areas far beyond their immediate environs. It also stressed the need for integrated rural-urban development because of the need to strengthen "economic interdependence between towns and surrounding rural areas" (Planning Commission, 1961: 689).

It is also in the Third Five Year Plan that the key role of urbanization in stimulating social and economic transformation has been realised and the need to plan the urban centres stressed (Planning Commission, 1961). Consequent upon this increasing emphasis on urban development, master plans have been prepared for 322 towns/cities and their immediate region in the country as a whole. These master plans have been prepared by the Departments of Town Planning of the respective States and, therefore, lack a national focus. Even at the State level an integrated approach for a coordinated development of these towns is totally absent. As for instance in the State of Andhra Pradesh master plans of its three most important towns Hyderabad, Vijayawada and Visakhapatnam, have not been formulated as part of the overall urban system of the State. Despite this major drawback these master plans are a distinct advance over the previous plans as they treat the city and their immediate rural hinterlands as integral units for purposes of urban planning.

While the need for regional and metropolitan planning has been greatly emphasised in the Fourth Five Year Plan, it is the Fifth Plan which examines the problem in the national perspective and suggests the formulation of a national policy of urbanisation to minimize the pressure of urbanisation on metropolitan cities by promoting "the development of smaller towns and new urban centres". This focus on urbanisation at the national level has led to the formulation and enunciation of a National Urbanisation Policy by the Town and Country Planning Organisation of the Government of India.

The National Urbanisation Policy attempts to draw a framework for spatial planning as part of the strategy of national economic planning. (Town and Country Planning Organisation, 1974: 17). The Town and Country Planning Organisation of India sets out the following five principal aims of the National Urbanization Policy :

(1) "Evolving a spatial pattern of economic development based on regional planning and location of a hierarchy of human settlements;

(2) Securing the optimum distribution of population between rural and urban settlements within each region and also among the towns of various sizes;

(3) Securing the distribution of economic activities in small and medium towns and in new growth centres (to achieve) the desired population distribution and maximum economic growth;

(4) Controlling and where necessary, arresting the further growth of economic activities by dispersal of economic activities, legislative measures and establishment of new counter magnets in the region; and

(5) Providing minimum level of services for improving the quality of life in rural and urban areas and gradually reducing differences between the rural and urban life" (Town and Country Planning Organisation, 1974 : 17).

This is a welcome document in the sense that it clearly establishes the need to view the urban and metropolitan development problems in the national perspective. Despite a reference in this document that a "system of cities" ought to be developed for a successful spatial planning the document fails to highlight the pivotal role of settlement nodes to organize and integrate the regional economy at the macro, meso and micro levels. The document further fails: (i) to identify the existing system of metropolitan cities, (ii) to explain the organization of territorial system around these metropolitan nodes, and (iii) to explain the connectivity between the nodal and functional system. The document further overlooks the level of development of the national economy when it suggests that "towns and cities with a population ranging between 50,000 and 2,50,000 having developed infrastructure and necessary conditions for self sustaining growth should be designated as growth centres" (Towns and Country Planning Organisation, 1974 : 27).

The document shows unawareness of the dynamic role which the growth centres should play in transmitting impulses of growth, diffusing innovations, and transforming the regional economy through the cyclical movement of the nodal exchange system when it restricts the definition of growth centres to those settlements which have the favourable climate "for the development of industries" (Chandrasekhara : 1972).

Regional Surveys and Studies

Since the beginning of the Second Five Year Plan studies on regional planning both official and quasi-official were actively advanced through the initiative of the Indian Statistical Institute. Of the many studies conducted the following five have been briefly reviewed :

(1) The Pilot Regional Survey of Mysore State;
(2) Macro Regional Survey of South India;
(3) The Damodar Valley Survey;
(4) South-East Resource Region; and
(5) Indo-Soviet Research Project on Regionalisation.

The Pilot Regional Survey of the Mysore State (Karnataka) was a pioneering research carried out under the aegis of the Indian Statistical Institute (Learmonth *et al.*, 1962). The major contributions of this study, in addition to explaining the theoretical formulation of planning regions, was to highlight the "distinct regional structure and patterns within the Mysore State (now Karnataka)" and to identify its planning regions. The Indian Statistical Institute followed it up with a Macro-Regional Survey of South India, the aim of which was to account for disparities in the levels of development with the help of selected indicators. It is, however, valued more for it is the key variables for a scheme of economic regionalization at the macro scales.

The South-East Resource Region study is taken up by the Town and Country Planning Organisation "for organisation of planning and economic management of the resources of the area" (Town and Country Planning Organisation, 1968). This region, the study points out, possesses not only a certain degree of geographic, economic and social homogeneity but also "functional unity which will permit effective common foresight and policy in planning". Although the study does not offer any blue print for development it does, however, highlight significant development characteristics of the region. It draws pointed attention to the inadequacy of linkages of rural settlements with urban market and also to its inadequately developed central place system which is evident from the fact that on the average one urban settlement serves 570 villages. Consequently urban centres fail to act as foci of development. The South-East Resource Region, it is further pointed out in this study, is oriented towards Calcutta and to a lesser extent towards the port of Visakhapatnam in the south, because the other major settlements of the region fail to act as effective counter magnets to Calcutta. The study, therefore, proposes, and rightly so, that as against the creation of new towns as growth poles the existing and the emerging major urban centres be so functionally strengthened as to effectively counteract the drift to Calcutta (Town and Country Planning Organisation, Government of India, 1968 : 4.36). In a subsequent study of this region the authors have emphasised the "growth centre" approach to the planning of this region, in order to promote effective integration of the primary urban system consisting of the market service towns and the secondary urban system consisting of the growth centres and growth points (Chandrasekhara *et al.*, 1972 : 36-70).

While the South-East Resource Region Study cuts across the State boundaries, the Regional Planning for West Bengal confines its observation within the political boundaries of the State. It is explicitly stated in this work that "a metropolitan regional plan for Greater Calcutta would not be a complete instrument of public policy implementation unless it is supported by an overall regional plan for the State" (Calcutta Metropolitan Planning Organisation, 1967). While this study does maintain a clear regional perspective and recognizes the importance of urban centres in formulating a strategy for regional development, it however conceives narrowly the scope of regional planning programmes when it restricts to the promotion of "planned urban growth" and the prevention of "unplanned hasty sprawl of urbanism" (Calcutta Metropolitan Planning Organisation, 1967: 62). On account of this restricted approach to regional planning the document fails to indicate a clear-cut urban development policy to countervail or even to minimize the magnetic pull of Calcutta (now Kolkata). Jakobson and Ved Prakash in a critique of regional planning for West Bengal have also stressed the need to break Calcutta's magnetism by changing the existing transportation flow patterns converging on Calcutta. In addition to the radial east-west running transportation corridors to Calcutta they suggest the strengthening of the north-south running transport system oriented to the ports of Haldia and Paradeep. This perpendicularity of flow between the transport systems, they feel, "could contribute to a reduction of Calcutta's influence in its hinterland" (Jakobson and Prakash, 1966-67: 36-65).

The Tennessee Valley Authority inspired the Damodar Valley Survey which was initiated in 1959. This is one of the earliest diagnostic regional surveys but it did not make any headway beyond the diagnostic stage. The valley was divided into a number of sub-regions (upper, middle and lower) and survey reports of resource potential of the valley as a whole or of its three sub-regions were prepared without suggesting any strategy for development. It can serve as a handy reference material to scholars who intend to probe deeper into the matter.

The Indo-Soviet Project Report on Economic Regionalization of India is of great theoretical value. It starts with the assumption that "a correct delineation and articulation of economic regions in geographic terms is an essential prerequisite of economic development in a developing country and an aid to judicious investment and optimum utilization of scarce resources" (Gupta and Sdasyuk, 1968: II). It explains lucidly the need for economic regionalization in planning for the eradication of economic backwardness and minimization of disparities in the level of regional development. Five distinct types of economic regions have been identified based on (i) natural resource and natural regions, (ii) population characteristics and resource development, (iii) agricultural resources, (iv) industrial development, and (v) transport and urban nodes. (Gupta and Sdasyuk, 1968 : 25-26). It further explains the practical applicability of these schemes of regionalization to regional planning in India. This work is noted for its conceptual clarity, scientific methods and pragmatic approach and constitutes a significant contribution to the theoretical formulations on economic regionalization of India.

In addition to these institutionally sponsored studies on regional planning some scholars have also made a notable contribution in this field. A pioneering contribution in this respect was that of Deshpande who as early as 1948, even before the initiation of the five year development plans, suggested a scheme of planning regions for the then State of Bombay and stressed the need for regional approach to economic planning to achieve optimal level of development in each region based on its resource potential (Deshpande : 1948). The application of regionalization to economic planning was further advanced regional survey of the Mysore State (now Karnataka). The State was divided into 21 units by Prakasa Rao and Bhat, through their micro planning units which were regrouped into six planning divisions (Rao and Bhat).

Misra's edited volume on Regional planning includes a set of valuable articles relating to concepts, techniques, and policies on regional planning (Misra *et al.*, 1969). Expressing his own views Misra states that "regional and national goals should, at least in theory, coincide". He is against the idea of equalization in the levels of regional development for inter-regional differences must continue as they are due to differences of culture and resource potential (Misra). Bhat in his thesis on Regional Planning in India highlights that spatial framework for planning based on resource structure of regions is more realistic in terms of development planning than linguistic framework. Although planning regions ought to be a combination of both formal and nodal regions yet Bhat would like them to be derived more from nodal regions arranged in hierarchical order (Bhat, 1972).

The regional planning studies reviewed so far have advocated planning based on homogeneous (functional) regions. These functional regions do highlight interregional differences and can be of some help in formulating realistic plans to achieve balanced regional development. None of these studies, however, have discussed centering policy in regional planning and hence have failed to appreciate the integrating and transforming roles which towns can play on the market and metropolitan centres. Christaller's theory of a nested system of settlement hierarchy within a region (1933) (Christaller, 1966) and Francois Perroux' theory of growth poles (poles de Croissance, 1961) (Perroux, 1950 : 90-97) have stimulated a large number of planning studies oriented to a system of market or metropolitan centres. These studies reveal greater awareness of the key role of urban centres as agents of modernization, and centres for the diffusion of innovations. Their approach is pragmatic and of relevance to planning problems at different area levels. They have, therefore, gained momentum and wider acceptability.

Market Town, Growth Pole or Metropolitan Oriented Studies on Regional Planning

The National Council of Applied Economic Research (NCAER) initiated the first major study on market towns in order to work out a strategy for the social and economic transformation of rural areas through a network of market towns (National Council of Applied Economic Research, 1965). The study holds the inadequate development of intermediate level of urbanization in India as a critical factor in retarding the country's economic development. It, therefore, feels that the "transformation" process can be set in motion by "creating both cities and market towns to which villages could be functionally related". Hence the study suggests that the existing number of 1936 towns should be raised in number to 12,500-14,000. If the dualistic structure of our economy is to be eliminated, the national economy is to be spatially integrated, and the productive capacity of rural sector is to be significantly improved and surplus marketed. These points were stressed again in a seminar conducted by the NCAER in 1972. The Background Note on the Development of Market Towns presented at this seminar emphasised the need of "a well spread out network of intermediate towns, which are readily accessible to most villages; can function as processing and marketing centres for rural population within their zones" (NCAER, 1972). Johnson who directed NCAER's first Project on market town (1962) has re-emphasised, in this seminar, the need for intermediate level urbanization and "centrally located market towns where appropriate facilities will be provided and where a variety of ancillary services will be available (Johnson, 1972: 60). Furthermore, Johnson conceives of them as "investment clusters" where "rather full range of opportunities is available mechanical, clerical and entrepreneurial or professional" (Johnson, 1972 : 65).

It is also stipulated in his work that agro-urban communities should be linked through a hierarchy of central places for the eventual linkage of the rural community with the national economy. The NCAER proposal for a national strategy for the development of market towns was not pursued further and consequently no action followed.

Meanwhile the Planning Commission came out in a big way to support the study of metropolitan cities and preparation of their master plan because of their social, political and economic importance and also gravity of the problems. This naturally stimulated a number of metropolitan centred regional plans. The Master Plan for Delhi (1969) was the first of such regional plans (Delhi Development Authority, 1962).

The Master Plan for Delhi examines comprehensively the planning and development problems of the national capital at three levels viz (1) Central City; (2) Delhi Metropolitan Region; (3) National

Capital Region. This is a sound approach because the planning problems of Delhi, the national capital, have to be viewed in the wider context of its region. In order to arrest the growth of Delhi and counteract its magnetic pull the master plan for Delhi has stipulated the growth of a number of counter-magnets on the periphery of the National Capital Region. These counter-magnets will be fully developed metropolitan centres with diversified economic base and large employment potential. Unlike the Master Plan for Delhi, the Basic Development for Calcutta (1966-1970) does not look beyond the metropolitan district and effective counter-magnets to Calcutta (now Kolkata) have not been clearly visualized (Calcutta Metropolitan P.O., 1966). It may also be noted that despite all the development inputs Durgapur and Asansol cannot possibly counteract the magnetic pull of Calcutta. In this respect the suggestion of Jakobson and Ved Prakash referred to earlier sounds more reasonable.

The Kanpur Regional Study, which includes the papers and proceedings of an international seminar focused on the developmental problems of Kanpur, emphasizes the need to promote integration of city and countryside by spreading urbanization and securing adoption of non-traditional modes of thought by villagers (Desai *et al.*, 1969). In his paper presented at this seminar Berry suggested four tier K-7 (1-7-49-343) system of settlement hierarchy for the adequate spatial integration of the economy of the Kanpur region (Berry, 1969: 203-19). In the same seminar Johnson drew attention to the inadequate development of the central place system and intermediate level urbanization. He observed that with one town on the average serving nearly 450 villages within the region one cannot expect metropolitan Kanpur to operate and control efficiently the economy of its region. Hence he concluded that to maximize spatial integration the "goal of the regional development plan, therefore, be the creation of about 300 more urban centres in the Kanpur region" (Johnson).

Manzoor Alam and Waheeduddin Khan in their study on Metropolitan Hyderabad and Its Region, have strongly stressed the need to view the planning and development problems in the larger regional, State and national perspective. The study brings out the impact of metropolitan Hyderabad in transforming the economy of its immediate rural hinterland. However, it has been observed that despite this impact of the metropolis over the region, the interaction between them is not up to the desired degree and, therefore, the economy of the region is not adequately integrated with the metropolis. Alam and Khan have, therefore, suggested the development of growth centres and 42 "rural service centres" for the spatial integration of the regional economy with the metropolis. This strategy, it has been claimed, will improve the efficiency of the "trickle down" mechanism, quicken the pace of spread-effect which will thereby accelerate the regional development (Alam and Khan, 1972). Earlier Alam in his chapter on the "Re-alignment of the Urban System of Andhra Pradesh" examined the development of the urban system of Andhra Pradesh in its political context and suggested a multiple growth centre or alternatively a single growth pole strategy for the economic development of a backward region of the State of Andhra Pradesh, Rayalaseema (Alam, 1971: 499-501). Alam has further expressed the hope that through this development strategy the magnetic pull of the three metropolises—Madras (now Chennai), Bangalore and Hyderabad over this region can be countervailed and optimal spatial integration of the economy accomplished.

Wanamali in his work on the "Nagpur Metropolitan Region" has examined in detail the level of social facilities available in all the settlements located within the Nagpur Metropolitan Region (Wanamali, 1970). He observes a sharp decline in the level of social facilities between Metropolitan Nagpur and its rural hinterland. This 'developmental dualism', Wanamali observes, hinders spatial integration of the economy. Hence to accomplish an integrated development of the metropolis and its region the author has suggested the creation of seventeen service centres within the rural hinterland of Metropolitan Nagpur. These service centres, it is hoped, if approximately, linked with the metropolis can transmit efficiently, developmental impulses down to the lowest settlement unit within the region.

A number of studies in India on problems relating to urban and regional planning have focused attention on metropolitan cities and their regions and have used data on traffic, transport and communication flows to highlight planning and development problems. In the Interim Report of the Planning Commission on Traffic and Transportation Problems in Metropolitan Cities concern has been expressed over the hyper-concentration of passenger and commodity flows in metropolitan cities due to the "mounting cycle of concentration of economic activities in these few large urban centres" (Planning Commission, Government of India, 1967 : 11). As a solution commended "a rational distribution of future urban development into existing small and medium size towns within the metropolitan region" (Planning Commission, Government of India, 1967 : 11). This Report is vague on the concept of metropolitan region, but one, however, presumes that the region here implies major trade and traffic flow blocks of the national metropolises Delhi, Calcutta, Bombay and Madras. Berry's study of commodity flows also identified a set of regional economies organized around metropolitan centres. Each of the four national metropolises, according to Berry, commands the trade of a well defined region called the "trade blocks" (Berry, 1966). Areas within the macro trading regions vary in their ability to receive growth impulses which drop off with distance. Consequently in these trade blocks according to Berry, "the more commercialized village and town economies are found in the areas of good access, while isolated tribal economies prevail in the inaccessible peripheries" (Berry, 1971 : 122). Berry further observes that although at the national level, the urban centres of India conform to rank-size distribution, at the sub-regional levels they do not. This is due to disparities in the level of regional development and can be minimized by maximizing accessibility and establishing a well articulated system of settlement hierarchy. Reed in his paper on Indian Communication Flows using air passenger flow data and applying sophisticated statistical techniques identifies three chief types of flow regions which he suggests can be used as planning regions since they indicate the degree of connectivity and the volume of flow integrating the region (Reed, 1969 : 145-171).

Lewis, on the other hand, is apprehensive of the metropolitan centred growth approach since in many respects "full-blown metropolitan agglomeration is an appalling destination for India" (Lewis, 1964 : 217). He has, therefore, suggested a town centred approach as "towns in the 20,000-3,00,000 range offer the most congenial physical setting for a synthesis between traditional, rural and the western-urban stands of contemporary Indian culture" (Lewis, 1964 : 194). Lewis further stresses the point that it is only through town centred development policy that India can achieve its goal of organizing a "technologically progressive, politically integrated, but geographically decentralized society" (Lewis, 1964 : 217.) Lewis and Johnson seem to agree on decentralized development for India focused around towns.

The growth centre approach to regional planning has been strongly advocated in a paper on South-East Resource Region by Chandrasekhara and others. The authors of this paper feel that "agglomeration and urbanization economies are expected to accrue to investments if they are concentrated in such centres". (Chandrasekhara *et al.*, 1972 : 36-37). They lay greater emphasis on the development of the secondary sector and, therefore, tend to ignore the tertiary sector which can be equally relevant in promoting this strategy. Although the authors seem to suggest that integration of the primary and the secondary urban systems into two independent systems is logically incompatible. Misra's growth centre strategy is rather metropolitan oriented for he does not want investments to be made in non-metropolitan centres before the take-off stage. The main thrust of Misra's argument is that through growth poles and growth centres a nation can achieve maximum productivity, optimal pattern of population distribution and total integration of regions or nation's economy (Misra, 1972 : 1-22). Misra's prescription of linking up investments with take-off stage could rather lead planners into a vicious circle and development dilemma. His argument is fallacious as it overlooks the point that unless investment is pumped into a settlement it can never reach the takc-off stage. Moreover, Misra's argument is not supported by any empirical study.

The concept of growth centres has been advanced to cover rural settlements as well, and a number of micro-regional studies advocating intergrated area development focused around rural growth centres have also been undertaken. The National Institute of Community Development initiated a study on rural growth centres in Miryalguda Taluq (smallest viable administrative unit in a district) in Andhra Pradesh with a view to (i) developing methods for identifying growth centres and their hinterlands in our rural areas; and (ii) preparing a plan based on growth centres for an integrated development of the immediate study area (Sen, Wanamali *et al.*, 1971). This study discloses that even in such small administrative units a discrete three-tier hierarchy of service centres based on functional characteristics is discernible. In order to organize and integrate the economic space of this taluqa the study has proposed the establishment of two high-level service centres (one located outside the Taluq but within the District) linked to the individual villages through a chain of 4 middle order service centres and 15 lowest order service centres called "central villages". Based on this hierarchy of service centres a perspective plan for the development of Miryalguda Taluq has been proposed. This is no doubt a pioneering study, for it has for the first time explored the possibility of using the growth centre concept at such a micro level. However, some of the important problems which are likely to emerge in Miryalguda Taluq as a result of new developmental inputs have not been touched upon. A certain degree of intermediate level urbanization is likely to be generated with the growing agricultural prosperity of the Taluq consequent upon the introduction of canal irrigation. These new urban centres are also likely to function as market towns to serve as an outlet for the agricultural surpluses of the area. The perspective plan for Miryalguda as given in this study does not provide for this. There is also a reference in this study to development of "self-sufficient" villages which are located outside the influence of service centres. One would associate these self-sufficient villages with subsistence economy and as non-central function settlements. To include them in the higher level of K-4 system of hierarchy is methodologically unsound. Despite these drawbacks one cannot overlook the fact that this study on Miryalguda does provide a perspective for spatial integration at micro level through a nested system of central places.

The location of market settlements in the command area of an irrigation project has been emphasised by the Small Industries Extension Trading Institute (SIET) in its report on Integrated Development of Pochampad ayacut (Andhra Pradesh). This study has indentified 12 growth centres in the command area and would like these to "serve as market centres for industrial development in order to minimize waste of scarce resources and to optimize the use of the existing resources" (Small Industries E.T.I. Hyderabad, 1973). Bhat in his work on Karnal district has attempted to translate area development strategy into a spatial development framework" (Bhat, 1974). This economically prosperous, and topographically homoegeneous district provides a good example to discover the problem of spatial integration in an isotropic surface. Bhat has discovered wide gaps in the settlements hierarchy due to lack of functional development among the rural settlements. He has, therefore, prescribed the generation of a "three tier pattern of central places from among the rural settlements", (Bhat, 1974 : 126), for the total spatial integration of the economy in Karnal district. The assumption in this study, as in many others, is that the western system of hierarchy is considered as the standard and valid system for our socio-economic conditions as well. It would be of great theoretical value to test the validity of this basic assumption itself. At this stage one would like to postulate that the system of hierarchy develops in response to socio-economic conditions and, therefore, a uniform global system of hierarchy is not likely to be a valid concept.

Regional Planning and Urban System

This brief review of the studies and researches in regional planning does point out the fact that the scholars are more inclined to accept the nodal system of regions as a more pragmatic approach to regional planning. It is also evident that the validity of a growth-centre oriented strategy for spatial integration has been widely accepted. The role of urban centres and market towns as agents of social and economic transformation at all regional levels has been fully established and appreciated. In the light of these, it is surprising that no effort has been made so far to understand the totality of the urban system of India and the role which metropolitan settlements can play in integrating the economy spatially. Although the urban population of India has not been growing very fast, nevertheless the fact remains that the 2,641 urban settlements including 147 metropolitan settlements[1] organize and control the social and economic space of India. Because of the concentration of the major secondary and tertiary activities in and around these metropolitan nodes, their population during the last four decades has grown at a phenomenal pace and as per the 1971 census 56 per cent of the urban population is concentrated in them (Alam *et al*). In view of this growing importance of urban and metropolitan settlements we must have adequate understanding as to how effectively and in what manner the national network of urban settlements, including metropolitan, function as a system. This would enable us to appreciate the organization of our national and regional economies. One of the primary tasks, therefore, is to identify the national urban system of India and its sub-systems. This could lead to the formulation of an appropriate strategy to use the metropolitan settlements of different orders in order to accelerate intra-regional development and reduce inter-regional disparities. It is only then that we can formulate a national policy for the development of counter-magnets to arrest the growth and reduce the magnetic pull of the national metropolises. In this connection it might be worth examining the French policy to encourage the growth of regional metropolises as counter-magnets to Paris (French Embassy in U.S.A—New York, 1965) or the British policy of identifying the development regions in the United Kingdom and developing new towns within each of its nine development regions based on their respective needs (Ministry of Housing and Local Government of U.K., London, 1964).

It may be recalled that the studies on market towns have particularly highlighted the dichotomy in our rural economies and the consequent development of dualistic structure between the two sectors. This dualistic structure of economy exists even within the major metropolitan settlements and is evident from the fact that the jobs and work centres relating to high and low level of technologies coexist in such settlements with a minimal of mutual interaction. Such a situation prevents organic development of the metropolitan economy and ought to be eliminated to achieve optimal internal integration and maximum of studies relating to the dualistic structure of metropolitan economies and their impact on rural hinterlands.

REFERENCES

1. All cities with 1,00,000 + population are being treated as metropolitan cities. According to the Census of India, 1971, there are 147 such cities ranging in population from 1,00,000 to 70,00,000. These, however, can be broadly classified into three orders of settlements according to their size and functional importance.

I Order	20,00,000	Distinguished for their pronounced metropolitan character and including only the primate cities.
II Order	5,00,000 20,00,000	Including mature metropolises but lacking the characteristics of Primate cities
III Order	5,00,000	Nascent metropolises.

NOTES

Alam, Manzoor and Khan, Waheeduddin, 1972: *Metropolitan Hyderabad and Its Region—A Strategy for Development,* Asia Publishing House.

Alam, Manzoor, 1971: "A Note on the Realignment of the Urban System of Andhra Pradesh—Planning and Development of Backward Regions," *A Case Study of Rayalaseema*, Vol. I. Planning and Cooperation Department, Government of Andhra Pradesh, Hyderabad, pp. 499-501.

Alam, S. M. Mohan, Ram and Gopi, K.N.: Trends and Patterns of Metropolitan Development in India, *Occasional Paper No. 3*, Centre for Urban Research, O.U.

Berry, Brian J.L., 1969: "Policy Implication of an Urban Location Model for the Kanpur Region," pp. 203-19 in [Desai *et al.* (Ed.)]: *Regional Perspective of Industrial and Urban Growth (The Case of Kanpur).*

Berry, Brian J.L., 1966: *Essays on Commodity Flows and the Spatial Structure of the Indian Economy*, Chicago: University of Chicago, Department of Geography Research Paper No. 111.

Berry, Brian J.L., 1971: "City Size and Economic Development", p. 122 in Leo Jakobson & Ved Prakash (Ed.): *Urbanization and National Development.*

Bhat, L.S., 1972: *Regional Planning in India,* Statistical Publishing Society, Calcutta.

Bhat L.S., 1974: *Central Place Hierarchy for A Developing Agricultural Region* (Mimeographed), Delhi, pp. 126.

Calcutta Metropolitan Planning Organisation, 1966: *Regional Planning for West Bangal,* Government of West Bengal, Calcutta, pp. 62.

Chandrasekhara, C.S. *et al.,* 1972: "The Role of Growth Foci—Regional Development Strategy", pp. 363-64 in (Misra *et al.* (Ed.): *Urban Systems and Rural Development,* Part I, Mysore.

Chandrasekhara, C.S. *et al.,* 1972: "The Role of Growth Foci-Regional Development Strategy", pp. 36-70 in *Urban Systems and Rural Development'* edited by Misra, Mahadev and Jayashankar, Prasaranga, University of Mysore.

Chandrasekhara, C.S.; Mathur, G.D.; and Sundaram, K.V., 1972: "The Role of Growth Foci in Regional Development Strategy", pp. 36-37 (in Misra *et al.,* Ed.): *Urban Systems and Rural Development,* Mysore.

Christaller, W., 1966: *Central Places in Southern Germany,* Translated by C.W. Baskari, Prentice Hall, New Jersey.

Delhi Development Authority, 1962: *Master Plan for Delhi,* Delhi.

Desai P.B. *et al., (Ed.),* 1969: *Regional Perspective of Industrial and Urban Growth—The Growth of Kanpur,* Macmillan.

Deshpande, C.D. 1948: *Western India—Regional Geography,* Dharwar.

French Embassy in USA—New York 1965: *France: Town and Country Environment Planning.*

Gupta, P. Sen and Sdasyuk, Galina, 1968: Economic Regionalisation of India, Problems and Approaches—*Census of India 1961*, Monograph, New Delhi, p. ii, 25-26.

Johnson, E.A. 1972: "The Integration of *Agrarian*, Commercial and Industrial Activities in Functional Economic Area," pp. 60-65 in (NCAER: *Market Towns and Spatial Development*).

Johnson, E.A.J.: *The Integration of Industrial and Agrarian Development in Regional Planning,* pp. 171-190.

Jakobson, Leo and Prakash, Ved 1966-67: "Urbanization and Regional Planning in India," *Urban Affairs Quarterly,* Vol. 1966-67, pp. 3665.

Learmonth, A.T.A. *et al.*, 1962: *Mysore State Regional Synthesis,* Vol. II, Asia Publishing House, Bombay.

Lewis John, P., 1964: *Quiet Crisis in India,* Anchor Books Edition, pp. 194, 217.

Ministry of Housing and Local Government, U.K.—London 1964: *The South-East Study,* 1961-1981, London.

Misra, R.P. *et al.*, (Ed.) 1969: *Regional Planning—Concepts, Techniques, Policies and Case Studies.* The University of Mysore, Prasaranga.

Misra, R.P.: "Strategies for Regional Development," pp. 356-359 in *Regional Planning,* Edited by R.P. Misra.

Misra, R.P. 1972: "Growth Pole Strategy," pp. 1-22 in Misra *et al.* (Ed.), *Urban Systems and Rural Development,* Mysore.

National Council of Applied Economic Research, 1965: *Market Towns and Spatial Development in India,* New Delhi.

National Council of Applied Economic Research (NCAER), 1972: *Market Towns and Spatial Development in India,* New Delhi.

Perroux, Francois, 1950: "Economic Space, Theory and Application," *Quarterly Journal of Economics* (64), pp. 90-97.

Planning Commission, India, 1952: *The First Five Year Plan,* Government of India Press, New Delhi, p. 20.

Planning Commission, India, 1961: *The Third Five Year Plan,* Government of India Press, New Delhi, p. 689.

Planning Commission, Government of India New Delhi, 1967: *Traffic and Transportation Problems in Metropolitan Cities—Interim Report,* New Delhi, p. 11.

Rao, V.L.S.P. and Bhat, L.S.: *Regional Planning in Mysore—The Need for Readjustment of District Boundaries,* Indian Statistical Institute, 1960.

Reed Wallace, E., 1969: "Indian Commercial Flows—Hierarchy of Regions and Regional Planning," pp. 145-171 in Misra R.P. (Ed.), *Regional Planning.*

Sen, L.K., Wanamali, S. *et al.*, 1971: *Planning Rural Growth Centres for Integrated Area Development—A Study of Miryalguda Taluqa*, National Institute of Community Development, Hyderabad.

Small Industries Extension Training Institute, Hyderabad, 1973: *Integrated Development of Pochampad Ayacut—Report II* (Mimeographed) Hyderabad.

Town and Country Planning Organisation, 1974: *National Urbanisation Policy—An Approach,* Ministry of Works and Housing, Government of India (Mimeographed November), p. 17, 27.

Town and Country Planning Organisation, 1968: *South East Resource Regional Plan—Preliminary Report.* Government of India, Ministry of Housing and Urban Development, New Delhi.

Town and Country Planning Organisation, 1968: *South-East Resource Regional Plan—Preliminary Report.* (Mimeographed), pp. 4-36. Delhi.

Wanamali, S., 1970: *Regional Planning for Social Facilities, National Institute of Community Development, Hyderabad.*

8

Metropolitan Dominance Atrophies Rural-Urban Integration

The dominance of urban culture by metropolitan cities i.e. cities with more than one million population is a global phenomenon but it is far more marked in the developing countries, where they also exhibit parasitical tendencies by sucking in all developmental activities. The behaviour of metropolitan culture in the developing countries is epitomized in India which carries within its canvas highly developed urban areas. High order secondary and tertiary functions such as sophisticated large scale consumer goods, industries, major banking and insurance services, political, administrative functions of capital cities, administrative headquarters of corporate sector, tertiary education and research, tend to hyper concentrate in these metropolitan cities. As a consequence they emerge as primate cities atrophying the development of other urban centres within their zones of influence. The emergence of such dominant metropolitan cities is notably marked in India both at the national and State levels.

Since metropolitan cities in India are located in diverse geographical areas with varying production specialization they functionally complement each other. They are consequently interdependent. As a result strong inter-metropolitan trade, rail, road, air and telecom linkages have been developed. Because of their functional character metropolitan cities are both economic and demographic nodes. They are high income generating centres and excellent markets for consumer goods. They also attract large number of immigrants most of whom can neither be provided with jobs nor shelter. Because of their high order functional concentration metropolitan cities breed both extreme affluence and acute poverty.

Published in *IASSI Quarterly,* Vol. 10, No. 1, 1991, pp. 47-59.

In view of their nodal importance in industrial, commercial, banking, educational, political and administrative development of the country they also emerge as centres of innovation and transmit powerful developmental impulses to their respective hinterlands. As such they tend to integrate the economy of their hinterlands and draw them into the vortex of the national economic system. However, the desired degree of urban-rural integration is not achieved because of the parasitical tendencies of such cities and due to low quality or absence of infrastructure facilities in the villages of India.

In this chapter it is proposed to outline the emergence of the national metropolitan system of India, analyse the phenomenon of metropolitan dominance at the national and State levels and examine the nature and character of spatial integration of the metropolitan cities with their immediate rural hinterlands.

Metropolitan Dominance and National Metropolitan System

The urban population of India during the decade 1971-81 registered a sharp rise of 43 per cent from 109 to 156.2 million. This was largely due to accelerated increase in the population of Class I cities of India which include all urban settlements with population of 1,00,000 and above. These settlements which constituted only 5.6 and 6.7 per cent of the total urban settlements in 1971 and 1981 respectively contained a disproportionately large proportion of the total urban population (49 and 60% respectively). During the last 80 years the growth of population in Class I cities has been phenomenal, increasing from a mere 22 per cent of the total urban population in 1901, to over 60 per cent in 1981. The 216 Class I cities in 1981 contained 14 per cent of the total national population. This strong concentration of population in a small number of settlements has been largely due to clustering of high income generating activities with strong multiplier effect—economic, administrative, political, social, cultural, and educational functions, etc.,—in these settlements, which enhanced their attractiveness to the labour force from smaller towns and rural settlements. Consequently the population of smaller urban settlements was decimated during the period 1901-1981. In 1901 nearly 60 per cent of India's urban population lived in towns with less than 25,000 population. By 1981, their share had declined to a mere 15.6 per cent.[1]

The most notable characteristic of the growth of population in Class I cities is their overwhelming concentration in the metropolitan cities i.e. cities with population exceeding one million. In 1981, India had 12 such cities. These metropolitan cities together claimed 44.6 per cent of the total population of Class I towns in 1981. This is rather reflective of unhealthy parasitical growth tendencies in the urbanization process of India. It may be further observed that the metropolitan population tends to concentrate more and more in the multimillion national metropolises of Bombay, Calcutta, Delhi and Madras. Their shares of population among the million cities has increased phenomenally from 28 per cent in 1961 to over 65 per cent in 1981. These four cities thus constitute the real urban magnets of India. It is in these and the other million-cities, most of whom happen to be state capitals, that administrative, economic and political power of India is firmly entrenched.

The national urban system of India is dominated by the four national metropolises of Delhi, Bombay, Calcutta and Madras as identified by Alam and Geeta (1987) and later by the National Commission on Urbanization (1988). Delhi is the capital city of India, the other three are sea ports of national importance commanding the foreign trade of Western, Eastern and Southern India. These four national metropolises constitute the nerve centres of the national economic system. Within the urban systems of the country the supremacy of the four national metropolises is unchallenged. These four metropolises alone have nearly one-third of the total Class I cities population, nearly one-fifth of the urban population and their average size between 1961 and 1981 has increased almost twofold from 2.8 to 4.93 million. Highlighting the primacy of these national metropolises, Prakash Rao points out that "based on population size, metropolitan functional index, airline connectivity and the number of intercity flight connections per week, Bombay, Calcutta, Delhi and Madras are found to dominate the urban system –78 per cent of the industrial licences are concentrated in Bombay, Calcutta Delhi and Madras" (1983, pp. 108-109). The primacy of these cities within their respective metropolitan regions is demonstrated by their high 3 city indices of primacy (1981) Calcutta: 13.7; Bombay: 2.7; Madras: 2.3; Delhi: 2.5.[2]

Dominance of National and Regional Metropolises

The dominance of the national and regional metropolises over the economy of the country is evident from the fact that nine million cities (1971) together have nearly one-fourth of the total working population concentrated in them. The concentration in the productive and profitable sectors of 'Manufacturing other than household', 'trade and commerce', and 'transport and communication' are more marked. The four national metropolises by themselves, and the other million-cities which are State capitals, together contribute 30.7 and 38.3 per cent respectively of the total urban workforce in large scale manufacturing, 19.5 and 26.7 per cent respectively in construction, 22.5 and 29.1 per cent respectively in trade and commerce, 23.9 and 31.0 per cent in transport and communication; and 20.13 and 28.31 per cent in other services (Census of India, 1971). Furthermore, in 1975, 9 million-cities of India contained 34 per cent of the total scheduled banks of the country which claimed 70 and 75 per cent respectively of the total deposits and advances.

Table 8.1 : Distribution of Deposits and Advances of Scheduled Commercial Banks in 9 Million-Cities, December 1975

Name of City	*No. of Offices*	*Deposits*	*Advances*
1. Delhi	594	128,001	118,659
2. Calcutta	490	134,649	122,666
3. Kanpur	112	14,321	7,669
4. Ahmedabad	233	21,335	24,196
5. Bombay	729	217,078	203,666
6. Hyderabad	203	21,040	14,991
7. Bangalore	290	24,471	33,290
8. Madras	351	43,580	57,687
9. Poona (D)	138	15854	11,861
All India	20050	1,371,073	1,007,345
All metropolitan	6784	943,534	800,911
Percent of total India	34	70	75

Source: Banking Statistics—Volume of Basic Statistical Returns, December 1975.

The intensity of concentration of economic activities in these million-cities is evident from the Table 8.1. This is further stressed by the fact that these cities together contributed in 1974-75 over 30 per cent of the total food trade in India, and 50 per cent of total manufacturing Table 8.2.

Most of the quaternary functions are also concentrated in these metropolitan cities. For instance, a second order metropolitan settlement like Hyderabad City, which is the capital of Andhra Pradesh and its political, administrative and judicial headquarters, has six

Table 8.2 : Contribution of large cities towards trade in India (1974-75) in percentage

Name of City	Food products	Food material from primary	Raw Fuel	Coal Commodity	Agricultural material	Industrial products
1. Calcutta	9.87	5.69	4.07	3.41	6.08	18.20
2. Greater Bombay	9.85	2.36	2.95	12.27	9.13	13.13
3. Delhi	5.25	0.69	3.44	1.44	4.25	5.90
4. Madras	4.08	5.98	2.49	4.11	4.03	5.16
5. Hyderabad	2.20	0.25	9.24	0.76	2.03	2.09
6. Ahmedabad	0.59	0.32	0.77	0.25	0.90	1.26
7. Bangalore	1.81	0.14	0.64	0.53	1.28	1.76
8. Kanpur	0.93	0.43	1.74	2.66	1.06	2.38
9. Poona	1.25	3.39	0.36	1.04	1.04	0.69
Total	35.83	19.25	25.70	26.47	29.80	50.57

Source: Mooins Raza and Yash Aggarwal: *Transport Geography of India.* Concept Publishing House, Delhi, p. 171.

universities, a large number of research institutes of national and international importance, headquarters of the Andhra Bank and the State Bank of Hyderabad and regional headquarters of the Andhra Bank and the State Bank of Hyderabad and regional headquarters of Reserve Bank of India and of most of the nationalized banks. It has also the regional sales office of a number of corporate sector agencies. With this concentration of high order tertiary-quaternary functions, Hyderabad will continue to be both primate and parasitic, for it is linked more strongly with large urban centres outside the State than with the settlements in its own region. The present national policy seems to concentrate the economic power in these cities and is strongly supported by its system of air services and super fast train linkages. Corroborating the concentration of jobs in the million-cities Rakesh Mohan points out that "these cities attract factory jobs and those in the transport and tertiary sectors and particularly government employment which is significant at 5 per cent level regression. This obviously implies that Central Government jobs are concentrated in large cities and they do have multiplier effect" (1983).

Consequent upon this policy of the Union and State Governments to concentrate investments and multiply job opportunities in these million-cities, it is least surprising that the bulk of the migrants are also attracted to the four national metropolises, which also claim most of the highly educated migrants and those employed in superior positions in various services. The movement of migrants is directly related to the availability of jobs in them, but the volume of influx invariably exceeds the capacity of the city to absorb. Consequently the migrants constitute a high proportion of the population of metropolitan cities (Table 8.3).

Table 8.3 : Share of Migrants to Total Population of the Million-Cities of India, 1971

City	*Total population*	*Total in migrants*	*Percentage of inmigrants to total population*
(1)	(2)	(3)	(4)
1. Calcutta	7,081,382	2,276,985	32.28
2. Greater Bombay	5,978,575	3,395,095	56.86
3. Delhi	3,647,023	1,886,285	51.86
4. Madras	3,19,930	786,545	24.28
5. Hyderabad	1,796,339	409,980	22.82
6. Ahmedabad	1,741,522	769,780	44.20
7. Bangalore	1,658,779	624,215	37.74
8. Kanpur	1,275,242	471,360	36.96
9. Poona	1,135,034	533,735	47.02

Source: B.K. Roy: 'Internal Migration in India', Transaction of Institute of Indian Geographers, Vol. 2, No. 1, January 1980, Department of Geography, Poona University, p. 37.

The lower order Class I cities lack this magnetic quality because of their low level of economic development and weak economic base.

For want of data it has not been possible to examine the migrational patterns among all the Class I cities of India. A case study of two States of Maharashtra and Andhra Pradesh, which have primate city distribution systems, reveals that migrational flows are significantly influenced by the pull of the primate cities. Metropolitan Bombay, being located at the apex of one of the macro metropolitan systems of India, viz., the Bombay system, possesses a much higher degree of primacy than metropolitan Hyderabad which is located at the apex of one of the sub-systems within the Bombay system. The volume of immigration in Bombay during 1961-71 exceeded the total volume of immigration in the whole State of Andhra Pradesh, in the corresponding period. The number of immigrants in metropolitan Bombay is approximately 67 per cent of total immigrant workers in all the metropolitan cities of Maharashtra. The role of Bombay in capturing the bulk of the flow of migrant workers in both Maharashtra and the macro metropolitan system of Bombay is reflective of its role as the primate city of that system (Table 8.4).

The primacy of Hyderabad in the settlement system of Andhra Pradesh, though not as pronounced as that of Bombay is nonetheless well marked. It can be observed from Table 8.5, that Hyderabad attracted nearly one-third of the total migrants to Andhra Pradesh in 1971 and approximately fifty per cent of the highly educated and technically qualified migrants. It is thus obvious that in both the primate cities, Bombay and Hyderabad, there is a hyper concentration of migrants employed in senior professional and managerial cadres.

By virtue of rapid transit facilities, the hold of the metropolises on the production, distribution and consumption of the national economy is almost total. This is substantiated by the fact that the prices of poultry products in Hyderabad city are determined by the consumer demand in Bombay and the prices of such seasonal fruits and grapes, mangoes, oranges etc., are controlled by the consumer demand in the four national metropolises of the country. Similarly it has been noticed that the urban markets of Warangal in Andhra Pradesh and Mysore in Karnataka receive a significant portion of their vegetable supplies from the metropolitan cities of Hyderabad and Bangalore respectively. This pattern of economic interaction retards the economic development of the rural hinterland of non-metropolitan settlements and consequently distorts the pattern of economic development.

Metropolitan Dominance and Rural-Urban Integration

In order to appreciate correctly the urban-rural integration at the micro level we shall examine it in the light of a comprehensive study executed in the rural hinterland of metropolitan Hyderabad (Alam and Khan, 1972). This study examined the metropolitan-hinterland relationship based on certain key variables viz. transport linkages, telephone system, water and electricity supply system, supply of consumer goods to the metropolis from the region, and reflective variables which are mainly social and demographic. The Hyderabad study clearly highlights the fact that metropolitan impact brings about structural changes in the economy of its immediate rural hinterland

Table 8.4 : Maharashtra State: Cumulative Percentage Distribution of Migrants into Metropolitan and other Class I Settlements by High Level of Education and Services, 1971

Metropolitan settlements and Class I towns	Metropolitan Population	Total migrants	Total literate migrants	Level of education		Level of education		Higher order services	
				Graduate migrants	Post graduate migrants	Technically qualified & professional migrants	Professional & Technically related workers	Adminis-trative & executive workers	Production & related workers
(1)	(2)	(3)	(4)	(5)	(6)	(7)	(8)	(9)	(10)
Greater Bombay	53.69	59.69	59.82	59.04	59.98	55.93	59.70	52.21	70.16
Poona	63.88	69.07	69.95	71.65	72.10	70.08	68.03	75.05	77.46
Nagpur	72.25	75.08	75.93	79.14	82.05	77.47	73.69	80.71	82.16
Sholapur	75.83	77.20	77.59	80.43	83.07	79.06	75.34	81.41	84.08
Ulhasnagar	79.39	80.98	81.58	84.74	85.77	82.58	79.89	82.58	87.65
Nasik	81.83	83.27	83.88	86.53	87.13	84.69	82.18	86.20	88.95
Kolhapur	84.24	85.09	85.63	88.38	88.28	86.52	84.34	87.20	89.98
Thana	86.10	87.61	88.25	91.08	90.71	88.77	86.84	88.18	92.69
Sangli	87.92	89.29	89.70	91.97	91.32	89.91	88.64	88.88	93.69
Amaravati	89.66	90.91	91.38	93.53	98.81	91.69	90.55	89.33	94.46
Malegaon	91.38	92.10	92.11	93.79	93.96	91.98	91.14	89.53	95.88
Akola	92.89	93.51	94.68	95.22	93.74	93.74	92.89	89.90	96.67
Aurangabad	94.37	94.92	95.00	96.77	97.44	95.69	94.92	92.42	97.20
Ahmednagar	95.70	96.08	96.30	97.66	8.05	96.93	96.04	98.90	97.76
Dhulia	96.94	97.18	97.37	98.23	98.47	97.50	96.97	91.14	98.33
Nanded	98.08	98.10	98.14	98.97	99.03	98.28	98.15	99.47	98.97
Jalgaon	99.06	99.07	99.08	99.58	99.69	99.25	99.32	99.83	99.36
Bhushawal	100.00	100.00	100.00	100.00	100.00	100.00	100.00	100.00	100.00

Source: Compiled from Census of India 1971, Part I-D, Table III-D.

Table 8.5: Andhra Pradesh: Cumulative Percentage Distribution of Migrants into Metropolitan and other Class I Settlements by High Level of Education and Services, 1971

Metropolitan settlement and class I towns	Metropolitan Population	Total Migrants	Total Literate Migrants	Level of education		Level of education		Higher order services	
				Graduate Migrants	Post graduates Migrants	Technically Qualified & Professional Migrants	Professional & Technically related workers	Administrative & Executive workers	Production & related workers
(1)	(2)	(3)	(4)	(5)	(6)	(7)	(8)	(9)	(10)
Hyderabad	44.21	29.35	32.76	54.11	55.22	43.86	38.48	71.78	25.23
Visakhapatnam	53.16	41.15	45.00	65.53	66.20	58.69	49.00	85.04	38.53
Vijayawada	61.64	53.86	58.05	72.78	72.57	66.33	59.78	89.05	52.76
Guntur	68.29	62.68	66.03	79.06	79.18	73.89	67.53	91.77	65.26
Warangal	73.39	66.92	69.37	81.66	82.04	77.65	71.78	92.66	69.32
Rajahmundry	78.04	73.36	75.29	85.25	85.44	80.73	76.64	93.95	76.67
Kakinada	82.08	78.07	80.17	88.62	88.23	85.87	81.24	95.19	80.17
Kurnool	85.44	81.41	83.57	90.90	90.23	89.77	85.24	96.08	92.69
Nellore	88.73	85.44	87.69	92.92	91.99	91.79	86.93	96.92	860.27
Eluru	91.86	89.24	91.29	95.13	93.81	94.35	91.31	97.73	89.94
Nizamabad	94.73	92.91	93.36	96.18	94.90	95.63	93.69	98.48	94.44
Machilipatnam	97.47	96.51	96.91	98.51	98.36	98.80	97.03	99.28	97.09
Tenali	100.00	100.00	100.00	100.00	100.00	100.00	100.00	100.00	100.00

Source: Compiled from Census of India 1971, Part II-D, Table III-D.

which responds to the consumer demands of not only its own metropolitan market but also to the demands generated in other metropolitan cities as well. As for instance poultry farming and grape culture were taken up in Hyderabad on a small scale in the early sixties after the formation of Andhra Pradesh in 1956. By mid sixties they emerged as major economic activities not only catering to the consumer demands in metropolitan Hyderabad but were also exported extensively to Bombay, Calcutta, Delhi, and Madras (Alam and Khan, 1972, p. 42).

The integration of the hinterland economy with the metropolis is also demonstrated by the supply of such perishable commodities of daily needs as milk, vegetables, meat etc. In a detailed study of the demand-supply position with regard to vegetables, milk etc. from the hinterland of Hyderabad it was found in 1966 that the metropolitan community of Hyderabad received most of its supplies from within a radius of 40 miles or 60 km. (Alam and Khan, 1972). With the availability of refrigeration facilities the radius of milk supply increased to even 200 km. The impact of metropolis on its hinterland can also be measured by the expansion of the metropolitan network of suburban bus and train services, the spread of metropolitan telephone, electricity, water supply system into the hinterland. All these variables suggest an intense degree of spatial integration of the metropolitan economy of Hyderabad with its rural hinterland within a radius of 25-30 miles (40-48 km). However, the entire geographical space is not spatially integrated for the influence of Hyderabad on its hinterland extends to a radius of 50-60 miles (80-96 km). This is largely due to poor infrastructure facilities in the rural hinterland. The degree of integration declines with the distance away from the metropolis as well as from the main highways. In the light of the Hyderabad study it can be generalized that :

(1) The lightest intensity of metropolitan-hinterland integration is accomplished within a radius of 25-30 miles or 40-48 km. Within this radius every economic activity of the rural hinterland is determined by the consumer demands in the metropolis. The rural economy gets thoroughly modernized and benefits fully from the high income, growing metropolitan market; and

(2) Immediately outside of the 25-30 miles (40-48 km) radius, villages with high intensity range, having strong daily

interaction with the metropolis, are confined to a 5 miles or 8 km wide corridor along the main highways.

Of late the process of rural-urban integration is being strongly promoted and reinforced by the television network particularly in the electrified villages. Most of the villages within a radius of 100 km of metropolitan Hyderabad are electrified and are distinctly under its magnetic pull. The integration of hinterland-metropolitan economy is also amply demonstrated by the rising rural income, their diversified commercial economic activities in response to demands in the national metropolitan market and the emergence of a network of periodic markets which act as intermediary settlements between the rural hinterland and metropolitan settlements. They reflect clearly the degree of interaction metropolitan settlements have developed with the interior of their respective rural hinterlands despite poorly developed infrastructure facilities.

In the light of the aforesaid discussion it may be observed that metropolitan dominance has considerably distorted the economic system of India. It has prevented the total integration of the rural economy with the urban system. Integration of the rural economy with the metropolitan market has been achieved either completely or partially, within the metropolitan zones of influence only. The process of rural-urban integration will have to be accelerated if the distortions in the national economic system are to be eliminated. This can be achieved by a phased redistribution of the tertiary and secondary activities from the metropolitan cities to lower order urban settlements and a total revamping of the infrastructure facilities in rural India.

Conclusion

India is among the ancient urbanized civilizations of the world but the continuity in the historical process of its urban development was broken by the intrusion of the colonial factor which dominated the economy and polity of the country for nearly two centuries. This precluded the smooth transition of India's economy from pre- to post-industrial era and introduced new and alien elements to its urban mosaic. The dominance of the colonial system ceased with the advent of Independence. The economy and polity of the country has radically transformed since then introducing innovative and modern elements into the country's economic and urbanization processes.

The rapidly transforming economy of the country has altered the colonial bi-nodal metropolitan system to a multinodal system. However, the politico-economic system that has emerged since Independence has continued the colonial tradition of concentrating the developmental inputs into a few large-sized metropolitan nodes which are accentuating regional disparities and preventing the articulation of a meaningful system of settlement hierarchy. This hyper-concentration of functions in large metropolitan cities is also noticeable at the State level. It has atrophied the development of rural hinterlands and their full integration into the national economic system. This anomaly can be rectified through a proper investment strategy to boost development of lower order urban settlements; a location strategy to shift high order tertiary and secondary functions from the primate cities; minimization of wage differentials between the metropolis and settlements of lower order, and a strategy to foster the growth of a well articulated system of hierarchy of settlements by functions and by revolutionizing the infrastructure facilities of rural areas across the country. Otherwise, atrophied development of the system of cities in India cannot be avoided and rural India will not be fully brought into the vortex of the national economic system. The latter will continue to be deprived of developmental benefits due to metropolitan dominance.

A Note on Rural-Urban Distribution, 1991

Since the completion of the chapter, provisional data for rural-urban distribution at the Census of 1991 have become available (Paper-2 of 1991, Series-I, Census of 1991).

In the 1991 Census, 4,689 places were identified as towns as against 4,029 in 1981. The number of 'urban agglomerations' increased from 276 to 381. The total urban population in 1991 was 217.2 million, accounting for 25.72 per cent of the total population of the country, the corresponding figures for 1981 being 159.5 million and 23.34 per cent respectively. The decennial growth of urban population, which was 46.14 per cent during 1971-81, was 36.19 per cent during 1981-91. The annual exponential rate of growth during the two periods was 3.83 and 3.09 per cent and the annual rate of gain as percentage of urban population was 1.72 and 1.02 per cent, respectively.

The distribution of the urban population as between urban agglomerations/town in different size-classes in 1991 was as follows:

	Population (million)	*Percent*
Class I (100,000 and above)	139.73	64.89
Class II (50,000—99,999)	23.60	10.96
Class III (20,000—49,999)	28.71	13.33
Class IV (10,000—19,999)	17.00	7.89
Class V (5000-9999)	5.64	2.62
Class VI (less than 5000)	0.66	0.31

In 1991, 50.57 per cent of the population of Class I cities lived in 23 metropolitan urban agglomeration/cities with a population of more than a million each.

The population of urban agglomerations of more than a million increased from 18.1 million in 1961 and 27.83 million in 1971 to 42.12 million in 1981 and to 70.66 million in 1991, the decadal rates of increase in population being 53.75 per cent during 1961-71, 51.35 per cent during 1971-81, and 67.76 per cent during 1981-91.

The total population of the four largest urban agglomerations recorded at the Censuses of 1951, 1961, 1971, 1981 and 1991 was as follows:

	1951	*1961*	*1971*	*1981*	*1991*
Greater Bombay	3.0	4.15	6.0	8.24	12.57
Calcutta	4.67	5.98	7.42	9.19	10.92
Delhi	1.44	2.36	3.65	5.73	8.28
Madras	1.54	1.94	3.17	4.28	5.36

REFERENCES

1. Since figures for 1991 were not officially available at the time of preparation of this chpater they have not been discussed in this chpater. The provisional figures more or less reaffirm the dominance of metropolitan cities.
2. City index of primary is determined by dividing the population of their first ranked city by the cumulative population of next two ranked cities in the region. It is an index of population concentration and domination of the primate city in the region.

9

Distortions in Settlement System of India

Introduction

The settlement system of a country develops in response to its politico-economic system and level of economic development, and tends to organize integration of the agrarian sector with the urban and industrial sectors. The existence of dualism in the economic structure of India, break in the historical continuity of its evolving settlement system caused due to political factors, wide inter-regional disparity in levels of development, inadequacy of linkages between the urban and their surrounding rural areas and consequent malfunctioning of the supply and distribution system, dysfunctional development of urban settlements, haphazard development of services in the urban and rural settlements, and misconceived developmental strategies and policies of private and public sectors tend to disrupt and distort the evolution of the settlement system and thereby prevent spatial integration and optimization of the economy and proper articulation of settlement hierarchy. The settlement system is deemed to be distorted (1) if the distribution is marked by a significant clustering of large sized settlements in pockets or corridors of development, (2) if such settlements are disproportionately more in numbers, and (3) if the inter-settlement distance range of such settlements is much less compared to the settlements in the lower size range. These are symptomatic of weakness in linkages in the middle and lower order of the urban settlements implying thereby a breakdown of the information system and, therefore, they cease to function as effective links in a chain of settlement system and tend to become ineffective

Published in *Geographical Review of India,* Vol. 42, No. 4, December 1981, pp. 305-322.

centres of urban activities. It is proposed to highlight in this chpater some of the key factors distorting the evolution of settlement systems of India.

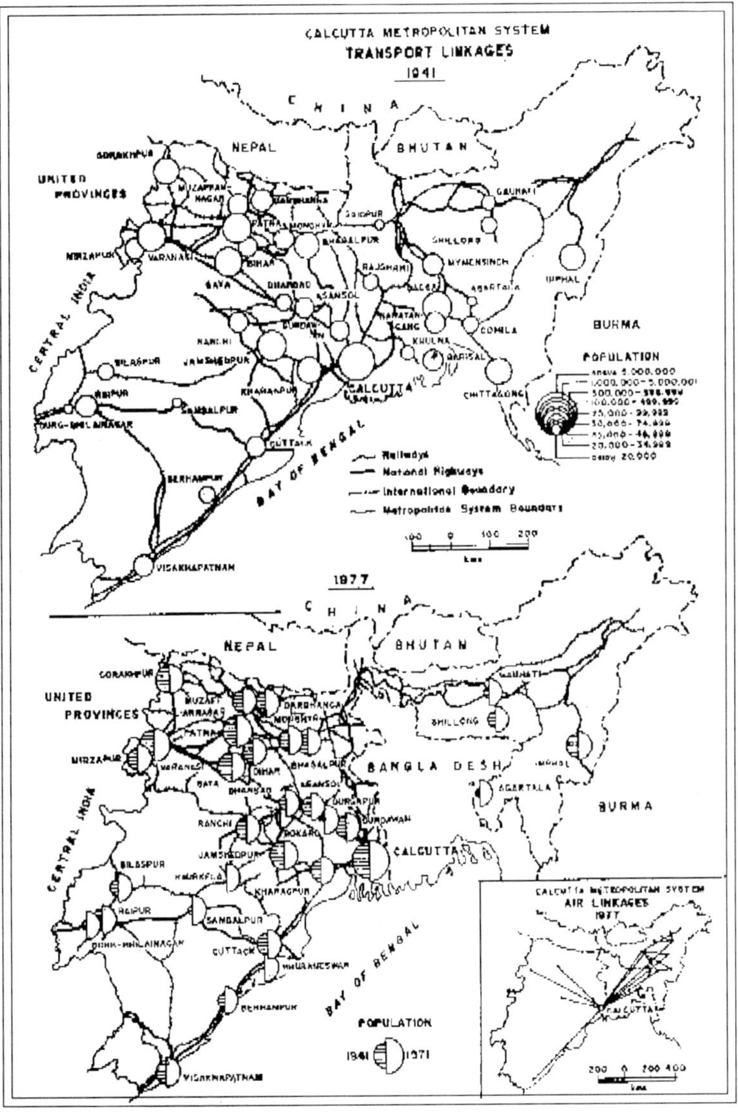

Fig. 9.1 : Transport Linkages of Calcutta Metropolitan System, 1941

Political and Historical Factors

The political and historical factors are among the most significant elements influencing the development of a country's settlement system. After the Second World War the changes in the international boundaries of India, and in the internal boundaries of its States have markedly influenced the patterning of its settlement system. The partition of India and its division into two sovereign countries of India and Pakistan disrupted the continuity in the evolution of the settlement systems of India. Although disruption had occurred on both the flanks of India, i.e. the west and the east, the effect has been maximum on the eastern wing since a major portion of the eastern settlement system, focused on the port of Calcutta, was politically and economically separated from its hinterland. The territory of Bangladesh, which was earlier known as East Pakistan, and its capital city Dacca, were part of the Calcutta settlement system. It was through this territory and its network of roadways, waterways, railways, that the north-eastern part of India was linked with Calcutta for the movement of people and goods. The removal of this territory from the sphere of influence of Calcutta constricted the linkage of Calcutta to the north-eastern periphery of its system either by air or through a narrow lane of roadways and railways from northern West Bengal to Assam (Fig. 9.1). The truncation of the eastern settlement system of India disturbed the process of spatial integration and the entire settlement system in the north-eastern periphery was placed in a state of flux. The north-eastern periphery has to look for a new regional focus after the political separation of Dacca. Gauhati is emerging as a regional centre for the entire north-eastern region but this cannot be accomplished unless the road network is realigned to converge on Gauhati. In order to reinforce and accelerate this process the capital cities of each of the States of this region will have to be linked with Gauhati through network of roadways, railways and airways. Till this linkage is established spatial integration of the economy of the north-east region cannot be achieved and the distortions which have appeared in the settlement system of this region through the truncation of the Calcutta settlement system cannot be rectified. (*see* Table 9.1)

The settlement systems are also disturbed and consequently distorted due to changes in the internal political boundaries of States or provinces within a country. Prior to its independence India was politically divided into Princely India and British India and each gave rise to its own settlement systems with little interaction between the

Table 9.1 : Calcutta Settlement System, Number of Settlements and Inter-settlement Distance by Size Range (1971)

	Size Range of Urban Settlement							
	20,00,000	*10,00,000 to 1,99,999*	*5,00,000 to 9,99,999*	*1,00,000 to 4,99,999*	*75,000 to 99,999*	*50,000 to 74,999*	*35,000 to 49,999*	*20,000 to 34,999*
No of Towns	1	—	1	30	12	25	37	88
Inter-town distance in km	—	—	—	231.42	318.66	249.04	188.42	159.83

two systems (Alam, Gopi and Parthasarathy, 1978). The abolition of princely states and reorganization of the States of India on linguistic basis in 1956 lent new dimensions to the development of settlement systems in India. The State of Rajasthan includes among others the erstwhile princely states of Jaipur, Jodhpur and Udaipur. These states developed their respective settlement systems focused around their respective capital cities which had a highly polarized and primate pattern of development, being the seats of supreme political and administrative power and centre for key economic activities. The abolition of these feudal states and their merger into a single State of Rajasthan and certainly ended their political entity, but not their cultural distinctiveness and polarized development of their principal urban nuclei which were also their capital cities. This poly-nucleated development of the settlement system of Rajasthan does not permit the degree of spatial integration expected in a mono-nucleated hierarchical pattern of settlement system (Fig. 9.2). Another instance of the disturbance in the settlement system of India has been when due to political decision settlements belonging to a particular system are realigned to a new economic, political and administrative nucleus. This has happened particularly in the State of Andhra Pradesh of which Hyderabad City is the capital. Hyderabad city was the capital of erstwhile multilingual state of Hyderabad. On the reorganization of States in 1956, Hyderabad became the capital of a monolingual Telugu speaking State. The Telugu speaking areas and their settlements which for a couple of centuries were aligned to the Madras Metropolitan System were alienated and realigned to the Hyderabad Metropolitan System. In such a situation political control and linguistic homogeneity may help political, administrative and cultural integration hut economic integration is difficult to accomplish particularly when the settlements of the realigned regions were earlier economically linked with a more dominant metropolitan city [Alam, 1976) [Fig. 9.3(a) and 9.3(b)].

Colonial Urbanization and Distortions in the Settlement Systems

The politico-economic system of the colonial period has stimulated the rise of primate cities which have in them a concentration of high order political, administrative, economic, cultural, educational and recreational functions. This particular pattern of development leads to a concentration of jobs of diverse types and multiple avenues of employment in a single city which eventually emerges as primate city overshadowing, functionally and demographically all other urban settlements in the State/ country. This is further confirmed by the two city indices of primacy of primate cities in certain selected countries (U.N.O., 1977).

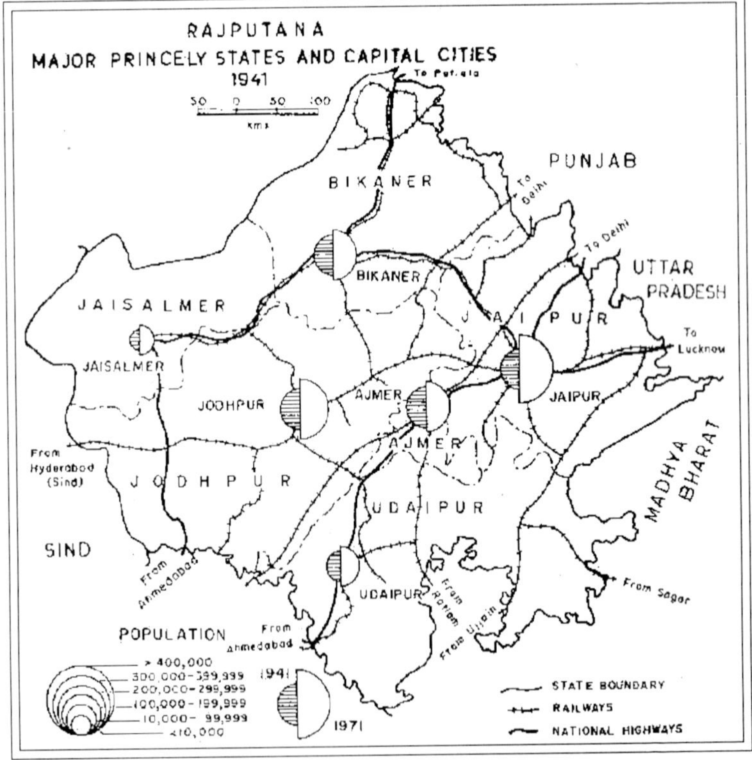

Fig. 9.2 : Rajputana : Major Princely States and Capital Cities

Sau Paulo (Brazil) 1.48; Buenos Aires (Argentina) 10.45; Lagos (Nigeria) 1.74; Nairobi (Kenya) 2.09; Rangoon (Burma) 3.79; Jakarta (Indonesia) 2.94; Colombo (Sri Lanka) 3.65; Calcutta (India within the Calcutta System) 11.59.

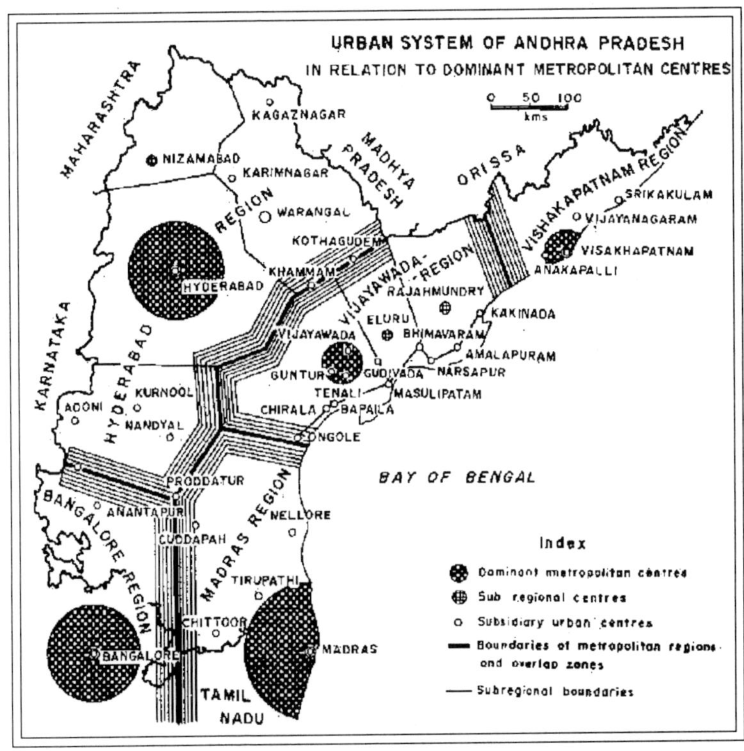

Fig. 9.3(a) : Urban System of Andhra Pradesh

The imposition of colonial economy on India after 1857 disrupted the established fabric of Indian economy and disturbed its settlement system which had evolved before the rise of colonial rule. It has been noticed that because of the colonial system "the centripetal pulls exerted by the inter-settlement linkages, which has evolved over time were replaced by the centrifugal pulls generated by the metropolitan economy through the establishment of new port towns and orientation of the internal commodity flows towards them. The old ports like Khambayat or Broach which had naturally grown over centuries were

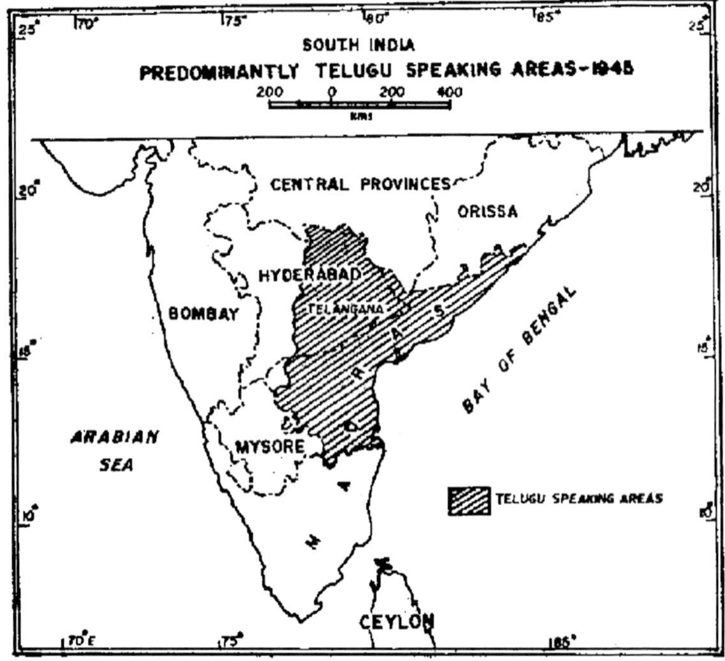

Fig. 9.3(b) : South India : Predominantly Telugu Speaking Areas—1945

destroyed, and in their place arose the colossus with four claws—Calcutta, Madras, Bombay and Karachi" (Raja *et al.*, 1976). An analysis of the growth of Calcutta, reveals that "the Calcutta conurbation registered an absolute growth rate of 90.39 per cent between 1872 and 1921, whereas, during the same period all the Class I cities of the hinterland combined, had an absolute growth of only 15.99 per cent and individually they either declined or registered a far lower growth than Calcutta" (Raja *et al.*, 1976). Lucknow, the second largest city in the hinterland of Calcutta, lost its population by 12.95 per cent during the period 1872 to 1921 and during the corresponding period the degree of primacy of Calcutta in its hinterland increased from 3.17 to 6.93. This primacy of Calcutta distorted the system of settlement hierarchy in its hinterland for "it developed not as the node of and along with the system but at the cost of it. It was not an instrument of urbanization but of urban atrophy" (Raja *et al.*, 1976). It has been observed in the case of

Bombay that its development has resulted in the loss of trade and traffic to the medieval ports of Karwar and Honavar since their hinterland has been annexed to the port of Bombay. Consequently, the natural pattern of hierarchical development of settlements oriented to these medieval ports have been disturbed with their realignment to metropolitan Bombay (Sita, 1972-73). During the colonial period metropolitan Bombay, like Calcutta, developed on parasitic lines and it still continues to do so because of its magnetic qualities as a metropolitan pole (Deshpande, 1973).

Hypertrophy of Metropolitan Centres

The Indian urban system is highly distorted, being dominated by large cities with population exceeding 100,000 (Alam, Rao and Gopi, 1974). These cities, constituting only 5.6 per cent of the urban settlements, contain 56 per cent of the total urban population. Although these cities attract most of public and private investments in industries, outside the resource base areas, yet they have a weak economic base as they are functionally dominated by low order tertiary activities. This over-burdening of the "nascent urbanization in India... by the expansion of the tertiary sector as against the experiences of the developed countries, which in their early stages of urbanization, enjoyed a growth of their secondary sectors" has weakened structurally the entire settlement system of India. However, this hypertrophy of several large centres "prevents the formation of system of towns" (Gohman *et al.*, 1976), and induces the growth and development of individual large urban centres but not the "system of Centres" (Raja *et al.*, 1976). The small and medium sized settlements are atrophied and cease to develop as centres of intervening opportunities (Khan, 1967). The cluster of small towns because of the accelerated growth of Class I towns "are not yet functioning as effective region forming nodes (Deshpande, 1973). Distortions in the settlement system due to hypertrophy of large sized settlements is further corroborated by the fact that the middle order settlements are much below the expected size in contrast to the higher order settlements which are disproportionately large in size (Fig. 9.4). Moreover, these large sized settlements are highly clustered, located closer to each other than the settlements in the lower size range, and contrary to the system of hierarchy the differences in the number of lower and higher order settlements does not conform to any accepted theoretical formulation (Table 9.2).

Table 9.2 : Metropolitan System of India

Population	*No. of Towns*			*Average Distance in km*		
	Bombay	*Delhi*	*Madras*	*Bombay*	*Delhi*	*Madras*
Above 20,00,000	1	1	1	—	—	—
5,00,000-19,99,999	5	6	3	428	214	176
1,00,000-9,99,999	36	32	31	81	90	72
50,000-99,999	39	49	48	122	106	192
20,000-49,999	164	147	146	65	61	41

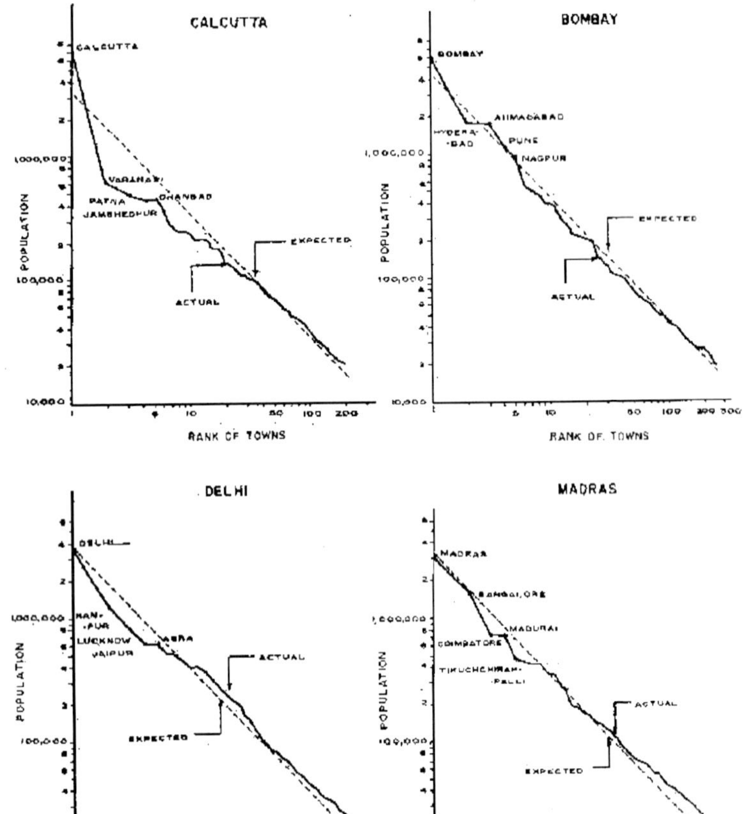

Fig. 9.4: Metropolitan Systems of India (Rank Size Distribution—1971)

The transport development policies of the State and Central governments are also oriented to strengthen the linkages between large cities, as against between cities and their regions. Almost all the State governments have introduced fast bus transport services linking the State capitals with their respective large cities having population exceeding one hundred thousand. In the State of Andhra Pradesh capital cities of the adjoining States viz. Bangalore (Karnataka), Madras (Tamil Nadu) and Bombay and Nagpur (Maharashtra) are thus linked. A similar situation is observed in the development of new railway services which are called fast express services. In the first instance Calcutta and Bombay were linked with the National capital—Delhi. Subsequently the national metropolises of Delhi, Calcutta, Bombay, Madras were interlinked by such services. These fast train services are also now available linking the State capitals with the national capital and with the other national metropolises (Fig. 9.5).

With the introduction of these fast train services travel time between the major metropolitan cities of India has been considerably reduced (Table 9.3). By virtue of rapid transit facilities the stranglehold of the national metropolises on the economy of the capital cities of the States is reinforced. This is substantiated by the fact that the prices of poultry products in Hyderabad city are determined by the consumer demand in Bombay, and of such seasonal fruits as grapes and mangoes by the consumer demand in the four national metropolises of the country. In turn the capital cities, at the State level, tighten their economic grip on the large urban centres within their respective political territories.

Table 9.3 : Saving of Time by Fast Running Train

	Travel Time			
Metropolitan Settlements	*Express Train*		*Fast Express Train*	
	Hrs.	*Mts.*	*Hrs.*	*Mts*
1. Delhi-Calcutta	25	45	16	30
2. Delhi-Bombay	25	00	16	55
3. Delhi-Madras	37	05	30	10
4. Calcutta-Madras	32	50	25	10
5. Bombay-Calcutta	35	45	29	45
6. Hyderabad-Delhi	32	30	23	25
7. Hyderabad-Bombay	18	20	13	20

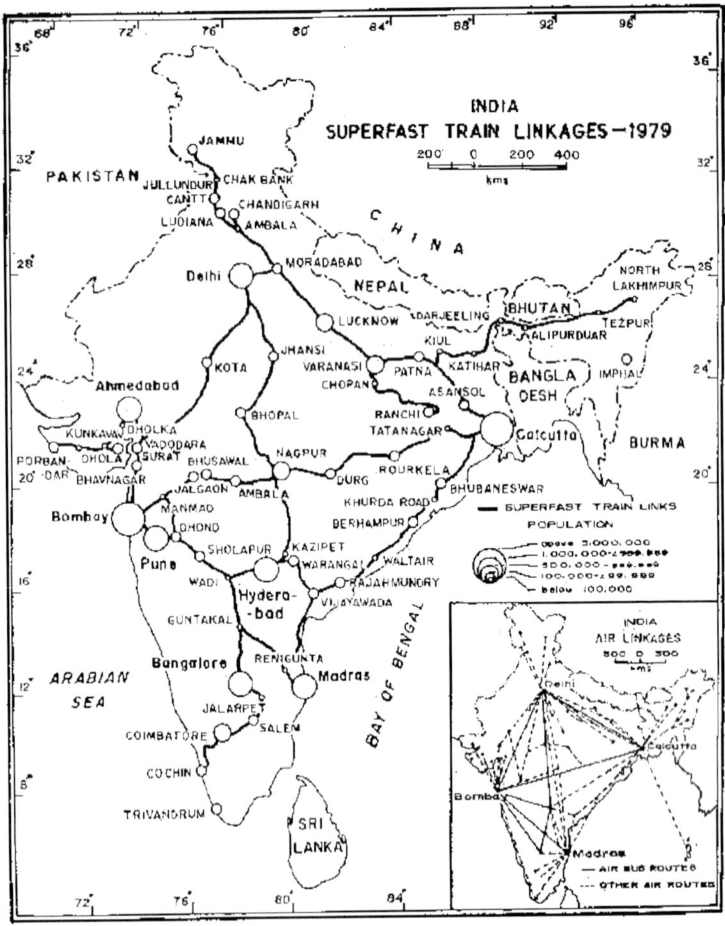

Fig. 9.5: India's Superfast Train Linkages—1979

This emphasis on the inter-linkage of the large cities in the transport development policy of the State and national governments has caused the concentration of the productive activities in the urban and peri-urban areas of large cities. Moreover, the absence of inadequacy of linkages of these cities with their immediate rural hinterlands has precluded the percolation of development impulses to the settlements in the rural hinterland of these cities. Consequently, the economies of hinterland of most of these large cities are not spatially integrated with their respective central cities. This pattern of urban development, where inter-city linkages are strong, and weak between the cities of their immediate rural hinterlands has led to the dominance of the markets of subdominant urban centres even in the supply of perishable commodities and particularly vegetables by the dominant metropolitan centres of the region. It has been noticed that the urban markets of Warangal in Andhra Pradesh, and Mysore in Karnataka receive a significant portion of their vegetable supplies from the metropolitan cities of Hyderabad and Bangalore respectively. This pattern of economic interaction between cities minimizes the inflow of goods from the hinterland to the central city and consequently retards the economic development of its rural hinterland which eventually gives rise to distortions in the settlement system.

Rural Hinterlands of Large Cities

Absence of spatial integration which leads to serious distortions in the settlement systems is notably marked in the rural hinterlands of most of the major metropolises of India.

This is best represented in the rural hinterland of Hyderabad city, a metropolitan settlement with more than 2 million inhabitants. A large part of its rural hinterland is not easily accessible (Fig. 9.6.) (Alam *et al.*, 1972). The metropolitan impact and the high level of urban, industrial, and agricultural development is confined to a radius of 32 km. from the metropolis. Outside this radius rural-urban dichotomy is sharp and economic development is confined to the high accessibility corridors.

The rural hinterland outside this radius is not developed much above the subsistence level which is substantiated by the survival of a large number of periodic markets which are not integrated with the metropolitan economy and are located in areas of marginal agricultural surplus consequently the central places are unevenly distributed resulting into a distorted system of hierarchy (Fig. 9.7). This has also resulted "in the inadequacy of the spread effect of the metropolitan economy and is evident from the fact that except for Hyderabad West and Hyderabad East Taluq, the metropolitan Taluq of Hyderabd Urban is fringed by "under developed taluqs" (Alam *et al.*, 1975). A similar situation has been observed in the hinterlands of Dhanbad a coal-mining town, and Rourkela, a steel town. Both these settlements have a population of more than 200,000 but they interact very little with their immediate hinterland because of poor transport linkages.

Consequently, even for their essential items of daily consumption such as vegetables they have to depend on the other neighbouring urban settlements or even metropolitan Calcutta (Bulletin, 1972).

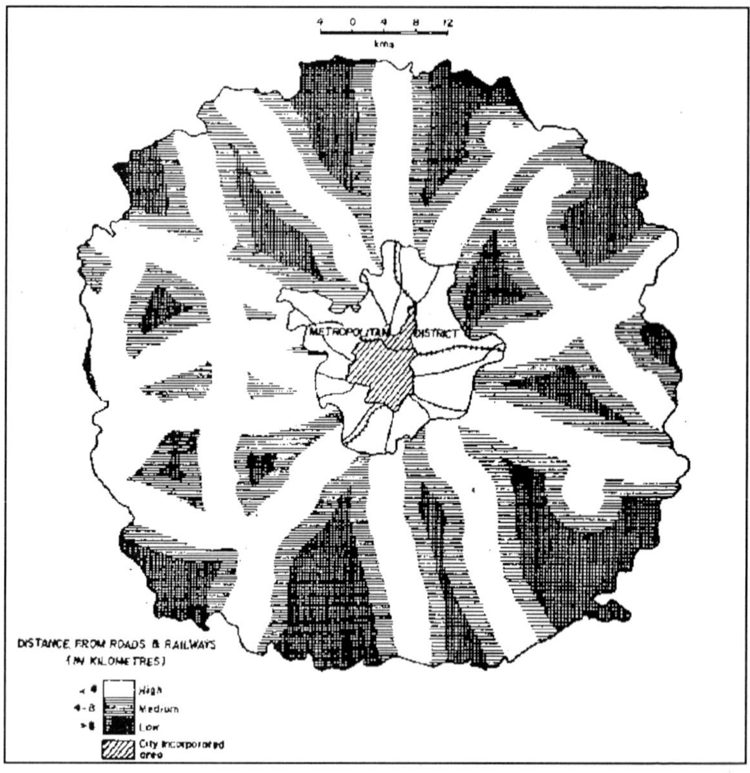

Fig. 9.6 : Hyderabad Metropolitan Region

Disparities in Levels of Development

Disparities in the levels of regional economic development are notably marked in India. This is partly a colonial heritage and partly also due to wrong priorities and investment strategies adopted by the central and State governments. During the colonial period the impact of modern industrial and agricultural development was discernible only in isolated pockets centred around parts of Calcutta and Bombay, and in areas suitable for plantation agriculture or canal irrigation for commercial farming.

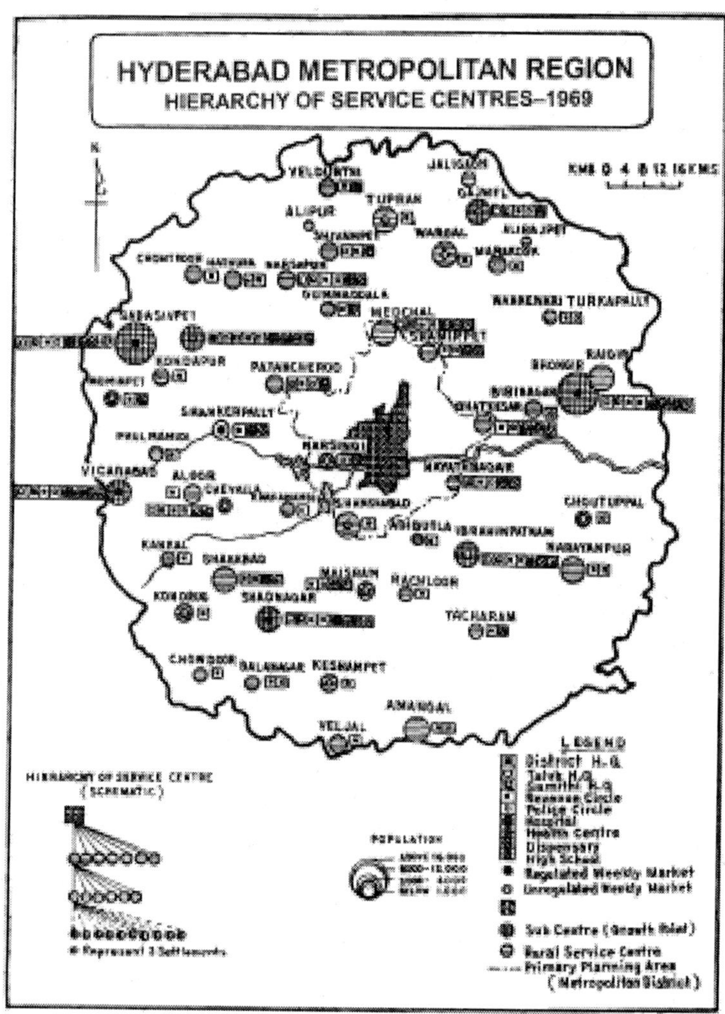

Fig. 9.7 : Hyderabad Metropolitan Region : Hierarchy of Service Centres—1969

During the colonial period the Indian economy was largely organized on dualistic pattern with a sharp division between the modern and traditional sectors and only marginal interaction in between the two sectors. The modern sector catered primarily to the imperial market, whereas the traditional sector catered to the shrinking indigenous market. These regional disparities have been further accentuated since independence as the public and private sector investments have largely moved into the already developed regions of the country. These widening disparities eventually led the Planning Commission of India to develop criteria to identify backward districts and to evolve a strategy for their development in order to minimize regional disparities in the levels of development (Roy Burman, 1971). These disparities are strongly reflected in the levels of infrastructure facilities. Inadequacy of infrastructure facilities prevent the articulation of the hierarchy of settlement systems which are consequently distorted. This is well exemplified in Andhra Pradesh where regional disparities are wide (Fig. 9.8) and pattern of hierarchy in each of its socio-political regions is highly distorted as is brought out by the Tables 9.4 and 9.5 (Alam *et al.*, 1975).

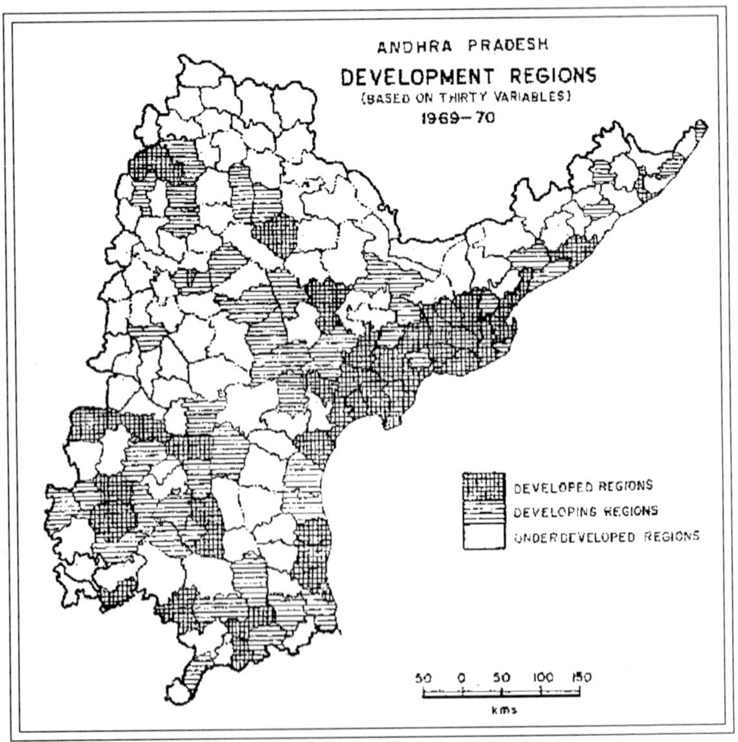

Fig. 9.8 : Andhra Pradesh : Development Regions (Based on Thirty Variables)—1969-70

Table 9.4 : Andhra Pradesh—Distribution of Taluqs by their Levels of Development and Regions (1969-70)

			Level of Development		
	No. of Districts	*Total No. taluqs*	*Developed*	*Developing (numbers denote taluqs)*	*Under-developed*
Regions					
Andhra Pradesh	21	195	49	49	97
(i) Coastal Andhra					
(a) Delta Districts	4	40	25	10	5
(b) Non-Delta Districts	4	40	8	10	22
(ii) Rayalaseema	4	42	11	15	16
(iii) Telangana	9	73	5	14	45

Table 9.5 : Andhra Pradesh—Number of Urban Settlements by Order of the Hierarchy (1971)

State/Region	*Hierarchical Order*				
	First	*Second*	*Third*	*Fourth*	*Fifth*
Andhra Pradesh	1	4	5	7	190
Regions					
(a) Coastal Andhra	—	4	4	4	87
(b) Rayalaseema	—	—	1	4	38
(c) Telangana	1	—	1	—	65

The Planning Atlas of Andhra Pradesh (Alam *et at.*, 1975) reveals:

(a) that there are marked disparities in the levels of regional development leading to a highly distorted system of urban hierarchy at the State level and even within its sub-regions, and

(b) absence of spatial integration of the economy even in the development taluq of the State because of the lag between economic development and provision of infrastructure facilities.

Conclusion

Distortions in the settlement system of the developing countries and particularly that of India were the direct outcome of the colonial policy to concentrate investments and administrative and political power in a few large urban centres which resulted in their hypertrophy and prevented "the formation of the systems of towns embracing the entire settled territory of a country, and also of regional urban sub-systems" (Gohman *et al.*, 1976).

The colonial capitalistic system also induced the growth of monopolistic production and finance capitalism which have "taken control of the primate metropolitan hierarchy in India. Hence, it is subjected to behave exactly according to law of the capitalist accumulation and concomitant forms of urbanization" (Chakraborty, 1975). The control of monopolistic production and finance capitalism on metropolitan economy has continued even after Independence and, therefore, the pattern of urban and metropolitan development in Independent India is not much different from colonial times. Such a metropolitan growth arrests wider diffusion of technology, causes stagnation of hinterland economy and prevents the adequate articulation of a hierarchical system of settlements. To generate a more dynamic system of urban and metropolitan economy and to rectify the distortions in the system of settlements the government must intervene to restrain the role of finance capital, prevent polarized development of metropolitan centres, accelerate the growth and development of the middle order urban centres, and initiate a public policy to promote the percolation of developmental impulses to the lowest level of settlements in the system.

Acknowledgement

I would like to acknowledge my gratitude to Dr. Waheduddin Khan, Dr. Afzal Mohammad and Dr. K.N. Gopi for constructive criticism. I am also grateful to Fatima Ali Khan and C.K. Aruna who read through the text and offered helpful suggestions. The text, however, reflects my thinking and I own full responsibility for its shortcomings.

NOTES

Alam, Manzoor (1976): A Note on Realignment of the Urban System of Andhra Pradesh, in V.C. Misra *et al.* (ed): *Essays in Applied Geography*, University of Sagar, Sagar, pp. 177-185.

Alam, Manzoor *et al.*, (1975): *Planning Atlas of Andhra Pradesh*, Chapter V, p. vi.

Alam, Gopi and Parthasarathy (1978): Pattern of Urban Development and Morphology of Indian cities (Paper submitted at the Indo-French Seminar held in Delhi, December).

Alam, Manzoor and Khan, Waheeduddin (1972): *Metropolitan Hyderabad and its Region*, Asia Publishing House, Bombay.

Alam, Rao and Gopi (1974): Trends and Patterns of Metropolitan Development in India, *Occasional Paper No. 3*, Centre for Urban Research, Dept. of Geography, O.U. Hyderabad.

Bulletin of the Heidelberg University (1972), South Asia.

Chakraborty, S. (1975): Development and Primate Metropolis: Some Value Questions, in Alam and Reddy: *Socio-Economic Development Problems in South and Southeast Asia*, Popular Prakashan, Bombay, p. 103.

Deshpande, C.D. (1973): The Suburbs of Greater Bombay, *Occasional Paper No.* 2, Centre for Urban Reasearch, Deptt. of Geography, O.U. Hyderabad.

_________(1973): Trends in Cities and Towns of Western India, Alam-Pokshishevsky (ed): *Urbanization in Developing Countries*, p. 136.

Gohman, Lappo Mayergoiz & Mashbets (1976): The Economic Geographic Aspects of World Urbanization and its Specific Features in the Developing Countries, in Alam-Pokshishevsky: *Urbanization in Developing Countries*, pp. 40-41.

Khan, Waheeduddin (1976): Growth and Stagnation of Small and Medium Sized Towns in Telangana—An Exploratory Enquiry, in Alam-Pokshishevsky (ed): *Urbanization in Developing Countries*, pp. 367-402.

Roy, Burman B.K. (1971): Towards Integrated Regional Frame, in Economic and Socio-Cultural Dimensions of Regionalisation-Census of India, *Census Centenary Monograph*—7, pp. 27-50.

Raza, Moonis and Habeeb, Atiya (1976): Characteristics of Colonial Urbanization—A Case Study of Satellite Primacy of Calcutta (1850-1921) in Alam-Pokshiskevsky (ed): *Urbanization in Developing Countries*, pp. 187, 196-197, 218.

Raza, Moonis, Habeeb Atiya and Kundu, A. (1976): Some Aspects of the Dysfunctional Character of Urbanization, in Alam-Reddy: *Socio-Economic Development Problems in South & South-East Asia*, Popular Prakashan, Bombay, p. 148.

Sita, K. (1972-73): Some Aspects of Urbanization in South Konkan, *Bombay Geographic Magazine*, Vol. 20-21, pp. 31-48.

U.N.O. (1977), *Demographic Year Book*.

10

The National Settlement System of India

Although many of the urban settlements in India are of great antiquity, a national settlement system only emerged during the period of colonial rule in the mid-nineteenth century with the building of the railway network. This network increased the mobility of goods and people, reduced physical distances between settlements, and enhanced their interdependence. The evolution of a national settlement system was further reinforced with the rapid development of a road transport system in India in the post-Second World War period. While recognizing the fact that recent factors are more relevant to an understanding of the settlement system-forming processes in India, the national system can be better appreciated if it is examined in historical perspective, because of the antiquity of the country's urban civilization.

Historical Growth and Development

The origin of the settlement pattern lies far back in the early valley-stage civilization (Basham, 1971). Valuable information regarding the distribution of settlement units lies scattered in various mythological and religious literature and in records of archaeological research. One can conclude on the basis of these sources that by about the fourth century BC, the whole subcontinent had come to possess a fairly large number of settlements of varying functional character. More than 600 settlement units (163 towns and 441 villages), spread over the whole country, have been referred to in ancient Puranic and Buddhist literature as existing by AD 700 (Law, 1954).

Published in *Urbanization and Settlement Systems—International Perspectives,* Edited by L.S. Bourne, R. Sinclair and K. Dzeiwonski, Oxford University Press, Oxford, 1984, pp. 453-472.

Villages were the functional socio-economic units. Various size-groups of villages were recognized—*Gamaka* (small), *Gama* (ordinary), *Nigamagama* (big), *Dvaragama* (Suburban), *Panchhantagama* (a frontier/border village) (Dube, 1967). These units ranged in size from 2-3 house clusters to villages of a thousand families. That considerable thought had been given to the study of villages differentiated on the basis of their form (such as open bowl, circular etc.), is evident in Jain canonical texts (Mukerjee, 1972).

Functional categorizations of villages have also been made. Puranic literature refers to villages as *Grama* (without market), *Pura* (with market), *Durga* (fort), *Pattana* (port), *Ghosa* (milkmen settlement), *Khata* (agricultural), and *Khamata* (near merkets). There are many references in the Tamil Sangam literature (the earliest *Sangam* is dated 3000 BC) to the territorial organization of the peninsula into five geographic divisions and the associated characteristics of communities and settlements in these regions. Here again functional categories of settlements and their spatial structures are described. Studies of ancient Tamil poetry of the earliest Sangam period lead us to the conclusion that peninsular India must have had even by this time a well organized and clearly demarcated settlement structure consisting of numerous well planned *nagarams* (towns) and *gramas* (villages). Madurai, Vanji, Poompuhar, for example, which exist today, date back to Sangam days (Basham, 1971).

As seen in the works cited above, the fertile, alluvial plains of the Indo-Gangetic system and riverine tracts, and the coastlines in peninsular India were dotted with numerous settlements. As agricultural communities prospered, accumulated wealth, and acquired technology and power, the political system and trade activities came to play a prominent role in shaping settlement patterns. Settlements located in appropriate sites developed into capitals or commercial towns. But political systems were subject to frequent changes which were reflected in the changing location of capital cities, fortresses, or defence towns.

Urban centres date back to prehistoric days, but there is no record of continuity in the urban tradition, at least where urban form or distribution is concerned (Smailes, 1968). What is clear and well substantiated is that cities of the historic period were expressions of imperial expansion and the intrusion of conquerors who sought security in urban concentrations. The fortresses and trading posts attracted accretions of indigenous peasant communities. Thus one can conclude that ancient urban centres acted as nodes which integrated communities and settlements directly or indirectly within the jurisdiction of the authority housed in the urban centre. As both agriculture and trade were the chief economic activities large numbers of market towns came to be established in pre-industrial India. In the south especially, trade connections across the Indian Ocean led to the emergence of many littoral kingdoms, such as the Kalinga, Pallava, Chera, and Pandyan, each with its capital city and leading ports. Port towns and inland towns, well connected with each other through natural routes, added another component to the settlement structure of this early period in South India.

Periods of political stability also stimulated religious and cultural activities. Religious establishments such as temples, monasteries, and *dargahs* (shrines of Muslim saints), and cultural centres like universities added to the importance of the settlements, transforming them into urban status. The construction of national highway, well maintained with shade-giving trees and rest houses, stimulated inter-regional traffic and many *serai* towns came into existence (Sinha, 1976). But these were the capital cities which dominated and organized the settlement system in any region with roads converging on/and radiating from them. These roads served administrative, military, trade, religious, and cultural traffic and stimulated the growth of new towns as well. It is during Moghul rule, especially in Akbar's reign (1556-1605), that a systematic division of the country led to a proliferation of administrative and garrison towns all linked to the capital city, Agra, by national highway (Naqvi, 1969). Western India and the Deccan showed a spurt in the growth of urban centres (new forts and administrative headquarters) as a result of Shivaji's (1646-1680) defence and administrative measures and the rise of Deccan kingdoms on the break-up of the Bahmani Kingdom.

The later Maratha kingdoms (1680-1707), the Sultanates of Eastern India and the Deccan, each added to the complexity of the urban mosaic in this period. But in general the earlier pattern formed by the administrative headquarters of the provinces or *Subas* (made up of major urban nodes, and sub-nodes of market towns within an agriculture-oriented economy), was not much disturbed. It can be said to underlie even the present regional settlement pattern in many parts of the country. The earlier urban centres, with a much reduced jurisdiction, still serve as nodes of mini-settlement systems.

Urbanization Factors during the Colonial Period—1757-1946

The break-up of the Moghul Empire, expansion of British political control over India after 1857, the development of rail and canal networks since the mid-nineteenth century, the commercialization of crop culture, the emergence of the expatriate settlements of Calcutta, Bombay, and Madras as the key ports of India and as centres of finance, banking, and industry, and the political division of the country into British India and princely India, each with distinctly different political and economic systems, markedly influenced India's urban mosaic during the colonial period.

The expansion of British political control gave a new dimension to urban development in India. Unlike the feudal cities of medieval India which were largely consumption-oriented the British introduced production-based urban centres with a monetary-based economic system typical of the development of towns in a capitalist society. The concentration of investment in industries and commerce in and around the port towns of Calcutta and Bombay led to their development as powerful urban magnets and primate cities. While the fort towns represented defence settlements during the medieval period, the British established a large number of unwalled garrison towns or cantonments as discrete urban units exclusively for the use of the armed forces of the British rulers. These were complex, such as in Meerut, Poona, Allahabad, and Bangalore, or were founded as independent new towns such as Secunderabad, Sagar, Mhow, and Kamptee.

The greatest incentive to urbanization during the colonial period was provided by the twin and almost simultaneous development of the rail network and the irrigation canal systems during the mid-nineteenth century (Schwartzberg, 1978). During the initial phase of rail development (1853-75) Bombay was linked with its agriculturally productive hinterland, which also possessed canal irrigation facilities, and with strategically important towns such as the capital cities of major princely states, Baroda, Hyderabad, Gwalior, Bangalore. By 1925 a mature rail network had emerged serving the cotton belt of India, and the canal irrigation areas of Cauvery and Krishna-Godavari deltas in the south and the Indo-Gangetic plains in the north. By then Calcutta, Bombay, Madras, and Delhi were interlinked. The emergence of these rail lines reoriented the inland trade routes of India, and encouraged new centres of production, trade and commerce.

The railway system was focused around Calcutta and Bombay primarily to serve the defence and commercial needs of the colonial powers in India. The railway lines were also instrumental in inducing the growth of a number of independent towns. The influence of the railway network on the distribution of towns and their size is underlined by the fact that, except for the hill towns of Shillong and Srinagar, all large towns with populations exceeding 100,000 are located along the rail lines.

The introduction of the modern canal system between 1850-1900, in the Cauvery and Krishna-Godavari deltas in south India and in the Indo-Gangetic plains in the north, laid the foundation for commercial agriculture and, supported by the rail network, stimulated the development of market settlements and agro-industrial based urbanization. Numerous towns in the Punjab (Bhatinda, Jalalabad) and Rajasthan (Suratgarh, Padampur) are the outcome of the transformation of purely agriculture-based rural settlements into a system of urban market centres based on agricultural surplus. Canals could not generate extensive urbanization without the supporting facilities—largely the railways—for the bulk movement of surplus agricultural products. Thus the major commercial towns of India, excluding the million population cities, such as Vijayawada, Kumbakonam, Hapur, Ludhiana, are located both in the canal-irrigated zone and along the railways. Agriculturally prosperous pockets in India are positively correlated with a well-established canal and rail network, have a fairly high level of urbanization, are noted for large clusters of medium to small size urban centres, and possess a well articulated system of settlement. This is fairly well susbtantiated by the settlement systems of the Punjab (Bhat, 1976) and the Krishna-Godavari deltas (Alam, 1976).

The introduction of tea plantations in Assam in the early nineteenth century and the cultivation of cash crops such as jute and cotton exclusively for export, created new pockets of economic prosperity and urban development (Munsi, 1980). They generated the rise of the plantation settlements of Shillong and Darjeeling and indeed the growth of small and medium-sized urban settlements in the cotton belts of Maharashtra and Tamilnadu. Sholapur and Coimbatore are good examples of towns in this category.

The emergence of industries based on cash crops—jute and cotton—around the expatriate port cities of Calcutta and Bombay and the concentration of export-import trade and banking in these cities, supported by the rail and road network which linked them to their hinterlands, induced hyper-concentration of urban centres around these cities leading to the formation of conurbations. Consequently, Calcutta and Bombay became the most attractive urban settlements for job seekers. They eventually emerged as primate cities within their respective urban systems, commanding an extensive and productive hinterland. Barring a few isolated inland industrial towns such as Kanpur, Ahmedabad, and Coimbatore, the major manufacturing belts were focused around these two parts and, to a minor degree, around the port of Madras in south India.

Another important factor influencing the pattern and character of urbanization in India was the political division of the country, prior to Independence in 1947, into British India and Princely India. The Princely states of India were essentially consumer-oriented societies and were marked by their low level of agricultural and industrial development and consequent low level of urban development. Being a feudal society the development was concentrated in the capital cities, and, therefore, most of them had a primate-city pattern of development. These primate cities in the Princely states developed as parasites on their agricultural hinterlands. In British India urbanization had spread outside the primate cities of Calcutta and Bombay into those relatively better developed prosperous areas based on either plantation agriculture or cash crops and supported by canal irrigation. Even the district headquarters in British India had gained urban status with a tertiary economic base. Hence, in 1901, those cities with populations exceeding 100,000 were concentrated in British India (Figure 10.1).

Post-Independence Urbanization Factors

In the post-Independence periods the introduction of Five Year Development Plans since 1951, as well as the creation of new States and the multiplication of administrative districts and *taluqs/tahsils* (lower revenue administrative units) in each State, has led to the rise of new capital cities for the newly created States and to an increasingly wide scatter of urban settlements supported largely by a weak tertiary base (Alam, Rao, and Gopi, 1974).

The impact of the Five Year Development Plans has left its mark on the urban pattern of the country, but this has been more an incidental outcome of the implementation of sectoral programmes than the consequence of any clearly defined goals of urban development. The increased tempo of economic development, particularly of industries in the inland centres along railway lines, was conducive to both the rise of new towns and the accelerated growth and development of old established towns. The expansion of the road network and road transport, which facilitated the collection of agricultural surpluses at market centres and their distribution to centres of consumption led to the emergence of a number of *mandi* (small growth centres) towns, such as Hapur in Uttar Pradesh and Anakapalli in Andhra Pradesh, and reinforced the growth of existing urban settlements. The urban network has spread further in India with the extensive development of major irrigation and multi-purpose projects in Bihar, Rajasthan, Andhra Pradesh, and Karnataka.

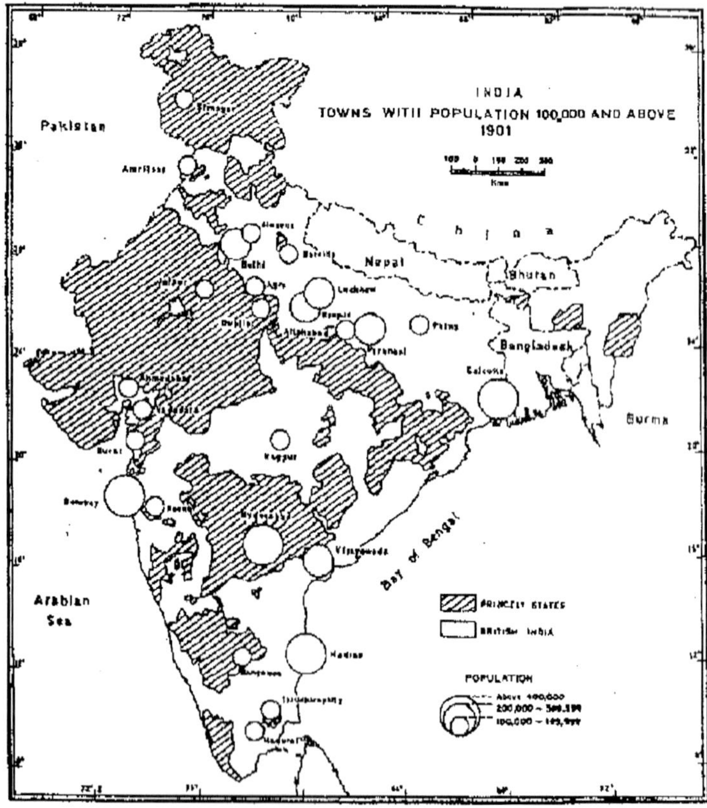

Fig. 10.1 : Towns with a Population of 100,000 and above, 1901

The planners' emphasis on large-scale mineral and industrial development has had two types of spatial consequences. First, the stepping up of mining exploration, prospecting, and exploitation resulted in the rise of a large number of mining towns, such as Khetri in Rajasthan, Neyveli in Tamilnadu, and Kothagudem in Andhra Pradesh. Second, the large industrial complexes, together with associated residential developments, either provided the nucleus of new towns in the hitherto economically backward regions (Rourkela, Bihar) or were established as suburban settlements on the peripheries of large towns, such as Bharat Heavy Electricals' Townships on the periphery of Bhopal and Hyderabad, New Bombay near Bombay, Gandhinagar near Ahmedabad, and Faridabad and Ballabhgarh near Delhi. These new settlements were instrumental in the accelerated growth of their senior settlements, but they were equally responsible for complicating their planning and development problems.

Urban Pattern of India and Metropolitan Development—1901-71

Although rural settlements (525,938 in 1971) far outnumber the urban settlements (2636 in 1971) the settlements system of India is dominated by the urban settlements. It is largely through these urban settlements that the settlement systems of India are being integrated (Figure 10.2). During the period 1901-71, the number of urban settlements increased by 42 per cent from 1851 to 2636, but the urban population increased by a much larger margin of 322 per cent. Towns in the upper three categories (25,000+ inhabitants) recorded the highest increase both in the number of settlements and in population (Table 10.1). As can be seen from the table, these settlements constitute approximately 33 per cent of all urban settlements, but contain over 80 per cent of the urban population. The concentration of population in the metropolitan or Class I settlements with populations exceeding 100,000 is most marked. These settlements constitute only a minor fraction (5.6%) of the total number of urban settlements (in 1971), yet they dominate the urban population. The share of metropolitan population in the total urban population has been rising progressively since 1931, and by 1971 it had almost reached 50 per cent. The concentration of population in metropolitan settlements is further emphasised by the fact that this handful of large settlements contained over 10 per cent of the nation's total population in 1971. The explosive rise in the proportion of the metropolitan population is indicative of the distinct trend towards a greater concentration of investments and developmental activities in such settlements.

The declining trend in the growth rate of small towns as a class, though not unique to India, is causing grave concern in view of the poor industrial and economic base of most of the metropolitan cities. It is all the more disturbing that despite their weak economic base they are able to attract large numbers, indeed most migrants, resulting in phenomenally high growth rates Table (10.2 and 10.3).

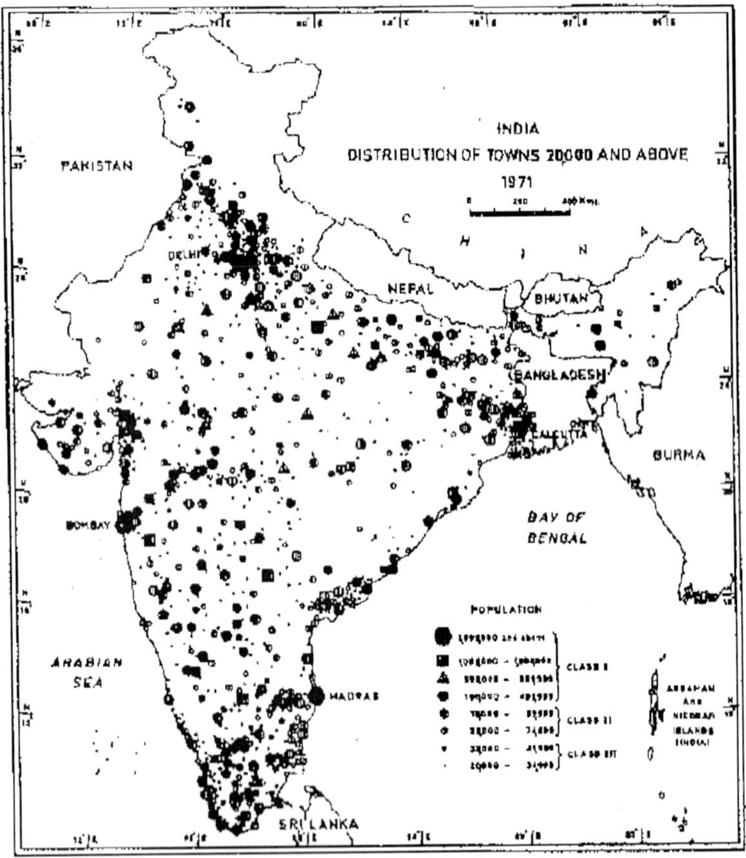

Source: Census 1971.

Fig. 10.2 : Distribution of Towns with a Population of 20,000 and above, 1971

Table 10.1 : *Growth in Number of Towns and Urban Population by Size Category of Towns*

	Number of Towns				*Population*			
	1901		*1971*		*1901*		*1971*	
	Number	*% of Total Towns*	*Number*	*% of Total Towns*	*Pop. in '000*	*% of Total Urban Population*	*Pop. in '000*	*% of Total Urban Population*
All Classes	1851		2336		25,852		109,094	
I 100,000+	25	1.35	148	5.61	5,692	22.02	53,381	48.93
II 50,000-99,999	42	2.27	183	6.94	2,948	11.48	14,712	13.49
III 25,000-49,999	136	7.34	582	22.08	4,382	16.95	19,947	18.28
Total of I to III	203	10.97	913	34.63	13,022	50.37	88,040	80.70
IV 10,000-24,999	395	22.34	873	33.12	5,847	22.62	13,961	12.80
V 5,000-9,999	756	40.84	678	25.72	5,752	20.63	6,197	5.68
VI <5,000	497	26.85	172	6.55	1,650	6.38	8,952	0.82
Total of IV to VI	1648	89.03	1723	65.37	12,829	49.73	29,116	193.30

Source: Compiled from Census of India, General Population Tables, 1971

Table 10.2 : Distribution of Urban Settlements with High Growth Rates by Size Class, 1971

Size Class	*A* *No. of Towns*	*B* *No. of Settlements with Growth Rate of over 50 per cent*	*B as Percentage of A*
I	148	65	43.91
II	185	40	21.85
III	582	98	16.84
IV	873	105	12.02
V	678	48	7.08
VI	172	22	12.79
All Classes	2638	—	—

Table 10.3 : India—Urban and Metropolitan Population, Growth Per Annum (in %)

Period	*Total Population Growth*	*Total Urban Population Growth*	*Metropolitan Population Growth*
1901-31	0.6	1.0	1.4
1931-51	1.5	4.3	9.5
1951-71	2.6	3.7	7.8

Source: Census of India, 1971, India: Final Population Tables.

Dominance of Metropolitan Settlements at the State and National Levels

The development of metropolitan settlements in each State of India is strongly influenced by the State's political, social, and economic conditions. There is, therefore, a wide variation among the States in the proportion of metropolitan to total urban population, as is shown in Table 10.3. Nonetheless, except for a few States, the urban pattern at the State level is dominated by the metropolitan settlements. Further, the share of metropolitan population in each State, except West Bengal, has increased. The decline in West Bengal is minimal.

The tendency towards primate city development is most notable at the State level. The leading cities of all the States have, by and large, maintained a high level of primacy. Table 10.4, giving the three city index of primacy, reveals that primacy is pronounced: (i) in States with expatriate settlements which originally linked India commercially with Britain, (ii) in States with a strong feudal background and, (iii) in the peripheral States where all development activities are concentrated in a single city.

Table 10.4 : Proportion of Metropolitan Population to Urban Population and Three City Index of Primacy by States, 1961 and 1971

State	Capital/First Ranked Cities	1961		1971		Per capita income 1969-1970 (rupees)
		Proportion of Metropolitan to Urban Population	Index of Primacy	Proportion of Metropolitan to Urban Population	Index of Primacy	
1. Andhra Pradesh	Hyderabad	40.58	3.7	45.41	3.3	544
2. Assam	Shillong	11.00	7.92	12.66	5.02	586
3. Bihar	Patna	35.15	0.7	32.32	0.9	402
4. Gujarat	Ahmedabad	42.42	2.10	54.09	1.7	740
5. Haryana	Chandigarh	8.07	—	12.82	—	N.A.
6. Himachal Pradesh	Simla	—	2.59	—	1.45	N.A.
7. Jammu & Kashmir	Srinagar	65.54	—	66.79	—	503
8. Kerala	Cochin-Ernakulam*	26.96	0.60	42.32	0.59	643
9. Madhya Pradesh	Indore*	31.56	0.60	41.06	0.67	495
10. Maharashtra	Bombay	60.49	2.9	64.76	3.5	736
11. Manipur	Imphal	—	11.50	—	6.97	N.A.
12. Karnataka	Bangalore	36.77	2.40	45.37	2.10	545
13. Orissa	Bhubaneshwar	13.19	—	30.04	—	571
14. Punjab	Amritsar	37.71	0.80	39.90	0.86	1002
15. Rajasthan	Jaipur	37.83	0.90	40.95	1.50	478
16. Tamil Nadu	Madras	37.76	2.4	43.80	2.7	591
17. Uttar Pradesh	Kanpur*	50.45	0.80	53.05	0.80	497
18. West Bengal	Calcutta	55.48	14.0	54.91	14.5	706
India	—	44.50	—	48.93	—	590

Source: Census of India : General Population Tables 1961 and 44.50—1971.

Note: * Non-capital cities; N.A. Not available.

Rank-Size Distribution System of Urban Settlements in Indian States

The Indian urban system covers a diversified culture and economy which is clearly reflected in the system itself and particularly in the size distribution of its urban settlements. At the national level the distribution has been consistently log-normal from the beginning of this century. This is because the settlement system of India has been treated as mono-nodal with Bombay and Calcutta included as part of the same system. If the urban settlement system of India is disaggregated and examined at the State level three distinct rank-size distributions can be identified [Fig. 10.3 (a), (b) and (c)] :

(1) Primate city distribution,
(2) Log-normal city distribution,
(3) Decentralized or polynucleated distribution.

Primate City Distribution

The States which exhibit this pattern of distribution include West Bengal, Andhra Pradesh, (Figure 10.3a). These States have as their capital or primate cities, centres which were formerly (i) the expatriate colonial ports such as Bombay, Madras, and Calcutta, (ii) the headquarters of plantation agricultural areas (Shillong), and (iii) the capital cities of the erstwhile princely states such as Hyderabad (Hyderabad State), Bangalore (Mysore State), and Srinagar (Jammu and Kashmir), or the capital cities of the newly constituted backward hill States. In this category Ahmedabad, the capital of Gujarat State, is the solitary exception, being one of the early industrial nodes of India.

Log-Normal Distribution

In this category included the States of Uttar Pradesh and Rajasthan (Figure 10.3b). They have distinct but not overwhelmingly dominant first order cities in their respective States. It has recently been observed, however, that Jaipur is tending to emerge as a primate city.

(a) Primate City Distribution

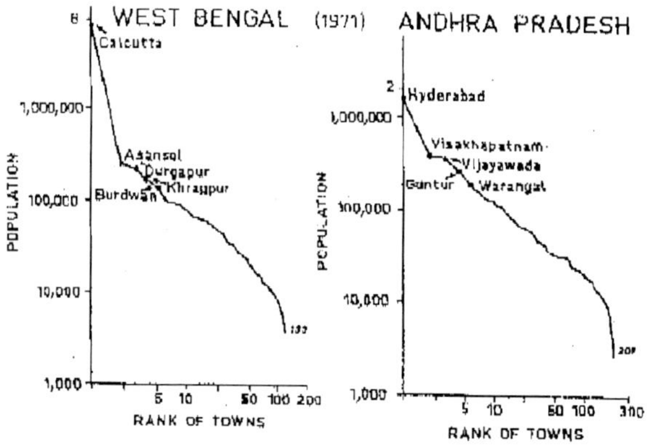

(b) Log-normal Distribution

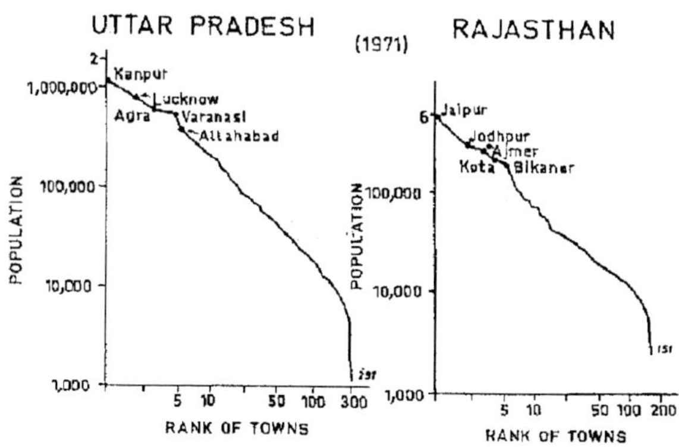

(c) Decentralised Distribution

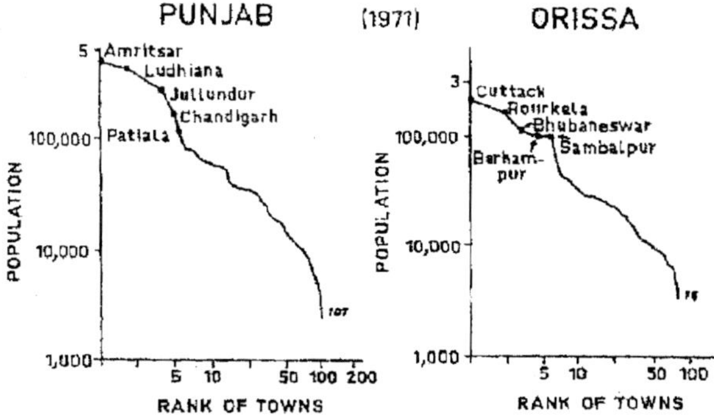

Fig. 10.3 (a), (b), and (c) : Rank-Size Distributions in Selected Indian States, 1971

Decentralized or Polynucleated Distribution

The States which conform to this pattern are Punjab and Orissa (Figure 10.3c). The settlement system seems to be decentralized, focussed around two or more major cities. It has not yet crystallized around any single metropolitan city. The States in this category, with the exception of Punjab, which has a high level of economic development, are relatively less developed economically as is reflected in their low per capita income (Table 10.4).

Dominance of National and Regional Metropolises

The dominance of the national and regional metropolises in the economy of the country is evident from the fact that the nine 'million' cities together contain nearly 25 per cent of the country's total working population. The concentration in the more productive and profitable sectors of 'Manufacturing other than household', 'Trade and Commerce', and 'Transport and Communication' are more marked. The four national metropolises—Calcutta, Bombay, Delhi, and Madras and the other 'million' cities together contribute 30.7 per cent and 38.3 per cent respectively to the total urban workforce in large-scale manufacturing, 19.5 and 26.7 per cent respectively in construction, 22.5 per cent and 29.1 per cent respectively in trade and commerce, 23.9 per cent and 31.0 per cent in transport and communication, and 20.13 per cent and 28.31 per cent in other services.

The intensity of this concentration of economic activities in the nine 'million' cities is evident from their control over national commodity flows, trade and commerce. These nine cities together contributed in 1974-75 over 30 per cent of the total trade of India, 45 per cent of total manufacturing and 30 per cent of the country's construction trade. In addition they are the centres of concentration of the quarternary functions since they are the main or regional headquarters of most of the national banks, of multinational firms, and of the regional offices of the Government of India. For instance, Hyderabad city which is the capital of Andhra Pradesh and its political, administrative, and judicial headquarters, has five universities, a large number of research institutes of national and international importance, the headquarters of the Andhra Bank and the State Bank of Hyderabad, and the regional headquarters of the Reserve Bank of India and most of the nationalized banks. It also has the regional sales offices of a number of national commercial agencies. With this concentration of high order tertiary and quaternary functions Hyderabad will continue to be both primate and parasitic for it is linked more strongly with large urban centres outside the State than with the settlements in its own region. The present national policy seems to be to concentrate economic power in these cities and is strongly supported by the system of air and fast train services, and by bank deposits and advances (Table 10.5).

Table 10.5 : Distribution of Deposits and Advances of Scheduled Commercial Banks (as on 31st December, 1975)

	City	Number of Offices	Deposits	Advances
1.	Delhi	595	128,001	118,659
2.	Calcutta	490	134,649	122,666
3.	Kanpur	112	14,321	7,669
4.	Anmedabad	233	21,335	24,196
5.	Bombay	729	217,078	203,666
6.	Hyderabad	203	21,040	14,991
7.	Bangalore	290	24,471	33,290
8.	Madras	351	43,580	57,687
9.	Poona	138	15,854	11,861
	Total Nine cities	3,141	620,329	594,685
	Total All India	20,050	1,371,073	1,007,345

Source: Banking Statistics—Basic Statistical Returns, Volume 5, December 1975, Reserve Bank of India.

National Metropolises and Metropolitan System of India

At the national level the economy of the country is spatially organized by four metropolitan cities—Bombay, Calcutta, Madras and Delhi. The transportation system of India is also focused around these four metropolises which have, therefore, assumed national importance. While interacting strongly themselves, they also have a core area of their own metropolitan dominance within which they shape and direct the economic activities of their respective urban sub-systems. It is, therefore, wrong to assume the metropolitan system of India to be mono-nodal and to define its size distribution on that basis (Berry, 1971). Of the four national metropolitan centres, the first three were developed as expatriate settlements in the early eighteenth century by the British rulers. Although Delhi has an ancient origin, New Delhi was built by the British as the new capital of India in 1910.

City Primacy

A primate city growth pattern is discernible in all of the four metropolitan systems of India, but is most pronounced in the Calcutta metropolitan system (Table 10.6). In the other metropolitan systems there is not much difference in their indices of primacy. The primate city pattern of these four systems is further substantiated by the concentration of urban population in the apex settlement of their respective systems. Here again the position of the city of Calcutta is unique claiming the largest concentration of urban population within its system.

Table 10.6 : Three City Index of Urban Primacy, 1971

Metropolitan System	*Index of Primacy*	*Primate City Population as Percentage of Total Urban Population of the System*
Calcutta	6.4	35.37
Bombay	1.7	21.70
Madras	1.3	15.68
Delhi	1.7	16.09

A high degree of primacy is usually associated with the parasitic growth of the major city, a low level of regional economic development, and a lack of spatial integration of the economy within the metropolitan system. This is best exemplified by the Calcutta metropolitan system which includes the vast north-east region, one of the most underdeveloped areas in the country. Besides, political factors also seem to have contributed significantly to the high primacy of Calcutta. As a result of the partition of the country in 1947 the whole of East Bengal, which was formerly part of the Calcutta metropolitan system, was separated from it. This disturbed the structural integration within the metropolitan system acquired during the pre-partition period. The entire transport system had to be reorganized; but still continues to be weak. This further distorted the settlement system focused on Calcutta and accentuated its primacy. The other metropolitan systems were not much affected by this political division of India.

Inter-Settlement Distances

An analysis of inter-settlement distances helps to achieve a better understanding of the hierarchical system of settlements. In a well-developed and functionally integrated hierarchy of settlements the number of settlements increases and inter-settlement distances tend to decline regularly from the higher to the lower levels of hierarchy. Any significant deviation would mean distortion in the system of settlements.

It may be observed, however, that in a dynamic system of settlements the inter-settlement distances within the same size range do not remain constant. This is corroborated by an earlier study of settlements with populations of 100,000 and above (Alam, Rao and Gopi, 1974). The straight line inter-settlement distances by size class for the settlements in all the four metropolitan systems are given in Table 10.7, highlighting two distinguishing features common to them all. In all of the systems between the size ranges 100,000-499,999 and 75,000-99,999 the number of settlements has declined and distances have increased with a fall in the size range. This is contrary to the accepted principles of the hierarchical ordering of settlement and is presumably due to the clustering of settlements in higher size ranges which has developed in the economically prosperous pockets of the country. This substantiates the earlier results obtained though the analysis of rank-size graphs, regarding the skewed development of the hierarchy of settlements in the four metropolitan systems. The Madras and Delhi metropolitan systems suffer from similar distortions in the size class 35,000-49,999, producing a rise in the inter-settlement distances above the preceding size class. These inter-settlement distance distortions are a reflection of the wide disparities in levels of regional development which distort the hierarchy of settlements. It must be emphasized that the four metropolitan systems of India should be considered as emerging systems. There are bound to be distortions in these settlement systems until they reach the stage of maturity. A mature settlement system with a well-articulated hierarchy can develop only if regional disparities are minimized and a rural-urban continuum is fully established.

Distortions in the Settlements System

The settlement system of a country develops in response to its politico-economic system and level of economic development, and tends to organize the integration of the agrarian sector with the urban and industrial sectors. Such factors as the economic structure of India, the break in the historical continuity of its evolving settlement system

Table 10.7 : Metropolitan Systems of India : Number of Settlements and Inter-Settlement Mean Distances between Settlements of Same Size Class, 1971

Population Size	*Madras System*		*Calcutta System*		*Bombay System*		*Delhi System*	
	Number of towns	*Average distance in km*	*Number of towns*	*Average distance in km*	*Number of towns*	*Average distance in km*	*Number of towns*	*Average distance in km*
Above 2,000, 000	1	—	1	—	1	—	1	—
1,000,000-1,999,999	1	—	—	—	3	616	—	—
500,000-999,999	2	170	1	—	2	335	5	399
100,000-499,999	31	122	30	231	36	187	32	213
75,000-99,999	10	268	12	319	13	298	15	287
50,000-99,999	38	160	25	249	36	232	34	203
35,000-49,999	42	175	37	188	40	226	42	211
20,000-34,999	104	117	88	160	124	155	105	159

due to political factors, wide continuity of its evolving settlement system due to political factors, wide inter-regional disparity in levels of development, the inadequacy of linkages between urban centres and their surrounding rural areas and consequent malfunctioning of the supply and distribution system, the dysfunctional development of urban settlements, the haphazard development of services in the urban and rural settlements, and misconceived development strategies and policies of private and public sectors, have tended to disrupt and distort the evolution of the settlement system and thereby prevent the spatial integration and optimization of the economy and a proper articulation of settlement hierarchy.

The settlement system is deemed to be distorted if : (1) the distribution is marked by a significant clustering of large-sized settlements in pockets or corridors of development, (2) such settlements are disproportionately more numerous, and (3) the inter-settlements distance range of such settlements is much less when compared to the settlements in the lower size range. These are symptomatic of weaknesses in the linkages among the middle and lower orders of the urban settlements implying thereby a breakdown of the information system. Therefore, they cease to function as effective links in the chain of settlement systems and tend to become ineffective centres of urban activities.

Conclusion

Distortions in the settlement system of the developing countries and particularly that of India were the direct outcome of the policy during colonial rule to concentrate investments and high-order administrative and political functions in a few large urban centres. This resulted in their hypertrophy and prevented the formation of the systems of towns embracing the entire settled territory of the country, and also the formation of regional urban sub-systems (Raza and Atiya, 1976).

The colonial capitalistic system also induced the growth of monopolistic production and finance capitalism which have 'taken control of the primate metropolitan hierarchy in India. Hence, it is subject to behaviour exactly according to the law of the capitalist accumulation and concomitant forms of urbanization' (Chakraborty, 1978). The control of monopolistic production and finance capitalism of the metropolitan economy has continued even after Independence and, therefore, the pattern of urban and metropolitan development in independent India is not much different from that in colonial times. Such a metropolitan growth arrests the wider diffusion of technology, causes stagnation of the hinterland economy, prevents adequate articulation of a hierarchical system of settlements, and induces the exodus of people from surrounding rural areas and middle-order urban centres to the metropolitan centres. To generate a more dynamic system of urban and metropolitan development and to rectify the distortions in the system of settlements, the government must intervene to provide disincentives to the growth of metropolitan settlements, accelerate the growth and development of the middle-order urban centres, and initiate a public policy to promote the percolation of developmental impulses to the lowest level of settlements in the system.

Acknowledgements

The author acknowledges with graceful thanks the assistance given by Dr. K.N. Gopi, Miss C.K. Aruna, and Miss Zubaida Begum, in the preparation of this chapter.

NOTES

Alam *et al.* : *Trends and Patterns of Metropolitan Development in India*, Hyderabad, Osmania University, Centre for Urban Research, 1974 (Occasional Paper 3).

Alam, S. Manzoor : Distortions in the Settlement System of India, *Geographical Review of India*, 42(4), 1981, pp. 305-322.

Alam, S.M. *et al.,* 1976. *Planning Atlas of Andhra Pradesh,* Hyderabad: Government of Andhra Pradesh.

Alam, S.M.; Rao, R.M.; and Gopi, K.N., 1974. 'Trends and Patterns of Metropolitan Development in India', Occasional Paper No.3, Centre for Urban Research, *Department of Geography*, O.U., Hyderabad.

Basham, A.L., 1971. *The Wonder that was India*, London: Fontana.

Berry, B.J.L., 1971, 'Internal Structure of the City', in Larry S. Bourne (ed), *Internal Structure of the City,* London.

Bhat, L.S. *et al.* : *Central Place Hierarchy for a Developing Agricultural Region*: A Report of a study sponsored by I.C.S.S.R., New Delhi, in: Micro Planning, New Delhi, K.B. Publication, 1976.

Bhat, L.S., 1976. *Micro Level Planning,* New Delhi: K. B. Publications.

Chakraborty, Satyesh : Development and Primate Metropolis. Some valuable questions, in: S. Manzoor Alam and G. Ram Reddy (ed), Socio-Economic

Development Problems in South and Southeast-Asia, Bombay, Popular Prakashan, 1975, pp. 76-104.

D'Souza (Victor S.). Green Revolution and Urbanisation in Punjab during 1961-71, in: S. Manzoor Alam and.V. Pokhishevsky (ed.), *Urbanisation in Developing Countries*, Hyderabad, Osmania University, 1976, pp. 455-474.

Dube, B., 1967, 'Geographical Concepts in Ancient India', *National Geographical Society of India,* Varanasi.

Gopi, K.N. : *Urban Growth and Industrial Locations*, New Delhi, Oxford and IBH Publishing Co., 1980.

Kumar, Pramila : *Agricultural Changes in Urban Fringe*, New Delhi, Rajesh Publications, 1980.

Law, B.C., 1954, *Historical Geography of Ancient India,* Paris: Societe Asiatique de Paris.

Mukerjee, A.B., 1972, 'Rural Settlements in Sivalik Hill Tract of Punjab', *N.G.J.I.*, XVIII, pp. 57-63.

Munsi, S. K., 1980, *Geography of Transportation in Eastern India Under the British Raj,* Calcutta: K.P. Bagchi & Co.

Naqvi, H.K., 1969, *Urban Centres of Industries in Upper India (1556-1803 A.D.),* Bombay; Asia Publishing House.

Raza, M. and Atiya, H., 1976, 'Characteristics of Colonial Urbanization—A Case Study of Satellite Primacy of Calcutta (1850-1921)', in Alam-Pokshishevsky, *Urbanization in Developing Countries,* Hyderabad: Osmania University 1976: 187-209.

Schwartzberg, J. E. *et al.*, 1978. *A Historical Atlas of South Asia,* Chicago: University of Chicago Press.

Sinha, S. N., 1976. *The Mid-Gangetic Region in the 18th Century,* Allahabad: Shanti Prakashan.

Smailes, A. E., 1968, 'The Indian City—A Descriptive Model', IGU Symposium on Urban Geography, Varanasi.

Part III : Urban India : Household Energy Consumption—Policy Issues

11

Urban Household Energy Use in India : Efficiency and Policy Implications*

Introduction

Urbanization has become an integral part of the socio-economic growth of developing countries. The levels of urbanization vary across countries and continents, but population growth is much faster in cities than in rural areas due both to higher natural increases and to net migration. Cities tend to be the focal points of economic activity and as Asian countries develop, their cities are likely to act as magnets for investments, industrial production and other economic activities. Urban lifestyles are much more similar across countries and continents, by comparison, rural ones tend to differ markedly even within the same country.

In urban and rural areas, energy is needed for the same end-uses-cooking, water heating, space heating in colder climates, lighting and other electricity end-uses, but their energy carriers tend to be very different. The carriers in a rural setting are determined by the local availability of resources; while in a city a wider selection of fuels and equipment is available for use.

Of all sectors, the household sector experiences the most pronounced changes in its patterns of fuel use over time. Typically a household may shift from using biomass, to kerosene, LPG and finally to electricity for specialized cooking. On the other hand, it may

---

* This paper was jointly written with Jayant Sathaye, Lawrence Berkeley National Laboratory, Berkeley, California, USA: and Doug Barnes, The World Bank, Washington DC, USA.

Published in *Energy Policy*, Vol. 26, No. 11, 1998, pp. 885-891.

shift from biomass to electricity for water heating. (Sathaye and Taylor, 1991). This shift phenomenon is often referred to as a 'fuel transition' from traditional (biomass-based) to modern household fuels. Past studies consistently indicate a strong correlation between household income levels and the types and amounts of fuel used for cooking (Cecelski *et al.*, 1979; Leach, 1988; Reddy, 1990). Based on this observation, researchers have developed the notion of a "fuel-income ladder" to explain the shift to more convenient and higher-quality fuels as household incomes pass certain thresholds (Reddy and Reddy, 1994).

Household fuel transitions often accompany changes in economic activity and lifestyles, and are a central focus of national and State government policy. The primary goal of government intervention in household fuel markets is to improve the availability of modern fuels at affordable prices. Government intervention usually takes the form of subsidies for fuels. The relative costs of using fuels, however, do not consistently appear to contain household fuel choices. Various studies have concluded that many poor households actually pay more for their fuels, on an energy-content basis, than do higher income households (Bhatia, 1988).

This chapter reports on the findings and policy implications arising from a household energy survey of the city of Hyderabad, India. The purpose of the survey was to assist the government in establishing more targeted policies for the provision of energy services in large metropolises and to validate the transition related to the supply and demand of household fuels for a large Indian city.

Background on Hyderabad

Hyderabad, with a population of five million, ranks sixth among the 16 Indian metropolises with a population exceeding one million. It is one of the historic cities of India founded in 1591. Its modern phase of development commenced in 1956, when it was declared the capital of the State of Andhra Pradesh. The population of Hyderabad has grown rapidly from 1.25 million in 1961 to 4.74 million in 1991, a 279 per cent increase in 30 years at an annual rate of 4.4 per cent, which has increased steadily, and averaged at 7.2 per cent between 1981 and 1991. The population growth has been accompanied by an increase in built-up area, which has more than doubled since 1971.

Hyderabad economy appears stagnant and over 40 per cent of the population lies in the low-income brackets. The literacy level is only 76 per cent and most of the literates are not educated beyond the high school level. The size of the household is unusually large (6.5 persons per household) for a metropolitan settlement and has not changed much over the last three decades. The dependency ratio is high with one earner for every four non-earners on the average in a household.

Methods

In order to validate the transition related to the supply and demand of household fuels for a large Indian city, we conducted an in-depth energy survey of 3,000 households and small commercial establishments in Hyderabad, India. The survey was conducted through a stratified random sampling of 2,000 households in the municipal area, and another 800 in the suburbs. The size of the sample was 0.38 per cent of the total number of 1991 households in Hyderabad. Because earlier energy surveys were carried out in 1966 and 1982 in Hyderabad, this work generated information on long-term household energy use trends (Alam, 1967; Alam *et al.,* 1983). The survey specifically examines issues related to fuel choice, household income, urban scale, and the energy-decision making process. The research examined the adoption of modern fuels for cooking, water heating, and the penetration of electricity and electric appliances in relation to socioeconomic characteristics and locations of households. It focussed particularly on energy use in low income households (slum dwellers), and examined factors that serve to reduce the poor households' access to fuels like the electricity.

Key Findings of the Survey

Hyderabad households have witnessed dramatic increases in modern fuel use in years. Changing patterns of household activity and livelihood underline this growth. Biomass fuels, until recently a dominant household energy source in Hyderabad, play only a limited role in current household activities. Even the dominance of kerosene appears to be diminishing as fuel-wood-using households opt for LPG over kerosene. The survey reveals that this increased reliance on modern fuels arises from a preference among consumers for more convenient and readily available fuels. Government policies have played a key role in spurring this transition through subsidized prices and the controlled availability of kerosene and LPG. These policies have also hurt the poor and reduced the overall efficiency of household fuel use in India.

Establishing household energy use patterns, requires a thorough understanding of the socio-economic characteristics of the surveyed households. The survey included data on income levels, household sizes, and education levels. These characteristics explain why households choose certain fuels, why they use certain amount of electricity, and why they purchase certain types of appliances.

Household Income

The economy of Hyderabad has had a very skewed development with extremely uneven distribution of income. This is borne out by the fact that about 43 per cent of the population is in the two lowest income groups. There is excessive concentration of wealth in the highest income group, who constitute 6 per cent of the population. Average household income in Hyderabad was surveyed to be Rs. 3,885 (US $110 @ Rs. 34 = 1 US $) per month. The survey data was stratified by ten income per capita categories, which were aggregated into five income groups. Household income varied almost six-fold from Rs. 1,455 to Rs. 8,184 per month across income groups.

The main finding regarding income growth is that household income in 1994 was higher compared to that in 1967, but significantly lower in real terms compared to 1982 (Table 11.1). Monthly income (at 1982 prices) declined from Rs. 382 per household in 1982 to Rs. 313 in 1994. The decline in real income is probably a combined effect of the lowering of State income for 1994 and strong inflation between 1982-1994.

The lower income also has been accompanied by a worsened income distribution since 1982. The lowest two of the five income groups account for about 43 per cent of the population. Their real income has decreased by almost half from the income levels of 1982. As a consequence, one-fourth of the city's population lives below the poverty level of Rs. 264 per capita per month. On the other hand, the real per capita income of the two uppermost income groups increased by 82 per cent for the top group and 20 per cent for the next one.

Table 11.1 : Changes in Hyderabad : Household Income

Year	*Income per household (Rs. per month)*	*Income per capita (Rs. per month)*
1967	187	30
1982	382	62
1994	313	47

Note: Deflators used to calculate income at 1982 price levels:
Consumer price index for industrial workers.
Consumer price index for urban non-manual employees.

Fuel Choice

Much of the energy used by Hyderabad households is mainly channelled towards two end uses: cooking and water heating, and to a lesser extent for space cooling, especially during the hot dry summer months. Space heating is not important because the climate is hot with little variability, and an occasional need is satisfied by short-term use of electric heaters. Two fuel transitions, which occur simultaneously, characterize the choice of cooking fuels in Hyderabad households: (1) replacement of biomass and solid fuels with LPG and (2) kerosene with LPG. A third transition, that from biomass to kerosene, which usually occurs at low-income levels and has been observed in earlier surveys (Sathaye and Tyler 1991), is no longer evident in Hyderabad. About 17 per cent of the households are involved in the direct transition from fuelwood to LPG, which occurs at a low monthly income per capita of about Rs. 250. Various factors affect the speed at which these transitions occur: income levels, the availability of fuels, government policies, cuisine, and household activity patterns. With the liberalization of the economy, the availability of LPG has considerably increased which in turn has helped speed the transition to this fuel.

According to the survey results, household fuelwood use declined drastically from a previously high level of 67 kg per capita in 1982 to low or insignificant levels, 14 kg per capita in 1994 (Table 11.2). The reduced use of fuelwood was offset by the increased use of both LPG and kerosene. Kerosene use increased 20 per cent and reached 23 litres per capita by 1994, and LPG use increased 15 per cent and reached 15 kg per capita (Table 11.2). Because of the increased use of LPG and kerosene, whose efficiency of use is several-fold that of fuelwood, the input energy consumption for cooking declined from 29 kgoe per household (hh) per month in 1982 to 22 in 1994. The corresponding output energy consumption increased only marginally, from 9.2 kgoe per hh per month to 9.5 during this period.

Table 11.2 : Average Fuel Consumption Per Capita by Type, Hyderabad

Fuels	*1982*	*1994*
Fuelwood (kg)	67	14
Kerosene (litres)	19	23
LPG (kg)	13	15

Our survey data shows that the decline in household fuelwood consumption is offset by a corresponding rise in its use in the non-household sector, which includes commercial establishments, crematoria and wedding halls, and small or tiny scale industries. In these applications, fuelwood is used in bulk quantities in the open air, where fire control is easier and smoke is quickly dissipated.

Electricity Consumption

Electricity demand has increased rapidly in Hyderabad in recent years. Higher appliance saturations and more intensive lighting, despite the decrease in household income, have spurred this growth. The incomes of the top two income groups have increased since 1982, however, which coupled with a drop in appliance prices may explain this seeming paradox. Electricity is available to all households in Hyderabad, but it is subject to frequent load shedding, blackouts, and voltage fluctuations. The survey revealed that over 30 space illuminating and conditioning, entertainment, water heating and kitchen gadgets and appliances are in use in Hyderabad households. The saturation rate of appliances is similar to that found in another Indian city, Pune (Kulkarni *et al.*, 1994), although the water heater saturation is lower.

Electricity represents over one-fourth of the total energy consumed in the household sector. The rich consume far larger quantum of electrical energy than the poor. The average monthly per household and per capita consumption of electricity is only 90 and 15 kWh, respectively. The consumption level of the rich and the poor households varies widely. Monthly consumption ranges from 180 and 41 kWh per household and per capita in the highest income group to 57 and 7 kWh, respectively in the lowest income group.

Energy Pricing

LPG, kerosene, coal, and biomass in various forms constitute the primary fuels used by the Hyderabad households. Coal use is small in households but significant in small commercial establishments. The availability and prices of each fuel vary across the surveyed households. Subsidized kerosene is available through ration shops at a price of Rs. 3 per litre. The average price paid by a Hyderabad household was surveyed to be Rs. 3.46, indicating the households purchase some proportion of the kerosene in the open market. The survey also revealed that the lowest-income group pays the highest average price at Rs. 3.6 per litre, implying that they purchase about a quarter of their kerosene on the open market. In contrast, households in the highest income group pay an average price of Rs. 3.33 per litre while purchasing about 12 per cent of their kerosene in the open market.

LPG is sold at a subsidized price of Rs. 7.57/kg. It is available on the open market at a much higher price of about Rs. 13/kg. The price and supply of fuelwood is not regulated and its surveyed price was Rs. 1.1/kg. Table 11.3 shows the prices of each of the three cooking fuels. LPG is clearly the most expensive in terms of its price per unit of input energy.

Table 11.3 : Fuel Prices adjusted for Combustion Efficiency

Fuels	*Subsidized Prices (Rs./unit)*	*Subsidized Prices (Rs./kgoe of input energy)*	*Subsidized Prices (Rs./kgoe of useful energy) Col.4*	*Market Prices (Rs./kgoe of useful energy) Col. 5*
Fuelwood*	1.1/kg	2.90	19.4	19.4
Kerosene	3.0/l	3.7	10.5	19.2
LPG	7.6/kg	7.14	11.9	20.0

Note: All prices are market prices. Fuelwood is not subsidized.

Of the three fuels, kerosene and LPG, prices are subsidized and fuelwood reflects its market price, which, therefore, turns out to be the most expensive fuel, when combustion efficiency is accounted for

(Table 11.3, column 4). If subsidies are eliminated, the prices of kerosene and LPG, adjusted for combustion efficiency, are almost the same and are close to the market price of fuelwood (Table 11.3, column 5).

The average price of electricity paid by surveyed households was Rs. 1.10/kWh. It varies only slightly from Rs. 1.08 to Rs. 1.15 from the lowest to the highest income group. The cost of supply to Hyderabad households is estimated to be Rs. 1.27/kWh, which amounts to a subsidy of Rs. 0.17/kWh.

Energy Expenditure Patterns

The average household monthly expenditure on all sources of energy is Rs. 211, and varies from Rs. 323 in the highest income group to Rs. 165 in the lowest one. As a percentage of household income, however, the poorest group has to allocate 14 per cent of its income for purchasing energy, while the richest allocates only 3 per cent for the same purpose. Households spend almost half their energy expenditure on electricity. On an average, households spend 44 per cent of their energy expenditure for electricity, 27 per cent for LPG and 23 per cent for kerosene. The expenditure on fuelwood is a mere 5 per cent. The share of expenditure on the three fuels varies with income. While the lower income groups spend more on fuelwood (23%) and kerosene (66%), the higher income groups spend nearly 92 per cent on LPG. Across income groups, the expenditure on electricity remains fairly high: the rich allocate 60 per cent and the poor 34 per cent of their energy expenditure for electricity.

Policy Implications

The Government of India administers the supply of kerosene, LPG and coal. It limits the amount of kerosene available at subsidized prices. Consumers with legal residences may purchase subsidized kerosene using ration cards provided to them by the government. Because the government does not give ration cards to households in illegal squatter settlements, these low income consumers must purchase kerosene at higher prices in the open market or use alternate fuels such as fuelwood or charcoal. Government restrictions used to limit each household to one subsidized LPG cylinder in the past, which when emptied could be exchanged for another. In the 1990s, LPG supply has been liberalized and the fuel has become available on the open market at prices that are nearly double those of subsidized supply. The fuelwood market in Hyderabad, however, is well structured and highly organized; it operates freely and efficiently without any direct government intervention.

Effects of Existing Policies

Despite the good intentions of policy-makers, the supply of energy to Hyderabad consumers remains inequitable where the poor do not have as good an access to subsidized fuels as the rich. The fuel subsidies do not appear to be needed since they primarily benefit the well-to-do. The electricity supply is unreliable and generates inadequate revenue to finance future improvements to the APSEB system. We explore these issues in more depth below.

Public Distribution System not well directed to help the poor

Although the ration card system is intended to make kerosene more affordable and available to the poor, it is not very well targeted. It benefits more the wealthy—and middle-class households. The poorest households without addresses cannot gain access to ration cards, and hence, pay much higher market prices for kerosene, or use inefficient and consequently very expensive fuelwood for cooking. In addition, the ration shops get kerosene only periodically and in limited quantities, so the supply routinely runs out before the next allotment, leaving the poor to either purchase open market kerosene or use fuel-wood.

Electricity Supply under increasing strain

Electricity supply to Hyderabad city, and to the State of Andhra Pradesh, is provided by the Andhra Pradesh State Electricity Board (APSEB). It generates, transmits and distributes electricity to urban and rural areas of the State. As a policy of the State government, aided by the national government, the APSEB supplies power to rural agricultural customers at highly subsidized rates. The loss in revenue is made up largely by subsidies from the national government, and in part by higher rates for industrial and commercial customers. Electricity supply to households is subsidized at a surveyed estimate of Rs. 0.17/kWh. In recent years, the APSEB, along with other SEBs, is under increasing financial strain as it is pressured to provide more service with less revenue. In Metropolitan Hyderabad alone the subsidy on electricity amounts to Rs. 150 million annually. The large subsidies coming to the SEB mean that it is more concerned with meeting government targets regarding the number of villages electrified as opposed to providing quality service to customers. The consequence is that public opinion regarding the SEB is extremely low. Focus group interviews of middle class and higher income households reveal support for reforming and liberalizing the distribution of electricity, even if it meant higher prices. There was not a similar level of support from the poor, so special consideration needs to be given to dealing with their problems.

Subsidy on Energy

The markets for energy in urban Hyderabad are influenced extensively by government policies that provide household fuel subsidies. The difference between the market price and the administered price of a fuel has been assumed to be the amount of subsidy on that fuel. We estimate that LPG, kerosene and electricity are subsidized to the extent of Rs. 5/kg (Rs. 4.6/kgoe), Rs. 2.5/*l* (Rs. 2.4/kgoe) and Rs. 0.17/kWh, respectively. Taking into consideration the household consumption of each of these energy sources, the subsidies in urban Hyderabad are massive, over Rs. 800 milion per annum, and are likely to grow as more people switch to "modern fuels". These subsidies are meant to help the poor, but the majority of the subsidies end up in middle- and upper-class households, who can afford to pay market rates for fuels. Likewise, policies to limit imports of fuels create periodic local scarcities. In scarcity, it is the poor who are last to gain access to the fuel, as evidenced by the fact that they had limited access to kerosene until LPG became more widely available for higher income households. Restricting the subsidy to the low income target groups would save the government a significant sum of Rs. 573 million annually.

Good Impact of Forest Policy

Our survey included an assessment of the vegetation cover in areas surrounding Hyderabad. Both aerial maps and ground truthing was done to ascertain the ground cover. The analysis of these data showed that because of (1) significant transition away from wood, (2) forestry policies that stress conservation of forests, and (3) changing land use patterns, deforestation in the Hyderabad region has slowed considerably. This is very good news, and existing land use and forestry policies should be strengthened to maintain this healthy, desirable and environment friendly trend.

Policies to Improve Energy Markets

Accessibility of LPG and Kerosene should be enhanced.

The policies to open up the petroleum markets for LPG and kerosene in urban households should be continued and supported. The availability of kerosene at world market prices has helped the poor gain access to kerosene, a fuel preferred over wood. In addition, the increased import of LPG has meant that the market for this product has expended among the middle and higher income consumers. The survey finds that the middle class and rich appreciate the convenience of LPG, and will continue to use it even if subsidies are removed altogether and all LPG has the benefit of freeing up the subsidized kerosene for the urban poor. Thus, the general recommendation is to continue to liberalize imports and to allow price competition of kerosene and LPG at competitive world market prices.

Price of Electricity should be raised and the APSEB made financially viable.

Middle and higher-income households are willing to pay more for an assured and reliable electricity supply. Raising electricity prices would help the SEB become financially viable. However, this cannot be done on an ad hoc basis, without assurance that service for all sections of society will be improved. It is clear that the public is skeptical that this can be achieved with the existing distribution system and management. An alternative would be to allow electricity distribution to be taken over by private companies, who would eliminate illegal connections and increase bill collections.

Fuelwood Trade based on Market Principles functioning efficiently

The fuelwood trade in Hyderabad is already based on market principles and this should not be changed. The forestry department should continue programmes that encourage farmers to grow (and harvest) trees on their own farms, since this is the main source of fuelwood for Hyderabad city. Since commercial enterprises are increasingly using wood, it is recommended that the coal subsidy and allocation system be eliminated and coal distribution should be based on market principles.

Policies to Help the Process of Fuel Transition among the Urban Poor

The subsidies that are currently given across the board to all households in urban Hyderabad can be reduced and still benefit the poor urban households. Although the targeting of these subsidies can be a problem, the following recommendations can be of more direct benefit to the poor than the current policies.

The poor can be targeted effectively through lifeline rates for electricity. The reason for this is that the poor use very little electricity. A lifeline rate can be designed based on the household load compared to their income. The findings of the survey are that a lifeline rate of 50 kWh per month would assist the poorest 23 per cent of the households, who have problems paying for electricity. In addition a policy to keep charges for new connections for minimal service very low would be efficient, if it is combined with strict enforcement and policing of illegal connections. A grace period of one billing period should be given before disconnection due to non-payment of bills. The combination of these policies would not constitute a burden on the APSEB and would be equitable.

For LPG, the poor and lower middle class households can be effectively targeted through making initial LPG service more affordable. This could be accomplished through the distribution of LPG in smaller bottles and by incorporating the costs of initial connection fees (bottle and stove) in the monthly bill. This credit could be given for one year, or it could be incorporated into the price of LPG. Retailing the LPG in smaller bottles would cost slightly more than LPG in standard containers, however, the unit price of LPG in both types of containers should be the same, in order to avoid leakage from one to the other.

The policy for kerosene is more complicated. In view of the existing level of poverty in the city, subsidy for kerosene ought to be retained to benefit the poor. Under the existing policy, the middle class and the rich are benefiting the most from the subsidy on kerosene; the poor are not able to get from ration shops the quantity of kerosene they need when they need it. It has been observed, therefore, that it is mostly the poor who purchase kerosene from the open market to fulfil their requirements. In view of this it is recommended that the sale of kerosene through the ration shops for the rich and middle income groups (pink card holders in AP) be totally stopped and only the target group (white card holders) should be entitled to avail of this facility. Simultaneously the sale of kerosene through private retail outlets be encouraged from where the middle and upper income groups may be able to purchase their requirement of kerosene.

An alternate approach would be to halt the sale of kerosene in the ration shops. All sales of kerosene should be made through the retail markets. Small distributors of the fuel should be encouraged, and a coupon should be issued only to poor ration card holders that will entitle them to purchase kerosene from a retailer at a subsidized price. The consequence of this policy would be to more directly target the poor with the kerosene subsidy. It would also open up the market of the fuel and would simultaneously discourage diversion of subsidized kerosene to other sectors.

The poorest of the poor are still using fuelwood for cooking. Improved stove programmes would be an effective policy to help the poor since it would reduce their cash outlay for fuels.

Conclusions

The household sector in cities of developing countries has witnessed the most pronounced changes in its patterns of fuel use. Our survey of 3,000 households in Hyderabad, India, highlights that despite the city's poverty and weak economic base, the sector has reached an advanced stage of energy transition, and the share of fuelwood in total energy consumption is much lower than before. There is a keen desire among the low income groups to shift to LPG, which is distinctly preferred over other fuels for cooking. Policies that help remove the barrier of high cost of obtaining LPG will speed this transition.

Energy supplies such as LPG, kerosene, and electricity are highly subsidized. Although the poor constitute the target group, it is the rich who benefit the most from the subsidies. It is mostly the poor who do not have the ration cards and, therefore, purchase kerosene at market prices. In view of this, subsidies on commercial fuels do not appear to be justified.

Electricity constitutes almost half the household energy expenditure, with its share being greater in higher income households. The saturation of electric appliances has risen since the earlier surveys, despite a decline in household income. This may be due to both lower prices for some of the appliances and a change in tastes whereby expenditure on entertainment and comfort is valued more than on other items. Despite the growing importance of electricity to households, its supply is the most erratic among all the major energy sources. Brownouts are frequent and supply during the dry season is limited to a few hours a day, when it is most needed. Policies ranging from higher charges, privatization of distribution, and the use of more efficient appliances and lighting are needed to ensure adequate supply in the future, which will require the political and organizational will to enforce appropriate policy measures that have been lacking thus far.

NOTES

Alam, M. (1967): Household Energy Survey of Hyderabad.

Alam, M.; Dunkerley, J.; Gopi K. and Ramsay, W. (1983): *Fuelwood Survey of Hyderabad,* Resources for the Future, Washington DC.

Bhatia, R. (1988): Energy Pricing and Household Energy Consumption in India, *The Energy Journal,* 9, 71-105.

Cecelski, E.; Dunkerley, J.; Ramsay, W. (1979): *Household Energy and the Poor in the Third World,* Resources for the Future, Washington D.C.

Kulkarni, A.; Sant, G.; Krishnayya, J. (1994): Urbanization in Search of Energy in Three Indian Cities. *Energy* 19, 549-560.

Leach, G. (1988): Residential Energy in the Third World. *Annual Review of Energy 13,* 47-65.

Reddy, S. (1990): *The Energy Sector of the Metropolis of Bangalore.* Ph.D. thesis. Department of Management Studies, Indian Institute of Science, Bangalore, India.

Reddy, A.K. and Reddy, B.S. (1994): Substitution of Energy Carriers for Cooking in Bangalore, *Energy* 19, 561-572.

Sathaye, J. and Tyler, S. (1991): Transitions in Household Energy use in Urban China, India, the Philippines, Thailand and Hong Kong. *Annual Review of Energy and Environment, 16,* 295-335. Sathaye, J and Tyler, S (1991), *op. cit.*

12

Fuelwood Use in the Cities of the Developing World : Two Case Studies from India

Introduction

In recent years there has been increasing, if belated, recognition of the important role of traditional fuels (fuelwood and crop and animal wastes) in the energy system of developing countries. Despite this interest, the structure of supply, distribution and consumption of traditional fuels is poorly documented compared with the now extensive data available on major commercial fuels such as electricity, gas and petroleum products.

A number of studies on traditional fuel supply and demand in rural areas have been undertaken, but little has been done to make comparable studies for urban populations. There are several reasons why this gap needs to be filled. First, as we shall see, traditional fuels are an important source of energy for urban households and, therefore, need to be taken explicitly into account in the formulation of policies governing household fuel use. Second, urban use of fuelwood contributes to the environmental deterioration associated with deforestation. About one-third of total fuelwood in India is currently used in urban areas, and this share could conceivably rise in future as consumers respond to higher prices of competing fuels. Moreover, urban consumption of fuelwood may contribute disproportionately to deforestation as it takes the form of logs from felled trees rather than the twigs, roots and branches used predominantly by rural populations. Third, major investment programmes for forestry and fuelwood at present being prepared by national government and donor

Published in *National Resources Forum (UN)*, Vol. 9, No. 3, August 1985, pp. 205-215.

organizations could benefit from increased undertaking of fuelwood markets.

The two case studies of urban fuelwood use and markets discussed here signal the commencement of attempts to fill this gap.[4] Though carried out for neighbouring Indian cities—Bangalore in Karnataka and Hyderabad in Andhra Pradesh—at the same period of time the two groups of researchers were not aware of each other's work until the projects were virtually completed. The simultaneous decision to study urban fuelwood use, arrived at independently, underlines the growing realization of its importance. Furthermore, the lack of contact between the two research teams adds weight to the strikingly similar findings of the two studies.

The objectives of both case studies were very similar—to study the entire fuel cycle including the generation and production of fuelwood supplies, their transport and distribution, and utilization. In both cases, however, most of the research emphasis was on the last two stages. This involved :

(1) estimating the quantities of fuelwood use in the cities for a given year;
(2) identifying the suppliers of this fuelwood;
(3) identifying the importance of the different transport modes supplying fuelwood;
(4) tracing the channels of distribution within the city; and
(5) identifying the major consumers of fuelwood.

Comparison of the Two Case Studies

Quantities of Fuelwood Supplied and Consumed

In both studies, the quantity of fuelwood was arrived at by making independent estimates of the amounts handled by suppliers, distribution channels and final consumers. In the case of Bangalore, the three estimates were very similar, implying a high degree of confidence in the estimates. In Hyderabad there was considerable difference in the amounts supplied and traded on the one hand, and total consumption on the other, suggesting that part of the supplies had not been adequately accounted for in the questionnaires covering arrivals and trade (*see* Table 12.1).

Table 12.1 : Estimates of Firewood Arrivals and Consumption, 1980-81 (in tonnes)

	Bangalore	*Hyderabad*
Suppliers	409,530	98,956
Distribution channels	451,140	101,850
Consumers	454,250	197,731
Consumption per capita (kg)	182	101

Sources: M. Alam *et al.* (1984) and A.K.N. Reddy and B.S. Reddy (1983).

In both cities, the estimates follow a similar pattern through the fuel cycle. The lowest estimates are those for supplies arriving at the city. The estimates derived from distributors are higher, and those based on consumption higher still. This pattern suggests that not all supplies arriving in the city are covered by survey of fuelwood arrivals or distribution channels. This could stem from an underestimation of bullock cart and head load arrivals, and, in the case of Hyderabad, by the generation of significant supplies within the metropolitan area. It also suggests that final consumers obtain part of their supplies direct from suppliers rather than through the wholesale and retail markets. This direct trade is particularly noticeable in the case of Hyderabad. The pattern of low supply and high consumption estimates suggests that more reliable and comprehensive estimates of total fuelwood consumption are to be derived from consumption rather than arrivals data.

Estimates of total firewood supplies and consumption for the two cities are given in Table 12.1 and Fig. 12.1. They show that both cities consume a substantial amount of fuelwood—almost 200,000 tonnes in Hyderabad in 1981 and 450,000 tonnes in Bangalore. The size of these amounts indicates that firewood is a major item of trade in the urban economies of these two major cities, and by no means a casual, small-scale activity.

An interesting feature of firewood in the two cities is the considerable difference in total consumption between them. Bangalore uses almost twice as much firewood as Hyderabad. Part of this difference is explained by Bangalore's higher population (2.5 million compared with 2.1 million). However, per capita consumption in Bangalore (at 182 kilos per year) is still 80 per cent higher than in Hyderabad (101 kilos). Further examination of this difference could throw valuable light on the determinants of firewood consumption. Insofar that it stems from a different composition of household energy

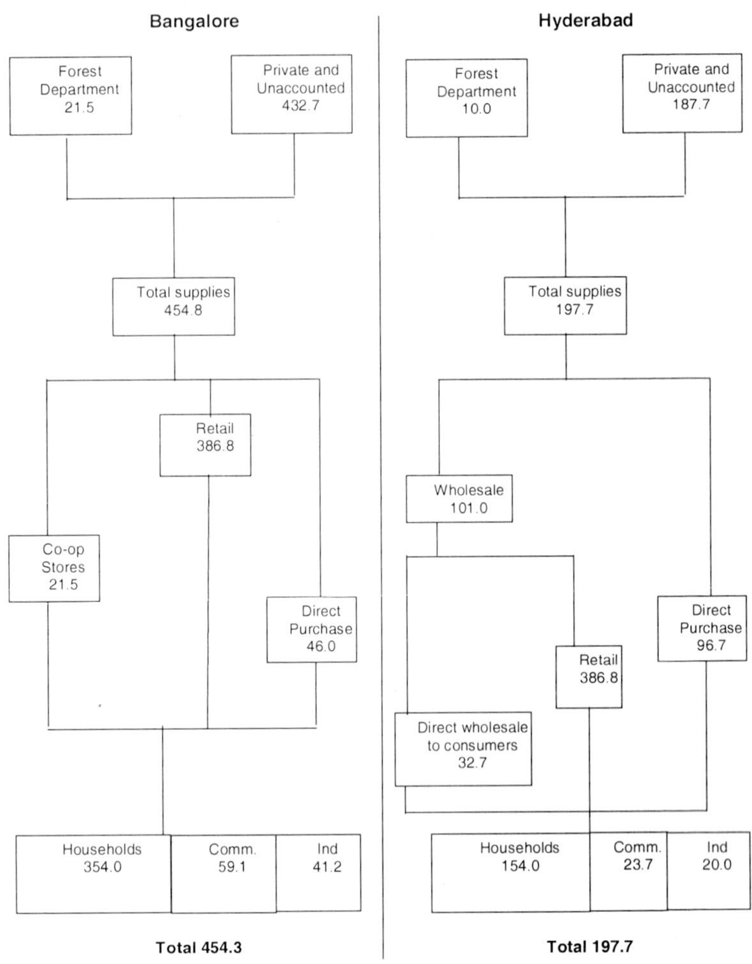

Fig. 12.1 : Firewood Supply and Demand in Bangalore and Hyderabad, 1980

use between the two cities, forthcoming studies of household energy use as part of the Bangalore urban ecology project could provide part of the answer.

Firewood Suppliers

The examination of sources of firewood supplies for these two cities leads to two important conclusions. First, the predominant suppliers of firewood are private contractors obtaining supplies largely from private land-owners. Government Forest Departments are minor sources, supplying directly (*see* Table 12.2) only 5 per cent of total supplies. Part of private contractors and unaccounted supplies may also come from government auctions, but the bulk of supplies originate in private lands.

The second conclusion is that a major part of firewood supplies originate from considerable distances. In Bangalore, for example, one half of total supplies come from between 120 and 300 km from the city, and 17 per cent from distances up to 700 km. In Hyderabad 55 per cent of total supplies comes from areas over 100 km from the city. The weighted average distances of origin could be about 100 km in Hyderabad and over 200 km in Bangalore. These long distances mean that the firewood trade in these, like trade in other commodities, will have important economic and environmental impacts on areas far distant from the cities.

Means of Transport

Given these distances between point of origin and consumption, transportation is of major importance. Four modes of transport are used: trucks, rail, bullock carts and head loads. In both cities truck transport predominates, accounting for about 85 per cent of the total in Bangalore and 94 per cent in Hyderabad. Despite lower costs of rail transport (about Rs. 0.44 per tonne kilometre for 200-250 km by truck compared with Rs. 0.15 by rail) rail transport has only a minor role due to the greater flexibility of truck transport in picking up and delivering relatively small loads. Bullock carts and head loads are also of small quantitative importance, transporting mainly local

Table 12.2 : Sources of Firewood Supply 1980-81 (in tonnes)

	Bangalore	*% of total*	*Hyderabad*	*% of total*
Government Forests	21,535	4.7	10,000	5.1
Private contractors	387,995	85.4		
Unaccounted	44,720	9.8	187,731	94.9
Total	454,250	100.0	197,731	100.0

Sources: M. Alam *et al*. (1984) and A.K.N. Reddy and B.S. Reddy (1983).

supplies of low quality firewood. The predominance of the most highly energy intensive mode (trucks) in firewood transport means that significant amounts of petroleum products are used in the firewood delivery system (see table 12.2).

Distribution Channels

In both cities there appear to be two parallel distribution systems: one organized by governments, and the other by private traders. In Bangalore the government segments in the form of co-operative societies which receive monthly allotments of firewood from the Forest Department for sale to ration card holders. In Hyderabad the government distribution system takes the form of agreements between industrial users and the Forest Department for specified supplies. As we have seen, in both cases the governmental distribution system accounts for a very small part of total supplies. By far the largest part of total supplies is distributed through private traders—commission agents who auction supplies as they arrive in the city, wholesalers and retailers. In Bangalore, consumers purchase most (85%) of their supplies from retailers. Direct purchases from co-operative societies account for 5 per cent. In Hyderabad, the share of purchases made directly from suppliers may be much higher—as much as 50 per cent of the total. Again further investigation of this apparent difference between the two cities could add greatly to our knowledge of fuelwood market organization.

Consumers

The structure of firewood consumption in the two cities is remarkably similar (Table 12.3). In both cases households are the major consumers,

Table 12.3 : Consumption of Firewood (in Tonnes)

	Firewood consumed	*% of total*	*Firewood consumed*	*% of total*
Households	354,000	77.9	154,031	77.8
Commercial	59,100	13.0	23,700	12.0
Industry	41,150	9.1	20,000a	10.1
Total	454,250	100.0	197,731	100.0

Source: M. Alam *et al.* (1984) and A.K.N. Reddy and B.S. Reddy (1983).

accounting for 78 per cent of the total, followed by commercial, social and ceremonial uses (hotels, bakeries, restaurants, cremations) about 13 per cent, and industry (plywood, bricks, tea, soap, packing cases etc.) about 10 per cent.

Household

Sample surveys of household in both cities suggest first that firewood is used largely by poor households. In Bangalore, for example, 80 per cent of lowest income families (casual labourers) depend wholly on firewood for both cooking and water heating. On the other hand, in families with income above Rs. 1,000 a month, 88 per cent use fuels other than firewood for both cooking and water heating. Of the total number of household totally dependent on firewood, 85 per cent are low income. At the other end of the scale only 3 per cent families with a monthly income of Rs. 1,000 or more use firewood. In Hyderabad, 60 per cent of the lowest income families (those with average incomes below Rs. 500 per month) depend primarily on firewood for cooking and water heating. In families with incomes of over Rs. 1,000 per month, 90 per cent use fuels other than firewood for cooking.

Table 12.4 : Monthly Mean Firewood and Total Household Energy Consumption in Hyderabad for Cooking and Water Heating, 1980

Income group (Rs.)	*Firewood (kgoe)*	*Total household energy (kgoe)*	*Fuelwood share as % of total (per cent)*
0-500	48	77	62
501-750	37	78	47
751-900	43	88	49
901-1000	32	80	40
1001-1250	42	92	47
1251-1500	39	91	43
1501-2000	26	83	31
2001-2500	33	91	36
2501-3000	27	90	30
3001-4000	19	82	23
Over 4000	24	109	22
Total sample	35	86	40

Source: M. Alam *et al.*, (1984).

Second, both studies indicate that firewood is the major form of cooking fuel in poor households. The Hyderabad household study which includes consumption of other fuels show that in the lowest income groups (under Rs. 500 household income per month), firewood is the single most important fuel accounting for 63 per cent of total cooking energy consumption (Table 12.4). At high incomes this share falls to 20 per cent. Furthermore, Table 12.4 also shows that the absolute amounts of firewood consumed per household decline as income rises. Thus, the lowest income households (under Rs. 500 per month) consume twice as much per month as the richest households. The Bangalore study indicates some increase in household use of firewood at lowest income, but over the whole range of income, the Bangalore and Hyderabad studies both indicate a negative relationship between household income and consumption of firewood. More specifically, both studies suggest that a 10 per cent increase in household income is associated with 7 per cent decline in firewood use. In other words, firewood is considered to be an inferior fuel by consumers who shift to preferred fuel such as bottled gas and kerosene as their incomes rise.

There are several reasons for the unpopularity of firewood. It is bulky and, therefore, difficult to store, it generates smoke and leaves ashes—all inconvenient factors in an urban household fuel. Wood stoves are often large, unwieldy and cannot be immediately extinguished after the cooking operation is terminated. Finally, the use of wood for cooking is forbidden in an increasing number of rental properties because of fire hazard. Despite these disadvantages, at present there appears to be little alternative cooking fuel for the poorest households.

Table 12.5 : Prices of Household Fuels, 1980

	Bangalore		*Hyderabad*		*Assumed combustion efficiencies*	*Efficiency adjusted prices*	
	Rs per GJ	*Index LPG= 100*	*Rs per GJ*	*Index LPG=100*		*Bangalore Rs per GJ*	*Hyderabad Rs per GJ*
Firewood	26.89	37	33.57	40	17	158	197
Charcoal	34.49	48	40.60	48	20	172	203
Kerosene	44.80	62	53.64	64	48	93	112
LPG	71.97	100	84.45	100	60	118	142

At first the main reason for firewood's popularity in poor households, despite its many inconveniences, is its cheapness. As Table 12.5 shows, in both Bangalore and Hyderabad firewood expressed in units of calorific content is cheaper than the alternative fuels. In both cities, firewood is 60 per cent cheaper than LPG, the favoured fuel for cooking, and 40 per cent cheaper than kerosene. Furthermore, firewood burning stoves are under Rs 5 are much cheaper than kerosene stoves (Rs. 30-90) and LPG stoves (Rs. 325-1500). These fuel prices and appliance comparisons, however, leave out the important poir.. of appliance efficiency.

The efficiency of cooking appliances using different fuel varies considerably, and it is generally agreed that the efficiency of wood stoves is lower than that of LPG and kerosene stoves. Part of the apparent cheapness of using wood may, therefore, be lost in low efficiency wood burning stoves. To illustrate this point the prices of Table 12.5 have been corrected to take into account assumed efficiencies (17% for firewood, 20% for charcoal, 48% for kerosene and 60% for LPG) of the various cooking devices. This procedure suggests that far from being the cheapest fuel, firewood, by virtue of the low efficiencies of firewood using stove, is substantially more expensive than either kerosene or LPG. The choice of the efficiencies chosen here can be debated, but the assumed efficiency of the wood burning stove is higher than usually cited so that there should not be any under bias in favour of the other fuels. If firewood were to be as cheap as kerosene and LPG on an efficiency corrected basis, efficiencies of firewood stoves would have to be as high as 20 to 30 per cent, well above the range of efficiencies usually quoted. The choice of firewood as a favoured fuel by poor households must, therefore, rest on the low initial cost of the appliance rather than the total cost of cooking with fuelwood.

Expenditure on cooking fuels represents a considerable financial burden for poor households. In the lowest income households in Hyderabad—those most heavily dependent on firewood—it accounts for 10 per cent of total family expenditure. A finer breakdown of the poorest households available from the Bangalore study illustrates the burden on the poorest groups even more dramatically. In the very lowest income group, expenditure on firewood accounts for 17 per cent of total income. The average for the lowest income households is 11 per cent, or about the same as in Hyderabad. As household income rises, the share of expenditure on cooking fuels declines sharply. In Hyderabad, for example, it accounts for just over one per cent in the highest income households.

Other Consumers

Although household use is predominant in both cities, commercial activities and industry together account for just over 20 per cent of total consumption. Commercial activities (13% of total consumption) typically use firewood for cooking and water heating in restaurants, hotels, bakeries etc. For industry, process heat is the major use.

Policy Implications

We have seen from these case studies that firewood is a significant item of trade in both cities, comes largely from private lands, is transported for considerable distances mainly by truck, is auctioned and distributed largely by private traders, is used mainly for cooking and water heating by low income households, is the main form of cooking for these households, and that expenditure on fuel wood represents a significant part of the monthly incomes of poor households.

What are the policy implications of these findings? The first concerns provision of firewood supplies. The question here is whether current and anticipated future levels of consumption can be that city firewood supplies are based primarily on logs from felled trees rather than the twigs, roots and branches from standing trees predominantly used in the countryside. Neither case study included direct observation of the state of the forest resource in supply areas. However, assuming that all Bangalore and Hyderabad firewood (643,000 tonnes annually) is obtained by felling trees and that each hectare yields about 120 tonnes then 5,358 hectares of forest land would have to be cleared and replanted annually to provide fuel wood for these cities and further provide charcoal. If firewood is to be truly renewable fuel, however, the acreages needed to support supplies at this level on a sustainable basis would be much greater—over 35,000 hectares and over 3 million trees would have to be planted annually.

While we do not have data on deforestation or replanting rates in this area (indeed, the two case studies could, with advantage, be extended to an examination of these issues), some degree of deforestation seems most probable. This is a particularly serious matter in semi-arid Bangalore and Hyderabad where forest regeneration and growth is slow.

This situation could become worse in the future. Trends in fuel wood consumption will depend on population, level and distribution of household income, the relative prices and availabilities of other fuels, and government policies with regard to the provision of domestic fuels. Urban populations in both cities have been increasing by about 3 per cent a year, and are expected to continue rising in future. This factor would, therefore, tend to increase fuelwood consumption. On the other hand, rising household incomes could depress firewood consumption as consumers move to preferred fuels. This distribution of income is also important for firewood consumption as a worsening income distribution leads to a disproportional rise in poor families who are the major consumers of firewood. The relative prices of firewood and other cooking fuels also affect firewood consumption. Any reduction in the price of firewood compared with other household fuels such as kerosene prices rising faster than firewood prices, would encourage an increase in consumption in industries and commercial establishment as well as in households. There are many uncertainties, but a reasonable scenario would be an increase in consumption of about 2 per cent a year representing a 50 per cent increase between 1980-81 (the year of studies) and the end of the century. Such as increase would impose additional strain on forest resources.

These possibilities underline the need for greater attention to forest resources, whether government or privately owned, including improved knowledge of the existing resource, increased replanting of both government and private lands, and efforts to improve the productivity of forest lands. Part of this will no doubt be undertaken by private farmers acting in response to changing market conditions. But the government could take a lead through the development and provision of improved seedlings, the regeneration of depleted forest lands, and the development of sources of supply (green belts) close to the cities. So far, government forestry policies have leaned towards production forestry to meet the requirements of forest-based industries and other commercial crops, or towards general environmental improvement. What is needed now is additional emphasis on fuel wood as such.

Another set of policy issues concerns the transport and distribution aspects of the firewood trade. As we have seen, firewood is transported considerable distances largely by truck, thus straining the capacity of an already overloaded transport system and using petroleum products, part of which are imported. In the Bangalore study for example, it was estimated that 2.2 million litres of diesel fuel were used each year to transport firewood to the city. Using similar estimating procedures, almost another million litres may be used in transporting fuelwood supplies to Hyderabad. Together these transport fuels, assuming that two-thirds are imported, could amount to some $ 400,000 a year in foreign exchange. If we assume for illustrative purposes that Bangalore and Hyderabad represent some 3 per cent of the total urban population, and if we assume further that they are typical of urban firewood supply situations throughout India, total foreign exchange costs of firewood transport could amount to $13 million annually and would rise in future as fuelwood consumption rises and as supplies are transported from more distant locations. These considerations reinforce the attractiveness of 'green belt' firewood developments and also raise the question of the merits of converting wood from distant locations to charcoal which is cheaper to transport. As charcoal making is typically closely regulated by States, they may need to revise some regulatory practices and investigate more efficient forms of charcoal production.

Throughout the distribution chain we need to inquire whether firewood markets are competitive and able to provide consumers with a product which is as cheap as possible, consistent with efficient service. As firewood is the staple fuel of the poor, it is important that prices should not be inflated either by excessive profits or by an otherwise inefficient distribution system.

While it is not possible on the basis of our present data to arrive at a definitive decision about market competitiveness, some preliminary conclusions are suggested by the data. The first is that the retail end of both the trades—firewood and charcoal trade—appears to be reasonably competitive. It is relatively easy to enter the firewood retail trade. Licensing is required, but this is apparently cheap and routine. The amount of capital is not large, though for many it may still be difficult to raise even small amounts. On balance, the large number of retail outlets suggests that entrance is easy and that, consequently, it would not be possible for a few suppliers to dominate prices at the retail level. Furthermore, there is evidence that final consumers can and do bypass firewood retailers by buying directly from suppliers.

The consumer has the additional protection of switching to other forms of fuel if firewood is considered too expensive. This may not be a viable solution for the poor because of the cost of changing appliances, though they could benefit indirectly by the switching of other higher income groups. All this assumes of course that supplies of other fuels are made available.

While there may be some competitive protection for consumers at the retail level of the fuelwood trade, the position in Hyderabad at least is more ambiguous at the wholesale level. On the face of it, the process is quite competitive. Supplies from all sources arrive at the informal auction sites for immediate disposal by the commission agents. However, very little is known about the working of this market, or whether there is complete freedom of entry into the commission agent business. One possibility of achieving greater knowledge of the process without unduly disrupting the existing system would be for the Forest Service with important data and information on the working of the wholesale market process. In other words, the Forest Service could use its influence to ensure that markets are more transparent. As in Hyderabad, the Forest Service is currently transporting the cut wood to a site convenient for loading by the forest contractor. The transport of this cut wood to the auction site would not be a major extension of Forest Service's existing activities.

Finally, there are issues of social policy. As firewood is the major household fuel, and as expenditure on firewood represent a very high share of expenditures in low income households, ways of providing low cost energy for cooking and water heating are of the greatest priority. There are a number of possibilities. The most obvious, given the low efficiencies, is the introduction of improved cooking stoves. Designs already exist which provide overall efficiencies of 40 per cent, over twice as high as the efficiencies assumed here. From our previous analysis it appears that the initial cost of appliance is an important factor in determining choice of fuel. If improved stoves are to be adopted they must continue to be low cost. The introduction of such stoves, however, could reduce firewood consumption sharply (by about 250,000 tonnes) and thus relieve pressure on forest resources. The resulting environmental benefits would justify substantial subsidies (such as kerosene) in being confined to the target population—in this case the poor.

An alternative is to promote the use of other fuels for cooking. We have seen from the analysis of household energy use that firewood is not a preferred fuel. Low income households would presumably be as eager as other households to shift to cleaner and more convenient forms of cooking fuels if they could afford them. Due to the differences in efficiencies, the displacement of all firewood in the two cities (about 500,000 tonnes) could be replaced by a relatively modest quantity (140,000 tonnes) of LPG. However, the provision of alternative fuels such as LPG and kerosene involve the expenditure of foreign exchange. They also have high initial costs—such as gas cylinders, gas or kerosene burning stoves. If these alternative fuels and/or their appliances were to be subsidized to a level which the poor could afford, richer households would also benefit from the subsidized prices, thereby increasing the cost of the subsidy programme.

One possibility which was considered in the 1960's is soft coal. This fuel has the advantage of being domestically produced and does not, therefore, represent a drain on foreign exchange. Soft coal is of low quality and is usually not a preferred fuel for households, especially if the alternative fuel is cheap LPG. However, the ready use of soft coal by institutional users suggests that it may be possible to extend soft coal use in households. What may be needed to accomplish this aim is research on soft coal cooking appliances which could minimize the disadvantages of the fuel—dirt and ash content. Thus improved, soft coal's greater compactness may make it an attractive substitute for wood.

As we have seen, the urban trade in fuelwood is a significant economic activity with actual and potentially major impacts on deforestation, the transport sector and social polity. Until recently, this trade has attracted little attention. Its role in deforestation and the consequent environmental deterioration was slow in being appreciated. In the era of low oil prices, the cost of transporting wood for long distances did not attract attention. In the realm of social policy, low kerosene prices offered the poor an attractive alternative to fuelwood.

In recent years these conditions have changed. Deforestation is now a major policy concern. The increase in oil prices has focussed attention on the need to economic consumption of transport fuels (which accounts for 40% of total consumption of petroleum products in India) and the difficulties of promoting kerosene as cheap fuel for domestic purposes. All of these considerations suggest a reassessment of the urban fuelwood trade and its relationship to these trouble spots. Suggestions emerging from these case studies include :

- the promotion of 'greenbelt' plantations where supplies of fuelwood for urban markets could be cultivated in nearby areas, thus improving the local environment and reducing environmental pressures of distant supply areas, as well as reducing consumption of transport fuels;
- the monitoring of market conditions to check whether markets are performing efficiently and that there are no unreasonable margins charged to traders; and
- the introduction of improved and if necessary subsidized wood burning stoves and the promotion of superior alternative fuels where feasible.

REFERENCES

1. *Dr. Alam* is an expert in urban studies concentrating his researches on cities in India and east Africa. Before taking his present post as Vice Chancellor of Kashmir University, he was Professor of Geography and Founder Director of Indian Ocean Studies Centre and Centre for Urban Studies at Osmania University, Hyderabad, India.
2. *Joy Dunkerley,* an economist, is a Senior Fellow at Resources for the Future, Washington, D.C., USA. She is working on a series of projects related to energy in developing countries and co-author (with William Ramsay, Lincoln Gordon and Elizabeth Cecelski) on Energy Strategies for Developing Nations. The Present article is based on work carried out in collaboration with the Centre for Urban Studies. Osmania University, Hyderabad, India (the Principal Investigator Manzoor Alam).
3. *Amulya Kumar Reddy*, a Physical Chemist, is Professor at the Indian Institute of Science in Bangalore, India. He is associated with ASTRA (the Centre for Applied Science and Technology for Rural Areas) and the Karnataka State Council for Science and Technology. This article was prepared when he was a visiting Senior Research Scientist at the Centre for Energy and Environmental Studies, Princeton University, USA.
4. The two studies are Manzoor Alam, Joy Dunkerley, K.N. Gopi, William Ramsay with Elizabeth Davis *Fuelwood in Urban Markets,* Concept Publishing Company, New Delhi 1984 and 'Energy in a Stratified Society: Case Study of Firewood in Bangalore by Amulya Kumar N. Reddy and B. Sudhakar Reddy In *The Economic and Political Weekly*, October 1983. The Bangalore fuel wood study is part of a wider study investigating many aspects of urban ecology.

13

Fuelwood as a Source of Domestic Energy in Urban India : The Case of Metropolitan Hyderabad and Raipur

Introduction

Despite of the availability of commercial sources of energy such as electricity, oil, diesel, coal and LPG, the non-commercial or traditional sources of energy still constitute the main source of domestic (cooking) energy in rural India and an important source in urban India. According to the Advisory Board of Energy (ABE) 95 per cent of rural households and 37 per cent of urban households in India are dependent on fuelwood, agricultural residue and dung cake for their cooking energy. Of these traditional sources, fuelwood is predominant catering for 56 per cent of rural households and 31 per cent of urban households. The National Commission on Agriculture (1976), the fuelwood Committee of the Planning Commission (1982), and the Advisory Board on Energy (1985) have all estimated significant rise in the consumption of fuelwood by the turn of this century as shown in Table 13.1.

Fuelwood is also being increasingly used in social functions such as marriages, and in solemn religious ceremonies such as cremating the dead. The fuelwood trade is being rapidly monetised in rural areas

---

This paper is jointly written with Joy Dunkerley, Senior Analyst, Office of Technology Assessment, Congress of U.S.A., Washington, DC.

Molly MaCauley, Fellow, Resources for Future, Washington, DC; and M. Naimuddin, Professor of Economics (Retired) Osmania University, Hyderabad.

Published in *The Annals of the National Association of Geographers India (NAGI),* Vol. 10, No. 2, December 1990, pp. 21.

with its growing use in urban settlements and industries. Consequent upon this large scale consumption of fuelwood in the domestic sector as also for industries, approximately 1.5 million hectares of forest area are getting depleted every year (ABE). In view of the poor technical quality of *chulhas* (stove) being used for fuelwood in India, their level of efficiency, according to the Advisory Board of Energy, does not exceed 8 per cent.

Of the total consumption of 120-130 million tonnes of fuelwood per annum in India, a little over 50 per cent is in urban India (ABE). Industries and the household are the principal consumers with the latter dominating. This rise in consumption has been despite a significant degree of substitution of fuelwood in household by kerosene and LPG in the cities of India with more than 100,000 populations. As for instance in Hyderabad city alone the proportion of household dependency on fuelwood markedly declined from 72 per cent in 1964 to 41 per cent in 1982 in terms of useful energy (Alam-Dunkerley *et al.*, 1984). Nonetheless the consumption of fuelwood in urban areas has been increasing because of rise in industrial consumption (paper, fibre, packaging, construction and mining), rise in the consumption at crematoria and in social functions such as marriage where mass cooking of food is undertaken to feed sometimes thousands of guests, and because of the rise in the number of urban poor who are the main consumers of fuelwood in urban India. Further, the substitution of fuelwood by commercial fuels, particularly LPG, is confined to medium and large sized urban centres with population exceeding 50,000. In these settlements they cover only a fraction of the total households. Inadequate substitutes account for the rising use of fuelwood as a source of cooking energy in urban India. This is clearly brought out in two studies on

Table 13.1 : Present and Projected Consumption of Fuelwood in India by Different National Agencies in India

Source		Present Consumption	Projected Consumption
1. National Commission on Agriculture	1970-71	150 million m^3	225 million m^3 (240 m^3 per 1000 caput) in 2000 A.D
2. Planning Commission Committee on Fuelwood	1982	150 million tonnes by 112 million households	180 million tonnes by 150 million households in 2000 A.D.
3. Advisory Board on Energy	1985	120-130 million tonnes	300-330 million tonnes by 2204-05 A.D. (per capita: 680 Kcal) consumption

Hyderabad and Raipur. It is proposed to highlight in this chapter, in a comparative perspective the basic findings of these two studies.

Metropolitan Hyderabad, the capital city of the State of Andhra Pradesh has a population exceeding 2.5 million (1981 Census). It is located in the Semi-arid Deccan Plateau in South India. Raipur is the divisional headquarters of the State of Madhya Pradesh. With a population exceeding 300,000 (1981 census), it is located in the intensively irrigated Chattisgarh plains of the Upper Mahanadi Basin in Central India. Climatically, it is sub-humid and claims dense forested areas within a radius of 30-100 km from where it draws its supply of fuelwood. In contrast, because of the semi-arid conditions, Hyderabad city draws its supply of fuelwood from distant forest zones of Karimnagar, Warangal and Adilabad located within a range of 50-200 km from the city. Economically and culturally the two settlements are sharply contrasted. Raipur is a monocultural centre located in the heart of Hindi speaking belt. Commerce and agro processing industries constitute its economic base. Hyderabad being a metropolitan settlement enjoys national stature. It is marked for its multi-lingual character with Telugu, Hindi and Urdu as the major languages. It has a diversified economic base and is a leading national centre in industries, banking, trade, commerce, administration, and education. It is one of the leading national centres with 7 universities and numerous national and international research centres in Sciences and Social Sciences. Hyderabad has now emerged as a mature metropolis whereas Raipur is a city in transition. Because of these basic differences in the economy of the two cities, Hyderabad's per capita income of Rs. 296, and per household monthly income of Rs. 1,709 (1981) at current prices are significantly higher than Raipur's per capita and per household income of Rs. 212 and Rs. 1400 per month respectively. The difference in their cultural setting, economic outlook and income level seem to be reflected in their respective fuel consumption patterns as brought out in the studies on Hyderabad and Raipur (Molly Mcaulay-Naimuddin *et al.*, 1987 mimeographed).

The Hyderabad study (1984) was taken up to look into the organizational structure of the fuelwood market, identify the principal consumers of fuelwood, analyse the changes in fuel mix over a period of time, examine the relationship between income, household size and fuel consumption pattern and highlight the policy implications. The Raipur study (1987) was an offshoot of the Hyderabad study with identical objective. This study was also undertaken to examine if differences in income, economic, cultural and physical environment and size of the settlements affect the consumption of fuelwood. Further based on these two studies in different social, cultural, physical and economic environment, we would be able to offer some generalizations on fuelwood consumption pattern and on the nature and character of fuel substitution from energy inefficient to energy efficient fuels in a transitional urban society of a developing country. An understanding of the fast change in fuel mix scenario in urban India will help in policy formulations.

The data were collected through structured questionnaires based on sample surveys. In the case of Hyderabad stratified random sampling procedure was adopted since homogeneous social and morphological areas were identified in earlier studies (Alam, 1965; Alam-Khan, 1972) whereas for the Raipur study households were picked up in accordance with random sampling principles covering all the 44 Municipal wards. A total of 1978 Municipal households plus 362 slum households were canvassed in Hyderabad during 1981-82 while questionnaires were administered to 500 households in Raipur during 1985-86.

Fuelwood Requirement and Source of Supply

The consumption of 154,000 tonnes of firewood per annum by the households in Hyderabad is more than three times the households' consumption of 44,600 tonnes in Raipur which is largely due to differences in their respective number of households i.e., 333,000 and 48,000. However, the per household consumption of fuelwood of 80 kg per month in Raipur far exceeds the average household monthly consumption of 35 kg of fuelwood in Hyderabad. Further, the dependence of Raipur on fuelwood as a source of cooking energy is notably marked since more than 50 per cent of its households depend on it as a primary source of energy (Table 13.2). Of the three major sectors consuming fuelwood in both Hyderabad and Raipur, the dominance of the domestic sector is conspicuous with 86 per cent of the total consumption in Hyderabad and 73 per cent in Raipur. The fuelwood consumption figures for commercial establishments in Raipur and Hyderabad are not comparable. Unlike the Raipur survey of 1985 which includes all categories of commercial consumers viz., bakerics, restaurants and hotels, tea stalls, hostels, and sweetmeat shops, the Hyderabad survey (1981) covered only consumption in hotels and restaurants. A more realistic and comparable picture emerges in Table 13.3, which highlights the fact that compared to Raipur, Hyderabad has over four times the number of commercial establishments using fuelwood but their consumption is only two and a half times that of Raipur. It is significant to note that except for hotels the per unit consumption of fuelwood is much less in Hyderabad compared to Raipur. Presumably this reflects the operation of the economy of scale in Hyderabad where bakeries, hotels and restaurants are much large in size than Raipur.

Table 13.2 : Hyderabad-Raipur : Fuelwood Consumption in Metric Tonnes

City	*Fuelwood as per cent of total fuel require-ments*	*Domestic*	*Marriages & Deaths*	*Commercial*	*Total*	*% of total supply accounted*	*Distance range for fuelwood supply (in km)*
Hyderabad	41	1,54,000 (86.5)	10,000 (5.6)	3,700* (7.8)	1,77,000	55	55-250 km
Raipur	54	44,600 (73)	3,200 (5.6)	13,200 (21.6)	60,400	21	30-100 km

Note: Figures in parenthesis denote percentages.

Table 13.3 : Raipur and Hyderabad : Consumption of Fuelwood by Commercial Establishments (in Quintals per month)

Type of Establishment	*Raipur (1985)*			*Hyderabad (1988-89)*		
	No. of Establi-shments	*Quantity of Fuelwood*	*Per Unit consump-tion of Fuelwood*	*No. of Establishments*	*Quantity of Fuelwood*	*Per Unit Consump-tion of Fuelwood*
1. Bakeries	29	1518	52.3	212	3661	17.2
2. Hotels	22	316	14.4	101	4848	48.0
3. Restaurants, Hotels & Tea Shops	360	7910	22.0	1381	17303	12.6
4. Sweetmeat stalls	61	1090	17.9	214	1243	5.8
Total	472	10384	22	1908	27055	14.2

It may also be noted from Table 13.2 that in both Hyderabad and Raipur a significant proportion of supply received is unrecorded and thus unauthorised. The proportion of unaccounted arrival is far higher in Raipur (79%) where the supply and price of the wood are controlled by the State Government. Unlike Raipur, free market economy system operates in the supply and sales of firewood in Hyderabad. Its supply, however, is monitored at the various checkposts along the major highways converging on Metropolitan Hyderabad.

[For details on sampling design and organization of fuelwood market, see the following :

S.M. Alam-Joy Dunkerley *et al.*, *Fuelwood in Urban Markets*, Concept, (1984) and Molly Macauley Niamuddin *et al.*, (1987) Raipur Fuelwood Survey Report (Mimeographed), Resources for Future, Washington. Includes consumption figures for restaurants and hotels only].

Income Distribution, Fuelwood Consumption and Income Relationship

There seems to be a strong relationship between the level of development and per capita income and energy consumption pattern. The per capita energy consumption of the developed economies like USA, Canada, West Germany, France, Japan and Australia, is far above the per capita energy consumption in the developing countries such as India, Indonesia, Pakistan etc. Further the developed countries use exclusively modern or commercial 'sources of energy such as electricity, oil and gas whereas the developing countries use a mix of modern and traditional sources of energy. The relationship of energy with income is also strongly reflected in the domestic sector at the household level and has been explained in the following paras.

Although Hyderabad and Raipur are located in widely varying physical and cultural settings and have contrasting economic bases, they nevertheless reflect common Indian urban characteristics of similar pattern of income distribution with a high concentration of low income groups (Rs.1,500), over 60 per cent in Hyderabad and nearly 75 per cent in Raipur (Table 13.4). The similarity in their middle and upper income groups' distribution is also noticeable. However, the middle income class including the lower middle income class is stronger in Hyderabad (34.4%) compared to Raipur (22.8%).

Table 13.4 : Hyderabad and Raipur: Income Distribution Pattern by Households

Broad Income Group	Hyderabad			Raipur		
	Number of Households	*Per cent of total (1981)*	*Cumula-tive per cent*	*Number of Households*	*Per cent of Total (1985)*	*Cumulative per cent*
1. Low Up to Rs.1500 per month	1009	60.8	—	368	74.4	—
2. Lower Rs.1501-2500 per month	395	23.8	84.6	67	13.6	88.0
3. Middle Rs. 2500-4000 per month	175	10.6	95.2	45	9.2	97.2
4. Upper: Rs. 4000 and above	80	4.8	100.0	14	2.8	100.0
	1659	100.0	—	494	100.0	—

Note: Rs. 1500 has been treated as the ceiling for low income groups. This coincides with the ceiling of upper income among the slum dwellers who constitute the poorest section of metropolitan community.

Principal Fuels and their Consumption Patterns

Electricity, fuelwood, LPG, Kerosene, Charcoal and Fuel constitute the main sources of domestic energy in both Hyderabad and Raipur. Electricity is primarily used for lighting, electrical fans, electric iron, toasters, geysers, air-coolers and air-conditioners in the domestic sector. Fuelwood, charcoal, kerosene and LPG are the main sources of energy for domestic cooking and their consumption in the aforesaid two cities is given in Table 13.5.

Table 13.5 : Consumption Pattern of Household Energy (Input in Million BTU and Per Cent of Total Cooking Energy Consumed)

City	Wood		Charcoal		Kerosene		LPG		Total
	BTU	*Per cent of total*	*BTU*	*Per cent of total*	*BTU*	*Per cent of total*	*BTU*	*Per cent of total*	
1. Hyderabad (1982)	0.5	4.1	00.61	5	0.378	31	0.290	24	1.229 MBTU
2. Raipur (1985)	1.1	6.1	0.2	10	0.2	9	0.2	12	1.8

It looks anomalous that Raipur with one-eighth of the population of Hyderabad consumes more energy than Hyderabad. This is presumably due to the greater dependence of Raipur on less efficient traditional sources of energy. In contrast Hyderabad uses in a significantly larger proportion the two more efficient sources of energy viz., Kerosene and LPG. This is further confirmed if we examine the consumption of useful energy or energy output in both Hyderabad and Raipur. In both the cities the output of cooking energy per household is much the same. (Table 13.6).

Table 13.6 : Consumption of Useful or Output Energy in Million BTU Per Household

City	*Wood*	*Charcoal*	*Kerosene*	*LPG*	*Total*
Hyderabad (1982)	0.08	0.012	0.18	0.174	0.45
Raipur (1985)	0.2	50,000 BTU (+0,000 BTU Coal)	0.1	0.1	0.5

It may, therefore, be concluded that Hyderabad because of its higher level of economic and cultural development and higher income base utilizes superior and efficient sources of energy for domestic cooking.

The relationship between income and fuel mix of households is expressed in Table 13.7 which gives the number of households using different fuel-mix by income groups. Households in metropolitan Hyderabad using superior fuel mix is evident by the fact that 65 per cent of the total number of households use Kerosene, LPG or Kerosene-LPG mix. Individually Kerosene is the most important domestic fuel for cooking followed by LPG.

Even among the lower income groups below Rs. 500 per month kerosene is the dominant fuel as against fuelwood. The desire of even the lower income groups to switch over to superior fuels is evident from the use of kerosene-LPG as a domestic cooking fuel in the income range Rs. 751-900. Such households may also be having undisclosed source of income such as remittances from abroad, and can afford to use superior and less polluting fuel mix. In contrast energy consumption in Raipur is dominated by wood-kerosene, LPG or LPG-Kerosene mix. It may be observed from the table that the average energy input in Raipur far exceeds that of Hyderabad at similar income levels but the consumption of useful energy, barring a few exceptions, is almost similar. This implies that there is more

Table 13.7 : Number of Households by Income Groups and Fuel Mix

Income	Wood				Kerosene				LPG				Wood-Kerosene		Kerosene-LPG	
	Hyderabad		Raipur		Hyderabad		Raipur		Hyderabad		Raipur		Hyderabad	Raipur	Hyderabad	Raipur
	1		2		3		4		5		6		7	8	9	10
	No. of Households	MBTU Consumed	No. of Households	MBTU Consumed	No. of Households	MBTU Consumed	No. of Households	MBTU Consumed	No. of Households	MBTU Consumed	No. of Households	MBTU Consumed	No. of Households	No. of Households	No. of Households	No. of Households
0-500	55	0.68	10	1.26	52	0.28	1	0.12	10	0.04	0	0.02	38	44	2	1
501-750	35	0.53	4	1.33	93	0.43	1	0.16	9	0.06	0	0.02	36	50	12	2
751-900	37	0.61	6	1.19	88	0.45	0	0.19	31	0.12	3	0.11	45	47	28	5
901-1000	15	0.45	2	1.15	45	0.41	0	0.19	31	0.25	3	0.17	28	29	28	4
1001-1250	14	0.60	0	1.23	41	0.40	1	0.19	29	0.24	2	0.32	31	16	26	4
1250-1500	—	—	1	1.09	41	0.39	—	0.16	36	0.31	6	—	31	17	37	7
1501-2000	10	0.37	2	0.95	54	0.37	3	0.19	—	0.41	5	0.41	20	12	82	8
2001-2500	14	0.47	0	0.74	21	0.31	0	0.08	40	0.43	2	0.72	12	3	47	1
2501-3000	5	0.38	0	0.59	18	0.37	0	0.15	26	0.49	6	0.65	7	3	37	5
3001-4000	3	0.27	0	0.34	10	0.31	0	0.12	38	0.57	1	0.80	6	2	25	1
4000	5	0.34	0	0.21	8	0.34	0	0.10	33	0.72	5	1.00	7	0	27	1
Total	**219**	—	**25**	—	**471**	—	**7**	—	**347**	—	**32**	—	**271**	**213**	**351**	**39**

MBTU—Million British Thermal Units per month.

wasteful utilization of energy in Raipur because of its dependence on firewood which, according to ABE, has an extremely low level of efficiency of 8 per cent. At the higher income level, however, the table reveals, that both the cities use diversified energy mix consisting largely of efficient sources of energy. The higher income groups, however, do consume a substantial proportion of fuelwood which presumably is considered a more dependable and accessible source of energy. The transition from inferior to superior fuels seems to be rather slow in Raipur which may partly be due to its lower per capita income and partly due to its social conservatism which precludes change in fuel mix. The metropolitan character and culture of Hyderabad makes the transition easy and acceptable.

Since Raipur uses a larger proportion of inefficient sources of cooking energy, it spends, on the average, almost twice as much on cooking energy as Hyderabad. It may be noticed further that the lower income groups spend higher proportion of their income on input energy than the higher income groups. In Hyderabad the expenditure per household ranges from 10.7 to 1.5 per cent between the lowest and highest income groups. In Raipur the respective percentages are 14.7 to 8.1 (Table 13.8). That the lower income groups tend to spend a larger proportion of their income on input energy is also confirmed by a sample survey of squatter settlements in Hyderabad (Table 13.9).

On the average the slum dwellers spend 9.8 per cent of their income and their maximum and minimum expenditure range from 24.4 to 6.49 as against the Hyderabad city average of 3.6 and the corresponding maximum and minimum expenditure percentages are 10.7 to 1.5. The per household energy input for the slum dwellers is much above the energy input for the municipal households for the corresponding income groups. This is because firewood is the primary source of cooking energy for the slum dwellers who constitute the poorest segment of the metropolitan community of Hyderabad.

The Hyderabad and Raipur studies confirm beyond doubt that fuelwood is the primary source of energy for the urban poor. This is despite the fact that it is the most inefficient source of energy, and in real terms the most expensive also. The cost of fuelwood to match the output energy of 15 kg. of LPG is almost twice that of the cost of LPG. Further, the large quantity of fuelwood required will cause storage problems (Table 13.10).

Table 13.8 : Monthly Mean Household Energy Consumption and Expenditure by Income Group

Income Group	*Mean Monthly Energy Consumption*		*Mean Total Useful Energy*		*Mean Energy Expenditure (in Rupees)*		*Mean Energy Expenditure (percentage of income)*	
	Hyderabad	*Raipur*	*Hyderabad*	*Raipur*	*Hyderabad*	*Raipur*	*Hyderabad*	*Raipur*
0-500	1.10	1.4	0.298	0.3	42.6	53.0	10.7	14.7
501-750	1.11	1.7	0.354	0.4	46.8	64.0	7.1	10.0
751-900	1.25	1.8	0.408	0.4	53.6	75.8	6.4	9.1
901-1000	1.14	1.9	0.430	0.4	56.3	78.5	5.6	7.9
1001-1250	1.32	1.9	0.455	0.5	60.8	90.1	5.2	7.6
1251-1500	1.30	2.1	0.476	0.5	63.2	95.8	4.4	6.5
1501-2000	1.19	1.8	0.495	0.5	64.2	95.2	3.5	4.9
2001-2500	1.29	1.8	0.504	0.5	68.2	111.8	2.9	4.5
2501-3000	1.28	1.7	0.542	0.6	70.4	1115.9	2.5	3.9
3001-4000								
4000								
	1.28	2.6	0.546	0.8	71.3	170.4	2.0	4.5
Total	1.56	2.1	0.683	0.7	91.0	150.8	1.5	2.5
Sample	12.3	1.8	0.453	0.5	60.2	85.7	3.6	8.1

Source : Alam-Joy Dunkerley *et al.*, Fuelwood in Urban Market and Molly Mcauley, Naimuddin *et al.*, Raipur Fuelwood Study Report (Mimeographed), 1987.

Table 13.9 : Hyderabad : Energy Consumption and Expenditure of Slum Households (1973)

Income group	*Size of house-hold*	*Mean monthly per capita income (Rs.)*	*Mean monthly energy consumption (BTU)*	*Mean Energy expenditure per household Rs.*	*Energy expenditure as % share of income per household*
100	2	45.0	0.481	31.0	34.4
101-250	3.6	51.7	0.747	37.2	20.02
251-500	4.8	52.58	0.861	49.5	12.27
501-750	5.0	116.92	1.16	54.4	9.26
751-900	6.8	128.80	1.51	68.5	7.77
901-1000	7.5	151.50	1.57	69.6	6.12
1001-1250	5.2	105.60	1.15	54.28	9.8

The comparative costs per household per month of the three basic fuels used in domestic cooking for Hyderabad and Raipur, as reported in the two studies, also demonstrate the uneconomical nature of firewood as energy source (Table 13.11).

Table 13.10 : Relative Combustion Efficiency and Cost of Firewood and LPG Hyderabad (May 1988)

	Input and Output energy of 1 kg. in BTU		*Output Energy of 15 kg*	*Cost of 15 kg each of LPG and fuelwood*	*Quantum & Cost of Firewood required to match 15 kg LPG Output energy*	
	Input	Output		Rs.	kg.	Rs.
LPG	43,569	26141.0	392115.0	65.95	115	65.95
Fuelwood	14,250	2422.7	36337.5	10.70	161.80	11330

Table 13.11 : Costs of Different Fuels : Per Household Per Month

	Hyderabad (1982) Rs.	*Raipur (1985) Rs.*
Firewood	187	198
Kerosene	106	163
LPG	134	160

This persistence with firewood as a source of cooking energy by almost all the income groups in the urban society of India seems largely due to its reliability and easy availability, and its apparent low cost. The high capital cost of LPG installation (Rs.100 per unit—ABE estimate) and restricted supply of kerosene have further ensured the continued use of fuelwood in the households particularly among the lower income groups. The higher income groups and particularly those with large size households also use firewood in substantially large quantity and will continue to do so because of their rural background and also they want alternative fuels always to be available to them in case of the breakdown in supply of LPG/Kerosene.

Income-Fuel Mix and Consumption Relationship

When measured statistically through regression analysis the relationship between income and fuel mix prove quite significant and provide a useful measure of the responsiveness of the household useful energy consumption and to change in income. The model chosen to represent the relationship between income and household energy consumption is a standard log-linear formulation.

$$log\ E = A + b\ log\ Y — C\ log\ H$$

Where E is quantity of cooking fuel demanded by one household; Y is the household income, and H is the number of household members. The results of the regression for Hyderabad and Raipur are given in Table 13.12.

The regression analysis for both Hyderabad and Raipur reveal that income elasticities with regard to input energy is either low as in Raipur (0.09) or negative as in Hyderabad (0.05). The consumption of useful energy increases with income in both Hyderabad and Raipur but elasticity is much less in Hyderabad: 26, each than in Raipur: 45. In other words a 10 per cent increase in household income leads to only 2.6 per cent rise in consumption of useful energy in Hyderabad whereas in Raipur it leads to a rise of 4.5 per cent. The household expenditure on energy also rises with income but again the elasticity is much lower in Hyderabad, 0.205 compared to Raipur 0.47. While Hyderabad shows a very strong negative relationship between rise in income and expenditure on energy, Raipur shows negative relationship between the consumption of wood and rise in income, and positive relationship between rise in income and expenditure on LPG. The elasticity in consumption of wood in Raipur is more pronounced i.e. 4.3 per cent decline in fuelwood consumption with 10 per cent rise in

Table 13.12 : Municipal Sample Household Coeffficients Estimated using Multiple Regression Analysis: Hyderabad (1981) and Raipur (1985).

Equation No.	*Dependent variables*	*Hyderabad (1981) Coefficient*				*Raipur (1985) (T Statistics)*			
		R^2	*Monthly*	*H.H. Size*	*Constant term*	R^2	*H.H. Income*	*H.H. Size*	*Constant term*
1.	Monthly households energy consumption (1000 BTU)	24	–0.054 (–3.04)	0.6115 (23.3)	6.27 (52.3)	0.18	0.09 (2.36)*B*	0.48 (8.28)*C*	12.84 (52.28)*C*
2.	Monthly household end use energy consumption (1000 BTU)	27	0.256 (18.3)	0.224 (10.8)	3.80 (40.2)	0.46	0.45 (16.43)*C*	0.18 (4.35)*C*	9.57 (53.42)*C*
3.	Household expenditure on energy (Rupees)	0.28	0.205 (14.5)	0.325 (15.6)	1.96 (20.5)	0.45	0.47 (15.85)*C*	0.20 (4.49)*C*	0.87 (4.54)*C*
4.	Household energy expenditure as per cent of total	0.64	–0.795 (–56.0)	0.325 (15.5)	6.56 (68.6)	—	—	—	—
5.	Monthly household expenditure woods as per cent of total expenditure	—	—	—	—	0.06	–0.43 (4.84)*C*	—	0.47 (0.97)*C*
6.	Monthly household expenditure	—	—	—	—	0.02	–0.17 (1.81)*A*	—	–0.80 (–4.77)*C*

Note: Hyderabad: equations in the logs of all variables. Analysis based on survey covering household bearing Municipal numbers.

* The unstandardized regression coefficient is reported for each independent variable and constant term is also given;

T Statistics are in parenthesis.

All the *T* Statistics for Hyderabad are significant at 95 per cent of confidence level;

A: Significant at 10 per cent level, *B*: at 5 per cent and *C*: at 1 per cent level.

income whereas the rise in the consumption of LPG is only 1.7 per cent. The Hyderabad and Raipur regressions confirm each other and help us to generalize that in urban India households tend to shift to superior fuels with the rise in income. Fuelwood is the primary source of energy for low income groups. However, it may be reiterated that because of social, cultural and reliability factors fuelwood is also used in the higher income groups. Metropolitan Hyderabad, because of its higher level of urban development, has already passed through the transitory phase and, therefore, its elasticity is much lower than Raipur which is experiencing its period of transition from inferior to superior fuel types.

Projection : Fuelwood Consumption

The historical and cross-sectional information for Hyderabad and cross-sectional data for Raipur confirm the following trends in domestic consumption of cooking energy :

(1) Declining energy consumption (over time or across rising income levels) if measured in unadjusted BTU.
(2) Consumption of useful energy increase over high income levels.
(3) Declining shares of fuelwood and increasing shares of LPG in total energy consumption.

While keeping these trends in mind the fuelwood projection for Hyderabad for 2000 A.D. is based on the assumption that there will be no change in the size of households and that mean household income will annually increase in real terms by 2.5 per cent. Based on this assumption, it has been estimated that by the year 2000 A.D. the consumption of input energy in Hyderabad will decline by 14 per cent between 1981-2000 from 1.23 million BTU to 1.06 million BTU whereas the consumption of output energy for the corresponding period will increase by 10 per cent. The projected scenario of domestic cooking energy consumption and its constituent fuels likely to emerge is shown in Table 13.13. We have projected a significant decline in the consumption of fuelwood by the Municipal households in Hyderabad during the next 19 years (1981-2000). This, however, does not imply that there will be decline in the consumption of fuelwood in metropolitan Hyderabad. The other important consumers of fuelwood are slum dwellers, hotels, restaurants, marriage functions and cremation of the dead among the Hindus and Sikhs.

Table 13.13 : Hyderabad and Raipur: Projection of Household Firewood Consumption in 2000 A.D.

Figures in metric tonnes per annum

Sector	*Hyderabad*		*Raipur*[1]	*Hyderabad*[2]	*Raipur*[3]
	1988-89	*1985*	*2000 A.D.*	*2000 A.D.*	
1. Households	1,54,000	—	44,500	1,60,000	58,500
				1,90,000	76,000
2. Institutions	13,700	32,467	13,200		
3. Other (Social unaccounted)	10,000	—	3,000	—	—

Source: Alam-Dunkerley *et al.* (1985), p. 75, Raipur are from MeCauley Naimuddin *Raipur Fuelwood Survey Report*, 1987, Projected by Naimuddin.

The squatter settlements tend to concentrate in metropolitan cities. We have, therefore, assumed that slum population of Hyderabad will maintain its present proportion of 20 per cent of the metropolitan population. The slum dwellers on account of their low income will not be able to change their existing fuel mix of wood and kerosene, the former being the dominant partner. With no substantial rise in the per capita income of slum dwellers a rising slum population at the current rate of 3.3 per cent per annum and the quantum of fuelwood consumption remaining unaltered i.e. 600 kg of fuelwood per household per annum, the fuelwood requirement of slum dwellers will rise from 43,800 tonnes to 68,302 tonnes per annum by 2000 A.D. Thus the total demand for fuelwood in Hyderabad by the year 2000 for the household sector including slum households may range between 1,60,000 and 1,90,000 tonnes per annum. Based on similar assumptions, the consumption of fuelwood in the household sector of Raipur has been projected to rise to 58,500-76,000 tonnes by 2000 A.D.

The aforesaid projection takes care of the fuelwood required for cooking by the domestic sector including both municipal and slum households. In the absence of time series data on consumption of fuelwood by commercial establishments, marriage functions and crematoria no projection has been attempted. However, time series data are available for fuelwood consumption in restaurants and hotels in Hyderabad.

Table 13.14 : Fuelwood Consumption in Restaurants and Hotels in Hyderabad

1966	*1981*	*1988-89*
11000	13700	21,000 Tonnes

Source: Alam *et al.* (1984), p. 76; Naimuddin: 1988-89 survey.

They demonstrate that during the 15 years period 1966-81 restaurants and hotels in Hyderabad registered rather low average annual increase of 2700 tonnes in fuelwood consumption. Whereas in the following period covering 1981-89, it increased phenomenally by over 7000 tonnes per annum. This has been largely due to the rising population of Metropolitan Hyderabad at the rate of 4 per cent per annum, and rapid growth in its floating population because of its increasing importance at the State and national levels. In view of the aforesaid trend it is being assumed that fuelwood consumption in restaurants and hotels for the decade 1990-2000 will increase at the same rate as during 1981-89. Hence the projected annual consumption of fuelwood in Hyderabad by restaurants and hotels alone may be in the neighbourhood of 30,000 tonnes by 2000 A.D. There is also likely to be a significant rise in fuelwood consumption in marriage functions at crematoria and other commercial consumers. If this trend of rising fuelwood consumption continues, it will have an adverse ecological impact on the environs of these cities.

Although their consumption patterns are different, Raipur and Hyderabad have striking similarity in their input and expenditure elasticities unlike metropolitan cities because of the persistence of poverty and of traditional social customs. This continued and rising consumption of fuelwood raises some basic policy issues which have been briefly discussed in the following paras :

Policy Implications

While making energy policy in India it must be borne in mind that fuelwood is the energy resource for the urban poor and will continue to be so in the foreseeable future. The planners and policy makers must ensure the supply of fuelwood to the urban consumers at affordable prices. The fuelwood prices are being adversely affected by the competing use by industries such as paper, fibre packaging etc. These industries ought to be provided with alternative resources so that the minimum fuel needs of the urban poor is not adversely affected. Further, large scale consumptions of fuelwood in metropolitan settlements of India will lead to depletion of forest resources and consequent environmental deterioration in their rural hinterland. The ecological consequences of fuelwood consumption in urban settlements should be constantly monitored to prevent environmental degradation without, however, disturbing the continuity of fuelwood supply. There is a need, therefore, to intensify fuelwood plantation under social forestry and other afforestation programmes.

There is a large section of population both in Hyderabad and Raipur, above the income level of Rs. 1,500 per month, willing to change over to viable fuels such as LPG but are not able due to short supply, particularly in metropolitan cities such as Hyderabad, Bangalore etc. The Gas Authority of India must make a concerted effort to increase its network of supply particularly in the urban markets to relieve the pressure on fuelwood consumption. Kerosene is a rationed commodity and is made available to the consumers through the public distribution system in a limited quantity at highly subsidized rates. Its price per litre has also increased by a small margin from Rs. 1.87 to Rs. 2.60 in 1988. It can easily replace fuelwood as a domestic cooking medium provided its supply is enhanced and the poorer sections of the urban community are helped to buy the improved kerosene stoves through bank loans, on easy terms, to install the LPG connections. These measures will go a long way to induce the urban folks to substitute fuelwood by superior or more efficient sources of energy such as Kerosene and LPG particularly in the large cities reducing, thereby substantial demand for fuelwood. In addition large scale installation of improved firewood *chulha* (stove) and electric crematoria will also reduce the demand for fuelwood.

The rising consumption of fuelwood in cities and towns of India, have also adversely affected the rural poor. Fuelwood is being gradually monetised in rural areas while until recently the rural folks could freely collect their fuelwood requirements from their immediate neighbourhood. They have now to travel longer distances particularly women to collect fuelwood. In order not to upset the supply position in rural India, fuelwood plantations have to be expanded considerably.

Conclusions

The two studies on Hyderabad and Raipur bring out striking similarity in the consumption behaviour of their respective households with regard to cooking energy and allow us to offer some broad generalizations. The households tend to shift over to more efficient sources of energy with the rise in income. Fuelwood as the dominant source of cooking energy of the lower income groups in urban India will continue to be so in the foreseeable future. Outside the domestic sector substantial quantity of fuelwood is also being consumed in marriage functions and for the cremation of the dead. No change is anticipated in the consumptions of fuelwood in these respects in the next two decades.

It has been observed that because of its higher per capita income and metropolitan functions Hyderabad has switched over substantially to more efficient fuel mix. Hence, its elasticity compared to Raipur is much less. Raipur is only a large regional urban centre. Until the transition is complete, fuelwood will continue to be Raipur's dominant source of cooking energy. Presently its households consumption of fuelwood is more than double the average household consumption in Hyderabad.

It has been estimated that by 2000 A.D. the households fuelwood consumption in Hyderabad and Raipur will approximately be 200,000 and 80,000 tonnes respectively. This rising consumption of fuelwood in urban settlements of India, metropolitan and non-metropolitan, raises the basic policy issue of its availability to the urban poor at affordable price.

The competing demand for fuelwood by the poorer urban and rural households on the one hand and by the industries and commercial establishments on the other hand are raising the fuelwood prices above the level of affordability both for the urban and rural poor. In the absence of alternative sources of energy this may cause energy crisis for the poorer urban and rural households. The demand and supply position of fuelwood has to be monitored consistently to avert the crisis. This conflict of interest has to be reconciled by increasing substantially the area under fuelwood plantation and by encouraging the spread and use of more efficient energy sources such as Kerosene and LPG in the urban settlements of India.

NOTES

Advisory Board on Energy (ABE) Government of India, New Delhi: *Recommendations*, (1983-84).

Alam-Dunkerley *et al.*: *Fuelwood in Urban Markets*, New Delhi, Concept Publishing Co., 1984.

Amulya Kumar Reddy and B. Sudhakar Reddy: "Case Study of Firewood in Bangalore: Energy in a Stratified Society", *Economic and Political Weekly,* Bombay—8th October, pp. 1757-70.

B. Bowander, V.V.R. Prasad and S. Prasad: *Fuelwood Consumption in Hyderabad: Policy Issues*, 1985.

Energy Conservation Challenges and Opportunities, August 1986.

M. Naimuddin : Fuelwood Consumption in Commercial establishments in Hyderabad (Mimeographed), 1989.

Manzoor Alam, Joy Dunkerley, Amulya Kumar Reddy, "*Fuelwood in Cities of the Developing World: Two Case Studies from India", Natural Resources Forum* United Nations, New York, August, 1985.

National Commission on Agriculture, Government of India, Ministry of Agriculture, New Delhi: *Report on Forestry*, Vol. IX, (1976).

Planning Commission, Government of India, New Delhi: *Fuelwood Policy Committee Report*, (1982).

Towards a Perspective on Energy Demand-Supply in India in 2000 A.D. 05 May 1985.

Part IV : Other Topical Themes

14

Geopolitical Importance of the Indian Ocean

The Indian Ocean is one of the smallest oceans but historically among the earliest used as an artery of trade and commerce, and strategically among the most important, being bounded on three sides by developing countries which provide essential and strategic raw materials, mineral and agricultural resources to the developed economies of the West. The location of highly developed economies like Australia and South Africa within the Indian Ocean realm adds further to the geopolitical significance of the Indian Ocean.

The countries of the Indian Ocean realm have diverse resources and are drawn from varying political, economic and ethnographic characteristics. Based on these they can be grouped under three broad categories as suggested below. A discussion of these countries, by categories, will highlight their distinctive characteristics and bring out their emerging trends which must be adequately appreciated in order to promote maximum intra-regional interaction.

- *Category I :* Developing economies and producers of primary products—politically independent:
  Persian Gulf States, East and Central Africa, Pakistan Bangladesh, Ceylon and South-East Asia, Mozambique.
- *Category II* : Developing economy with a diversified economic base, and a rising level of technology-politically independent : India.
- *Category III* : Developed economies with high levels of technology, and colonies of European Powers—politically dominated by Europeans :

Published in *Indian Journal of Politics,* Department of Political Science, Aligarh Muslim University, Aligarh, India, June 1973, pp. 13-26.

(a) Australia, South Africa (the last two are ethonographically dominated by the non-European population).

Category I: Developing Economies and Producers of Primary Products—Politically Independent

The countries included under this category are marked for the richness and diversity of their agricultural and mineral products and are equally known for their dependence on the U.S.A. and West European countries, both for capital resources and for marketing of their products. These countries, based on their resource endowment, can further be sub-classified as :

(a) The oil-rich countries of West Asia around the Persian Gulf—Iraq, Iran, Saudi Arabia, Bahrain, Kuwait, etc.;
(b) The East and Central African countries of Tanzania, Kenya, Uganda, Zambia, Malawi and Malagasy with their prosperous plantation agriculture of cotton, sisal, coffee and sugar, and rich reserves of high grade phosphate (Uganda and Tanzania) and copper ore (Zambia);
(c) The South and South-East Asian countries of Pakistan, Ceylon, Bangladesh, Malaysia, Singapore and Indonesia with their rich resources of cotton, sulphur and rock salt (Pakistan), tea and coconut (Ceylon) jute and tea (Bangladesh), rubber, palm oil, and tin (Malaysia), and rubber, coffee and sugar-cane (Indonesia).

Oil and the Indian Ocean

Of the raw materials produced in the region, oil is by far the most important and nearly 60 per cent of the total trade both in value and tonnage passes through the Indian Ocean. The states around the Persian Gulf are among the premier producers of crude petroleum, contributing a little over one-third of the world petroleum production. In addition to being significant producers they also possess 81 per cent or 31,000 million metric tonnes of the known world oil reserves, distributed as follows :

Iran (4,700); Iraq (3,000); Kuwait (8,600); Saudi Arabia (7,200); other West Asian countries (6,860).[1]

Table 14.1 : Persian Gulf Countries : Export of Petroleum and Growth of Oil Revenue

Country	*Export value of Petroleum (Per cent of total export) (1969)*			*Growth of Oil Revenue (Million U.S. Dollars)*			*% Increase 1958-68*
	Total Export Value	*Export Value (absolute)*	*Petroleum (per cent)*	*1958*	*1963*	*1968*	
1. Iraq (value in Million Dinar)	367.0	344.0	93.0	80.0	110.0	174.0	121.0
2. Iran (million Rial)	146.0	114.0	78.0	247.0	385.0	712.0 (1967)	188.0
3. Saudi Arabia (million Saudi Rial)	7853.0	6341.0	81.0	298.0	607.0	927.0	210.0
4. Kuwait (million Dinar)	20.86	20.86	100.0	160.0	191.0	238.0	49.0

Source: International Trade Statistics—U.N. 1970.

Petroleum industry is the basic economic activity of these countries and in most cases constitutes over 90 per cent of their total export value. This economic boom experienced by these countries is exclusively dependent on the phenomenal rise of their oil revenues. This is highlighted by Table 14.1 which reveals that increase in oil revenue over the decade 1958-68 has ranged from nearly 50 per cent in Kuwait to over 200 per cent in Saudi Arabia. This rise in oil revenue of the producing countries has been partly due to increase in the rates of royalty paid to them but largely on account of increase in production both of crude petroleum and petroleum products which increased respectively from 66 and 33 million tonnes in 1948 to 559 and 91 million tonnes in 1968. However, the most significant point is that American and European Economic Community oil companies control oil production in the Persian Gulf region (excepting Iran and Iraq). Consequently, a large proportion of revenue derived from petroleum production and its marketing is netted by the oil producing companies which is substantiated by a phenomenal rise in their oil income from a mere 150 million dollars in 1948 to nearly 3,500 million dollars in 1968, a staggering rise of a little over 100 fold per annum. The recent nationalization of Iraq Petroleum Company by the Government of Iraq is indicative of a growing realization among the Arab countries of the naked exploitation of their resources by the developed West. These developed countries such as the U.S.A., Canada, Britain, West European states and Japan are also the major customers of petroleum whereas in addition to other uses it is used as raw material to support large complex of petro-industries. The U.A.E., which is one of the largest producers of crude petroleum, annually imports nearly 90 million tonnes. The vested interest of these capitalist countries in the oil industry of the Persian Gulf region is, therefore, deeply entrenched.

Excluding an insignificant proportion of oil which is channelled through pipelines to the coasts of the Levant, the Persian Gulf oil is tanker-transported. The Indian Ocean is the main artery of movement for the oil traffic. Its strategic importance for oil movement can be realized by the fact that on the average over 100 million metric tonnes are annually transported across the Indian Ocean. Of this, 70 million tonnes used to pass through the Suez Canal. Since the closure of the Suez Canal in 1967 the volume of oil traffic through the Indian Ocean has greatly increased and nearly 40 per cent of the world petroleum trade passes through this Ocean to Japan, Australia, U.S.A., France, Italy, U.K., West Germany, etc. Despite a rich strike of oil in the

North Sea[2] and across the Chinese Coast[3] the Persian Gulf countries retain their primacy among the oil producing regions of the world. The North Sea region can, however, meet only 15 per cent of the total oil requirements of the West European countries and the U.S.A. and possesses 7 per cent only of the world oil reserves as against 81 per cent by the Gulf states. Hence for oil trade the strategic importance of the Indian Ocean will continue to grow with the rising dependence of the capitalist countries on the Persian Gulf oil.

The Persian Gulf states are also becoming increasingly aware of the geopolitical importance of the Indian Ocean. They seem to realize the fact that their progress and prosperity is vitally linked with the security and freedom on navigation in this Ocean. Iran, economically the most advanced of the Persian Gulf states, seems to be the most conscious of this situation. The then Shah of Iran recently declared unequivocally that "the sea contiguous to the Gulf of Oman—the Indian Ocean—recognizes no frontiers" Iran is, therefore, contemplating to cast a wider "security perimeter" in the Indian Ocean in order to protect its vital economic interests from Chach Bahar to Abadan.[4]

Agricultural and Mineral Resources in Central and East Africa

In addition to oil, the countries of the Indian Ocean realm are a store house of strategic minerals and agricultural raw materials which are vital to the economic prosperity of the developed Western economies and in which the latter have a big stake. On the western fringe of the Indian Ocean are the East and Central African countries of Kenya, Tanzania, Zambia, Uganda, Malawi, Mauritius and Malagasy with their important plantation crops of coffee, cotton, sisal, tobacco and sugarcane developed with the Western capital. This is brought out by the fact that "in 1962 Europeans and Asians formed less than 3 per cent of the East African population but received 3/5th of the total monetary income."[5] This is strongly corroborated by O'Connor[6] who points out that in Zambia, "European agriculture expanded at an even more rapid rate that in Kenya during 1950s, and it has continued to expand, even if much more slowly during the 1960s". "In Kenya", according to Grove, "Three quarters of agricultural exports in 1965 were produced by European and Asian farmers."[7] In most cases the value of European and Asian farm products rose mainly through increased yields, and trebling of the value of livestock and dairy product sales".[8] In contradistinction the farms managed by the natives stagnated and consequently the value of their farm products did not rise even marginally. The contrasting positions of farms managed by Europeans and natives is exemplified by their pattern of development in Rhodesia where, on the European farms, the total value of sales rose from $ 98 million in 1955 to $ 140 million in 1960 and $ 185 million in 1965. As against this the value of sales on African farms stayed at only $ 14 million in the corresponding periods.

These agricultural products are the backbone of the economy of most of these Central and East African countries as they constitute their major parts (Table 14.2). This export sector is vitally important for the economic growth of these countries as it attributes a significant proportion of their gross domestic product (Uganda 45%, Kenya 22%, and Tanzania 40%)

Table 14.2 : Principal Agricultural Exports from Selected Central and East African Countries

Commodity	*East African countries (Kenya-Uganda-Tanzania) (value in $'000)*		*Malawi (in $'000)*	*Mauritius (in million Rs.)*
	1960	*1968*	*1969*	*1968*
Total value of Exports	368,485.0	568,722.0	18,285.0	346.0
Coffee	96,807.0	192,357.0	—	—
Cotton (Raw)	56,168.0	42,221.0	—	—
Sisal	19,642.0	39,536.0	—	—
Sugar	—	—	—	321.0
Tea	—	—	4,763.0	—
Tobacco	—	—	6,323.0	—
Groundnut	—	—	2,795.0	—
Percent share of principal crops to total export value	60.2	57.8	57.8	93.0

Source : United Nations Economic Bulletin for Africa, Vol. I, June 1970.

In addition to these plantation crops the East and Central African countries are emerging as significant producers of some of the strategically important minerals. Africa contributes significantly to the world production of copper (22.2%), diamond (97%) and phosphates (26.4%). East and Central African countries have a dominant share in the production of these important minerals. The diamond mining industry is slowly gravitating to Tanzania. Tanzania and Uganda are significant producers of phosphates. The Tororo deposit of phosphate in Uganda with a proved reserve of 200 million tonnes (42% concentrate) is the largest in the Commonwealth. Zambia (formerly Northern Rhodesia) has the largest copper reserves in the world and in copper production it now far exceeds Zaire (Kinshasa or former Belgian Congo). Zaire and Zambia are the leading world producers of copper. They together produce over a million tonnes of copper valued at 1,500 million dollars—1969) and contribute two-third of the international trade in this commodity. Of these two Zambia leads with a production of 720,000 tonnes valued at 1,014 million dollars (1969). But copper mining in Zambia is under British control and over 60 per cent of the product is exported to U.S.A. The international trade of these African countries is also oriented to the developed Western economies (See Annexure I: International Trade of Selected East and Central African countries). This dual control on production activities and international trade exercised by the developed Western economies on the developing East and Central Africa has induced imbalances in the latter's economic structure and hampered their rational economic development. By virtue of this dual control the developed West is in a position to paralyse the economy of these African countries. It seems vitally important for the scientific development of the economy of these African countries that they must get out of the economic stranglehold of the West without in any way impairing the efficiency of agricultural and mineral development. Moreover, they must diversify their economic base in order to reduce their dependence on the export of primary products.[9]

These Central and East African countries find outlets to international market for their products through the Indian Ocean ports of Dar-es-Salaam and Mombasa on the east coast of Africa. The rail-road system of these countries is also oriented to these ports. The favourable ecological niches have also developed axially along these transport routes. Areas adjacent to the coast are the best developed and contain a relatively high density of population. These factors have in turn enhanced the importance of East African ports where both the port facilities and defence installations have been significantly increased with British and American assistance. Mombasa and Dar-es-Salaam are the principal ports for the exports and import of East African countries and are, therefore, of great strategic importance. The port of Mombasa has a separate oil jetty and deep water berths at Kalindinin and Kipevu to accommodate 13 ships with 33 feet draught. A new channel is under construction to permit access to oil tankers up to 65,000 tonnes. This has naturally resulted in the development, near the port (at Changamwe behind Kipevu), of a large refinery and oil depot to supply oil "to Kenya, Uganda and possibly Zambia and Mauritius".[10] The port of Dar-es-Salaam has deep water berth facilities and its first oil terminal was completed in 1966. An oil refinery is under construction which will supply Tanzania, Burundi and Zambia whence a pipeline is under construction.[11] The capital investment of the West in enhancing the port facilities in Mombasa and Dar-es-Salaam has further entrenched its vested interest in this area. It has, however, been recently reported that the Chinese are also assisting the development of the port of Dar-es-Salaam which can be ominous for the capitalist countries.

South-East Asian Countries

A similar situation exists with regard to the development and marketing of resources in South-East Asia. West Malaysia is a leading producer of natural rubber and tin, contributing more than 40 per cent and 30 per cent respectively of the world production in these commodities. These two premier exports are monopolized by the West European and American markets (75% rubber and 80% tin).In Indonesia too there has been, of late, a large influx of American capital. The revival of the Indonesia rubber plantation and petroleum industries has largely been due to financial and technical assistance provided by the U.S.A. The dependence of these countries on the developed West is highlighted by Table 14.3.

Table 14.3: Percentage Share of the Developed Economies of the Total Value of Principal Exports of West Malaysia and Indonesia (1968)

Country	*Value of total exports*	*Value of principal exports*		*Percentage share of developed economies of principal exports*
1. Indonesia (in million rupiah)	7996.0	1. Crude petroleum 2. Rubber	3,330 1,627	62
			4,957	
2. Malaysia (West) (in million Malaysian dollars)	4075.0	1. Rubber 2. Tin and Alloys	1,940 932	72
			2,872	

Source: International Trade Statistics—United Nations, 1970.

A notable feature in the movement of these commodities is that over 60 per cent of the cargo from South-East Asian countries passes through the Indian Ocean. Moreover, Malaysia and Indonesia are trying to reduce their dependence on Singapore and the Strait of Malacca by developing Port Swettenham (West Malaysia) and Tijilatjap (Indonesia) which are oriented to the Indian Ocean, with the capital and technical assistance of the United Kingdom and Australia respectively.[12]

Category II : Developing Economy with a Diversified Economic Base and a Rising Level of Technology—Politically Independent and Stable

India is the only country which falls under this category. None of the Asian and African developing countries fringing round the Indian Ocean can match its human and physical resources. In technology too India is far ahead of these countries. Hence, it stands as a class by itself which magnifies its strategic importance within the Indian Ocean realm.

India's association with the Indian Ocean dates back to ancient past. According to Panikkar, South India developed its civilization in the ancient period independent of North India and had strong trading contacts across the Indian Ocean with the Hebrew lands and the Roman Empire. It is clear from the Periplus that by the first century A.D. the Indian shore upto the mouth of the Ganga was known to the Roman and Egyptian traders. The sea water around the shores of India was called by the ancients as Indikon Pelagos or Mare Indicum. One of the most convincing evidence of ancient Roman trading contacts with South India had been the discovery of Roman trading station at Arikamedon near Pondicherry. The trading relationship between South India and the territories on western and northern periphery of the Indian Ocean continued even during the Arab hegemony and some of the earliest Muslim settlements in India were along the Malabar Coast. By the ninth century A.D. there were notable colonies of Muslim merchants on that coast.[13] The Indian Ocean was, therefore, one of the main arteries of India's external trade since early times. At present this dependence of India on the Indian Ocean for its foreign trade is almost total. India has, therefore, a big stake in the Indian Ocean. Any breakdown in this channel of communication can paralyse India's economy.

Among the developing economies, India is the only country which, on account of the diversity of its resources, the dynamic character of its population and its political stability, has a chance to emerge as a major Indian Ocean Asian power. While still a major producer of primary products, it has made rapid strides both in the development of capital and consumer goods industries and in the application of intermediate and sophisticated technologies. Hence, while on the one hand it exports its primary products such as tobacco, tea, hide and skin, iron ore, mica, manganese, etc., on the other hand sophisticated electrical goods, machine tools etc., are also among its export items. India has commenced exporting its technology and technical skill as well. Indian technicians are busy designing an oil refinery in Iraq, establishing a textile mill in West Malaysia and are rendering technical assistance to Ethiopia, Tanzania, Mauritius and Zambia in their developmental activities. This growing contact of India with the countries of Indian Ocean realm is inevitably linked with the freedom of navigation in the Indian Ocean which further emphasizes the strategic importance of the Indian Ocean for India.

Besides its trade, the defence of India is also linked with the safety and security of the Indian Ocean. Of all the countries of the Indian Ocean none, like India, has such a long stretch of over 2,000 miles of exposed coast line. While on the one hand this long coast line with its numerous large and medium ports stimulates foreign trade and directly contributes to the rapid economic progress of the country, on the other hand it makes the defence problem of India highly complex. There are very few sites along the Indian coast lines which do not provide a landing ground. Hence our coast lines are highly vulnerable. With the growing rivalry of the major powers in the Indian Ocean we must prepare ourselves to hold our own against any odds. It certainly calls for the development of a well equipped and powerful navy and establishment of a chain of naval stations to guard our coasts.

In our foreign trade, like the other developing economies of the Indian Ocean, we are also very strongly linked with the developed economies of the West. Nearly 60 per cent of India's external trade is with the U.S.A., U.K. and other West European countries and this is in spite of change in the direction of trade in favour of the U.S.S.R. and East European countries. A substantial change in India's pattern and direction of international trade may occur if the overland route between India and East European countries is allowed to operate freely across Pakistan.

Competitive Economy of the Indian Ocean Realm

The aforesaid analysis highlights the point that the developing economies of East and Central African, South and South-East Asian regions have striking similarity in their production pattern, caused partly by their tropical location but basically a reflection of the demand and consumption pattern of the former colonial powers. Hence their economies developed on supplementary lines and are consequently of competitive character. This naturally hinders intra-regional trade within the Indian Ocean realm. Trans-regional trading, therefore, constitutes the basic character of the movement of commodities within this realm. The economic structure of these countries is in response to the economic relationship imposed on them by the former colonial powers. Despite the loss of political control the colonial powers still control the productive machineries of their former colonies and are, therefore, in a position to prevent structural changes in the economy which are essential if the developing countries are to diversify their economic base and accelerate their rate of economic growth. The direction and pattern of international trade should be so altered as to promote intra-regional trade within the Indian Ocean realm. This can be accomplished by stimulating complementary development of their respective economies to the mutual advantage of the countries concerned.

In promoting the aforesaid idea India can play a pivotal role. We can achieve this objective more meaningfully if we can anticipate the developmental trends in these countries. Central and East African countries may eventually merge as a single trading block like the European Economic Community. The countries of this region together have as diverse and extensive physical resource endowment as India. Moreover, they are not handicapped, like India, from a high population density and complexity of a cultural legacy which inhibit development. Among the regions of the Indian Ocean realm the African region by virtue of its size, resource endowment, and favourable demographic situation has the highest potentiality for development. The countries comprising this region may, with bold policy planning and imaginative foreign policy, step up their level of economic development and eventually catch up with India in the not too distant future. In the background of their existing demographic situation they may be more inclined to develop capital intensive skill in order to accelerate their rate of economic growth. India should assist such a process which may generate complementary trade between India and these countries on lines similar to the trans-Atlantic trade between Western Europe and the U.S.A. The trend towards capital intensive development in countries similarly situated as Central and East African states is amply reflected in Iran. Among the Persian Gulf states, Iran is the only country which compares favourably with these African countries in its resource endowment. It is rapidly diversifying its economic base and is concentrating on capital intensive development particularly in the field of agriculture. This was recently emphasized by the Shah of Iran who declared that "a healthy economy would require maximum agricultural production with a minimum of human labour" and, therefore, he promised all incentives "for production of cash crops in vast mechanized estates employing little human labour".[14] This will bring about a structural change in the economy of Iran. India will have to take note of these basic changes in the economy of these developing countries if it desires to increase its trade with them.

Category III : Developed Economies with High Levels of Technology and Colonies of European Powers (Politically Dominated by Europeans)

This category includes the highly developed economies of Australia, South Africa and Rhodesia and countries which are still the colonies of European powers—Mozambique. In this category are also included the independent countries which are economically and geographically linked with South Africa (Swaziland, Lesotho and Botswanaland). It may be incidentally mentioned that Botswanaland is trying to reduce its dependence on South Africa and Rhodesia by increasing its linkage with Zambia.

Of the developed economies of the Indian Ocean realm, Australia and South Africa, the latter is more exposed to the Indian Ocean because of the location of its chief ports, Durban and Port Elizabeth. The port of Durban serves the Johannesburg industrial complex which contributes "over half of South Africa's industrial output".[15] South Africa is considered as one of the most developed countries of the world. A United Nations Report on South Africa points out that "the Republic has become to a degree self-sufficient and also able to finance military and police outlays on a massive scale". In the same Report it is also pointed out that "the Government's room to manoeuvre rests fundamentally, however, on the low wages of African labour", and for South Africa the continuance of this manoeuvrability is vital to its economic development. The low-paid native labour can be easily moved from point to point thereby enabling the European owners of factories and mines to keep their cost of production low. In order to maintain this, South Africa has entered into a longstanding agreement with the Portuguese Government whereas the former is allowed to recruit upto 80,000 Africans annually for work in Witwatersrand. The number of workers crossing into the Republic invariably exceeds the official quota.[16]

South Africa, the U.S.A. and West European countries have developed a strong vested interest in the Portuguese colony-Mozambique, because of their large investments in its developmental activities. South Africa, particularly, has invested heavily in exploiting the resource endowment of Mozambique such as water power, agricultural products and in improving the port facilities. Over 350 million dollars have been invested in the construction of Cabera Bessa Dam on the river Zambesi and on the comprehensive development of this river for irrigation, navigation and generation of electricity (2000 KW capacity).[17] South Africa is not only the principal financier but also the main consumer of the power generated and raw materials produced.

South Africa and its western allies have invested widely in the development of mineral resources of Swaziland—asbestos, iron ore and coal. In collaboration with Japan, which is the best purchaser of Swaziland iron ore, South Africa is constructing a railway line, 150 miles long, from Goba to the port of Lourenco Marques, traversing the rich mineral belt of the country through its entire length. This will facilitate both the exploitation of resources and their export. It is significant that the European population in Swaziland has trebled from 5,000 to 15,000 during the last 15 years and the developed areas of Swaziland are occupied by this section of the population.[18]

France and Britain, in collaboration with the U.S.A. have helped the development of the Mozambique ports of Lourenco Marques, Beira and Nacala. Lourenco Marques located in Delgao Bay is deemed to be the best harbour on the entire African coast and rivals Durban.[19] It has 12 square miles of sheltered anchorage area and can accommodate 30 boats each drawing 30 feet. Its hinterland extends to Rhodesia and Swaziland, and among its new facilities are a large sugar terminal and bulk loading equipment for iron ore from Swaziland. The port of Beira is important for its copper exports. Its hinterland extends to Katanga copper mines of Zaire with which it is directly linked by rail and river transport. Nacala is a fast developing port of Mozambique where facilities for ocean going ships were provided in 1953. Its hinterland upto Catur (45 miles inland) is an area of dynamic and intensive development with cotton and cashew-nuts as its principal products and exports.

The demographic factor is also a significant determinant of the political postures of West European powers in Africa from Rhodesia southward. The distribution of European-population in a few selected countries is given in Table 14.4.

Table 14.4 : Distribution of European Population in Selected African Countries

Country	Total population (Million)	European Population	
		Absolute (Million)	Percentage of total population
1. South Africa	13.0	2.5	19.2
2. Rhodesia	2.2	0.14	6.4
3. Malagasy	5.0	0.067	1.3
4. Mozambique	6.1	0.049	0.8

Every effort is being made to settle European population in the developed areas of these countries. It has already been observed that the already developed lands in Central and Southern Africa are completely Europeanised. The process of European colonization in the highlands of Mozambique has been accelerated of late. It is particularly attractive to poor Portuguese farmers who are struggling to survive in their own countries.[20] On the contrary they enjoy affluence in Mozambique with their rich tea and tobacco plantations.[21] The destiny of nearly 6 million European populations is linked with their political dominance in southern Africa. This is about twice the population of New Zealand and half the population of Australia. It would be naïve to expect the USA and Western Europe to act against this politically dominant white population. Moreover, the dominance of this white population in South Africa serves best the geopolitical interests of the USA and Western Europe. The control of the ports of these African countries is vital to the defence of the Indian Ocean and the protection of international trade of the developed West with East and Central African countries.

Special Strategy within the Indian Ocean

In the trans-oceanic movement of commodities certain locations in the Indian Ocean enjoy strategic importance of a high order. Most of these locations are already under the control of European powers. Since the closure of the Suez Canal, the importance of the Mozambique Channel has increased manifold for most of the oil traffic of the Suez Canal now passes through the channel. This has enhanced the locational importance of Mozambique's ports of Nacala, Beira and Laurenco Marques, and of the island of Malagasy and its natural harbour—Diego Suarez. The island of Reunion and Comoros in the Indian Ocean, controlled by France, are of equal strategic importance. It is now reported that with the change of regime in Malagasy, which is not too friendly towards France, the French Government is abandoning Diego Suarez in favour of the Comoros islands where a submarine base has already been built. Even the Soviet Union, of late, has become quite active in the Indian Ocean. This is partly to protect its nearly 100 merchant vessels and trawlers operating, at any time of the year, in the Indian Ocean and partly to forestall the Chinese from eroding Russian influence in the Indian Ocean realm.[22] The British also according to a Teheran weekly believe that "the Russians are all out to dominate the Ocean as a means of encircling China while also holding Western trade at ransom". The British further believe that the Russians were creating a "Sea Lane" around the Cape. The same weekly further states that the Russians have access to the facilities of the island of Massirah and a "number of littoral states (of the Indian Ocean) have provided Russia with naval facilities. There are at least half a dozen who would do the same if Moscow applied enough pressure on them".[23] The ever increasing interest of the super-powers in the Indian Ocean can constitute a serious threat to the defence and security and economic prosperity of the developing countries fringing the Indian Ocean. This threat cannot be minimized unless the developing countries themselves control the productive elements of their respective economies and intensify intra-regional trade.

The location of Ceylon in the Indian Ocean between the Bay of Bengal and the Arabian Sea makes it admirably suited to exercise vigilance on trans-Indian Ocean movement of ships. Consequently, its two ports of Colombo and Trincomalee are logistically significant. Colombo is strategically located on the convergence of shipping routes in the Indian Ocean. We should endeavour to evolve a common naval strategy with Ceylon for the friendship of that country is vitally important for the defence of the Indian coast line.

The projection of the Indian peninsula in the Indian Ocean and its consequent embankment makes it equally accessible to the East, West and South of the Indian Ocean. The extensive coast line of India allows us a high degree of naval manoeuvrability unrivalled by any other country within the Indian Ocean realm. In order to optimize the use of its strategic location in the Indian Ocean India must build strong (or strengthen its existing) naval bases in Cochin, Marmagoa, Bombay, Kandla on the West Coast, and Tuticorin, Madras, Visakhapatnam, Paradip and Calcutta on the East Coast. The Andaman and Nicobar islands have also to be adequately equipped for they guard the vital sea gateway—the Malacca Strait. The islands of Laccadive and Maldives have to be included within our naval defence inner perimeter in order to protect our vital interests in the Indian Ocean.

The strategic importance of India in the Indian Ocean is likely to be jeopardized since Malaysia and Indonesia are preparing to reduce their dependence on Singapore. Malaysia is developing port Swettenham and Indonesia port Tijilatjap on the southern coast of Jawa opening on the Indian Ocean. This reorientation of Malaysian and Indonesian external trade will reduce significantly the traffic through the Strait of Malacca since the Suez Canal is already closed. With this reorientation of South-East Asian trade the principal trans-oceanic highway may shift to the southern base of the Indian Ocean (south of Equator). This will be against the strategic and economic interests of India. However, this will not reduce the dependence of India on the Indian Ocean for international trade. Consequently, the vitality of our economy and the survival of our democracy are inevitably linked with peace and freedom of navigation in this ocean. The Indian Ocean also controls the life line of Pakistan, Bangla Desh and Ceylon. Hence it would be in the geopolitical interests of the countries of the Indian sub-continent to evolve a common naval strategy for the defence of their coast line and for the maintenance of peace in the Indian Ocean area which is vitally important for their security and economic prosperity.

Trade within the Indian Ocean realm is characterized by an unequal trading partnership between the developed West and the developing countries of this realm. The balance of trade is invariably in favour of the developed economies. This is the consequence of unnatural flow of trade generated through colonial rule against the dictates of geography. This has to be replaced by intra-regional trade if optimum benefits of the geographical setting of the Indian Ocean are to be derived by the countries fringing round. The ancients fully utilized this natural, permanent and inexpensive linkage in promoting their economic and cultural contacts with the countries of the Indian Ocean realm. The restoration of this natural area of interaction of trade and culture can generate traffic on lines similar to the trans-Atlantic traffic between Western Europe and Eastern sea-board of Canada and the United States. The Indian Ocean realm will thus emerge as a zone of co-prosperity for the countries which until recently were politically and economically exploited by the capitalist colonial powers.

REFERENCES

1. 'Growth & Structural Changes in Middle East', *The Middle East Journal*, Vol. 25, No. 3, 1971, pp. 309-324.
2. *Newsweek.*
3. The *Statesman*, November 1, 1972.
4. *Kayhan International* (Tehran) Airmail Edition, November 11, 1972.
5. Morgan, W.T.W., *East Africa—Its Peoples and Resources,* p. 276.
6. O'Connor, A.M., *The Geography of Tropical African Development* (1971), p. 47.
7. Grove, T., *Africa South of the Sahara*, p. 188.
8. O' Connor, A.M., *The Geography of Tropical African Development,* (1971), p. 47.
9. *Ibid.*, p. 75.
10. *Ibid.*, p. 267.
11. *Ibid.* p. 267.
12. *Statesman*, 28th March 1972, *Status of Malacca Straits.*
13. Pannikar, K.M. *A Survey of Indian History* (1971), pp. 66.
14. *Kayhan International* (Tehran), November 11, 1972 (*Airmail Weekly*).
15. Grove, T., *Africa : South of the Sahara*, p. 236.
16. *Ibid.*, p. 226.
17. O. Connor: *The Geography of Tropical African Development* (1971), p. 123.
18. Grove, T.: *Africa : South of Sahara*, p. 253.
19. Auguste Toussaint: *History of the Indian Ocean*, London (1966), p. 216.
20. O'Connor, A.M.,: *The Geography of Tropical African Development* (1971), p. 47.
21. Hance William: *The Geography of Modern Africa* (1964).
22. *Statesman*: September 21, 1972: V.M. Nair: *Russia and the Indian Ocean.*
23. *Kayhan International* (*Airmail Weekly*), November 11, 1972.

ANNEXURE I

International Trade of Selected East and Central African Countries

(Period is January to December 1969 unless Stated Otherwise)

(Figures in '000 U.S. Dollars)

S.No	Name of Countries	TANZANIA				KENYA			
		IMPORTS		EXPORTS		IMPORTS		EXPORTS	
		Absolute (a)	% of total (b)	Absolute (a)	% of total (b)	Absolute (a)	% of total (b)	Absolute (a)	% of total (b)
(1)	(2)	(3)		(4)		(5)		(6)	
	World Total	198742	—	232694	—	327168	—	176760	—
	Developed Areas	138448	69.66	134306	57.72	246507	75.35	115236	65.19
1.	E.E.C.	44320	22.30	29260	12.57	67966	20.77	36097	20.42
2.	U.K.	52891	26.61	59411	25.53	101626	31.06	40797	23.08
3.	U.S.A.	11582	5.83	17768	7.64	24447	7.47	14076	7.96
4.	Japan	18227	9.17	11479	4.93	26157	7.99	3600	2.04
5.	East Europe	4248	2.14	4936	2.12	6057	1.85	1981	1.12
6.	China	11098	5.58	10890	4.68	3212	0.99	1335	0.76
7.	India	6630	3.34	18490	7.97	8265	2.53	4063	2.30

Source: *Foreign Trade Statistics for Africa.* United Nations Publications Nos. 19 and 20 (171).

Annexure I—*Contd.*

		ZAMBIA				UGANDA			
		IMPORTS		EXPORTS		IMPORTS		EXPORTS	
S.No	Name of Countries	Absolute (a)	% of total (b)	Absolute (a)	% of total (b)	Absolute (a)	% of total (b)	Absolute (a)	% of total (b)
(1)	(2)	(7)		(8)		(9)		(10)	
World Total		455051	—	757038	—	127298	—	195676	—
Developed Areas		370777	8148	722909	95.49	103024	80.93	149327	76.31
1. E.E.C.		57608	12.66	243713	32.19	26931	21.16	14479	7.40
2. U.K		106385	23.38	223734	29.55	43484	34.16	44214	22.60
3. U.S.A.		46680	10.26	15005	1.98	5248	4.12	46305	23.66
4. Japan		25258	5.55	160851	29.25	17289	13.58	22934	11.72
5. East Europe		3992	0.88	7677	1.01	3389	2.66	11225	5.74
6. China		1479	0.33	2198	0.20	2509	1.97	1245	0.64
7. India		2187	6.48	7600	1.00	5230	4.11	6778	3.64

Annexure I—*Contd.*

S.No	Name of Countries	ZIMBABWE			
		IMPORTS		EXPORTS	
		Absolute (a)	% of total (b)	Absolute (a)	% of total (b)
		(11)		(12)	
	World Total	73919	—	43883	—
	Developed Areas	49117	66.54	32166	39.30
1.	E.E.C.	5785	7.83	3696	8.42
2.	U.K	21838	29.54	20180	45.99
3.	U.S.A.	2977	4.03	0749	6.26
4.	Japan	3636	5.19	86	0.20
5.	East Europe	212	0.29	—	—
6.	China	66	0.09	77	0.18
7.	India	750	1.01	75	0.17

15
Changing Geography

The responsibility to govern India under its federal polity is shared by the Central and State governments. This has occasionally caused friction in the Centre-State relationship and has, therefore, inevitably led to a continuing debate regarding either the enhancement of the Central control over the States of the dilution of its authority so that the States may enjoy a larger measure of autonomy. The debate was forcibly suppressed during the Emergency which stifled the freedom of expression. It has been restarted by Sheikh Abdullah and Jyoti Basu and is likely to catch up with greater vigour because of the ideological differences between the political parties in power in the Centre and the State of Kashmir and West Bengal. Sheikh Abdullah in his press conference held in New Delhi on 29th January, 1978, has again forcefully pleaded for the greater devolution of power to the States and has even suggested the extension of Article 370, under which the State of Jammu and Kashmir enjoys special status, be applicable to other States as well.

In view of this national debate on the problems of larger autonomy to the States and Centre-State relationships, it seems appropriate to examine *de novo* if in the light of advancing technology and changing geography, we can have an alternative to the federal politic system of the country which, while retaining its integrity and political unity, will lead to a more decentralized democratic system of government, will take democracy to the grass root level, will allow a more balanced and equitable social and economic development of the country, and will provide ample scope for the regional languages and cultures to flourish.

We have adopted a federal Constitution for India and reorganized our States on a linguistic basis in order to provide the maximum

Published in *The Seminar* (*Monthly*), New Delhi, India, June 1978, pp. 12-15.

opportunity to the various linguo-cultural regions to develop their own ethos and economy within the national framework. In this process we have created such small States as Goa and Pondicherry which contrast sharply with such large sized linguistic States as Andhra Pradesh, Maharashtra and Karnataka. While the smaller States with small populations and meagre natural resources show a greater degree of dependence on the central government, the larger States with diversified resources desire a larger measure of autonomy and freedom to shape the development of regional economy and regional culture.

The linguistic States are not free from social and economic tension. They include within their territories distinct sub-cultures which feel choked under the pressure of the dominant culture of the region and, therefore, demand autonomous territorial existence to manage their own affairs. The intensity of the feelings of these sub-cultures was amply demonstrated in the movement for a separate State of Telangana in Andhra Pradesh in 1969. This separatist movement also reflected the latent feelings in most other sub-cultures within the larger linguistic States.

This demand is further supported by the fact that small States, even of the size of districts in the larger States, do exist within the federal polity of India. Moreover, the direction of drift in the present political situation of the country may once again create a favourable political climate for encouraging demand for small States which eventually may be difficult to resist. This will of course be disastrous as the creation of these multiple small States with their inevitable and expensive ministerial and gubernatorial paraphernalia will throw our economy out of gear. We are certainly not in a position to waste our scarce monetary resources on such non-remunerative items of expenditure.

Economically, the linguistic States have failed to satisfy the aspirations of the people. The economic disparity between the developed and backward regions in most of the States has further widened. The powerful kulaks and entrepreneurs of the developed regions have successfully influenced the investment policy of the government and of the banks to suit their interest. Thus, the disparities in the levels of development have rather continued to grow and this agonizing process cannot be mitigated under the existing political system.

It is an unfortunate fact that the linguistic States have encouraged linguistic jingoism and have prevented the emergence of a national ethos. The people of each linguistic State tend to take more pride in their own regional language, regional culture and are more concerned about the development of their own region. Because of these divisive trends, the national perspective is being completely ignored and every problem is being viewed from the narrow regional angle. Regionalism has gone so deep into the body politic of each State that even such minor issues as the fate of Belgaum and Chandigarh or the distribution of river waters are viewed emotionally and never rationally.

In the field of education, linguistic regionalism has shown its most ugly face and rabid form. One does not deny the efficacy of the regional language as a medium of instruction, but its erroneous implementation is adversely affecting the economic interests of the student community of the State. While English is an alicn language, it is nonetheless a great asset. It is a powerful vehicle of communication at the international level and has internationally become the second language of the non-English speaking world. It is through the medium of this language that the scholars in India keep themselves abreast of the latest developments in their respective areas of specialization.

To reduce the importance of the English language at the post graduate and research level will imperil the progress of the country in the field of science and technology. And this is precisely what the linguistic fanatics are attempting to do. The whittling down of the stand of English has immeasurably damaged the standard of education at the post graduate and research levels. The insistence on regional language as the medium of instruction at the post graduate and research level will deprive our educated youth of an opportunity to find employment in the national and international employment market.

The more disastrous effect of this policy in the field of education will be to encourage inbreeding in the centres of research and higher learning in each State. The universities will thus be forced to recruit scholars for the teaching faculty from within the region and, therefore, cannot look for the best talent available in the country. The regional language medium policy at the university will undermine completely the idea of national integration and national ethos.

This regionalization of the total gamut of one's life and the complete absence of national perspective will generate an intense demand for a large measure of autonomy at the State level. The growing ambition of powerful leaders in the State finds the restriction and curtailment of their power and authority by central intervention exasperating. They crave, therefore, for a large share of power. There is an increasing possibility that the States will eventually succeed in getting a larger measure of autonomy, reducing the central control over the States to the minimum. Will this larger measure of autonomy serve the interest of the people, lend political stability and accelerate the pace of social and economic development? In short, will it serve the national interest?

Although we are living under a democratic political system, it is unfortunately heavily weighted against the illiterate poor who constitute over 70 per cent of the population. The system works in favour of politically dominant minority groups consisting of the industrial entrepreneurs and the rich sector peasants. These dominant minority groups control the political and administrative machinery in each State. It is these powerful groups which can financially provide support to the prospective candidates to fight elections.

These vested interests have powerful lobbies at the State legislature and, therefore, do not allow such legislations to be enacted which are inimical to their interests. Even if these are enacted, their speedy and effective implementation is prevented. Moreover, the bureaucracy which has to implement these programmes also belongs to the same class and is, therefore, sympathetic to their interest and consequently reluctant to move fast. The present democratic system is, therefore, working against the landless labourers, the poor peasants and the industrial labourers whom it is expected to serve.

Because of the federal polity in India we are subjected to a dualistic system of administration. We have the State sectors and central sectors in every important aspect of the social, political and economic life of the country. This dualistic pattern is deeply entrenched and so widely spread that sometimes we wonder if we are living in the same country for we have different salary scales, rates of Dearness Allowance, House Rent Allowance, City Compensatory Allowance etc., for the employees of the State and Central Governments for the same type of job in the same town. In view of the higher salary scales for the employees of the Central Government there is a growing demand to establish a larger number of new all-India services such as medical, educational etc.

Consequent upon this dualistic system, the union government has failed to develop a national economic policy which will be uniformly applicable to all the States of India. The country has no well defined industrial location policy. Because of this dualism of sectors we occasionally observe the absurd situation when industries in the central sector bargain for better terms with the State governments. The central sector industry gets eventually located in the State which offers the best terms irrespective of its economic feasibility and desirability.

The federal polity of the country has encouraged dualism in our political and economic system which has accentuated tension and friction in the State-Centre relationship. This perpetual state of tension will encourage divisive tendencies and hence will not be conducive to a healthy and vigorous national development. The situation now calls for a revolutionary change in the political and administrative set-up of the country. The technological revolution which has overtaken India can be effectively used to establish a decentralized democratic but a well knit unitary political, administrative and economic system in India.

The improvements in the communication system and transportation, the network have transformed the geography of the country, have annihilated distances, have brought together diverse lands and cultures of the country and have knit them together into an integrated unit. There is no part of the country which is more than 3 hours of jet flying distance from one another. Excepting for the north-east and the isolated west coast, the superfast trains have made the national capital accessible to even the remotest corner of the country within 40 hours. The telephone system has reached every district headquarters in the country. The rapidly developing television network in the country will finally bridge the gap among the peoples and cultures of India.

We are very close to achieving the national electric grid system which will enable the surplus in Bhakra Nangal area to be transferred to the deficit areas in other parts of the country. We are also contemplating the national river grid system so that the surplus in one area is utilized to meet the needs of the water famished areas in the country. The technological advances in India have advanced the frontiers of shared culture and we are on the threshold of achieving a truly national culture in India. It may thus be noticed that the technological advances in the country are leading us towards the formation of a truly well linked national political and economic system. This however, is being prevented by the political overlords in the States as they fear the erosion of their own power and care little for the interest of the people. Modern technology is, therefore, being grossly misused to centralize greater power in the State capitals.

The country, therefore, needs a political system which, while eliminating the existing dualistic system of government, will allow democracy to percolate down to the grass root level and where the people will genuinely feel that they have a share in the management of the country. We want a system where the government will be more responsive to the needs of the people and where the political leaders and bureaucracy will be able to communicate directly with the people they are expected to serve. We want a system where the *kulaks* and the entrepreneurs will not be able to form a powerful lobby at the State or national level to exploit the poor peasants and the industrial workers.

This may be feasible if the federal structure is replaced by a unitary system, the States are abolished and the district is made the basic political and administrative unit of a national system of administration. The modern system of communication which is being effectively used to centralize political and administrative powers in the capital cities of the States can be used with equal effectiveness to decentralize it. The telephone, tele-printer and wireless network can establish instantly the link between the district headquarters and the national capital.

In this new set-up as conceived here, the district will be directly represented in Parliament, and will also constitute a planning unit communicating directly with the Centre. The Centre will be directly responsible for the development of each district and can, therefore, adopt a more rational and scientific strategy for its development in order to reduce disparity between the developed and the backward districts of the country. This will lead to a serious effort on the part of the national government to encourage micro (district) level integrated planning. A truly national policy on planning will thus emerge.

This set-up also visualizes a national regrouping of the districts at the micro, meso and macro levels without the gubernatorial and the ministerial paraphernalia of the existing political set-up but with a considerable degree of decentralization of administrative, financial and planning powers at each level.

This change in the political system will need a change in the administrative set-up as well. The district administration may have to be democratized with a considerable measure of financial and administrative autonomy which will be guaranteed by the Constitution. The administration of the district will have its development authority which will be the only agency responsible for the integrated development of the district. The problems of the backward communities including scheduled castes, scheduled tribes and minorities can be viewed in their proper perspective at the district level and be dealt with more comprehensively and satisfactorily by the District Development Authority.

There will be no bar to the development of the regional languages and regional culture and the three language formula can be more effectively applied to the district level. In fact, this will lead to a more healthy and rapid development of the regional language which at the district level will be the language of its administration.

While we have envisaged in this note a wholesale reorganization of the national political system, we cannot ignore the key role which the national capital will play in this reorganized set-up. The national capital will symbolize the national ethos and will reflect the wants and desires of the nation, its strength and weaknesses, its aspirations and achievements, its cultural diversity and dignity in adversity. The capital of India which should be the nerve centre of the nation and should reflect its culture-mix should be shifted to a more central location which is notably marked for its confluence of cultures. Despite its historicity and the halo that is built around it, Delhi because of its peripheral location in a mono-cultural area, fails to fulfil its legitimate role as a national capital. If Delhi is eliminated, then the choice lies between Nagpur which is the geographical centre of India, and Hyderabad, which besides its high degree of centrality in the network system of India, is already a crucible of Indian cultures.

The transformation of the federal polity of India into a democratized and decentralized unitary system will, on the one hand, eliminate divisive tendencies and, on the other, maximize economic development and reduce socio-economic disparities at all levels. The abolition of the States of India and the emergence of the districts as the planning, administrative and political units of the country will transform radically the political, social and economic setting of the country. The foci of social and economic development will shift from the State capitals to the district headquarters from where the developmental impulses can effectively trickle down to the village level.

The bureaucracy will owe loyalty to a single national government and the people of India will look towards this national government to solve the problems of their agonizing backwardness and appalling poverty. There will be no State and Central sectors, no concurrent and State list, and no Central and States' services. All these anomalies will vanish and will give way to a well articulated and highly democratized national system with, distinct but well coordinated national policies on education, administration, industrial and agricultural development, etc. The plurality of Indian culture will flourish but it will be subsumed by a broader national culture and will be perceived in the national context.

16

The Historic Deccan– A Geographical Appraisal

The Deccan is a historic entity and a geopolitical concept. In the ancient and medieval periods its political boundaries were unstable. This instability was largely the result of topographical and historical factors. This chapter examines briefly, the evolution of the historic Deccan and the validity of its geopolitical concept in the context of the existing conditions.

Geographically the term Deccan, which means the south, is coterminous with the peninsular tableland that lies south of the Tropic of Cancer. It is defined in the north by the Vindhyan and Kaimur Watersheds and its outer boundary is marked by 300 metres contour line. The peninsular tableland includes two major geologic-physiographic regions—(1) a plateau of basic igneous rock (*lava*) weathered into rich black soil, and the other (2) a peneplained gneissic region with infertile red soils interrupted by numerous granitic hills. The historians do not accept this geographic definition of the Deccan. To them, the Deccan is a political entity but they among themselves are not agreed on its precise territorial definition. Vincent Smith defines it a territory "south of Narmada ...in which Malabar and the Tamil countries of the extreme south are not included".[1] According to Dr. Raychaudhuri the Deccan "stretches from the Sahyadriparvat (Satmala Range)... and the expanse of hill and plateau that connects it with Mahendragiri and forms the watershed between Mahanadi and Godavari in the north, to the Krishna and Tungabhadra in the south, and from the Arabian Sea in the west to the Bay of Bengal in the east".[2] For the French historian Dr. Jouveau Dubreuil, the Deccan comprises "the large tract of country which is bounded on the north

Published in V.K. Bawa (Ed.) *Aspects of Deccan History*, Institute of Asian Studies, Hyderabad, India, 1975, pp. 16-29.

by Narmada and the Mahanadi, on the east by the Bay of Bengal, on the west by the Arabian Sea, on the south by the Nilgiri Hills and the Southern Pennar".[3] In Dr. Raikar's opinion, the Deccan extends between the "Vindhyas and the Tungabhadra".[4] Dr. Bhandarkar narrowed its limit to the Marathi speaking area between the Godavari and the Krishna.[5] In contrast Sardar Panikkar extended its limit to the whole of the Peninsula south of the Vindhyas. Excepting this last, all other definitions have implied political connotations. Dr. Bhandarkar was perhaps the only historian who attempted to substantiate on political and historical grounds his definition of the Deccan. He recognized only the lava region, north of the Krishna, as the Deccan because of the domination therein of an Indo-Aryan culture and language. This definition ignores the historical fact that foci of north Indian culture such as Bidar and Hyderabad also developed in the central and eastern sectors of the geographic Deccan. The rest of the definitions, by implication, define the Deccan as that part of South India which was under the political control or influence of the northern imperial powers. These definitions are vague and fail to bring out the political concept of the Deccan which can be understood only in the context of its historical evolution.

Historical Evolution of the Deccan

The historical and political connotation of the Deccan evolved with the expansion of the political control, south of the Vindhyas, of the northern imperial powers—from the Nandas to the Moghuls. This is evidenced by the absence of references to *Dakshinapatha* in the early Vedic hymns. The composers of the early Vedic hymns were ignorant of the natural and human conditions south of the Vindhyas. Even in *Kaushitaki Upanishad*, the mention of *Dakshina Parvata* in all probability meant the Vindhyan Mountains. In *Aitareya Brahmana*, a Vedic work, the reference to *Dakshina disha* means the land south of the River Chambal.[6] In the *Markandaya, Vayu and Matsya Puranas* the *Dakshina* or *Dakshinapatha* denoted the whole peninsula to the south of the Narmada.[7] It is, therefore, obvious that during the period of the *Vedas*, *Upanishads* and *Puranas* the *Dakshina Disha* or *Dakshinapatha* signified a territory totally different from the political Deccan as defined by the scholars of Indian History. During these periods the *Dakshinapatha* was divided into numerous independent tribal territories. It was practically cut off from the north because of the natural obstacles such as mountain ranges covered with dense forests. Being thus shaded off from the civilizing influence of the Aryas, the *Dakshinapatha* had by then not acquired any political significance for the powers in the north.

The emergence of the political Deccan is clearly linked with the Aryanisation of the south and the rise of imperial powers in the north which desired control of the *Dakshinapatha.* The penetration of Aryan influence in the south commenced during the epic period of the *Ramayana* which "when purged of all exaggerations, interpolations and anachronisms, is evidence of the solid central fact that Rama championed the cause of Aryan culture... and that he gave an impetus to the spread of Aryan ideals and institutions in the Deccan".[8] These gains were consolidated during the *Mahabharata* period as "Sahadeva, the youngest of the Pandu princes, is represented in his career of conquest to have gone to *Dakshinapatha* after having conquered the king of the Pandayas".[9] In this account the *Mahabharata* clearly distinguishes the *Dakshinapatha* from the far south. It was only after the epic periods that Aryan imperialism developed into a potent threat for the lands south of the Vindhyas as the epic had nurtured the concept of Indian unity.

It is thus evident that since the end of the *Mahabharata* period the degree of Brahmanical influence from the north considerably increased on the south and culminated in the rise of the Nanda and Maurya empires which controlled political territories in South India and encouraged within it the development of Aryan culture. These twin elements of political control and cultural influence have contributed to the shaping of the historic Deccan.

The vision of politically united India was conjured up during the period of the epics and has remained since one of the principal motivations in the movements of Indian history. There have been a few occasions in ancient Indian history when the southern rulers (Satavahanas) also made incursions into the north but as a rule the Indo Gangetic empires, from the Nandas to the Moghuls, because of their vastly superior human and material resources and geographical locations always tend to dominate a large part of peninsular India. This territory, south of Vindhyas, defined by the political control of these Indo-Gangetic powers came to be termed as the Deccan. The territorial jurisdiction in the south of each of the powers was different from the other. As for instance, the southern limit of the Mauryan Empire was marked by the River Pennar, whereas that of the Khiljis almost touched Cape Comorin but that of Tughlaqs extended only upto the Cauvery. Hence, there are many loosely defined Deccans such as those of the Mauryas, Khiljis, Tughlaqs and Moghuls (Fig. 16.1). Despite this deep penetration of the northern Imperial powers into South India, their area of effective political control in the region remained largely confined to the north of the Krishna. This is confirmed by the fact that the political jurisdiction of the Deccan Kingdoms such as the Satvahana, the Bahmani, Hyderabad etc. (Fig. 16.2 and 16.3) which emerged respectively on the disintegration of the Mauryan, Tughlaq and Moghul empires did not extend south of the boundaries of the North Indian Kingdoms which once held important positions in their respective imperial courts.

An examination of the various definitions of the Deccan and of the Figures 16.1, 16.2 and 16.3 would reveal three distinct geographical regions of the Deccan (Fig. 16.4) :

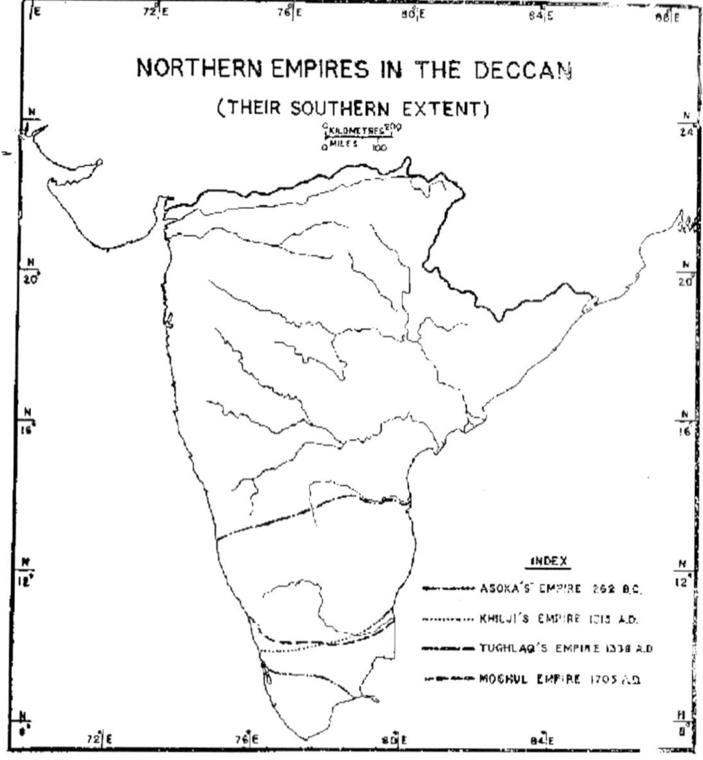

Fig. 16.1 : Northern Empires in the Deccan (Their Southern Extent)

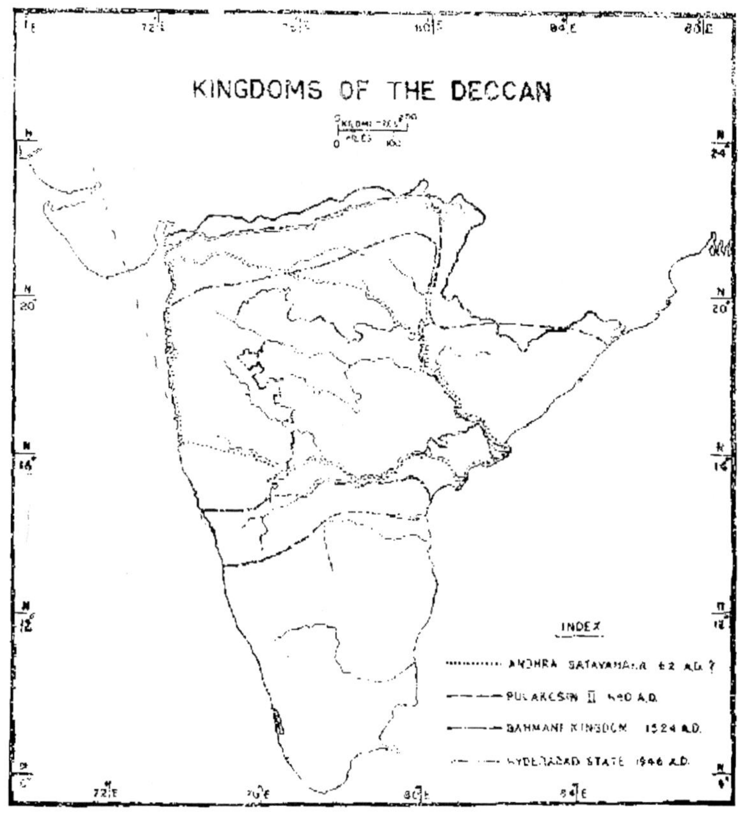

Fig. 16.2 : Kingdoms of the Deccan

(a) The Marchland Deccan or the Area of Political Assimilation.
(b) The Heartland Deccan or the Area of Political Control.
(c) The Peripheral Deccan or the Area of Political Influence.

The Marchland Deccan or the Area of Political Assimilation

The Marchland Deccan, located between the Vindhyas and the Godavari ethnically belongs to the North. Political control of the Marchland was essential for access to the Deccan and hence it always served as a springboard for invasion of South India. As for instance Akbar's consolidation of control over Berar and Khandesh enabled Shah Jahan and Aurangzeb to wage war against the kingdoms of the Deccan. The political association of the Marchland Deccan with the north was so frequent and strong that it lost its cultural identity and this distinguished it from the other parts of the Deccan.

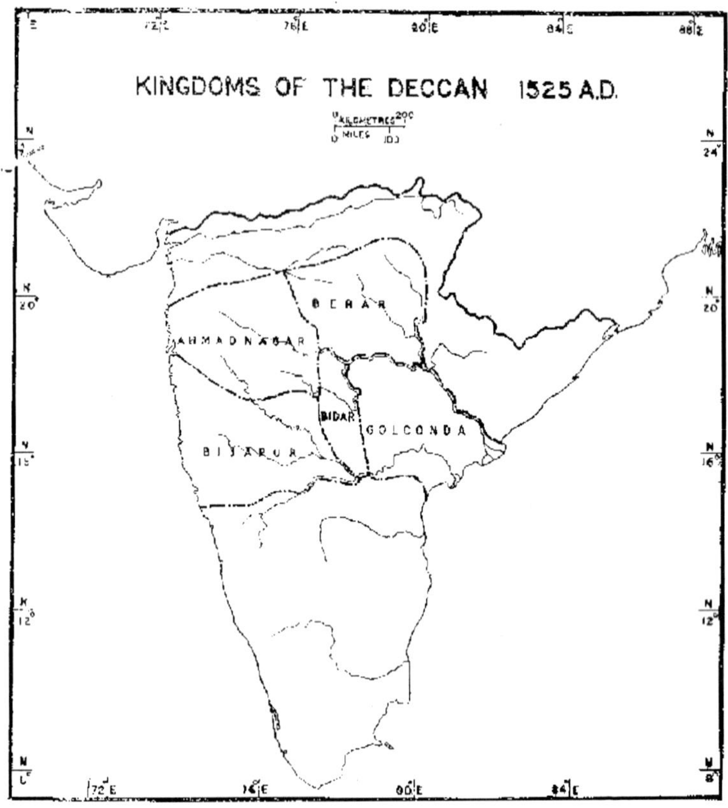

Fig. 16.3 : Kingdoms of the Deccan—1525 A.D.

The Heartland Deccan or the Area of Political Control

A careful examination of Figures 16.2 and 16.3 would reveal a core area of peninsular India between the Godavari and Krishna which served as the nucleus for the rise of the Deccan kingdoms from Satavahanas to the Asaf Jahis. This core area which formed part of all the kingdoms of the Deccan may be called the Heartland Deccan and is marked out by the following characteristics :

(1) It has been under the direct administrative control of the northern imperial powers through their governors.

(2) Being a fertile region supporting a large population it has served as a nucleus for the rise of powerful kingdoms.

(3) Racially and linguistically it is a transition zone between the Indo-Aryan North and the Dravidian South.

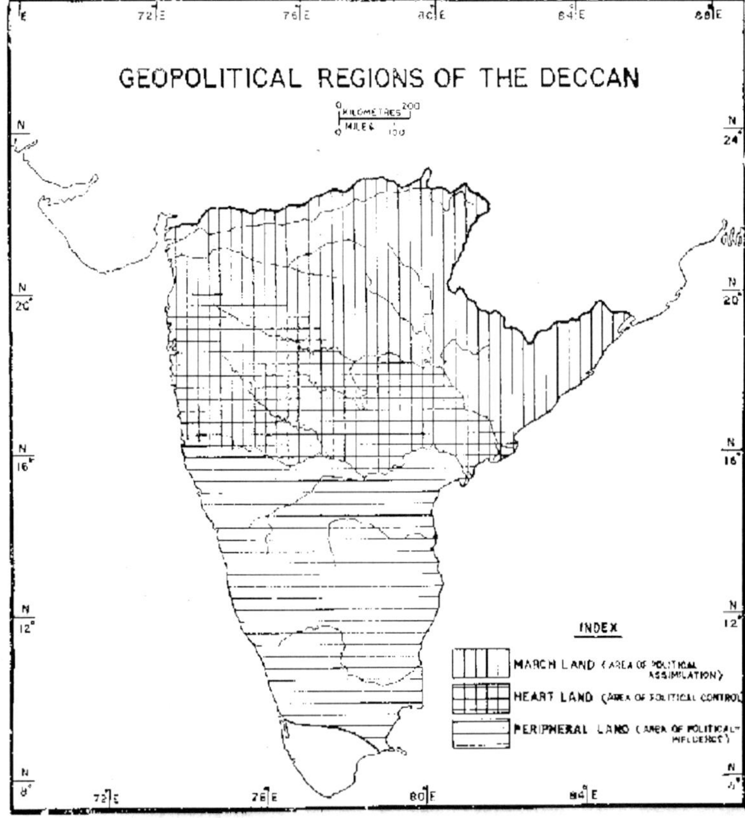

Fig. 16.4 : Geopolitical Regions of the Deccan

The Heartland Deccan (Fig. 16.4) because of its pivotal position in controlling the Deccan, was always a coveted possession of the imperial powers and, therefore, they preferred to rule over it either under their direct supervision (as was done by Mohammad Bin Tughlaq) or through their trusted officers (Nizmul Mulk Asaf Jah was appointed Governor of the Deccan by Aurangzeb). As a result the Heartland Deccan became also the area of effective political control of the northern imperial powers in South India. The Deccan, south of the Krishna, was seldom effectively controlled by these powers.

The Heartland possessed all the ingredients of becoming the nucleus of a powerful state. Its fertile black cotton soil and the fertile valley of the Krishna and the Godavari which traverse it were capable of supporting a large population. Its nearness and accessibility to the important ports on the west and the east coasts made it all the more an economically viable region. It is, therefore, not surprising that this central core, between the Krishna and the Godavari, served as the base for the rise of the Deccani kingdoms established by the nobles and generals of the declining imperial powers. The Satavahana Empire (220 B.C. to 220 A.D.) was built on the ruins of the Mauryan Empire. The rise of the Bahmanis (A.D. 1347-1500) is attributed to the fall of the Tughlaqs and the Asaf Jahs ruled over the State of Hyderabad after the fall of the Moghul Empire. It is also within the Heartland that the capitals of these Deccani Kingdoms were located such as Paithan, Bidar, Ahmadnagar, Bijapur, Gulbarga and Golconda-Hyderabad. These capital cities in turn became strong foci of north Indian cultures. Their absence south of the Krishna is conspicuous.

Racially and linguistically it is a transition zone between the Indo-Aryan Marchland and the Dravidian Periphery. It is this zone which in ancient days was called "Arya Nadu"—for it was here that the Aryans first settled[10] in the south and as a result the "Aryan and non-Aryan languages fused to create a Prakrit dialect which obtained wide currency".[11] Sociologically it is a mixed zone of cultures and races and these features are as significant in distinguishing the Heartland from the other two geopolitical regions of the Deccan as any other characteristics.

The Peripheral Deccan or the Area of Political Influence

The Heartland acted as the pivotal point for the annexation of the region south of the Krishna. Despite the penetration of many imperial powers into the far south their political control of this region was only nominal. The native rulers, though they paid tributes and owed allegiance to the imperial power, by and large, retained control of their respective states. This is corroborated by the facts that the principal centres of north Indian culture are not found north of the Heartland and that no Deccan kingdom had its origin south of the Krishna. Thus the Peripheral Deccan, an ethnically Dravidian area, remained only within the sphere of influence of the northern imperial powers and was never effectively ruled by them.

Unstable Political Frontiers of the Deccan[12]

The power of the northern empires was based on land resources while the southern kingdoms such as Chera, Pandya, Chola were maritime powers. The strength of the Deccani kingdom was based on both the factors. The need for a strong army arose out of the proximity of powerful kingdoms to the north and south. As the principal overland trade routes of the Deccan such as Surat-Aurangabad-Masulipatnam or Delhi-Aurangabad-Hyderabad-Masulipatnam and Goa Bijapur-Hyderabad passed through alien territories the political control of the adjoining coastal areas was considered essential by the Deccani powers to maintain the lifeline of overseas commerce and trade. Thus, access to and control of the Konkan and Coromandel coasts had been of supreme importance in the geopolitical strategy of the Deccani kingdoms and was uniformly pursued by the Satavahanas,[13] the Bahmanis,[14] the Qutb Shahis and Asaf Jahs.[15] Consequently political boundaries parallel to the coast lines were always unstable. In contradistinction, the northern and the southern frontiers remained relatively stable except during the periods of imperial expansion.

The centrifugal forces encouraged by topography, distance from the capital and lack of proper communication damaged the central authority and caused disruption of the kingdom and the instability of its political boundaries. The downfall of the Chalukyas and the Bahmanis was followed by their dismemberment into many kingdoms.

In ancient and medieval Deccan there were frequent shifts in the location of capital cities mainly because of topographic difficulties. With the expansion of their kingdom to Kalinga the Satavahanas shifted their capital from Paithan to Amraoti, near the Krishna Delta.[16] The Bahmanis moved to Bidar from Gulbarga[17] and the Asaf Jahs from Aurangabad to Hyderabad.[18] A classic example in this regard was the creation by the Chalukyas of a subsidiary capital Vengi in the east, in addition to Badami in the west, when their kingdom expanded in that direction.[19]

Formation of linguistic boundaries seems to be an old-standing tradition in the Deccan and they proved fairly stable. The three principal kingdoms of the Deccan, Ahmadnagar (Marathi), Bijapur (Canarese) and Golconda (Telugu) after the disintegration of Bahmani kingdom were more or less linguistic states. Even earlier than this the split of the Chalukya kingdom into Yadavas (Marathi), Hoyasalas (Canarese) and Kakatiyas (Telugu) was based on linguistic factors.

Of the natural frontiers, rivers have lent more stability to the political boundaries and have rather conditioned the lateral alignment of the kingdoms of the Deccan such as those of the Satavahanas, the Bahmanis and the Asaf Jahs. The longitudinal alignment of Western Ghats clashed with the inevitable urge of the Deccani kingdoms to reach the sea and thus their efficacy as frontiers was considerably reduced.

The Historic Deccan—Geopolitical Concept and its Validity

In the Republic of India, the historic Deccan has ceased to be a political factor. The old geopolitical concept of the Deccan as the bridge between the North and South has no relevance now. Despite the disintegrating influences generated by the formation of States on linguistic basis, the integrating factors of economic development are much more potent now than ever before. With the Chinese threat the historic Deccan has assumed new geopolitical significance for India. It provides "defence in depth" against any invading forces from the north. But it is vulnerable against sea attack especially on the east and hence the creation of a strong navy to defend India's 2,500 miles coastline is imperative.

In conclusion it may be observed that the historic Deccan, which is a geographic, ethnic and political entity played a significant role in shaping the Indian History. Originally it was "a laboratory of relations between the Aryan civilization of the north, and the historic Dravidian civilization of the south." It can now be used to weld them together and bring about emotional integration which is vital to national unity.

REFERENCES

1. Vincent Smith: *The Kingdoms of the Deccan*, p. 439.
2. Hemchandra Raychaudhuri: "Geography of the Deccan", in *The Early*

History of the Deccan, edited by G. Yazdani OUP, London, 1960, p. 3

3. Jouveau Dubreuil: *Ancient History of the Deccan, Pondicherry, 1920*, p. 5.
4. Y.A. Raikar: *Indian History—A Study in Dynamics*, p. 8
5. R.G. Bhandarkar: *Early History of Deccan*, 1920, p. 2.
6. Hemchandra Raychaudhuri: "The Deccan in Scriptural and Epic Tradition", in *The Early History of the Deccan*, p. 14.
7. R.G. Bhandarkar: *op. cit.*, p. 1.
8. G. Venkata Rao: "Pre-Satavahanas and Satavahanas", in *The Early History of the Deccan, p. 67*
9. R.G. Bhandarkar: *op. cit.*, p. 2.
10. Hemchandra Raychaudhuri: *loc. cit.*, in *The Early History of the Deccan*, p. 21.
11. G. Venkata Rao: *loc. cit.*, in *The Early History of the Deccan*, p. 70.
12. Although it is difficult to trace the precise frontiers (boundaries) of the Deccani kingdoms, it would nonetheless be wrong to assume that in ancient and medieval India the concept of frontier (boundary) was non-existent. As early as the fourth century A.D. the land of the Vakataka kingdom was "carefully surveyed" A.S. Altekar: "The History of the Vakatakas", in *The Early History of Deccan*, p. 196. Todarmal had Akbar's Empire thoroughly surveyed before he introduced his land revenue system. Tavernier in his *Travels* mentions the use of certain trees to define the boundaries of the Qutb Shahi Kingdom.
13. Vincent Smith: *The Kingdoms of the Deccan*, p. 441, OUP.
14. Haroon Khan Sherwani: *The Bahmanis of the Deccan*, p. 11.
15. In the early twentieth Century the Nizam negotiated infructuously with the British Government for access to Masulipatnam.
16. T.L. Shah: *Ancient India*, Vol. I, Chapter VI, pp. 146-187, 1938.
17. Haroon Khan Sherwani: *op. cit.*
18. Manzoor Alam: Cities of Hyderabad and Secunderabad—Their Geographical Forms and Functions—First chapter of unpublished thesis—Edinburgh, 1962.
19. S. Krishnaswami Ayyangar: *Ancient India*, p. 43.

Index